INDEPENDENCE AND DETERRENCE
BRITAIN AND ATOMIC ENERGY, 1945–1952
Volume I: POLICY MAKING

INDEPENDENCE AND DETERRENCE

BRITAIN AND ATOMIC ENERGY, 1945-1952

Volume 1
POLICY MAKING

by
MARGARET GOWING

assisted by
LORNA ARNOLD

Macmillan

First published 1974 by
THE MACMILLAN PRESS LTD
London and Basingstoke
Associated companies in New York
Dublin Melbourne Johannesburg and Madras

SBN 333 15781 8

Printed in Great Britain by
WESTERN PRINTING SERVICES LTD
Bristol

Contents

1947–1951

1951-1952

List of Plates

between pp. 146 and 147

The above are reproduced by permission of the following: Keystone Press Agency Ltd (1 and 7); Central Press Photos Ltd (2 and 5); UK Atomic Energy Authority (3); Photoreportage Ltd (4); Antony Barrington Brown (6); Camera Press Ltd (8, photograph by Tom Blau); Lotte Meitner-Graf (9).

Preface

THESE two volumes are a sequel to my *Britain and Atomic Energy,
1939–1945*;* they are a further instalment of the history of the
British atomic energy project commissioned by the United Kingdom
Atomic Energy Authority. The volumes do not speculate on the
question whether the world would have been a better or a worse
place if man had learned neither to release energy from the fission of
uranium nor to make plutonium, an extremely toxic material unknown in nature and with a radioactive half-life of 24,000 years.
They deal with problems whose scale is microscopic by comparison:
why and how Britain developed her atomic project in the years from
1945 to her first bomb test in the autumn of 1952. Volume 1, *Policy
Making*, is concerned with 'Why' and Volume 2, *Policy Execution*,
with 'How'. Volume 2 takes the answers to 'Why' as given in
Volume 1; that is, the scientists and engineers who were responsible
for carrying out the project, like the vast majority of the British
population at that time, accepted the need for atomic weapons and
power.

Atomic policy is an important thread in the post-war history of
Britain; it is woven into almost every part of that history – international, diplomatic, Commonwealth, military, constitutional, political, administrative, economic, social, scientific, technological and
medical. The making and execution of policy involved almost every
layer of government and society from the Prime Minister through to
the military and civil hierarchies of Service officers, administrators,
executives, scientists, engineers, draughtsmen and building workers.

The volumes would clearly have been unmanageable if I had
strayed too far into adjacent territories and I have therefore written
only the necessary minimum about, for example, the Cold War or
the production of aircraft to carry atomic bombs. I have omitted
some things in the atomic story for lack of space and time: for
example, many parts of the scientific work and (equally vital) the

* Macmillan, 1964.

role of the manual workers.* Even with these limitations, the great bulk and diversity of topics and material are largely responsible for the time taken to write these volumes and for their length; the detailed 'nuts and bolts' account of the project in Volume 2 seemed the more necessary because studies of sophisticated large-scale scientific and technological enterprises are still only too rare.

The arrangement and presentation of so complex a story have been difficult. *Policy Making* is mainly, though not wholly, presented as a chronological narrative as seen from Whitehall. *Policy Execution* is arranged by topics, and includes a detailed description of the work on the plants and the weapon; this was the only way of describing the load on the men in the project team. To help non-scientific readers, the same technical appendix is included in both books.

There is inevitably an overlap between the two volumes and some overlap within each volume. This is particularly true in *Policy Execution*; for example, nuclear power has a chapter of its own (Chapter 19) but power problems have an important place elsewhere, for instance in the discussion of Harwell's role (Chapter 18) and in the discussion of relationships with private industry (Chapter 17). Choosing the best order for the chapters was also difficult; in Part Two of *Policy Execution* ('The Enterprise') I have grouped together the chapters about those activities which were predominantly Harwell's, although this arrangement meant separating the Harwell chapters from chapters on the factories with which Harwell scientists were intimately concerned. Perfect solutions to such problems of arrangement are rarely found and historians, like engineers, have to seek the best compromise.

The books are official history in accordance with the terms explained in the preface to *Britain and Atomic Energy, 1939–1945*.† They are the first official history for the peacetime years to be authorised for publication by Her Majesty's Government. Although the volumes are not part of the new series of peacetime official histories which is being prepared in the Historical Section of the Cabinet Office,‡ the same general principles and procedures have

---

* I had also hoped to make a statistical analysis of the background of the scientists and engineers in the project. However, I leave this as an interesting topic for a social scientist.

† The 'closed' period for public records is now thirty years. It was reduced from fifty in 1967.

‡ See HOC Deb., 18 Dec 1969 (written answers, vol. 813, cols. 411–12).

been followed. I have been given free access to the same range of official documents. I made no attempt to write the history of atomic intelligence and the subject is almost entirely excluded. Sir Alan Bullock has acted as honorary consultant to the UK Atomic Energy Authority to ensure the maintenance of professional historical standards, but I alone am responsible for the statements made and the views expressed.

The volumes were circulated for official comment to interested Government Departments who, for reasons of public policy which I accepted as compelling, suggested a very few omissions of technical detail and an extremely small number of other alterations.

Writing contemporary history has advantages and disadvantages. I have sometimes envied historians working on earlier periods since the people they write about cannot answer back. However, I am convinced that on balance contemporary history has enormous advantages, provided there are adequate documentary records by which personal memories can be checked. The circulation of drafts to people who took part in the project has yielded important historical data – not only new facts but also evidence from leading individuals that they knew very little about crucial decisions until they read my volumes.

It would be invidious to mention by name the many scientists, engineers and administrators to whom I am indebted for their in-exhaustible patience, helpfulness and clarity of exposition. I wish I had been able to talk to even more of them. The assistance of Mrs Lorna Arnold of the UKAEA, whose name appears on the title-page, has been indispensable. I am deeply grateful for her devoted work in research and writing as well as in more humdrum tasks; nothing has ever been too much trouble for her. The archives sections of the various atomic energy establishments have given un-wearied help. The manuscripts put a heavy load on the duplicating and typing sections of the Authority's London office, and I thank them all, especially Mrs Patricia Suckling. Finally, my sons Nicholas and James deserve some thanks for their tolerance and understand-ing of the anxieties of authorship.

MARGARET GOWING

Linacre College, Oxford
October 1973

List of Abbreviations

ACAE   Advisory Committee on Atomic Energy
AEB   Atomic Energy Board
AEC   Atomic Energy Council
AE (DR)   Atomic Energy (Defence Research) Committee
AECL   Atomic Energy of Canada Ltd
AE (M)   Ministerial Committee on Atomic Energy
AE (O)   Official Committee on Atomic Energy
AERE   Atomic Energy Research Establishment (Harwell)
BEA   British Electricity Authority
Bepo   British Experimental Pile O (Harwell)
CAE   Controller, Atomic Energy
CDA   Combined Development Agency
CDT   Combined Development Trust
CEA   Commissariat à l'Energie Atomique
COS   Chief of Staff
CPAE   Controller of Production, Atomic Energy
CPC   Combined Policy Committee
CPR   Companhia de Radium Limitada
CRL   Chemical Research Laboratory
DCPAE   Deputy Controller of Production, Atomic Energy
DRPC   Defence Research Policy Committee
DSIR   Department of Scientific and Industrial Research
EBR 1   Experimental breeder reactor No. 1 (U.S.)
Gleep   Graphite low energy experimental pile (Harwell)
ICI   Imperial Chemical Industries Ltd
JCAE   Joint Committee on Atomic Energy
MIT   Massachusetts Institute of Technology
PAC   Public Accounts Committee
RCC   The Radiochemical Centre, Amersham
ROF   Royal Ordnance Factory
SCE   Select Committee on Expenditure
UKAEA   United Kingdom Atomic Energy Authority
UKCC   United Kingdom Commercial Corporation
UKGSM   United Kingdom Geological Survey and Museum
UNAEC   United Nations Atomic Energy Commission
USAEC   United States Atomic Energy Commission

A Note on Documentation

In accordance with the practice of the official war histories, references to official papers that are not yet publicly available have been omitted: notes are confined to published material. The complete documentation will, however, be available in confidential print and will be accessible to scholars when the documents concerned are open to the public.

The author is grateful to the Controller of HM Stationery Office for permission to reproduce and quote Government documents. She also acknowledges her indebtedness to the authors and publishers of all those books that have been mentioned in this work.

M.G.

1 August 1945: Retrospect and Agenda

THE two atomic bombs dropped on Japan had brought the Second World War to an abrupt end. Hiroshima had been utterly destroyed by one bomb, without warning, on 6 August and Nagasaki on 9 August: on 10 August Japan had agreed in principle to surrender.

The atomic bomb had shown itself to be the supreme weapon which could terrify into instant submission a country which did not possess it. Less than fifteen years earlier, nuclear physics had still been pursued as the purest of pure science, without much thought of practical applications,* although in the 1930s some scientists – Fermi, Joliot-Curie and Szilard – had been so impressed with the practical possibilities of nuclear energy that they had taken out patents. Now, in 1945, nuclear physics had produced a weapon that could determine the balance of power, the life and death of nations.

Britain had been the midwife of this bomb. If it had not been for the brilliant scientific work done in Britain in the early part of the war, by refugee scientists from Europe and by British scientists, the Second World War would almost certainly have ended before an atomic bomb was dropped. It had been the cogency and clarity of

* Rutherford's own views were not consistent. In 1903 he had made a 'playful suggestion' that, could a proper detonator be found, it was just conceivable that a wave of atomic disintegration might be started through matter 'which would indeed make this old world vanish in smoke'. In 1904 he wrote of the possibility that an enormous amount of energy might be obtainable from a small quantity of matter. In 1916 he said that if the energy from radium could be released and used, it would be possible from 1lb. of material to obtain as much energy as from 100 million lb. of coal but that fortunately at the present time we had not found a method of so dealing with these forces; personally he was very hopeful that we should not discover it until man was living at peace with his neighbours. But in 1907 Rutherford said he did not believe we were ever likely to be able to control atomic energy so that it was of commercial value and that 'our interest in the matter is purely scientific'. In 1933 he made his well-known remark that expectations of sources of power from atomic transmutations were 'merest moonshine'.[1]

the British Maud Report* in 1941 which had persuaded the Americans of the practical possibility of an atomic bomb and the urgency of making one.

It was ironic therefore that the atomic bomb more than anything else emphasised the change during the Second World War in the relative power of the United Kingdom and the United States, even though it did not cause this change. This was part of the shift in world power which had been foreseen by writers from de Tocqueville onwards and which had been gradually taking place from the end of the nineteenth century: a shift of power away from Western Europe towards a bipolarity with America at one end and Russia at the other.[2] But this shift had been delayed and disguised in the years from 1918 to 1939 by American withdrawal into political isolation and by Russian withdrawal from the international scene to cope with the aftermath of revolution and civil war.

Now, in 1945, the United States and Russia had emerged from the Second World War as the great military powers. But there the similarity between the two countries seemed, at that moment, to end. The United States, in spite of an immense expenditure of resources on the war, had emerged from it with losses that were relatively very small and with an economy immeasurably strengthened. The war had released her vast productive powers which had been languishing in the 1930s, so much so that her strength in relation to the rest of the world was at that moment perhaps greater than that of any other country or empire in medieval or modern history. No feat seemed beyond the capacity of her industry and technology. For a time after the war, however, most Americans were very reluctant to accept their world role in peacetime. The Russians were less reluctant, yet Russia had suffered most terribly in the war in terms of both lost lives and devastated land, towns and factories. Her military strength seemed to the world at large and to other governments to consist almost entirely of sheer numbers of men, backed by mass production of routine weapons. Her strength in terms of industrial, scientific and technological performance was believed to be far behind that of the United States – and indeed of Britain.

This belief helped to conceal from Britain in the immediate post-war years some ineluctable facts of the change in the world balance

---

* The Maud Committee, consisting of eminent scientists, was set up in April 1940 to study the feasibility of an atomic bomb. A full account of it is given in *Britain and Atomic Energy, 1939-1945.*

of power. There was no possible doubt about the shift in power towards the United States, for wartime experience had made it only too clear. Britain had mobilised for war, with extraordinary efficiency and at the cost of great strain, a higher proportion of her economy for a far longer period than the United States. But she had been able to do so only because of the flow of food, materials and munitions from North America. Without immediate help from the United States at the end of the war she was 'virtually bankrupt and the economic basis for the hopes of the public non-existent'.* Until 1943 Britain's fighting forces had exceeded those of America, but at the end of the war America's fighting strength was overwhelming. The changed balance of power had also become abundantly clear in the Anglo-American conferences and military planning of the last year or so of the war: whatever the façade of consultation, American views on operations and political settlements had almost always triumphed.

This shift of power had been dramatically emphasised by the atomic bomb. The early British work embodied in the 1941 Maud Report was decisive in getting the American atomic bomb project off the ground,[3] but Britain had then become only a junior partner in the business, contributing significantly in various ways but present largely on American sufferance. Britain had simply not had the resources to develop the atomic bomb, which had become the terrifying symbol of America's industrial, scientific and technological strength. There, a $2,000 million project of the greatest complexity had been inserted into the war effort with administrative genius but without great difficulties over capacity. Even the decision to drop atomic bombs on Japan – one of the most fateful decisions of the war – was primarily an American decision, although the British Government had been asked to agree.

After Hiroshima and Nagasaki, the Manhattan Project lost impetus despite General Groves's efforts. The future was uncertain; the single objective of the war years was gone, and morale was low; scientists were drifting away, especially from Los Alamos; contracts were running out. When the Atomic Energy Commission took over in 1946 they found the nation's strength in nuclear weapons to be far less than they had been led to believe.[4] Nevertheless, at the end of the war the United States was the only country possessing an

---

* Lord Keynes's words in a paper submitted to the War Cabinet on the day Japan surrendered.

atomic bomb capacity and Britain was only too conscious of the implied disparity in power. But the atomic bomb which symbolised America's immense strength also seemed to symbolise Britain's status in any league tables of power. Britain may have been only a junior partner in the American bomb project, but she had after all shared in it and knew much detail about many, though not all, parts of it. Her own work and the work of her scientists in North America made it reasonable to assume that Britain was nearer to nuclear power status than any other great power. Some early estimates (see Chapter 3) suggested that Russia might have an atomic bomb three years after the end of the war, but such calculations seem to have had little impact. No one seems to have seriously believed that Russia would explode atomic bombs before Britain. Although Russia was an infinitely greater power than Britain in terms of land mass and size of armies, she was generally believed to be inferior in science and technology and in industrial resources to support them. The most shattering* moment of truth for Britain in the early post-war years was the first Russian bomb test, three years before the first British test.

The Russian bomb test in August 1949 lifted Russia to the status of a super-power, another power moving on the level of the United States. Britain would never be on that level, but she still stood above the rest of the world. All the other countries of Western Europe had been war-torn and politically divided while Britain felt, and was felt by Europe to be, great on many counts. Her superiority in atomic know-how was only one item but an important one in the reckoning. It is tempting, if futile, to speculate on the what-might-have-beens of history. Would Britain have come to terms sooner with her status in the post-war world if her own and her refugee atomic scientists had been less clear-sighted in 1940 and 1941, if the Maud Report had never been written and if she had played no part in a wartime atomic project?

As it was, Britain's newly elected Labour Government was faced in August 1945 with formulating atomic policies, plans and programmes. It was beset with a multitude of other desperately urgent problems: the reconstruction of the British economy and the need for American financial help, the occupation of Germany, the future

---

* It was shattering, even though some very accurate estimates of Russian capabilities had been made (see Chapter 7).

of India, and war in Palestine, were only some of them. But the chief Ministers in the new Government were at least familiar with the outlines of these other problems while almost none of them had even heard of atomic bombs before July 1945. Mr Churchill had vigorously insisted that knowledge of the atomic bomb be kept to the smallest possible circle of Ministers and advisers. About seven Ministers* in the wartime coalition had been involved in the bomb project in varying degrees and at varying times, but only two of them, Sir John Anderson and Lord Cherwell, knew continuously and in detail about the whole business. The Deputy Prime Minister, Mr Attlee, was not included in this select band to whom the secret was confided, nor was Mr Bevin, a leading member of the War Cabinet, who was to become Labour's Foreign Secretary. Sir Stafford Cripps, another Labour Minister and a scientist by origin, had tried as Minister of Aircraft Production to take some interest in it but had been warned off. Mr Churchill gave little thought to the post-war implications of the atomic bomb, except in so far as Anglo-American relations were concerned, but even if he had done so it is unlikely that he would have foreseen or imagined the difficulties of a totally unprepared and uninformed Labour Government in office when the first bombs were dropped.

It was the more unfortunate that the number of properly informed advisers was also very small: it comprised a few individuals in the Cabinet Office, the Foreign Office, the Department of Scientific and Industrial Research, the Treasury and the Raw Materials Department of the Ministry of Supply. The Chiefs of Staff had been given only the barest outline, while Mr Churchill had refused in the last years of the war to allow any atomic information to go to Sir Henry Tizard, who was then writing a report on the future of defence research and who was to become the Labour Government's chief adviser on defence research policy.

What was the atomic legacy of problems, policies, projects and plans which the Labour Government inherited in July 1945? The chief problem was only too clear: having ended one war with atomic bombs, how was the world to avoid blowing itself to pieces with some more? No progress whatsoever had been made towards answering this question before the war ended. Niels Bohr's

* Sir John Anderson, Lord Cherwell, Mr R. A. Butler, Colonel Llewellin, Colonel Moore-Brabazon, Mr Eden, Lord Hankey. None was a member of the Labour Party.

initiatives[5] had been fruitless and there had been no consultations
between the West and Russia even though Russian interest in the
atomic business was well known. We now know that Russian
scientists were already planning a bomb project, while information
about the British and American projects had been transmitted to
them by the various atomic spies. Yet the possibility of this bomb
was the big unmentionable subject that never reached the agenda of
any of the meetings of Roosevelt, Stalin and Churchill at which
they discussed the post-war world. It was simply referred to, and
then obliquely, in a fleeting remark by Truman to Stalin at Potsdam
only two weeks before the first bomb was dropped on Japan. International control of atomic energy was an unexplored subject when
the war ended.

There were already other international ramifications of atomic
energy enmeshing Britain in a web of obligations and relationships
that were sometimes conflicting and always obscure. First and foremost was Britain's atomic relationship with the United States. This
relationship had been close in 1941 and the early months of 1942,
but had then been repudiated by the Americans so that it amounted
to nothing for nine months. On Churchill's insistence it had been
resurrected and enshrined in the formal Quebec Agreement of
August 1943 between President and Prime Minister. This had said,
firstly, that the United States and the United Kingdom would never
use the atomic bomb against each other; secondly, that they would
not use it against third parties without each other's consent; thirdly,
that neither country would communicate any information about
Tube Alloys* to third parties except by mutual consent; fourthly,
that any post-war advantages of an industrial or commercial character should be dealt with as between the United States and Great
Britain on terms to be specified by the President of the United States
to the Prime Minister of Great Britain; fifthly, that various arrangements would be made to ensure full and effective collaboration
between the two countries in bringing the project to fruition,
including the setting-up of a Combined Policy Committee which
would *inter alia* agree on the programmes of work in the two countries and allocate materials. This agreement had led to the migration
to the United States of many of the British scientists and engineers

---

* The British wartime code name for the atomic energy project. In this
clause Tube Alloys was inferred to mean atomic energy in general and not
just atomic bombs.

working on atomic energy (including the naturalised refugees);* one other team was already lodged in Canada. But the Quebec Agreement itself had some real obscurities: the first clause by including the word 'never' seemed to refer to infinity, the second and third had no reference to time, the fourth referred to after the war, while the fifth dealt only with the war or, rather, with bringing the project to fruition.

British doubts about post-war collaboration, however, seemed to have been put to rest by the Hyde Park Aide-Mémoire which the President and Prime Minister signed in September 1944. This promised that full collaboration between the two countries in developing Tube Alloys for military and commercial purposes should continue after the defeat of Japan unless and until terminated by joint agreement. The doubts were at rest only briefly, for six months after the agreement was signed the President was dead and no other American knew of its existence until told by the British. Even if there was doubt about the validity or even the meaning of formal agreements, there was no doubt about British desires. All the British who knew about the project were passionately anxious that collaboration should continue. There was some self-interest in this since the American project was vast and could yield invaluable information, but there was also the belief that such collaboration would be but one facet of a profound Anglo-American understanding which would be a foundation of stability in the post-war world. This had become the main tenet of Mr Churchill's faith and it was shared by the scientists in varying degrees. Sir James Chadwick,† who had been more responsible than any other individual for the close and friendly relations of the British and Americans in atomic energy in the last two years of the war, felt this especially strongly:

I think it is impossible to exaggerate [he wrote] the benefits to both parties and the world in general of future collaboration in this project. I am not thinking at all of the selfish interest of collecting information or getting the benefit of US experience and ideas. I am quite sure help from the US is not necessary to enable us to carry out this project in England. We can stand on our own feet.

* Almost all the academic groups went to North America. However, important development work was proceeding at various establishments of ICI Ltd, and most of the scientists and engineers so employed stayed in Britain.[6]
† Britain's greatest living nuclear physicist, discoverer of the neutron.

What I am anxious to do is to preserve our good relations and to extend them into the future.

During the war the Anglo-American atomic relationship had been not bilateral but triangular, with Canada as the third point. Canada possessed rich uranium deposits which the British and Americans wanted. Apart from that, Britain had asked Canada to join the atomic energy project in 1942 in order to provide a North American home for the Anglo-French team of scientists which had been working on slow neutron reactions at Cambridge. This work had been considered important primarily because of its possibilities for nuclear power, although the Cambridge team had foreseen that in the course of these slow reactions a new element, later to be called plutonium, could be produced, which would be fissile and thus another potential explosive for bombs. By 1942 it had been clear that the Americans were moving ahead in this whole field very fast indeed. The British had now wanted to move their teams to the United States, but the Americans had refused to have them. The team would have been very much out of the picture if they had stayed in England, and therefore Canada, so near the United States laboratories, had seemed a good home.

The National Research Council of Canada had welcomed the team and had financed first of all a laboratory at Montreal and then the construction of nuclear piles at Chalk River. The team had finally become an integrated Anglo-Canadian one, including within itself some naturalised British citizens who had been refugees from Fascism and five French citizens. Eventually the team had been given considerable support in supplies, materials and information by the United States. In the last eighteen months of the war the project had flourished under the leadership of Professor Cockcroft, who had come out from England to be its head. Its existence had given Britain the foundations of a peacetime nuclear reactor programme, and Canada a flying start into the nuclear age, with all the implications this held for her science and industry. It also brought Canada a seat at the top diplomatic tables. She had not been a signatory of the Quebec Agreement but she was a full member of the important bodies set up under it, and was the only one of the British Dominions fully participating in atomic energy at the end of the war.*

* General Smuts of South Africa also knew of the project on a personal basis. This was partly because of his individual status and partly because of the hope that uranium deposits would be found in South Africa.

Anglo-Canadian atomic co-operation was working well by the end of the war, but some difficult questions loomed for the post-war period. What was going to happen to the Anglo-Canadian project, in which Canada had invested so much, if the British brought their scientists home to start a native programme? What part was Canada, torn between her ties with Britain and the United States, going to play if Anglo-American collaboration diminished after the war? Could the preferential treatment of Canada in atomic secrets be justified to the other Dominions?

Britain's other international atomic entanglements at the end of the war were with Europe and most especially with France. French scientists under Joliot-Curie had been in the forefront of work on slow neutron chain reactions in 1939. When France fell in 1940 two of them, Halban and Kowarski, had fled to Britain carrying with them their precious stock of heavy water and some patents on their early discoveries, and had been installed at the Cavendish Laboratory at Cambridge. It was the Cavendish team that, in 1942, had gone to Canada where three other Frenchmen joined it. But for the arrival of Halban and Kowarski neither the British nor the Canadians would have embarked during the war on a slow-neutron project, which was to be the indispensable basis for the production of power and plutonium.

On the other hand, the Frenchmen, by participating in a large project in North America, had been able to do and learn a great deal. The British had been so impressed by the value of the early French work that they had signed an agreement carving up the world rights in the French patents after the war. However, they could go no further towards plans for post-war collaboration with France for, largely because of American mistrust of Halban, the French atom scientists had become a source of bitterness and misunderstanding between the United States and the United Kingdom. Joliot had visited Sir John Anderson early in 1945 and had emphasised that it would be very dangerous if any one nation occupied a dominant position in atomic energy after the war. If France was not to be admitted to collaboration with the United States and Britain, he said, she would have to turn to Russia: inquiry had been made of Russia as to whether she was interested and the answer had been 'yes'. Joliot had been sure that France and Britain together could 'hold the position vis-à-vis America better than either alone'. Anderson had urged upon Churchill the need for some understand-

ing with the French during the war, but the Prime Minister had
vehemently refused to ask the United States President to permit the
slightest disclosure to France or Russia. General de Gaulle had been
told nothing about the work by the American or British Government, though we now know that he was briefed by the French
scientists.[7]

So the war had left unsettled mutual ties and obligations between
the British and the French. There were other ties of varying strength
in Europe. Britain had been largely responsible in 1944 for an agreement with the Belgian Government pre-empting the whole of the
uranium output of the immensely rich Belgian Congo mines for ten
years ahead. Was Belgium going to ask for some *quid pro quo* after
the war, and if so what?* Finally, there was a strong personal
atomic energy link with Denmark left from the war: Niels Bohr
had returned to his homeland, and would certainly be in the forefront of its atomic energy planning.

After the war there was often talk of the three overlapping circles
of Britain's international commitments – Britain and America,
Britain and the Commonwealth, Britain and Europe. These three
circles certainly existed in the wartime atomic energy story. But the
Anglo-American circle was to the British in 1945 by far the most
important; the other two were subsidiary orbits.

The international ramifications of atomic energy were not of
course the only legacy of the war. In the reckoning there was also
Britain's state of preparedness for a project of her own. Apart from
the work that continued at various ICI establishments, nearly all the
rest of the British project had emigrated to North America by the
end of 1943 and the knowledge of these scientists and engineers was
the product of their work overseas. The Americans had produced
the two different kinds of fissile material – uranium-235 and
plutonium. The British had been concerned with two of the methods
for producing U-235, electromagnetic separation and gaseous diffusion. They had worked so intimately with the Americans on electromagnetic separation that they knew everything there was to be
known about this process, but it was recognised that this might well
be an uneconomic method of separating U-235 in peacetime. The
British also knew a good deal about the American gaseous diffusion
project for separating U-235, in its early, though not its later, stages

* Britain had also been buying the uranium mines in Portugal, but there
was as yet no understanding with the Portuguese Government.

of construction. They had supplied the material for the membranes in the American plant. Plutonium was a different story: the British had never had access to the United States large-scale plants at Hanford where plutonium was produced, nor to the plants for separating and purifying it.* However, irradiated fuel rods had been supplied by the Americans to the Canadian project for work on the separation of plutonium.

The basis for British post-war work in this field was the Anglo-Canadian project, where a pilot pile was being constructed – though it did not operate until after the war – and where laboratory work was being done on a method for separating plutonium. Since the United States was associated with the Canadian project there had been some access to the United States laboratories and technical advice, as well as to supplies of materials. The pile being built in Canada was, however, a heavy water pile and it was clear that, if only for lack of heavy water, Britain's own piles after the war would have to use a graphite moderator as Hanford did. Nevertheless, the British had been able to do a great deal of the planning for their own post-war pilot graphite pile in Canada during the war. They had also been able to let their minds range over many possible systems for producing nuclear power.

Britain's knowledge was not confined to the production of fissile material. Most of her scientists in the United States project had been employed in the holy of holies, Los Alamos, where the methods of making fissile material into bombs were devised. They knew between them most of what there was to know on the subject, although their knowledge of the metallurgy of plutonium was very limited. One of the team, Dr Penney, was in one of the aeroplanes over Nagasaki when the plutonium bomb was dropped.

So the British had acquired a great deal of atomic know-how in North America when the war ended. In Britain itself, ICI had completed much of the basic design work and flowsheets for a low-separation gaseous diffusion plant, and a pilot plant was under construction to produce membranes for it. There was also some experience, again in ICI, of large-scale production of uranium metal. In other directions, however, progress had been disappointing. For a year or so before the end of the war, the senior scientists in the projects in North America and in the Tube Alloys organisation had

* Chadwick alone had been permitted visits to the reactors and some of the laboratories.

been discussing a possible post-war atomic energy programme for Britain. It had been generally assumed that Britain would wish to make atomic bombs after the war as well as pursue the possibilities of atomic power. But there had been disagreement about Britain's route to the production of fissile material – whether she should produce plutonium or U-235 and by which method.

On Chadwick's advice a decision had been postponed. He had felt that to begin serious preparatory work for large-scale production in Britain before the war ended would create a very bad impression in America. He had reiterated how important it was for future agreement and collaboration between Britain and the United States that it should be manifest that the wartime effort had been a co-operative one, and that there should be no serious divergence of opinion through which isolationists in the United States could drive a wedge between the two countries and prevent any post-war collaboration. An attempt by Britain to divert any major effort to a project of her own while war was still being waged would, he had thought, provoke this divergence of opinion. But Chadwick had believed that in any case such an attempt would be premature. For the United States had produced both kinds of fissile material, plutonium and U-235, and they had used three different methods for making the latter.* It would not be clear which fissile material Britain should first produce, and which method she should use if she produced U-235, until the bombs had been tested or used.

On one point all the scientists, together with Sir John Anderson's Tube Alloys Consultative Council, were agreed well before the end of the war: on the need for a decision to set up a research establishment, and for preliminary planning such as the selection of a director and other staff, the choice of a site and so forth. Unfortunately there had been unconscionable delay in taking this basic decision from the time Chadwick had first proposed it in May 1944. Nothing had been firmly decided when the war ended. Chadwick had also proposed in 1944 the establishment of a central laboratory to deal with all radioactive substances – that is, with radioisotopes. Discussions on a scheme had proceeded through 1945.

So, as the atomic bombs fell and Japan surrendered, the week-old Labour Government was faced with a heavy atomic energy agenda. This had to be added to the agenda for settling the affairs of the war-shattered world and the war-shattered British economy and for

---

* The third was thermal diffusion, which was a subsidiary method.

fulfilling those promises of a better world which had sustained war-time morale and led to the Labour Government's election. The atomic energy agenda comprised world affairs on a cosmic scale – the international control of this terrifying new power – plus world affairs in terms of Britain's atomic energy relationships with other countries. It also overlapped the defence agenda. Was Britain to make atomic bombs? If so, how many and with what priority over other weapons? Then there were specific problems about pro-grammes: programmes for raw material supplies, for research and for the production of fissile material – programmes for the most complicated technology yet known in advanced industrial countries. The first item of this formidable agenda seemed the most mundane and yet it had to be settled first in order that progress could be made on all the others. This project was going to extend its tentacles into foreign affairs, Commonwealth affairs, defence, intelligence, indus-try, fuel policy, civil science policy, the universities, medical research, the health and safety of the population. How was it going to be fitted into the machinery of government? What powers of control would the Government take over it?

Appendix 1

STATEMENTS BY THE PRIME MINISTER AND MR CHURCHILL ON THE ATOMIC BOMB, 6 AUGUST 1945

Statement by the Prime Minister

1. Everybody will have seen the important statements which have been made by President Truman and by Mr Stimson, the United States Secretary for War, about the atomic bomb. The problems of the release of energy by atomic fission have been solved and an atomic bomb has been dropped on Japan by the United States Army Air Force.

2. President Truman and Mr Stimson have described in their statements the nature and vast implications of this new discovery. Some account is now required of the part which this country has played in the remarkable scientific advances which have now come to fruition. Before the change of Government Mr Churchill had prepared the statement which follows and I am now issuing it in the form in which he wrote it.

Statement by Mr Churchill

3. By the year 1939 it had become widely recognised among scientists of many nations that the release of energy by atomic fission was a possibility. The problems which remained to be solved before this possibility could be turned into practical achievement were, however, manifold and immense, and few scientists would at that time have ventured to predict that an atomic bomb could be ready for use by 1945. Nevertheless, the potentialities of the project were so great that His Majesty's Government thought it right that research should be carried on in spite of the many competing claims on our scientific manpower. At this stage the research was carried out mainly in our Universities, principally, Oxford, Cambridge, London (Imperial College), Liverpool and Birmingham. At the time of the formation of the Coalition Government, responsibility for co-ordinating the work and pressing it forward lay in the Ministry of

Aircraft Production, advised by a committee of leading scientists presided over by Sir George Thomson.

4. At the same time, under the general arrangements then in force for the pooling of scientific information, there was a full interchange of ideas between the scientists carrying out this work in the United Kingdom and those in the United States.

5. Such progress was made that by the summer of 1941 Sir George Thomson's Committee was able to report that, in their view, there was a reasonable chance that an atomic bomb could be produced before the end of the war. At the end of August 1941 Lord Cherwell, whose duty it was to keep me informed on all these and other technical developments, reported the substantial progress which was being made. The general responsibility for the scientific research carried on under the various technical committees lay with the then Lord President of the Council, Sir John Anderson. In these circumstances (having in mind also the effect of ordinary high-explosive which we had recently experienced), I referred the matter on 30 August 1941, to the Chiefs of Staff Committee in the following minute:

> General Ismay for Chiefs of Staff Committee.
>
> Although personally I am quite content with the existing explosives, I feel we must not stand in the path of improvement, and I therefore think that action should be taken in the sense proposed by Lord Cherwell, and that the Cabinet Minister responsible should be Sir John Anderson.
>
> I shall be glad to know what the Chiefs of Staff Committee think.

The Chiefs of Staff recommended immediate action with the maximum priority.

6. It was then decided to set up within the Department of Scientific and Industrial Research a special division to direct the work, and Imperial Chemical Industries Limited agreed to release Mr W. A. Akers to take charge of this Directorate, which we called, for purposes of secrecy, the 'Directorate of Tube Alloys'. After Sir John Anderson had ceased to be Lord President and became Chancellor of the Exchequer, I asked him to continue to supervise this work, for which he has special qualifications. To advise him, there was set up under his chairmanship a Consultative Council composed of the President of the Royal Society, the Chairman of the

Scientific Advisory Committee of the Cabinet, the Secretary of the Department of Scientific and Industrial Research and Lord Cherwell. The Minister of Aircraft Production, at that time Lord Brabazon, also served on this Committee. Under the Chairmanship of Mr Akers there was also a Technical Committee on which sat the scientists who were directing the different sections of the work, and some others. This Committee was originally composed of Sir James Chadwick, Professor Peierls, and Drs Halban, Simon and Slade. Later it was joined by Sir Charles Darwin and Professors Cockcroft, Oliphant and Feather. Full use was also made of University and industrial laboratories.

7. On 11 October 1941, President Roosevelt sent me a letter suggesting that any extended efforts on this important matter might usefully be co-ordinated or even jointly conducted. Accordingly all British and American efforts were joined and a number of British scientists concerned proceeded to the United States. Apart from these contacts, complete secrecy guarded all these activities and no single person was informed whose work was not indispensable to progress.

8. By the summer of 1942 this expanded programme of research had confirmed with surer and broader foundations the promising forecasts which had been made a year earlier, and the time had come when a decision must be made whether or not to proceed with the construction of large-scale production plants. Meanwhile it had become apparent from the preliminary experiments that these plants would have to be on something like the vast scale described in the American statements which have been published today.

9. Great Britain at this period was fully extended in war production and we could not afford such grave interference with the current munitions programmes on which our warlike operations depended. Moreover, Great Britain was within easy range of German bombers, and the risk of raiders from the sea or air could not be ignored. The United States however, where parallel or similar progress had been made, was free from these dangers. The decision was therefore taken to build the full-scale production plants in America.

10. In the United States the erection of the immense plants was placed under the responsibility of Mr Stimson, United States Secretary of War, and the American Army administration, whose wonderful work and marvellous secrecy cannot be sufficiently admired. The main practical effort and virtually the whole of its

prodigious cost now fell upon the United States authorities, who were assisted by a number of British scientists. The relationship of the British and American contributions was regulated by discussion between the late President Roosevelt and myself, and a Combined Policy Committee was set up.

11. The Canadian Government, whose contribution was most valuable, provided both indispensable raw material for the project as a whole and also necessary facilities for the work of one section of the project which has been carried out in Canada by the three Governments in partnership.

12. The smoothness with which the arrangements for co-operation which were made in 1943 have been carried into effect is a happy augury for our future relations and reflects great credit on all concerned – on the members of the Combined Policy Committee which we set up; on the enthusiasm with which our scientists and technicians gave of their best – particularly Sir James Chadwick who gave up his work at Liverpool to serve as technical adviser to the United Kingdom members of the Policy Committee and spared no effort; and not least, on the generous spirit with which the whole United States organisation welcomed our men and made it possible for them to make their contribution.

13. By God's mercy British and American science outpaced all German efforts. These were on a considerable scale, but far behind. The possession of these powers by the Germans at any time might have altered the result of the war, and profound anxiety was felt by those who were informed. Every effort was made by our intelligence service and by the Royal Air Force to locate in Germany anything resembling the plants which were being created in the United States. In the winter of 1942–1943 most gallant attacks were made in Norway on two occasions by small parties of volunteers from the British Commandos and Norwegian forces, at very heavy loss of life, upon stores of what is called 'heavy water', an element in one of the possible processes. The second of these two attacks was completely successful.

14. The whole burden of execution, including the setting-up of the plants and many technical processes connected therewith in the practical sphere, constitutes one of the greatest triumphs of American – or indeed human – genius of which there is record. Moreover, the decision to make these enormous expenditures upon a project which, however hopefully established by American and British research,

remained nevertheless a heartshaking risk, stands to the everlasting honour of President Roosevelt and his advisers.

15. It is now for Japan to realise in the glare of the first atomic bomb which has smitten her, what the consequences will be of an indefinite continuance of this terrible means of maintaining a rule of law in the world.

16. This revelation of the secrets of nature, long mercifully withheld from man, should arouse the most solemn reflections in the mind and conscience of every human being capable of comprehension. We must indeed pray that these awful agencies will be made to conduce to peace among the nations, and that instead of wreaking measureless havoc upon the entire globe, they may become a perennial fountain of world prosperity.

Note: The 1945 White Paper from which this extract is taken is out of print.

2 Labour's Machinery of Government

BECAUSE of the magnitude and complexity of atomic issues, policy-making was to seem, both to the Labour and Conservative Governments* of the post-war decade, inappropriate to the normal machinery of government. The same was true in the United States and France. How, then, and by whom were policy decisions to be taken and executed? There had to be some forum where Ministers together would decide high policy issues; ministerial and departmental responsibility for organising and supervising the project had to be allocated; interdepartmental co-ordination of policy among senior officials was essential; the department to which atomic energy was allocated had to work out a suitable organisation. In the event, under neither the Labour nor the Conservative Government was the machinery planned as an interlocking whole. It just grew.

Ministers and their Advisory Committees

To take the top level first. Early atomic energy decisions are frequently cited as examples of the move away from Cabinet government towards government by the Prime Minister in a presidential mode.[1] The facts are more complicated than this, but it is true that Mr Attlee's full Cabinet had almost no part in those decisions. Here was a new force which held the threat of annihilation and conceivably the long-term promise of cheap and plentiful power at a time when inadequate coal supplies were strangling the British economy; a force that was intertwined with defence policy and with most important questions of foreign and Commonwealth policy. Yet during the six years of Mr Attlee's Government atomic energy or bombs appeared less than ten times on the agenda of Cabinet meetings. Half these appearances – five – were in the first six months of

* The organisation of the project under the Conservative Government in 1951–2 is dealt with in Chapter 12.

the period, and were concerned mainly with the Truman–Attlee
talks in November 1945 (see Chapter 3). Two were in December
1950 at the height of the Korean War when Mr Attlee flew to warn
Mr Truman against dropping atomic bombs, and one was in the
autumn of 1951 when the Americans were pressing that more
stringent security procedures should be adopted for people employed
in the British atomic energy project. On only three of the occasions
when atomic energy was on the Cabinet agenda was it there for
purposes of discussion: twice in connection with the talks of
November 1945 and once in connection with the security procedures.
On the other occasions, members of the Cabinet were simply being
informed. Moreover, the words 'atomic bomb' were rarely mentioned, even indirectly, in the various Cabinet discussions on defence
and foreign policy in these years, although once at a Cabinet meeting
an objection was raised to the exclusion of atomic energy research
from the Defence Estimates.

Apart from Mr Attlee's two, partly 'atomic', visits to Washington,
the Cabinet as a body was completely excluded from all the major
decisions on atomic policy in these years.* It took no part in the
decisions to establish a research establishment, to build piles to produce plutonium, or, later, to build gaseous diffusion plants to separate
uranium-235; no part in the decisions to make and then test an
atomic bomb, and about the planned place of atomic bombs in
British strategy; in the decisions about priorities; in the decisions
concerning atomic relations with other countries, including the
important atomic negotiations with America after 1945. As we shall
see later, in the one year of the Conservative Government which
comes within the period of this book the Cabinet played a slightly,
though not dramatically, larger role. It was usual, during and after
the Second World War, for many other policy questions to be
formulated and settled within Cabinet committees and small groups
of Ministers. The difference in the case of atomic energy was that
major decisions were not reported to the full Cabinet but were, even
at that level, shrouded in secrecy.

The precedent for excluding the Cabinet from vital discussions on
atomic energy had been set by Mr Churchill during the war. It is

* The Prime Minister informed the Cabinet in advance of the statement he
was going to make in the House of Commons on 22 January 1946 about the
setting-up of an organisation to produce fissile material, but there was no
discussion.

possible that Mr Attlee was encouraged to continue the practice
partly because of the suspicions with which he and Mr Bevin undoubtedly regarded their left-wing colleagues in matters of defence
and foreign policy; the author has, however, seen no specific evidence on this point. Certainly, although Mr Attlee largely kept the
subject off the agenda of the full Cabinet, he did not take major
decisions single-handed. The machinery for ministerial consultation
was curious. For eighteen months there was no standing Ministerial
Committee on atomic energy, complete with specific terms of reference and membership. There was simply 'Gen 75'. Committees of
Ministers who gather together for certain *ad hoc* purposes are given
'Gen' numbers; although they have a formal secretariat and formal
circulation of papers, their existence and functions are not included
in committee books and organisation charts. It is possible that
Cabinet Ministers not attending Gen 75 meetings did not even know
of its existence.

Gen 75 consisted of an inner ring of senior Ministers: to begin
with, the Prime Minister, Herbert Morrison (Lord President of the
Council), Ernest Bevin (Foreign Secretary) and Stafford Cripps
(President of the Board of Trade), while soon Arthur Greenwood
(Lord Privy Seal) and Hugh Dalton (Chancellor of the Exchequer)
were added. Once it was decided that departmental responsibility
for the project should be lodged with the Ministry of Supply, the
Minister, John Wilmot, also attended Gen 75 meetings. Gen 75 was
during its lifetime a real forum for decision-making on atomic
energy policy. It began in August 1945 and held sixteen meetings in
the next sixteen months. It took decisions on plans for international
control of atomic energy; sometimes, though not always, on questions of Anglo-American collaboration;* and on the broad production and research plans for the British project. Although it had
only its somewhat science-fiction nomenclature, Mr Attlee referred
to it informally as the 'Atom Bomb Committee'.

This in itself was curious because until January 1947, the month
after the last meeting of Gen 75, no explicit decision had been taken
to make a British atomic bomb and then the decision was taken not
by Gen 75 but, as we shall see, by a rather smaller and different
collection of Ministers operating as Gen 163: the Prime Minister,
Herbert Morrison, Ernest Bevin, Lord Addison (Secretary of State

---

* The Committee did not discuss the breakdown of Anglo-American co-
operation in the spring of 1946, nor the McMahon Act (see below, Chapter 4).

for the Dominions), A. V. Alexander (Minister of Defence) and John Wilmot.

Shortly after this, at the beginning of February 1947, a proper Ministerial Atomic Energy Committee was set up to replace the Gen 75 meetings and 'to deal with questions of policy in the field of atomic energy which require the consideration of Ministers'. The members were the full roll-call from the last Gen 75 meetings plus the Minister of Defence and the Dominions Secretary, with the Prime Minister as chairman. Considering how many important policy questions were involved in atomic energy, it is surprising that the number of meetings of the Committee was few and diminishing: only five in 1947, two in 1948, four in 1949, two in 1950 and one in 1951. The Committee did not meet in 1952 after the Conservative Government took office.*

In practice there continued to be recourse to Gen meetings, with different title numerals, to settle some of the important specific questions of policy on atomic energy. One was assembled in February 1949 to consider a report by the Chiefs of Staff recommending an increase in the scale of production of fissile material; it consisted of the Prime Minister, Morrison, Bevin, Alexander and G. R. Strauss, now Minister of Supply, sitting with the Chiefs of Staff and atomic energy officials. Since this was a matter of great concern to the Chancellor of the Exchequer and to the President of the Board of Trade because of the demands on resources the new programme was bound to make, it is surprising that it was dealt with in such a narrow defence circle. A little later, in May 1949, another *ad hoc* committee was called to consider the priority of atomic energy in relation to priorities for other areas of defence research and development; this consisted of the Prime Minister, Alexander and Strauss plus the Chiefs of Staff and Sir Henry Tizard, who belonged to the Ministry of Defence and was chairman of the Defence Research Policy Committee. A year later another Gen committee was convened to consider a matter that seems well within the orbit of the Ministerial Atomic Energy Committee – the suggestion that responsibility for atomic energy should be removed from the Ministry of Supply and vested in some kind of public corporation. On this, the Prime Minister, Stafford Cripps (now Chancellor of the Exchequer), Emanuel Shinwell (now Minister of Defence) and G. R. Strauss met with official advisers. Similarly, the

* See Chapter 12. The Ministerial Committee was later resurrected.

Conservative Government was to set up a Gen committee at the end of 1952 to consider the organisation of the atomic energy project. The arrangements for security vetting for atomic energy employees were considered by both Labour and Conservative Governments in different Gen meetings.

The other ministerial forum where atomic energy entered into discussions was of course the Cabinet's Defence Committee, under the chairmanship of the Prime Minister.* The role of the atomic bomb was in particular a feature of the periodic reassessments of global strategy (see Chapters 6 and 7). In the early post-war days, when the possibility of atomic bomb attacks on Britain still seemed remote in time, it was not in the forefront of the reappraisals, but it became more and more crucial after the explosion of Russia's first atomic bomb in August 1949. Even so, the Defence Committee as such was not kept regularly informed of Britain's own programme for producing atomic bombs nor of the expenditure upon it. Not until 1950 did it take decisions on Britain's atomic programme; in that year, however, it was called upon to decide on important questions of priority between atomic and other weapons (see p. 231).

Thus although the full Cabinet played very little part in formulating atomic policies – whether in connection with bomb production or the big problems of international atomic relationships – Ministers acting together took the decisions on most major issues. The pattern of the decision-making process is confused since so many different groupings and titles were involved. The groupings overlapped in membership; the Prime Minister, the Foreign Secretary, the Minister of Defence and the Minister of Supply, with his departmental responsibility for the atomic project, belonged to nearly all of them, while other senior Ministers such as the Chancellor of the Exchequer, the Lord President of the Council, the Lord Privy Seal, the President of the Board of Trade and the Dominions Secretary belonged to some of them. Ten or so Cabinet Ministers, mainly those whose portfolios covered domestic policy, had virtually no opportunity for contributing to the decisions on atomic policy even though such decisions lay at the heart of Britain's foreign relations and her status in the world. The author has seen no evidence that

---

* The other members were: the Lord President of the Council, the Foreign Secretary, the Chancellor of the Exchequer, the Minister of Defence and the three Service Ministers, the Minister of Labour and National Service, and the Minister of Supply.

any of the men thus excluded complained or asked for information. However, the Prime Minister did not take the crucial atomic decisions by himself. Rather, there was an inner circle in the Cabinet who shared this responsibility with him and an outer circle who did not.

The Prime Minister exercised an especially close personal surveillance in this area. He did this with the blessing of his 'inner circle' colleagues and his role was defined, as we shall see in a moment, in the general discussion about ministerial and departmental responsibility for the project. However, there was another complication in deciding where ministerial responsibility should lie; this was the decision to retain the services of Sir John Anderson, who had been the Minister in charge of atomic energy in the wartime coalition Government, first as Lord President and then as Chancellor of the Exchequer. Sir John was Independent M.P. for the Scottish Universities, but although he refused to join the Conservative Party he sat on the Opposition Front Bench after the 1945 election and was in most affairs an implacable enemy of the Labour Government. However, Mr Attlee and he had worked closely together on home affairs during the war and had a warm regard for each other. Mr Attlee, possibly dazed by his own and his colleagues' ignorance of all that this appalling bomb meant, was therefore in a receptive mood when the Secretary of the Cabinet suggested, three days before the first atomic bomb was dropped, that he might care to consider an arrangement whereby Anderson, who was 'fully seized of the long complicated history' of atomic energy, would continue for the present to be associated with it, reporting direct to the Prime Minister on matters where ministerial decisions were called for.

Accordingly, at the first meeting of the Gen 75 Committee on the day the Japanese capitulation was announced, the Prime Minister urged the need for some continuity with the previous organisation, in particular in order to retain the fullest possible measure of co-operation with the Americans. He suggested that an Advisory Committee should be set up, like the committee the President of the United States had already established, to make recommendations on the general policy for the use of this new discovery and especially about the way its international aspects should be handled. The British committee should consist partly of Service and official representatives and partly of scientists associated with the work; the Prime Minister proposed that Sir John Anderson, with whom he had already talked, should be its chairman.

The Gen 75 Ministers* agreed to this while noting that these arrangements would not affect Ministers' responsibility for policy decisions and that the Prime Minister would generally supervise the work, consulting his colleagues from time to time as might be necessary. Letters were immediately exchanged between the Prime Minister and Sir John and the Committee was established, duly composed of Service and official representatives and scientists. In the first year or fifteen months after the war, this Advisory Committee on Atomic Energy was the key committee on the subject. Its terms of reference were wide: '(a) to investigate the implications of the use of atomic energy and to advise the Government what steps should be taken for its development in this country for military or industrial purposes; (b) to put forward proposals for the international treatment of this subject.' The committee was indeed responsible for making the recommendations which led to the first decisions on the shape of Britain's atomic programme and the attitude to international control. It was a very active committee until the autumn of 1946.†

The position of Sir John Anderson as chairman was especially important. He returned to an office in the Cabinet Office, enjoyed the services of its secretariat, and was a quasi-Minister. He was consulted on all important telegrams before they were sent off and on most questions of policy that had to be submitted to the Prime Minister. The High Commissioner in Canada and the British Ambassador in Washington continued to address telegrams personally to Sir John on atomic matters of special secrecy or importance, and it was Sir John who accompanied the Prime Minister on his atomic energy talks with President Truman in Washington in November 1945. Against the undoubted advantage of some continuity of knowledge and experience there were some very marked

* Only Herbert Morrison (Lord President), Ernest Bevin (Foreign Secretary) and Sir Stafford Cripps (President of the Board of Trade) were present at this meeting.

† It had ten meetings in the last four months of 1945 and eleven meetings in 1946, but only four in 1947 and none after May 1947. Its hard-core members were Sir Edward Appleton, Professor Blackett, Sir Henry Dale, Sir George Thomson (scientists), Sir Alan Barlow, Mr N. Butler (officials), Lord Alanbrooke and Lord Tedder (Services). Others who became members or attended meetings were Sir James Chadwick, Sir Robert Robinson, Sir Henry Tizard (scientists), Sir Alexander Cadogan, Mr Oliver Franks, Mr Roger Makins, Sir Archibald Rowlands (officials), Admiral Sir John Cunningham (Services).

disadvantages in this arrangement. The peculiarity of Sir John's quasi-status was reflected in his feeling that he could not attend ministerial meetings, so that there was no direct personal link between the Advisory Committee and ministerial deliberations on its reports and recommendations. An even greater disadvantage was that Sir John was given his new role well before any decision was taken about the peacetime departmental home for atomic energy. When this responsibility was allocated, inevitably the departmental Minister concerned was largely a cipher, and the administrative hierarchy was confused. Indeed, to those who recommend taking important matters out of party politics, the story of Sir John Anderson's responsibilities for atomic energy under the 1945 Labour Government is a warning rather than an encouragement.

Sir John was firmly back in the saddle when discussions began about departmental responsibility for atomic energy. Mr Attlee was inclined at first, even after Sir John had returned, to appoint a single Minister who would give his whole time to this subject. He should be a man of scientific attainments, able to get on with other scientists. He could be Paymaster-General and sit in the Lords, thought Attlee, who quickly added, thinking no doubt of Lord Cherwell whom he disliked, that the precedent for this arrangement was not good. Have we a man to take on the job, he asked? The Secretary of the Cabinet marshalled the disadvantages of appointing a Minister confined to atomic energy. His responsibilities would be limited. He could not deal with international policy, which was the responsibility of the Foreign Secretary, nor with strategy, which was the responsibility of the Minister of Defence. Policy must certainly be co-ordinated, but this must be done by a Cabinet committee at the ministerial level; the chairman of a committee dealing with a matter of such importance could hardly be anyone except the Prime Minister. At a lower level, the Advisory Committee under Anderson would ensure co-ordination. So it seemed that the duties would not be sufficient for a whole-time Minister.

Who then was to look after the project? The Department of Scientific and Industrial Research had been able to take responsibility in wartime because the sums spent were small, and the work was done mainly through research contracts with universities and industry. But they could not harbour a large establishment conducting research with a vital bearing on defence. The Secretary of the Cabinet suggested that the responsibility should be placed with the

Ministry of Supply, which had the experience and organisation for such affairs. Anderson's Advisory Committee had already made the same proposal. Professor Blackett, although very dubious whether Britain should produce atomic bombs, nevertheless felt strongly that since the building-up of research and development involved a large production effort, costing several millions of pounds, it must come under the Ministry of Supply, which had the necessary experience and resources and was in close touch with the chemical and engineering industries.

The Prime Minister and his Gen 75 colleagues endorsed the proposals of the Secretary of the Cabinet in October 1945. There was general insistence, especially by Ernest Bevin, that just as in the United States final authority in atomic matters lay with the President, so in Britain it must rest with the Prime Minister, who would 'consult from time to time with those of his colleagues principally concerned'. The Prime Minister would answer Parliamentary questions on the subject – though sometimes it might be desirable to try to get these removed from the order paper on security grounds. The Gen 75 meeting also agreed that the Government would continue to look for advice on all matters connected with the use of atomic energy to John Anderson's committee, which would still report to the Prime Minister. The responsibility for the research establishment would be with the Minister of Supply, who would appoint a full-time administrator responsible to him under the general supervision of his Permanent Secretary. Meanwhile, Ministers said, the Minister of Supply should give early consideration to any special measures necessary to safeguard the security of the project.

The situation was confused, to say the least. The Prime Minister had ultimate responsibility on all major questions and no major policy decisions were to be taken without his prior approval. A member of the Opposition Front Bench was chairman of the main working committee, handled at the working level key questions of internal and external atomic policy, and reported direct to the Prime Minister. The Minister of Supply had been given an assignment whereby the administration which was his responsibility was separated from the policy which it was to serve. Moreover the decision was taken before the shape of the project as a whole could be seen. In October 1945, when these matters were settled, only a research establishment had been authorised, but not large-scale

production, and when that was included the Minister's position was
to be more anomalous than ever. The fact that the first Minister of
Supply in the Labour Government was a weak Minister did not
help. In 1947 a stronger Minister, G. R. Strauss, took over, but by
then the pattern of management was settled.

We shall consider later the organisation of the project within the
Ministry of Supply. But first, how did the Prime Minister and the
quasi-Minister, Sir John Anderson, exercise the atomic functions
given to them? All the atomic energy policy questions were indeed
submitted to the Prime Minister, but Mr Attlee's personal initiative
in the business, after an initial burst, was limited. Immediately after
the bombs had been dropped on Japan Mr Attlee, as we shall see
in Chapter 3, himself wrote minutes, letters and telegrams on the
question that moved him profoundly – the international control of
atomic energy. Thereafter a great deal of paper about atomic affairs
was put before him and he took the necessary decisions quickly, but
there is little sign in the documents of close personal involvement,
nor did Mr Attlee himself write minutes suggesting or questioning
policy. His normal comment was 'I approve', 'I agree', or simply
his initials. The only exception was when matters of security cropped
up. Mr Attlee – and Mr Bevin and Mr A. V. Alexander as well –
became more and more opposed to the revelation of almost any
information about Britain's atomic project since they thought it
might help the Russians, and Mr Attlee sent a stream of tart personal minutes to the Minister of Supply objecting to visits to Harwell
or to the publication of photographs and information, however
innocuous.

In the autumn of 1947, for example, the Minister of Supply told
the Prime Minister that he was proposing to issue a series of photographs of Harwell to the press and to the Atomic Scientists' Association for their travelling train exhibition which was organised
with the support and co-operation of the Ministry; the photographs
had been carefully selected to ensure that they contained no classified
information. Mr Attlee was extremely cross and was not moved by
an appeal from his personal assistant that a reasonable balance
should be kept in matters of atomic secrecy and that it was just as
wrong to suppress information which was not dangerous as to
publish information that was. Mr Bevin was 'astounded' at the
release of information and photographs without regard to foreign
policy, the United Nations Atomic Energy Commission 'or any of

the other complicated things going on in connection with this business'. He had also disliked the BBC's week of programmes on the subject earlier in the year. Scientists appealed to Sir James Chadwick, who found the whole business a storm in a teacup and asked wearily whether it was really necessary for Bevin to deal with these matters himself. Official support (apart from what was irretrievably committed) and photographs were withheld from the scientists' train exhibition, and Attlee and Bevin agreed that in future they should be consulted personally on any similar questions. Bevin told his officials firmly that they were to note in future that 'nothing on atomic matters must be allowed to happen without both the Prime Minister and myself are informed'. Mr Attlee's almost invariable subsequent attitude was that he could not 'understand the constant requests for publicity'. As we shall see, people in the project became increasingly sure that this restrictive policy on publicity of any kind was a grave mistake.*

Sir John Anderson's involvement in atomic energy was very vigorous for a year or so but then it gradually petered out. Already by March 1946 there were feelings that the arrangement was unsatisfactory: it was a serious disadvantage that the chairman of the Advisory Committee did not attend ministerial meetings. Lord Portal, as we shall see in a moment, was just taking up office within the Ministry of Supply as Controller of Production, Atomic Energy – an appointment made by the Prime Minister and carrying a direct line of approach to him (see p. 40). It seemed that Portal would now be a more suitable link between ministerial and official levels. Moreover Portal needed a strong technical committee to advise him and was setting one up in the Ministry of Supply; it would be mere duplication to have two high-level advisory committees in the field. Anderson's committee in practice combined the functions of an advisory and an interdepartmental committee, and it was clear that these functions must now be split. Whatever the advantage of this arrangement at the start in dealing with a subject so new and so technical, it would be undesirable to discuss in a full advisory committee the many questions, especially those affecting defence and foreign policy, which were now arising. By 1946 informal *ad hoc* meetings of officials were already meeting to discuss them.

So in August 1946 a new standing committee was set up, the Atomic Energy Official Committee, 'to consider questions in the

* The whole question of secrecy is discussed more fully in Chapter 16.

field of atomic energy which call for discussion between Departments'. The Committee was normally to report direct to the Prime
Minister, but where a particular Minister such as the Foreign
Secretary was specially concerned, the report would be submitted to
the Prime Minister through him. The Committee consisted of
representatives of the Chiefs of Staff Secretariat, the Foreign Office,
the Treasury, the Dominions Office and the Ministry of Supply.

The terms of reference of the new committee specifically excluded
those questions appropriate to the committees presided over by Sir
John Anderson and Lord Portal. But in practice, from the time of
the appointment of the Official Committee, the Anderson Committee waned in importance, and Anderson's own position waned
with it. His committee remained formally in existence until
December 1947, when a decision about its future had to be taken
because of his own departure from it. The Ministerial Atomic
Energy Committee agreed that it was no longer appropriate that
Anderson should remain as chairman. No reasons are recorded, but
it seems likely that his criticism of Labour policy in other fields made
his position in atomic energy increasingly odd. Simultaneously
Anderson himself wrote to the Prime Minister a letter of resignation. He asserted with some pride that all the purposes for which
the Committee had been instituted had largely, if not entirely, been
achieved: the research establishment was a going concern, the lines
of large-scale development had been laid down, legislation establishing control at home was on the statute book, the problem of international control had been explored in all its aspects, the raw material
position was remarkably satisfactory. All this was true, although
the achievements were not all the result of the Committee's work.*
There were also personal considerations why Anderson wished to
go. When the Churchill Government fell, Anderson had been
invited to resume his directorship of ICI but had thought it incom-
patible with work on the Committee. Now the invitation had been
renewed and he had accepted.

By this time, the Atomic Energy Official Committee had become
the main forum for interdepartmental discussions of atomic policy as
they concerned Anglo-American relations, other foreign and

---

* See Chapters 4 and 11 for Sir James Chadwick's achievement on raw
materials. Anderson should have added the considerable achievements of his
Nuclear Physics Sub-Committee which promoted the study of nuclear physics
in the universities (see Chapter 18).

Commonwealth relations, international control and raw materials supply, although for some time it played little part in the discussion of production plans. The Committee had not been very dynamic during its first six months, but it underwent a marked change in March 1947 when Roger Makins* of the Foreign Office took over the chairmanship.† He had recently returned from Washington, where he had been responsible in the Embassy for atomic affairs, to become an assistant under-secretary – the third tier down in the official hierarchy. It was another of the administrative anomalies of atomic energy that someone at this level should be directly responsible to the Prime Minister, as Makins was in his capacity as chairman of the Official Committee. He did not report through the Permanent Under-Secretary or the Foreign Secretary, and the Foreign Secretary himself influenced atomic energy policy not departmentally but simply as a member of Mr Attlee's inner group of Cabinet Ministers. Makins carried a heavy load, for atomic energy was only one of his many duties as head of the Foreign Office General Division which included, *inter alia*, economic affairs. However, under him the Official Committee became a real focus of power: several civil servants of long experience found it one of the most effective committees they had ever known.

The dominance of the Official Committee had led directly to the decline of the Advisory Committee, but there were still some doubts about the wisdom of abolishing the latter. Such a move might arouse suspicions and indeed it was thought that there were 'a number of scientific personages' who would be likely to cause considerable embarrassment to the Government but for the fact that as members of the Advisory Committee they received information and had occasional opportunities for discussion and for giving their views to the Government. However rationalisation won and when Sir John Anderson gave up the chairmanship at the end of 1947 his Advisory Committee was disbanded. There was to be a new sub-committee on atomic energy of the Government's Advisory Council on Scientific Policy with Sir James Chadwick as chairman, and it was

* Minister at the British Embassy in charge of atomic energy policy 1945–7, Assistant and later Deputy Under-Secretary in the Foreign Office 1947–52, knighted as Sir Roger Makins 1949, later Ambassador in Washington 1952–6, and Chairman of the Atomic Energy Authority 1960–4, created Lord Sherfield 1964.

† For a short time he was nominally deputy chairman with Sir Edward Bridges as chairman, but in practice he always chaired the Committee.

hoped that Chadwick's unique experience and knowledge would now provide the chief link between the various advisory committees. Chadwick was anxious that Lord Cherwell should be a member of his sub-committee, and Sir Henry Tizard, the chairman of the main Advisory Council on Scientific Policy, known to be an antagonist of Cherwell's, thought there was a great deal to be said for this, but Mr Attlee gave a firm 'no'. Cherwell, he said, was very much more an Opposition politician than a scientist and it would be illogical to get rid of John Anderson and bring in Cherwell. However, throughout the period of the Labour Government Cherwell was in close touch with the project as a member of Lord Portal's Technical Committee in the Ministry of Supply.

Defence and Production

With these reorganisations in January 1948, the interdepartmental and advisory committees seemed to have become much more sensible, but there remained one gap which caused a good deal of resentment. In this era of the Labour Government, atomic energy was almost entirely a defence affair. Yet there were no adequate arrangements below the Prime Minister and his inner circle of Ministers for bringing the defence aspects of atomic energy together either with its foreign policy or raw materials aspects or with the other programmes of defence research and production. Atomic energy remained obstinately outside the Ministry of Defence's responsibility for supervising and co-ordinating defence programmes.

This was partly because the Ministry of Defence itself was not established until October 1946. Until then the strategic aspects of atomic energy were the business only of the Chiefs of Staff, who were at this stage concerned simply to reiterate their conviction that Britain must have atomic bombs, and that they must be made in the United Kingdom. However, atomic bombs belonged to the middle distance and the Chiefs of Staff were preoccupied with the immediate and pressing military problems of the aftermath of the war. Just before the war ended, a special *ad hoc* committee of scientists with Tizard as chairman had made a report on 'Future Developments in Weapons and Methods of War', but on Mr Churchill's instructions they had been forbidden access to any information about atomic bombs. Soon after the war ended, an Atomic Weapons Sub-Committee of the Deputy Chiefs of Staff Committee was set up to study and make recommendations about the use of atomic energy in weapons of war. It began by enthusiastically collecting information about atomic energy and bombs, but then it found that another Chiefs of Staff Committee, the Joint Technical Warfare Committee, was charged with revising the Tizard report on future weapons. So it turned over all its 'matters of fact relating to atomic energy' to this committee, went into suspension and never returned. The Technical Warfare Committee reported in July 1946 that, although it appreciated the profound changes in warfare that atomic energy had brought about, it did not seem likely that changes would take place until at least five years hence.

In October 1946 the Ministry of Defence was created. Tizard became its scientific adviser, and also chairman of the Defence Research Policy Committee set up in January 1947 to advise the Minister of Defence and the Chiefs of Staff on matters connected with the formulation of science policy. By this time, as we shall see, Lord Portal, former Chief of the Air Staff, was firmly in the saddle as Controller, and his atomic energy project was already regarded as something whose self-contained and elevated status was above debate: other departments and organisations could become involved in its problems only in order to help, never to question. At a very early meeting of the DRPC, Tizard reported that the responsibility of the Committee in atomic affairs was not sufficiently defined and other members emphasised their uneasiness. A Royal Air Force representative pointed out that aircraft were being designed in ignorance of the size and character of the missiles they might have to carry, while the Admiralty emphasised their great interest in atomic energy as a means of propulsion.

Early in 1947 the Secretary of the Cabinet and the Prime Minister's special assistant considered the relationship between Tizard and his committee and atomic energy. They believed that Tizard was not only concerned with committee relationships, but was toying with the idea that the administrative and executive responsibilities for atomic energy should come within his organisation. They saw in this the remains of Tizard's extreme soreness at his exclusion from atomic energy affairs during the war. However, both advisers cautioned the Prime Minister against such a change, if only because the eventual application of atomic energy might be as important for civil industry as for defence.

So it was generally agreed, and the Minister of Defence concurred, that the administrative and executive responsibility for atomic energy should stay put. The Defence Research Policy Committee was not to impinge on the preserves of Anderson's Advisory Committee, which was at that time still meeting and giving advice on production plans, but Tizard was to join it. The DRPC was, however, to review the conclusions set out in the 1946 report of the Joint Technical Warfare Committee, including the sections on atomic energy. This would enable the DRPC to discharge its responsibilities for seeing that the strategic consequences of atomic energy were properly appreciated by the Defence departments and that the planning of defence research programmes reflected these consequences.

Confusion persisted. A DRPC sub-committee on the strategic aspects of atomic energy was indeed set up to assemble all the latest information on the subject, but it was to be concerned not with policy but simply with setting out all the relevant facts. Tizard also joined Anderson's Advisory Committee, but it met only twice thereafter. The Prime Minister's office understood that Tizard was receiving full information about developments in atomic energy and that the relevant committee papers were going to him, but this was clearly not true. For in June 1947 Tizard said at a Chiefs of Staff meeting that no decision had yet been taken on the production of atomic weapons, which was, as the Chiefs of Staff well knew, a misstatement of fact, since the decision to make a bomb had been made in extreme secrecy in January 1947 just as the DRPC was born; Tizard, it seems, was excluded from the very small circle of people who knew about it. Nor did Tizard receive the papers from the top committees in the Department of Atomic Energy in the Ministry of Supply which discussed the project in any detail. Tizard did not know at quite a late stage who was responsible for collaboration with the United States in atomic energy. 'If I were the only one who was confused about these matters', he wrote, 'I should think it was merely due to my own stupidity, but the Minister of Defence is himself uncertain where responsibilities lie.' The DRPC was expected to report on the scientific research and development programmes and policies necessary to meet the global strategy laid down by the Chiefs of Staff. Yet in its first report at the end of 1947 the information available to it about the atomic programme was so meagre that its assumptions on the subject were nonsensical.

There was at the end of 1947 a renewed outburst of concern about the inadequacy of the arrangements for bringing the defence aspects of atomic energy within the scope of the central defence machine. No one seemed clear about the responsibility of the Chiefs of Staff for providing the strategic guidance which would govern the production of atomic weapons, nor about the responsibility of the DRPC for providing advice on the production of atomic weapons as part of its task of supervising and co-ordinating programmes of defence research and production. When the secretary of the Chiefs of Staff Committee tried, at the end of 1947, to explain the sequence of the decision-making process he found the task difficult, since in the interests of security little had been recorded and such records of meetings as existed had not been circulated. Not surprisingly, his conclusions about who had formulated atomic energy production policy were incorrect.

The Chiefs of Staff, Sir Henry Tizard and Lord Portal met to discuss the difficulties. Everyone agreed that it was the constitutional responsibility of the Chiefs of Staff to make recommendations to the Government on the strategic implications of atomic warfare. In fact, as Portal admitted, the scale of production of fissile material had not been related to strategic policy,* but he had kept the Chiefs of Staff fully informed of progress, and they had a representative on Anderson's Advisory Committee which had made the recommendations to the Government on the scale of the British project. Portal was willing to co-operate with the Chiefs of Staff to the fullest possible degree.

There was also agreement on the need to bridge the serious gap between the scientific effort devoted to atomic and to other weapons: atomic developments would affect developments in other types of weapons, and unless they could all be studied as a whole and in relation to each other there was a danger that the scientific effort might be misdirected. It seemed that a committee should be set up, whether or not under the DRPC, to reconcile the research priorities for atomic and conventional weapons. Portal agreed, since the existing general research priorities could not be maintained with the limited scientific effort available, but he assumed that the proposed committee would deal only with policy recommendations and not with the methods of implementation which must, he asserted, remain the responsibility of the Ministry of Supply.

When the atomic committee structure was reviewed at the end of

* See below, Chapters 6 and 7, for the formulation of the production programme.

1947, because Anderson's Advisory Committee was to be wound up, the Prime Minister agreed to the establishment of two new committees, only one of which, however, came under the DRPC. One was the Atomic Energy (Defence Research) – or AE(DR) – Committee, to review and report on the relations between defence research programmes as a whole and atomic energy defence research. Tizard was to be chairman and it would include Chadwick, the representatives of the three Services and some of the chief figures of the Ministry of Supply's Division of Atomic Energy. The second new committee, the Atomic Energy (Review of Production) Committee, came under Lord Portal and its job was to review the scale of atomic energy production in relation to the requirements of defence. Again it would include Chadwick, and representatives of the Services and Ministry of Defence and of the Division of Atomic Energy; there would also be a Treasury representative.

Tizard may have rejoiced that he had at last won some control over atomic energy, but in practice it still eluded him. For it was Portal's Review of Production Committee, with its clear and specific task, which proved important. The starting-point of the Committee's activities was, it is true, a report to the Chiefs of Staff in April 1948 from the Tizard–DRPC sub-committee on the strategic aspects of atomic energy, set up, it will be recalled, nine months earlier. However, this was simply a factual statement of the nature of atomic weapons, their potentialities, the means of delivering them and the estimated effects on various types of target. An inter-Services sub-committee was then set up to assess in the light of this report the strategic requirements for atomic weapons from United Kingdom production. On the basis of this assessment, the Review of Production Committee did its work.

This review of production itself led to attenuation of the functions of Tizard's AE(DR) Committee. If the Chiefs of Staff machinery concluded that a certain number of atomic bombs were strategically essential to Britain, it was very difficult for the AE(DR) Committee to reopen the question whether too much effort was being put into research for atomic, compared with other, weapons. The Committee's job therefore turned out to be something much more limited – to review the requirements of the atomic weapons programme that were put forward and to decide how these could be met with the least damage to other defence research and development programmes. Tizard became more and more irritated by his own inability to enter effectively into the atomic research arena. He repeatedly urged that the DRPC should have the same responsibility for atomic energy defence research and development as for all other defence research and development. Portal and the Ministry of Supply were, however, adamant in resisting this proposal and they were able to bring forward one weak but nevertheless compelling justification – that the prospects of better collaboration with the United States depended on maintaining an atomic organisation which was carefully circumscribed. In 1949 the Tizard–Portal argument became part of a renewed and much wider debate about the priority to be given to atomic bombs in the general strategy of the United Kingdom (see Chapter 7).

Departmental Organisation

So far this chapter has been concerned with the formulation of atomic energy policy at the top levels of government – by Ministers and by senior interdepartmental and advisory committees. We have seen that ministerial responsibility was curiously divided. It was accepted that the Prime Minister himself would supervise atomic energy work generally, and a Foreign Office official reported direct to him rather than to the Foreign Secretary on the policy questions involved; a quasi-Minister belonging to the Opposition benches, Sir John Anderson, was given special authority to deal with major matters of policy; this major area of defence research evaded the authority of the Ministry of Defence; the Minister of Supply was given executive responsibility for the project. What was the organisation for carrying out this responsibility?

On one point a decision was assumed rather than taken. In discussions during the war, some of the scientists, including Chadwick, had felt that it would be difficult to carry out the project as they conceived it within the usual framework of a Government department. They had inclined to the idea of a Government-controlled corporation or trust, like Power Jets. However, when organisation was discussed in the autumn of 1945, Ministers felt generally that control of research could not be divided from large-scale production and that it was 'undesirable that an enterprise of this kind should appear to be a commercial undertaking'. The scientists themselves felt that research in this field was of permanent importance for the future of the country and could not be left to private enterprise.

The organisation that evolved within the Ministry of Supply was affected by the order in which the early decisions were taken. Two decisions were taken by Ministers simultaneously – the decision to make the Minister of Supply responsible and the decision to set up a research establishment. As we have seen, the latter decision should have been taken during the war but it was one of the pieces of un-finished business left for the Labour Government. There was bitter disappointment that even then the decision was not taken immedi-ately but was left for two months. It was finally taken in October 1945 on the basis of the paper that Anderson's wartime Consultative Council had drawn up for Mr Churchill in the summer. How-ever, in the summer large-scale production of fissile material was not an immediate prospect, whereas in October it was. In the summer a decision on the organisation of the research establishment could have been taken on its own. But in October the organisation of the research establishment and of the large-scale plants needed to be considered together: it was essential that there should be the closest possible links between development and production and that the two functions should be under one and the same organisation. As it was, the director of the research establishment was appointed before it had been decided whether to build large plants or who should organise this side of the project.

It had always been recognised that the task of the director of the research establishment would not be easy. At first the establishment might be rather academic, but it would need to change its balance towards the technical development of processes and plants, while maintaining fundamental research so as to preserve a fresh and inquiring spirit. It must be able by the processes of cross-fertilisation to become an invigorating centre with a very wide influence. The director would have to arrange suitable contacts between the establishment, university and industrial laboratories and other Government institutions. The post would call for tact, judgement and wise discretion.

Since Chadwick himself did not wish to take the post, only one man had ever been seriously considered for the directorship – Professor Cockcroft. Chadwick had strongly urged his appointment in the summer. 'He has many virtues which would contribute to the smooth running of the Establishment', he had written,

and he would keep his hand on all the strings. In common with most scientists he also has many faults and those we must recognise from the beginning so that we can supplement him by a suitable choice of assistants. For example his knowledge is wide but it is not at all profound; his views are of rather a dull everyday hue. On the other hand his temper is so equable and his patience and persistence so inexhaustible that we can put in lively and relatively irresponsible men who have the real feeling for research without fear of upsetting the balance.

On one point all the scientists had been agreed: the establishment should enjoy greater freedom of action than was normally allowed to Government establishments. The reason was not only the unique importance of the project but the width and variety of its practical applications. It was argued that new technical discoveries arising from it could only be followed up quickly and effectively if use was made of all the best scientific talent in the country, including many scientists from universities and elsewhere whose help could only be obtained on a part-time basis. This would call for methods of administration and a degree of continuous improvisation which could not easily be reconciled with the normal routine of a government establishment. There could be no impairment of the usual Parliamentary control over expenditure of voted money, but some system of administration must be devised which would allow those responsible for administering the establishment a free hand in the allocation of available funds.

When Cockcroft was formally offered the directorship by the Permanent Secretary of the Ministry of Supply he made another stipulation that was confirmed in writing: subject to rules for safeguarding military secrets, the work of the establishment was to be carried on under conditions in which the exchange of views and publication of results would be similar to those in university research laboratories.

So Cockcroft was appointed in January 1946 and was responsible only to the Minister and his Permanent Secretary. His status was in no way affected by the decision Ministers made – at the same meeting when his appointment was confirmed – that the Minister of Supply would appoint a full-time administrator to plan and direct the atomic energy project. The transfer of responsibility to the Ministry of Supply was announced in Parliament at the end of October 1945[2] and plans were quickly put in hand for moving the Directorate of Tube Alloys people from their wartime home in the

Department of Scientific and Industrial Research to the Ministry. It became urgent to appoint within the Ministry a Controller of Atomic Energy, who must be a man of first-class capacity, recognised as such not only by Ministers but by Parliament and the public. A number of Army and Royal Air Force officers were considered, only to be dismissed as not available or as lacking the necessary competence for the job. At first it seemed possibly unwise to appoint a professional soldier, since this might seem to give too strong a bias to the military aspects: some scientists were already expressing alarm on this point. It was nearly the end of December 1945 when the Minister of Supply suggested Lord Portal, wartime Chief of the Air Staff, for the job. Portal was most reluctant to accept the post and felt that he lacked administrative experience outside the narrow limits of his career in the Royal Air Force. But the Prime Minister prevailed and Portal agreed to take the job from March 1946 for about two years.

There was some dismay among the scientists at this new organisation – the transfer of the project to the Ministry of Supply and the appointment of Portal. There was a disposition to blame Chadwick and Cockcroft who must, it was assumed, have been consulted about the new arrangements. As we have seen, the scientists on Anderson's committee had perceived the advantages of the Ministry of Supply. However, as Chadwick said, the transfer to this Ministry was accepted before he or Cockcroft could make any protests, and he himself felt so strongly about the whole business that he could hardly bear to write about it. But Chadwick did his best to dispel the apprehensions about Portal's appointment. He himself was very glad that Portal had taken the job – 'he impressed me more than anyone I have met for a very long time'. Chadwick did not think the appointment would emphasise too strongly the military aspects of the project, which were, in any case, bound to be to the fore now and perhaps for some time. It would be helpful in relations with other countries, especially with the United States, to have a man like Portal in charge. General Groves, who was still in charge of the United States project, was indeed impressed by the appointment.

Lord Portal belonged to the Ministry of Supply but his responsibility was to the Prime Minister rather than to his Minister; indeed, as we shall see, when Portal initiated discussions on the decision to make atomic bombs he informed the Permanent Secretary but would have been glad to keep the subject away from the

Minister. Portal had direct access to the Prime Minister, although he rarely used it. The title of Portal's post was Controller of Production, Atomic Energy, and he was asked to take the post on the understanding that his jurisdiction did not cover the research establishment at Harwell, or Cockcroft, who had been appointed before him. Indeed, Portal had no written terms of reference. Officials in the Cabinet Office and 10 Downing Street had hoped he would exercise general co-ordination of the project in Whitehall, and when the Atomic Energy Official Committee was established in the summer of 1946 they expected Portal to be chairman. But Portal saw his functions as strictly related to production and he flatly refused to extend them even in the face of intervention by the Prime Minister.

When Portal took over, another key appointment besides Cockcroft's had already been decided upon. At the end of 1945 Christopher Hinton, one of the great British engineers of his day, was due to leave the post of Deputy Director General of Filling Factories in the Ministry of Supply and to return to ICI. On ICI advice, the Ministry saw that he was the right person to organise the design, construction and operation of the large-scale production plants and he had agreed to do this, at a salary well below his ICI salary. He set up his headquarters at an old filling factory at Risley in Lancashire on 4 February 1946.

When Portal took over in March 1946, the embryo organisations of Cockcroft, for research, and Hinton, for production, already existed. There was also in the Ministry of Supply the organisation of the Directorate of Tube Alloys which had been transferred there. Sir Wallace Akers had recently returned to ICI but his deputy, Michael Perrin, who had also come from ICI, was still in post. There was also a very small group of Ministry civil servants looking after the normal administrative needs of the new project. When Portal arrived he quickly set out his proposals for his new department. He saw that, for rapid progress with minimum waste of effort, there must be the most intimate co-ordination of policy, coupled with the greatest possible decentralisation in execution. There were four aspects of the enterprise upon each of which the Controller required the advice of a responsible official:

(*a*) Scientific advice. Portal did not wish to become in any way responsible for the scientific research programme, but he must have an authoritative channel of scientific advice, and the right to pose scientific questions affecting technical policy and production and if necessary to have scientific research initiated for the purpose of getting answers to these questions.

(*b*) The organisation of design and production which would maintain direct liaison with the research establishment. Matters of major technical policy about the main plant would be referred to the Controller.

(*c*) Technical policy. The head of this section would be responsible for ensuring that the technical policy being followed accorded with the latest scientific information available. He would also formulate in the first instance any technical (as opposed to purely scientific) advice on atomic energy required by the Government Departments and would be responsible for liaison with them on technical policy.

(*d*) Administrative and non-technical policy to be provided by Ministry civil servants.

Cockcroft would clearly fill function (*a*) in addition to his own independent duties, and Hinton was already filling (*b*). Portal proposed Perrin for function (*c*).

When Chadwick was asked by Portal for his views, he was very critical on two main counts. Firstly, he felt it was a great mistake that was bound to lead to difficulties and hindrances if the production side under Portal was separated from the research and development side under Cockcroft. He could not understand how such a divorce had come about, unless because Cockcroft was apprehensive that he might find himself responsible not only to Portal but to a deputy. Chadwick was convinced that the whole effort should be under one head who should bear ultimate responsibility for all that was done or not done. The director of the research establishment must indeed have undisputed internal control of his laboratories, but matters of general policy would arise, especially over development, which would have a wide bearing on the project and would affect the production side. Surely, said Chadwick, the responsibility for decisions on these and allied matters must fall to the head of the organisation. Otherwise different parts of the organisation might pull in different directions at the same time, with resulting confusion and division of purpose.

Chadwick's other criticism concerned Portal's proposal for a

Deputy Controller (Technical Policy). Chadwick saw how important the post would be in assuring adequate contact and collaboration between the various parts of the project and in keeping Portal in close touch with its many aspects. It seemed that the powers Portal planned to give to this deputy controller would make him the king-pin of the organisation – 'your deputy in general and your other self' as Chadwick put it. Chadwick doubted the wisdom of appointing Perrin, for he remembered the difficulties of the wartime Tube Alloys directorate. Partly because of its ICI connections, some of the British scientists had been bitter about it and the Americans had been suspicious. Chadwick felt Perrin's appointment to the new post might compromise relations between Portal's office and many of the scientists in or out of Harwell, and would not ease collaboration with the United States and Canada. Cockcroft shared these doubts.

However, Portal's proposals went through intact. Perrin became Deputy Controller (Technical Policy). The division between control of research and of production remained and not until January 1950 did Cockcroft agree to become part of Portal's organisation. Coordination became even more important from 1947 onwards when Dr Penney was made responsible for the development and fabrication of an atomic bomb. It also became more difficult because Penney was already Chief Superintendent of Armament Research, responsible to the Controller of Supplies (Munitions) within the Ministry of Supply and with an additional functional line to the Chief Scientist of the Ministry. He now acquired dual allegiance – to Portal on atomic bomb matters and to the Controller of Supplies (Munitions) for other weapon affairs. Not until late 1950 were Penney's functions separated. Henceforward he was responsible only for atomic weapons and only to the Controller of Atomic Energy.*

Chadwick's misgivings about the organisation proved justified and the ambiguities of responsibility in the first years left their mark. Fortunately, after some initial misunderstanding, collaboration at the working level, albeit between men of very different temperaments, proved surprisingly good during the period of this book (see Chapter 13). Nevertheless, there was never firm central control or guidance of the project, and this led to uncertainties over functions – over, for example, the balance and aims of Harwell's

* In late 1950 the title of the post was changed from 'Controller of Production, Atomic Energy' to 'Controller of Atomic Energy'.

research and development work – some of which were to persist for many years (see Chapter 18).

As Chadwick feared, Perrin's appointment was not popular within the project. He got on excellently with senior civil servants and was a great help to Portal in the execution of his central functions, for example in dealings with the Chiefs of Staff, especially over the review of production requirements, and was also, as in the war, extremely wise in intelligence affairs. But it was not easy for Perrin to act as the nerve-centre of the project and as the channel of communication between Portal and the different establishments. Portal himself was clearly no technical expert on atomic energy so that Perrin's hand was seen, whether rightly or wrongly, in any edicts which came from London. It was not only the scientists with their wartime memories who were unhappy. Hinton and his *de facto* deputy, W. L. Owen, had both come from ICI; Hinton had been senior to Perrin and Owen had been there very much longer than Perrin. Owen, faced with extremely heavy engineering responsibilities, was angry that Perrin should have a higher rank and salary than his own. Hinton was uneasy because Perrin had been primarily on the research, rather than the production, side of ICI. A retired air commodore was appointed under Perrin to progress the Risley organisation. Since he had no qualifications which would have enabled him to form sound judgements or to help in any way, his appointment was regarded as an insult; Hinton refused to allow him to visit the atomic factories. By contrast, the retired air vice-marshal, E. D. Davis, usually referred to as 'Dizzy', who was appointed under Perrin to progress weapon development and act as a central liaison with the Service users, was effective and useful.

Apart from Portal and his staff, there was in the Ministry of Supply's Division of Atomic Energy a small band of career civil servants who serviced the project – an under-secretary, an assistant secretary and two principals. They were not the usual Civil Service birds of passage moving quickly between jobs, but remained connected with atomic energy for unusually long periods. As we shall see, Hinton invited the assistant secretary concerned to join the key Risley committee, and from that time onwards a sympathetic rapport grew up (see Chapter 21). The project used the common services of the Ministry of Supply – contracts, housing, canteens, establishments – but otherwise it was an island unto itself within the Ministry. Its special security barriers made it known as 'the cage'.

Thus the overall direction and control of the atomic energy project within the Ministry of Supply was weak. Apart from the organisational difficulties, Portal himself was drained by the war, had no experience of a production organisation and had little taste for the atomic energy job. He presided most formally over bi-monthly meetings of the Atomic Energy Council which he set up within the Ministry of Supply; here the directors of the various bits of the project met and this provided some co-ordination, although, for reasons of secrecy, Penney did not attend these meetings until July 1948. He also instituted, as soon as he took office, a Technical Committee to replace the old Tube Alloys Technical Committee; it included outside scientists* to give advice on a whole range of problems. In general, however, he was remote and unbending and made little attempt to interfere. A scientist in the project wrote that those who had met Portal had been impressed by his personality and integrity, but, he added, 'how many of the atomic energy staff either in the research or production projects have ever seen him?' Portal came into his own in dealings with Ministers and the Chiefs of Staff. The Prime Minister and other senior Ministers had admired him in the war, and his views carried great weight with them. The Chiefs of Staff Committee was Portal's own territory; its members were his former subordinates and his prestige there was immensely high. Other people in the project probably never knew how tenaciously Portal fought with Ministers and Chiefs of Staff for a continued top priority rating for atomic energy in this period. He always succeeded. Portal's influence was strong in another direction: he believed the project should be turned over to a corporation and his opinion on this counted for much with Lord Cherwell.

Portal's limited role in the project is illustrated by his request, only

* The following served on it at various times: Sir Wallace Akers, Sir James Chadwick, Lord Cherwell, Dr Cockcroft, Sir Charles Darwin, Professor P. I. Dee, Professor H. J. Emeleus, Professor N. Feather, Mr Hinton, Professor M. L. Oliphant, Mr L. Owen, Professor R. E. Peierls, Dr R. P. Linstead, Professor M. H. L. Pryce, Sir Geoffrey Taylor, Sir Claude Gibb, Mr C. F. Kearton, Professor T. R. C. Fox, Dr W. B. Lewis, Dr H. W. B. Skinner, Professor F. E. Simon, Professor D. Hanson, Dr R. Spence, Dr W. G. Penney, Mr M. W. Perrin. On the question of industrialists' membership of the Committee, see Chapter 17.

eighteen months after he took over, to vacate it. He found that the
job was very spasmodic and did not take up the whole of his time.
At the same time his qualities – his high standing and reputation
especially with the Americans, his impartiality, and his ability to
present the broad aspects of atomic energy policy in high-level discussions – made him difficult to replace. Finally, Portal agreed to
stay but his post was recognised as part-time. There were disadvantages in the arrangement; for example, during crucial Anglo-
American discussions in 1949 Portal was touring South Africa for
Barclays Bank. Portal and Perrin both stayed on in the project until
the autumn of 1951.

It is convenient to add here the postscript to Portal's departure. It
was hoped to get another ex-Chief of Staff to do the job, but both
Lord Tedder and Lord Fraser absolutely refused. Lord Addison,
Dominions Secretary, felt strongly that the new Controller should
not be from the Services but the Minister of Supply felt it was an
advantage, although the reason he gave – that the Armed Services
played a predominant part in atomic energy affairs in the United
States – was not correct. The choice fell on a soldier, General Sir
Frederick Morgan. It was generally believed among the senior
people in the project that the post went to 'the wrong Morgan', that
the Prime Minister really meant Sir William Morgan who had
impressed him as representative of the Chiefs of Staff in Washington,
but that he confused the names and the letter had already gone to
Sir Frederick when the mistake was sorted out. Sir Frederick took
up the post but was generally regarded as a mere figurehead. Very
soon afterwards, however, the Government had changed and a
Minister with a very close personal interest in atomic energy, and
the wish to supervise it, was back on the scene – Lord Cherwell
(see Chapter 12).

This then was the organisation of the project within the Ministry
of Supply. There is one other section of the atomic energy organisation that must be mentioned – the organisation in Washington, for
negotiations with the Americans will be a constant thread in this
book. At the end of the war Sir James Chadwick was in charge of
the British atomic scientists in the United States project and was in
this capacity the link with its director, General Groves. He was also
adviser to the two British members of the Combined Policy Committee, the high-level forum for deciding upon Anglo-American
problems. One British member was, in the post-war years (though

not in wartime), the Ambassador in Washington* and the other was, first, Field-Marshal Lord Wilson, the British representative on the Combined Chiefs of Staff Committee while that body continued, and then Sir Gordon Munro, who was the Treasury representative in Washington and in charge of atomic energy raw materials.

Chadwick had performed his wartime task magnificently and indeed the British would not have played nearly such an important part in the American project if it had not been for the relations of trust and friendship he had established with General Groves.[3] His importance had been still greater because he had been the one constant link on the British side, amidst changes in the British Embassy and Combined Chiefs of Staff. In many ways the work had been uncongenial to him: he wrote sadly that he was overburdened with affairs of one kind and another 'for much of which I am fitted neither by temperament, training nor ability'. Now, after the war, he remained for a year, helping with the negotiations with the Americans, ensuring a smooth transfer of staff back to England, writing a long series of immensely wise letters to the authorities in Britain about production programmes and organisation, and to scientists about their misgivings or their personal problems. He had worn himself out – he had had only one day's holiday in three years – in the pursuit of Britain's interests and in the hope of post-war Anglo-American collaboration; the British Embassy was anxious that he should be persuaded to visit Washington once a year.† Chadwick's very great services to his country were inadequately appreciated: symbolically, when he arrived back at Southampton he was met by a relatively junior official and by a car whose chauffeur ran out of petrol on the journey and had no coupons to buy more. He and Lady Chadwick quietly finished their journey to Euston by bus.

After Chadwick left Washington, the technical adviser to the British Embassy, and the channel for technical communications, was the head of the United Kingdom Scientific Mission (a DSIR man) who had a member of the Ministry of Supply's Division of Atomic Energy to help him. Within the Embassy proper one senior official of Minister status spent a great deal of time on atomic

* Lord Halifax until May 1946; Lord Inverchapel, May 1946–May 1948; Sir Oliver Franks, May 1948–December 1950.

† Chadwick returned for some weeks early in 1947 as Scientific Adviser to the British delegate at the United Nations Atomic Energy Commission.

energy. Roger Makins was in charge of it in the last months of the
war and until he left Washington for London early in 1947. He
pointed out that the other duties of the post were extremely onerous
and that although he tried to give atomic energy first priority, it was
'frankly impossible' to do all that was needed. His urgent request
to the Foreign Office for an assistant had met with no response. It
was decided that when he left, his atomic work should be taken
over by Sir Gordon Munro who would be allocated another member
of the Embassy staff to help him. This was Donald Maclean, who
later fled to Russia. He was employed on atomic energy work, with
access to all the secret papers going to and from the Embassy on the
subject, from the end of 1946 to September 1948, and he became
British Secretary of the Combined Policy Committee. He was closely
involved in uranium negotiations and in this capacity had a pass to
the office of the United States Atomic Energy Commission.

The British atomic energy organisation in Washington did not
specifically cover defence affairs. Field-Marshal Lord Wilson held a
brief for them until he left early in 1947 and subsequently they were
handled by the chief military representative in Washington. There
was the same gap in Washington as in London between the atomic
project and Ministry of Defence responsibility for scientific research
and development. Sir Henry Tizard complained equally strongly
but equally ineffectively about this gap.

Legal and Democratic Control

The Ministry of Supply's powers to operate the atomic energy
project had to be given legal form. Moreover it was generally
recognised that atomic energy was an altogether exceptional field in
which special and far-reaching powers of control over anyone
operating in it were required: these powers too had to be translated
into legislation. Drafting of a Bill began early in 1946, in close
co-operation with Anderson's Advisory Committee, and after consultation with bodies such as the Federation of British Industries
and ICI the Bill was introduced into the House of Commons on
1 May 1946 and became law on 6 November 1946.[4] The positive
clauses were the first three, which gave the Minister of Supply
responsibility for promoting and controlling the development of
atomic energy, together with power to produce and use atomic
energy, to carry out research and to give financial assistance to other
persons engaged on this work. Clauses 4, 5 and 6 gave the Minister

power to acquire information about any materials or plant connected with atomic energy and the right to search for minerals and
other substances needed for its production. Under the next three
clauses the Minister might acquire compulsorily both the right to
work any such materials and also any materials, plant or contractual
rights connected with atomic energy. Under Clause 10 no person
might engage in any activities connected with the production and
use of atomic energy* except under licence from the Minister, who
must, however, ensure as far as practicable the availability of
materials and plant for research and educational purposes and for
commercial purposes not related to atomic energy. Clause 11
restricted the disclosure of information about atomic energy plants.
Clause 12 concerned control over atomic energy patents.

The Bill caused no major controversy, though the Atomic
Scientists' Association was concerned[5] about several points, in
particular the effect of Clause 11 on the scientists' interests in the
disclosure of information. The discussions leading up to the Bill are
interesting for the light they throw on a question that is often asked
today: why did the British Government, unlike the American
Government, make atomic energy a Government monopoly? In
fact the Act itself did not create a monopoly: it had no background
of political theory, it did not nationalise atomic energy or say that
private enterprise should take no part in its development or use. It
did enable the Minister to exclude private enterprise if he so wished,
by the use of his licensing powers, but no one doubted that such
powers were essential in a matter so potentially dangerous to safety
and security, and indeed the provisions for control in the United
States Act were more far-reaching in certain respects than those in
the British Act. Moreover, close control was essential in case a
scheme for international control was worked out.

The Government wanted to encourage atomic energy research by
outsiders, and at first it had hoped to persuade ICI to become an
agency contractor for the production of fissile material. The firm
adamantly refused, and it was they who urged that a Government
organisation should do the job: this story is related in Chapter 17.
Once production of fissile material had become the responsibility of
the Ministry of Supply, the feeling grew that the revolutionary
economic, military and international implications made the work
unsuitable for private firms, while there were also peculiarly serious

* This would have no effect unless the Minister made an order prohibiting
the activities, but no such order was ever made.

dangers from accidents. Such a large expenditure and production effort was involved and there was such uncertainty about the results and the timing that the project was indeed beyond the scope of any private interests, and for this reason alone was particularly suitable for a national enterprise. The scientists certainly agreed with this line[6] and so did the Conservative Opposition. As we shall see later, once the project got under way, its directors were anxious to, and did, sub-contract as much work as possible to industry, but often they could not find suitable takers. Later, when the first power-producing plants were being planned, there was a strong desire that private industry should help with nuclear design, construction and operation. The role given to private industry was dictated not by the Government's political theory but by military need and industrial structure.

What of the normal democratic controls over the Government in the exercise of its great powers over atomic energy – the controls of Parliament and of press comment? The project did not in the period of this book become a storm-centre of public controversy as it did in the United States. British indifference may have been due partly to the fact that the whole project was so much smaller than the American project and a much less immediate part of the basic security of the nation. Another reason was that the American concern and agitation was led by the atomic scientists,[7] while the British atomic scientists, who were few in number, had less strong feelings about questions of organisation and less apparent antipathy to the military, and were therefore less vociferous. Most of them were closely involved in the project as employees or advisers. They had formed an Association of Atomic Scientists, but it was a highly respectable body including Sir Wallace Akers and Lord Cherwell as vice-presidents and it largely confined its activities to valuable but inevitably small-scale education of the public. The Association's impact on the Government was minimal. One of the Prime Minister's Civil Service advisers recalled superciliously – and without understanding of the scientists' real concern for the future – his dealings with the Association: 'It is a curious but none the less important fact that extreme brilliance in scientific research is very frequently coupled with immaturity of outlook. It is no exaggeration to say that many of the young men engaged on atomic research who are hand-picked for their brilliance are adolescent in their approach to political and similar questions.'

Another reason for the lack of controversy was the extreme secrecy which shrouded the project (see Chapter 16). As we have seen, Mr Attlee and his closest colleagues wanted the public to know as little as possible lest an enemy learn even more. The minimum of information was given to Parliament and to the press, who for the most part accepted the situation with great, indeed excessive, docility. Here the contrast with the United States was most striking. In particular, Congress had a committee, possibly the most powerful of all its specialist bodies, to watch over atomic energy and the Atomic Energy Commission, while the press believed in as much public education, and indeed controversy, as was possible under the security rules. In the British Parliament, any interest by Members was warded off, despite original good intentions. In the autumn of 1946, for example, the Minister of Supply had said he was very alive to the need for the most active Parliamentary control 'in this most important matter': the Minister would have to give the House of Commons frequent and full information about what he was doing with 'the vast powers entrusted to him'.[8]

In practice, the estimates for expenditure on atomic energy, as on other defence research and development expenditure, were concealed from Parliament by burying them in general sub-headings of the Ministry of Supply vote[9] – a post-war development introduced for security reasons. It was not very happily accepted by the Select Committee on Estimates, which felt that it bore an unduly heavy responsibility on behalf of Parliament when so much of its information was given in strictest confidence and was largely unrecorded (see Chapter 14). The Select Committee in 1947 had recommended an impartial committee of the House to help the Minister of Supply in the discharge of his atomic energy functions, but the Minister did not think this would be helpful.[10] During the whole period of the Labour Government there was not a single House of Commons debate devoted to atomic energy, although occasional references were made to it in other connections such as foreign affairs or defence; Lord Cherwell initiated one debate in the House of Lords[11] but this was concentrated mainly on questions of organisation. Moreover the Opposition co-operated gladly in keeping atomic questions off the order paper. There were few MPs with scientific qualifications, but there were some assiduous questioners among the Labour members, in particular Emrys Hughes and Raymond Blackburn (the latter, it should be noted, a strong supporter of a

British bomb).[12] However, they met a stone wall. Emrys Hughes complained: 'When we ask questions about it [the atomic bomb] one would almost think that an atomic bomb has been dropped. When an Hon. Member asks the Prime Minister about the atomic bomb he looks at him as if he had asked about something indecent.'[13] After the first Russian bomb test in 1949, 34 MPs put down a motion asking the Prime Minister to take the initiative for a conference with heads of state to break the atomic deadlock. The Prime Minister thought it would be fruitless and dangerous to discuss the motion largely because it might give an impression of appeasement politics. Bevin wrote in a Foreign Office file 'keep it off' [the order paper]. At the end of 1950 Blackburn intended to raise atomic energy on the adjournment, but such a debate would, it was thought, prejudice talks in Washington. The Foreign Office approached the Speaker's secretary who thought the matter unlikely to come up but said that he would tell the Speaker it would not be in the national interest.

The comparison with indecency seemed to recur: another member found that the press was also aloof from the subject 'as from sex in the past'.[14] This situation had various causes; D-notices* were issued on certain topics but these did not account entirely for the inadequate press coverage.

Here too there was an extraordinary contrast with the United States situation, where press coverage of all aspects of atomic energy was full and well informed and newspaper debate and discussion were wide-ranging and uninhibited.† In 1945 there were some serious background articles in the British press (in, for example, *The Times, Daily Telegraph, Manchester Guardian* and *Observer*) on the theory of atomic energy, written by academic scientists, and among the popular dailies, the *Daily Express* produced an illustrated guide to nuclear fission. But there was nothing comparable to, for instance, the series of articles by a staff member of the *New York Times* who was detached for service with the United States War Department, at the latter's request, in order to explain the atomic bomb to the public.[16] There is in the British press less evi-

* The D-notice procedure for restricting publication in the press is described in Chapter 16.

† Though in 1945 a scientist from Columbia University was apparently told that he could be imprisoned for seventy years for an article stating that radioactivity would make the ground at Hiroshima unsafe for seventy years.[15]

dence of continuing concern with the science, politics and morals of atomic energy: the popular press indulged in trivialities or fantasies about atomic energy as a magic source of prosperity, with atomic-powered family cars,* cookers and labour-saving devices for all, while the more serious papers ignored the fantasies but often fell back on clichés. The Americans marvelled at the relative calm of the British leaders and press in the face of a discovery more dangerous to Britain than to any other great power.[17]

For a time after the bombing of Japan, British press and public concern about atomic energy was indeed tremendous and the British conscience was deeply stirred. 'An unceasing flow of correspondence' of which *The Times* published a selection testified to the profound public interest in the wide range of technical, strategic, political and moral problems, and the views of eminent men – Niels Bohr, Sir Henry Dale, Sir George Thomson, Sir Laurence Bragg, Professor Blackett, Professor A. V. Hill, Professor Oliphant, Professor J. B. S. Haldane – were published in full or quoted. But 'as soon as the appalling significance of the atomic bomb faded from minds steeped in horrors, apathy resumed its sway'.[18]

After this, British press references to atomic energy were some-times frequent, even abundant – especially in 1949, and in 1952 just before and after the Monte Bello test. They do not, however, con-stitute a debate on British policy or provide a picture of the develop-ment of the British programme. Ethical problems, and problems of control, were discussed from time to time but almost entirely in the context of American use of and possession of the bomb: as an American paper remarked,[19] the British, having had only about 200 men in the American bomb project, had not quite the same sharp sense of responsibility for having let the monster loose. But, as the *Manchester Guardian* said, 'the mere lack of a bomb does not absolve us from having any ideas about the political means of its control'.[20]

Amid this general talk of the atomic bomb, the press contained little discussion about whether Britain should have its own atomic bomb programme, though the *Daily Mail* and *Daily Express* vociferously demanded a British bomb as early as possible. The *Manchester Guardian*,[21] asking in 1949 whether Britain should

* *The Daily Telegraph* reported on 29 Nov 1945 that Mr Shinwell was to have a demonstration ride in a motor-car which the inventor claimed was atomic-powered. The test was a failure and the inventor alleged sabotage.

confine herself to peaceful uses of atomic energy or should make her own atomic bombs, argued that two years earlier the latter had been the only possible decision, but that this was no longer the case. In 1949 the *Daily Express* declared under huge headlines that Britain was to make bombs and that large-scale plutonium production at Sellafield would be mostly for defence.[22] Yet in announcing the first production of plutonium in Britain, only the *Daily Worker* and one other journal[23] had headlined it as a bomb ingredient, most papers referring to it as an atomic power material, while as late as March 1951 the *Economist*[24] cast doubt on a Press Association report that Britain was to manufacture atom bombs. In 1952 press reports of the Monte Bello test, while lavish, were commonly very incorrect and abounded in flattering assumptions that a British bomb could have been tested much earlier but had been deliberately delayed for the sake of major improvements and refinements. Some said it was much more powerful than any American bomb, some that it was much smaller, some that it had been tested in a guided missile. Exceptionally, the science correspondent of the *Daily Telegraph* was accurate and well informed on weaponry. The outcome of the test was greeted with chauvinistic pride by part of the press but elsewhere with somewhat modified rapture as a regrettable necessity due to the failure to integrate American and British defence, or as an expensive demonstration to secure American co-operation, or even as a sheer waste of resources.

For want of news from British sources, articles or news items in the British press concentrated on the United States project or on American views and activities. The British people usually knew American policy in this crucial matter but not their own Government's,[25] and the atomic debate was carried on mainly by American scientists, politicians and journalists. 'One could wish', said the *Manchester Guardian*, 'that the committees set up by our own government had a little more to say. . . . The silence of our own government does not encourage people to take this great problem seriously. There is a work of public education being done in the United States which has no counterpart here.'[26]

Why was British press coverage, compared with that of the United States press, so unsatisfactory? Newsprint was rationed and newspapers were very slim. There was also the familiar psychological reason that, while the Americans had the bomb and felt a proprietary interest and responsibility for atomic energy, the British did not.[27] Moreover, though a few pertinacious British journalists worked hard to get information and print it, in the United States the 'lynx-eyed newspaper men' did not relax their fact-finding efforts for an instant; and they enjoyed a freedom unknown in Great Britain, to obtain and use official information of the highest importance.[28] The systematic follow-through, and the thorough examination of issues in planned series of articles, is notable in the American press.

Inanition was the greatest problem of the British press. They were starved by the deficiencies of Parliamentary discussion,[29] and by the lack of nourishment from Government and official sources. Information about the British programme, as we shall see in Chapter 16, was withheld; even Harwell was not allowed to admit the press until July 1948. Britain's project was surrounded by a veritable lead shield of secrecy. By contrast, the US Atomic Energy Commission published semi-annual reports which President Truman commended[30] to every thoughtful person, while David Lilienthal, chairman of the Atomic Energy Commission, travelled up and down the land explaining the problems and possibilities of nuclear science.[31] Articles in British papers complained often but unavailingly about the secretive official attitude: 'Why the mystery? The Americans disclose abundant information.'[32]

Virtually everything about Anglo-American atomic relations that reached the British press came from United States sources, either from American papers or from British correspondents in Washington. Sometimes even news reports from Britain appeared first in New York and were then picked up by London papers; for instance, items about secret talks in June 1949[33] between Mr Churchill and Mr Attlee and leading members of his Cabinet on the breakdown of information exchanges with the United States. American correspondents in London had an unrewarding life; at times when Washington was all excitement, Whitehall was 'as non-committal as Brer Rabbit', admitting no more than that the British Embassy in Washington occasionally discussed atomic energy business with the United States Government.[34] Pressmen were passed from the Ministry of Supply to the Foreign Office, which had nothing to say,[35] and they found British officials circumspect to the point of neurosis.[36]

Atomic energy had been under Labour an exception to normal

principles and procedures of peacetime Cabinet, ministerial, departmental and Parliamentary government. It was to remain so under the Conservatives. To recapitulate: at the ministerial level, under Labour, several Cabinet members knew nothing about this vital and expensive project and the Defence Committee rarely mentioned it, while the main committee for atomic energy did not take some of the most important decisions. Two Ministers – the Prime Minister and the Minister of Supply – had direct responsibilities for the project, but in the formative years after the war a member of the Opposition was in charge of day-to-day policy questions. At the official interdepartmental level responsibility was also diffused, and even when much of it was concentrated into the Atomic Energy Official Committee, there was a gap in the co-ordination of the project with the other defence affairs with which it was so closely related. Within the Ministry of Supply itself the project was tight inside its cage but there was the same lack of coherence. The small band of able civil servants was successful in cutting many administrative knots. Research, production of fissile material and weapons work were, however, in three separate kingdoms inadequately co-ordinated by a part-time Controller who did not even altogether admit responsibility to his Minister. There was almost no real scrutiny of the project by Parliament or the press.

The prime reason for this treatment of atomic energy, so exceptional by any of the usual constitutional tenets, was awe and fear. There may have been other reasons. For example, Mr Attlee and Mr Bevin, conscious of the divergence of views within the Parliamentary Labour Party and the Government on foreign policy and defence, may have deliberately wished to keep knowledge away from their left wing. Or they may have wished to evade debate because they felt peculiarly vulnerable to criticism from Mr Churchill on a subject which he had guarded so closely from them and which he considered to be so peculiarly his own. But awe and fear were common to other countries besides Britain. They were aroused by an exceedingly complicated technical project which perhaps no British Minister and few civil servants really understood, a project of vast and horrifying potentialities, which went to the heart of national security and relationships with other countries and which might one day have great industrial importance as well. Therefore the atomic project seemed to demand very special treatment within the British machinery of government, and very special secrecy.

But the price of this special status, of the labyrinthine committee system and the excessive secrecy, was confusion in some quarters and ignorance in others, which reduced both efficiency and involvement. The author is left with the conviction that if it had not been for the extraordinary competence of three men at the working level – John Cockcroft, Christopher Hinton and William Penney – the project might have been an expensive fiasco. Instead it was to prove in this period of the Labour Government, within the objectives set for it, one of the most successfully executed programmes in British scientific and technological history.

Appendix 2

MAIN COMMITTEES DEALING WITH GENERAL ATOMIC ENERGY QUESTIONS

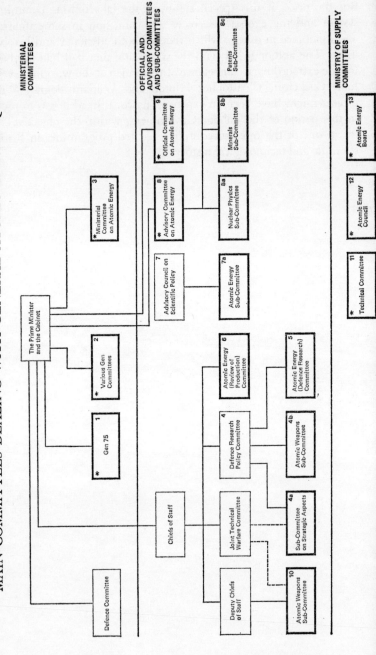

NOTES. This chart is merely for rough and ready reference and cannot properly represent a complicated and changing structure; for example the committees shown were not all co-existent. Membership overlapped to a great extent. Committees dealing solely with atomic energy are in heavy boxes; the most important are marked *.

* 1. *Gen 75* Aug 1945–Dec 1946. See p. 2.

** 2. *Various other Gen committees* 1947–52. See p. 2. Seven other Gen groups of Ministers dealt with the British bomb, atomic priority, organisation and security. (But see 3 below.)

* 3. *AE(M) – Ministerial Committee on Atomic Energy.* See p. 22. Feb 1947–end 1951. 'To deal with questions of policy which require the consideration of Ministers.'

4. *DRP – Defence Research Policy Committee.* See p. 33. Appointed Jan 1947 to advise Minister of Defence and Chiefs of Staff on science policy in the defence field. Fact-finding sub-committee on strategic aspects of atomic energy (4a) reviewed Joint Technical Warfare Committee's 1946 report, and sub-committee on atomic weapons (4b) collated information on weapon possibilities.

5. *AE(DR) – Atomic Energy (Defence Research) Committee.* See p. 36. Appointed Jan 1948 to report to DRPC on relations between defence research programmes and atomic energy defence research.

6. *AE(RP) – Atomic Energy (Review of Production) Committee.* See p. 36. Appointed Jan 1948 to report to Chiefs of Staff on scale of atomic energy production in relation to defence requirements.

7. *SP – Advisory Council on Scientific Policy.* Its Atomic Energy Sub-Committee, appointed Jan 1948, dealt with nuclear power. See p. 31 and Chapter 19.

* 8. *ACAE – Advisory Committee on Atomic Energy (Anderson Committee).* See p. 24. Sep 1945–Dec 1947. To advise the Government on development of atomic energy for civil and military purposes, and international handling. Its Nuclear Physics Sub-Committee (8a) was to 'make recommendations regarding the programme of nuclear physics to be pursued in this country as a whole'. See Chapter 18.

* 9. *AE(O) – Official Committee on Atomic Energy.* See p. 29. Aug 1947–Sep 1957. 'To consider questions in the field of atomic energy which call for discussions between departments.' Reported to the Prime Minister.

10. *Atomic Weapons Sub-Committee.* See p. 32. Set up in 1945 to report to Deputy Chiefs of Staff on use of atomic energy in weapons. Reconstituted in 1947 as DRP sub-committee (see 4 above).

*11. *TC – Technical Committee.* See p. 45. Mar 1946–Mar 1956. An advisory committee to the project; included many distinguished outside scientists and engineers.

*12. *AEC – Atomic Energy Council.* See p. 45. Mar 1946–Oct 1951.

*13. *AEB – Atomic Energy Board.* See Chapter 13. Replaced AEC in Oct 1951.

1945-1947

3 External Policy: Brief Hope of Interdependence

T HE purpose of all these committees and people and departments involved in the cumbersome machinery of atomic government was to evolve policy and to execute it. There were two main areas of policy – external relations with other countries which are the province of this chapter and Chapters 4, 5, 8, 9 and 10, and internal production policy, the province of Chapters 6 and 7. The two areas are interconnected: production policy influenced, and was influenced by, external relations. But interconnection did not mean interdependence. British production policy was primarily determined neither by international negotiations for the control of atomic energy, nor by the success or failure of negotiations for co-operation with the United States of America or any other countries. British production policy was largely the instinctive response of a country which had been a great world power and believed itself to be one still, and which had the knowledge and industrial resources to develop what was manifestly the new passport to first-class military, and possibly industrial, rank. Nevertheless, the external questions were of very great concern to Britain. She experienced the same mixture of feelings as other countries about international control – first great hopes, then fears mixed with reluctance. Her atomic relations with the United States were important to her not only because of the information she needed for her domestic programme but because they must be a key to the strength and balance of Anglo-American relations as a whole. Her atomic relations with other countries – with Europe and the Commonwealth – reflected their subordination to the Anglo-American relationship. Intertwined with external relations was the purchase of uranium, the raw material essential to the production programme; this is dealt with in Chapter 11.

In August 1945, as the pictures and stories of Hiroshima and

Nagasaki burned themselves on the world's consciousness, questions
of international control were uppermost in Mr Attlee's mind. No
attempt had been made during the war to discuss the problem
between the Americans, the Russians and the British. Niels Bohr's
single-minded struggle to persuade Roosevelt and Churchill to open
discussion had ended in complete failure.[1] Even if Bohr had succeeded, talks with Russia might have failed to bring the powers
together. However, the fact that they were not held before the
atomic bombs were dropped, before they presented an apparent
threat of duress to Russia, made it most improbable, if not impossible, that post-war talks on control could succeed. Before the war
ended, small groups of American and British officials had been
working independently to put down on paper their thoughts on
control, but they had not got very far. Meanwhile the United
Nations organisation had been planned during the war in total
ignorance of atomic energy, even among almost all the American
and British participants.

Mr Attlee felt so strongly on the importance of the whole question
of control that in August he wrote down his own thoughts with not
a word crossed out. 'A decision on major policy with regard to the
atomic bomb is imperative', wrote the Prime Minister.

> Until this is taken civil and military departments are unable to
> plan. It must be recognised that the emergence of this weapon has
> rendered much of our post-war planning out of date. . . . I noticed
> at Potsdam that people still talked of the line of the Oder–Neisse
> although rivers as strategic frontiers have been obsolete since the
> advent of air power. It is infinitely harder for people to realise that
> even the modern conception of war to which in my lifetime we
> have become accustomed is now completely out of date.

The Prime Minister had no faith in any suggestion that all nations
might agree to keep the bomb a secret in the hands of the United
States and the United Kingdom. 'The most we may have', he said,
'is a few years' start. The question is what use are we to make of
that few years' start.' He foresaw that any attempt to enforce an
Anglo-American world-wide rigid inspection of all laboratories and
plants was neither desirable nor practicable: to attempt to penetrate
the curtain round Russia would be to invite a world war. 'The only
course which seems to me to be feasible and to offer a reasonable
hope of staving off imminent disaster for the world', wrote Mr

Attlee, 'is joint action by the USA, UK and Russia based upon stark reality. We should declare that this invention has made it essential to end wars.'

There was no sign of any American initiative on international control. It was the British Prime Minister who suggested to his colleagues in the Gen 75 Committee that he should put the whole case to President Truman and propose that they should, together, consult Stalin. 'The time is short', he concluded. 'I believe that only a bold course can save civilisation.' Mr Bevin, the Foreign Secretary, agreed with these sentiments but not with the method of consultation proposed. He did not think the question should be raised with Truman and Stalin in isolation from the many different subjects at present under discussion between the three Governments. He suggested that the Prime Minister should as a first step send a confidential message to President Truman proposing that they should review world policy in the light of the atomic bomb.

A month of drafting and redrafting followed before Mr Attlee's letter to the President was ready. It repeated with a sense of urgency the points the Prime Minister had made to his colleagues. It acknowledged that the new outlook he was advocating, 'the new valuation of what are called national interests', would inevitably involve risks and would, to the countries possessing the temporary advantage, constitute an act of faith. Such an act would be even more difficult for the United States, who had expended such vast resources on the project, than for Britain. Mr Attlee sent a copy of the draft letter to Mr Churchill, who agreed with the Prime Minister's sentiments about 'the appalling gravity' of the matter and sympathised deeply with the anxieties it aroused, but disapproved with many reiterated negatives of the general tone. What, asked Mr Churchill, did the Government want the Americans to do?

> Do you want them to lay their processes before a conference of the United Nations? It would not (not) be easy for them to convene a conference themselves unless they were prepared to share their knowledge and the uranium etc. Do you wish them to tell the Russians? Is that what is meant by 'an act of faith'? If so I do not (not) believe they will agree and I personally should deem them right not (not) to and will certainly have to say so, if and when the issue is raised in public.

Mr Churchill went on to say that the responsibility for propounding a world policy clearly rested with the United States. He imagined they had a two or three years' lead and would have got further in that time:

> I am sure they will not (not) use their advantage for wrong pur-
> poses of national aggrandisement and domination. In this short
> interval they and we must try to reach some form of security
> based upon a solemn covenant backed by force viz. the force of the
> atomic bomb. I therefore am in favour after we and the United
> States have reached agreement of a new United Nations conference
> on the subject. I do not (not) however consider we should at this
> stage at any rate talk about 'acts of faith'. This will in existing
> circumstances raise immediate suspicion in American breasts.

Moreover, Churchill emphasised, Britain had a special relationship with the United States in this matter as defined in his agreement with President Roosevelt:

> This almost amounts to a military understanding between us and
> the mightiest power in the world. I should greatly regret if we
> seemed not (not) to value this and pressed them to melt our dual
> agreement down into a general international agreement consisting,
> I fear, of pious empty phrases and undertakings which will not
> (not) be carried out (see what happened about submarines).

In spite of Mr Churchill's admonitions, Mr Attlee's letter to Mr Truman (reproduced in Appendix 3) was duly sent on 25 September 1945.[2] There was concern that no speedy reply came: it was over three weeks before a letter arrived which, though friendly, showed no sign of haste to arrange talks. It seems that the President was anxious as to the effect on Russia of any announcement about atomic bomb discussions between the United States, the United Kingdom and Canada. The desire not to offend Russia was para-doxically mingled with reluctance and dilatoriness in talking to her about the atomic bomb. But British Ministers felt strongly about the delay. The issue overhung the whole field of international relations and it was important not to leave matters to drift until the Russians felt they had nothing to gain from co-operation with the United States and Britain. Mr Attlee telegraphed asking urgently for talks and a meeting was fixed in Washington for 9 November.

In preparation for the Washington talks, minds had to be cleared on two main points. Firstly, what was to be the attitude on atomic affairs to Russia? Secondly, if there was to be international control, what methods were practicable and politically feasible? Attitudes to Russia and to giving her information fluctuated on both sides of the Atlantic. American diplomacy leading up to the Cold War in its relationship to the atomic bomb is now a centre of historical controversy outside the scope of this book.[3] Truman's own attitude to the bomb and to British and Russian participation in atomic affairs was by no means always consistent. Early in September he agreed, 'we must take Russia into our confidence',[4] but less than a month later he made it clear that he might share scientific knowledge but not engineering secrets. The atomic bomb had become in his eyes America's 'sacred trust'. James Byrnes, his Secretary of State, had always strongly opposed atomic negotiations with Russia, favoured an American monopoly of the atomic bomb and was throughout consistent in his attitude to Russia – and to Britain. The President himself believed increasingly that the United States alone had the combination of industrial capacity and resources to produce a bomb. Even Einstein was prepared at this stage to justify the President's stand; he believed that no secret existed in the bomb, but insisted that the United States should maintain control until the world government he advocated was ready to function.

In Britain, the fluctuation in views was especially apparent in Ernest Bevin. On 11 October 1945 he was telling his colleagues at a Gen 75 meeting that there was everything to gain and little to lose by making Russia party to the knowledge of the atomic bomb process and by trusting to their good faith in observing an international agreement for the control of the weapon. Bevin believed that many of the difficulties encountered at the September 1945 meeting of the Council of Foreign Ministers could be attributed to Russian resentment at exclusion from this new development, and that agreement with the Russians on atomic energy might bring about a change in the whole atmosphere. 'We should take the risk of giving this information to the Russians in the interests of our foreign policy', he said.

This opinion was reinforced by advice from the British Ambassador in Washington, Lord Halifax, and the British Ambassador in Moscow, Sir Archibald Clark-Kerr.* Halifax agreed that those who mistrusted Russia were very likely right, but found himself

---

* Later Lord Inverchapel; he succeeded Lord Halifax as Ambassador in Washington in May 1946.

constantly reverting to two opposed expert opinions, one that Russia would get the bomb secret anyway before very long, and the other that Russia was years away from being able to translate knowledge into practice.* What was the point of incurring political resentment by refusing to consider disclosure when disclosure promised to be either superfluous or innocuous?

Clark-Kerr wrote from Moscow at the beginning of December 1945, describing the Russian state of mind towards the atomic bomb. The Ambassador recalled the almost unbearable tension that had strained Russian lives throughout the whole history of their movement, and which explained perhaps 'some of their abnormalities'. For years, he said, the Russians had been toiling after something like security for their country, their system and their own bodies. 'Nearly all who now govern Russia and mould opinion have led hunted lives since their early manhood when they were chased from pillar to post by Tsarist police.' Then came the intense and dangerous gamble of the revolution, followed by the perils and ups and downs of intervention and civil war. Survival remained extremely precarious through the internecine struggle after the death of Lenin and the purges. These people 'trembled for the safety of their country and their system as they trembled for their own'. They built up a machine that might promise the security they needed, but the German invasion caught them unready and swept them to the brink of defeat. Finally with victory came the conviction that national security was within their reach. 'There was a great exaltation of hearts that Russia could be made safe at last', while resounding success at last justified Russian faith in the permanence of their system.

Then, said Clark-Kerr, 'plumb came the atomic bomb', and at a blow the balance which had seemed set and steady was rudely shaken. 'Russia was balked by the West when everything seemed to be within her grasp'; and her 300 divisions were shorn of much of their value. Russian disappointment was tempered by the belief that their Western comrades-in-arms would surely share the bomb with

---

* For example, in September 1945 Halifax reported that General Groves thought Russia might now possess or at an early date obtain the requisite scientific data but was satisfied that for many years to come it would be impossible for them to marshal adequate technical industrial capacity to make the knowledge effective. On estimates of the date when Russia would have atomic bombs, see Chapter 7.

them, and the Ambassador believed the Kremlin hoped for this. 'But as time went on and no move came from the West disappointment turned into irritation and, when the bomb seemed to them to become an instrument of policy, into spleen. It was clear that the West did not trust them. This seemed to justify and quicken all the old suspicions. It was humiliation also and the thought stirred up memories of the past.'

However, well before he received this powerful reinforcement from overseas advisers, Bevin's original preference for conciliation with Russia through atomic sharing had been shaken. Only a week after his advocacy of this line in October 1945, he referred again at Gen 75 to the proposal to admit Russia to full knowledge of the bomb-production process. It must be clear, he said, what we should ask for in exchange for this knowledge. He had at first been inclined to attribute recent difficulties with Russia to the fears about the atomic bomb, but 'further study had convinced him that Russian policy had shown no variation'. This tougher line was supported by official advisers at home. The Foreign Office and the intelligence authorities believed that proposals to bid for Russian co-operation by taking them into full confidence were based on a misunderstanding of the Russian attitude. Russian policy, they said, was strictly realist in outlook and not influenced by motives of gratitude; they would regard such an offer with suspicion. This line was supported by other senior officials who were advising the Government.

Mr Attlee himself was converted to a tougher line, although he was not prepared to go too far along it. He amended officials' drafts of an aide-mémoire for his Washington trip to exclude references to the Russian threat. Nevertheless, before he went to Washington he had accepted the American view that practical know-how, as opposed to fundamental scientific knowledge, should not be shared with Russia. He did not think an offer to do so would be likely to change Russia's attitude to world problems, but would rather be regarded as a confession of weakness. The establishment of better relations should precede the exchange of technical information. Moreover, he said that because of the scarcity of raw materials no agreement for pooling them with Russia should be entered into except in return for substantial advantage.

When, in one of its rare incursions into atomic policy, the full Cabinet considered the problem just before Mr Attlee went to Washington, some (unnamed) Ministers were unhappy about this line. They felt that the practical know-how of manufacture of the atomic bomb must be shared with Russia as well as fundamental scientific knowledge. They thought it would be wiser to make an immediate offer to disclose information to the Russian Government since the true basis of lasting peace was mutual confidence; to create confidence, risks should be taken. 'If it was our policy to build world peace on moral foundations rather than on the balance of power we should be prepared to apply that principle at once to the atomic bomb.' These Ministers agreed that Russia was not fully co-operative in world affairs but thought this was due largely to suspicion of the West and to pre-war experiences; the urgent need now was to remove the causes of suspicion. There was much to be said, they believed, for offering full disclosure of the secret but linking the offer with discussion of means of co-operation in establishing an effective world organisation. The point was also made that tension had arisen between Russia and the United States over the atom bomb, and that Britain should seek to act as mediator and thereby rally round her those nations which feared the consequences of growing estrangement between the United States and Russia. Nevertheless, in spite of these misgivings, the Cabinet endorsed the general line Mr Attlee proposed to take.

The other point where Mr Attlee sought provisional conclusions before setting out on his journey was on methods of international control. Sir John Anderson's Advisory Committee had run through possible methods: agreement not to use the weapon; agreement to communicate to a central authority all scientific and technical atomic energy information; United Nations control of raw materials; a monopoly in the manufacture of active materials to be concentrated in a body set up by the United Nations. The political difficulties in any of these schemes would be very great indeed and no scheme would be effective without international inspection, which might not be workable and would be unpalatable to national opinion.

Ministers had found it all too easy to point out the snags in all the control methods. But when it had seemed that the Americans would put forward little in the way of constructive ideas on control at Washington and that the British might have to take the initiative, a committee of officials under Sir Edward Bridges, Secretary of the Cabinet, was asked to study the problem yet again. They produced a report in just over ten days. In it they considered three possible forms of control agreement: prohibition of the manufacture of bombs by all; restriction of the production of bombs to one international organisation; the restriction of bomb production to the Big Three (United States, Britain and Russia) or Big Five (including France and China). The officials concluded that no international agreement was likely to succeed which attempted to restrict the freedom of any of the major powers to produce atomic weapons. They suggested therefore that all nations should be left free to make bombs if they could but that use of the bomb should in effect be prohibited by a convention; if one power used the bomb, all the other signatories should go to war and use the bomb against the offender. Under this regime of collective retaliation and deterrence there would be full exchange of basic scientific information, though not of industrial information. The officials thought that any proposal to admit other countries to a share of the raw materials which the United States and Britain had acquired through secret agreements would mean substantial sacrifices, which should be made only in return for an important advantage.

The Prime Minister believed the officials' proposals were dangerously illusory and unrealistic. Was it suggested, he asked, that if war broke out between America and Russia they would fight to a finish without resort to atomic bombs? If one country in extremity used them, Britain would be bound to join in an attack on that country, even though in every other respect she deemed it to be in the right. 'What British Government in view of the vulnerability of London would dare accept the obligation of entering on atomic warfare against an aggressor who might be able, before going down, to destroy London?' Moreover, Attlee said, there was no means of knowing whence had come an atomic bomb or who was the culprit, and thus the effect of certainty of immediate counter-attack was lessened. In atomic warfare, he wrote, 'twice is he armed who gets his blow in first'.

Thus Mr Attlee was forced backwards to the elementary truth: there was no hope of controlling the use of atomic weapons unless the world laid aside nationalist ideas and strove without reservation to bring about an international relationship in which war was entirely ruled out. He proposed in talking to Truman simply to endorse the twelfth point in the President's recent statement of United States foreign policy – that peace required a United Nations organisation composed of all the peace-loving nations willing jointly to use force if necessary to ensure peace. He would suggest that no attempt should be made to restrict the development of atomic energy by any country in view of the impossibility of effective control, and that there should be no special convention to govern the use of atomic weapons to restrain aggression, but simply the determination to stick to the United Nations Charter and reinforce its authority by using atomic weapons against an aggressor if occasion arose. It was agreed that in a few years, perhaps three (see Chapter 7), Russia would be able to produce atomic bombs. In this period, said Attlee, a real attempt must be made to build a world organisation upon the abandonment of power politics.

These early discussions and thoughts of the Labour Government about international control of atomic energy contained the seeds of ideas and strategic theories that were to pervade discussions on control for the next twenty-odd years – inspection, non-proliferation, pre-emptive blows and so forth. They were founded on the truths learned from League of Nations days which had to be relearned in the subsequent quarter of a century: control of any weapons was impossible unless mutual trust existed between nations, while no world organisation could be strong unless the leading powers were united in wishing it so to be. But they also pointed the paradoxes and dilemmas of a world power in the nuclear age: while waiting for mutual trust to be established and Utopia to arrive, each such power must look to its own interests and make itself as strong as possible in nuclear weapons, even if thereby mutual mistrust was engendered and the chances of ultimate international control diminished.

Mr Attlee's own position illustrated the paradox. As he prepared to go to Washington he talked of the abandonment of power politics and of faith in the United Nations. 'The new World Order', he had written, 'must start now.' But he was also intent on making Britain's own atomic position as strong as possible, in particular by forging the strongest possible nuclear link with the United States. Official advice had been insistent on this. The Chiefs of Staff had emphasised that in the event of failure to secure international agreement, the possession of atomic weapons 'of our own' as deterrents would be vital to British security. They wanted the British production of weapons to start without delay. This conclusion was underlined by Sir Edward Bridges' committee which reported to Ministers on international control. The second essential in United Kingdom policy, they said, was to maintain the closest possible

co-operation with the United States. Any opportunity of reinforcing
a general system of international sanctions by a private understanding between Britain and the United States should certainly be taken.
The committee had urged that when he met the President the Prime
Minister should express the hope that the United States would be
willing to continue the general system of co-operation, and especially
the machinery for settling policy and exchanging information as set
up by the Quebec Agreement, and also combined raw material
control. He should also refer to Britain's intention to produce
bombs, to Britain's interest in atomic energy for industrial power,
and to the problem of Clause 4 in the Quebec Agreement (see Chapter 1) in the latter connection.

Mr Attlee said he would take up these points in Washington. At
this stage neither Mr Attlee nor the Gen 75 Ministers were prepared
to give the directive for the production of bombs for which the
committee of officials had asked. Mr Attlee intended to tell the
President, however, that Britain was 'naturally interested in
development of atomic energy both as a means of self-defence and
as a source of industrial power'. The Washington talks were thus to
cover two points: the first steps towards international control of
atomic energy and the future of Anglo-American co-operation. In
the three months between Hiroshima and his visit to Washington,
Mr Attlee had muted his idealist cries from the heart for a 'new
valuation of what are called national interests' and 'acts of faith'
and had moved to a more cautious position, much nearer to that of
President Truman and indeed of Mr Churchill. He was still concerned chiefly with the international aspects of atomic energy, but
he was showing a readiness to accept the principle implicit in his
officials' advice: that in a world of nation-states, each country must
look after its own interests first. He was increasingly apprehensive
of Russian intentions.

On 9 November Mr Attlee and the Prime Minister of Canada,
Mr Mackenzie King, went to Washington. For talks of such
importance the preparations seemed very inadequate. The Prime
Minister had purposely gone without a specific agenda and with no
document to submit to the President, but he was accompanied by
Sir John Anderson, who knew all the details of the business. On the
American side, however, none of the people hitherto concerned
with atomic energy had been consulted about the discussions as late
as 8 November; the President and Mr Byrnes, Secretary of State,

were keeping things in their own hands and no procedure had been worked out for conducting the meetings.

Nevertheless, there was little disagreement in the talks on the main topic of international control, and the only difficulties were drafting ones.[5] The three heads of government issued a declaration (see Appendix 4) composed from parts of the three draft texts prepared by the three different groups. It was based on Mr Attlee's assertion that the only complete protection for the world from the destructive use of scientific knowledge lay in the prevention of war. The leaders declared their willingness from the outset to proceed with the exchange of fundamental scientific information for peaceful ends, but they did not propose to share specialised information about the practical application of atomic energy until effective reciprocal and enforceable safeguards against its use for destructive purposes could be devised. They urged that the United Nations should set up a Commission to make recommendations for the international control of atomic energy.

The attitude to Russia implicit in this declaration and the increasing international mistrust had already emerged in Mr Truman's and Mr Attlee's minds in the weeks before they met. It was compounded of grave and growing doubts about Russian intentions and consequent resolutions to be firm, with a desire for conciliation if possible. One episode illustrates the more conciliatory attitude of the time. On 6 September 1945, Gouzenko, a cipher clerk in the office of the Soviet Military Attaché in Ottawa, had defected and revealed an extensive Russian spy network in Canada; one of its many assignments was to get information about the atomic bomb. This might have been expected to encourage the heads of government to be tough, but in discussing the case before the November Washington meeting Mr Attlee* and Mr Mackenzie King seemed extremely anxious to postpone taking any action in the case which might, by unwelcome publicity, prejudice an approach to Russia. The United States authorities led by Mr Dean Acheson shared this view. There were fears of two opposite possibilities. On the one hand public opinion, especially in Congress and the Canadian Parliament, might be so stirred that any co-operation with Russia might be difficult.

* Mr Bevin believed, however, that the right course was to go ahead with interrogation and prosecution, including 'Primrose' or Dr Nunn May, the British atomic scientist who was one of the spies. 'I think we are being too tender', he said (see Chapter 16.)

On the other hand public opinion, especially among scientists, might sympathise with Russia, who had been denied a share in this secret. The Government would not receive the wholehearted support they needed to prosecute the cases unless an offer of atomic collaboration had first been made to Russia. The business was discussed at the November meeting in Washington, but such evidence as there is suggests that there were still doubts about the political wisdom of letting the affair burst. Interrogations did not finally begin until February 1946. The news of the spy ring did not in itself make the three heads of government less forthcoming to Russia.

In the Washington talks the three leaders had concentrated on the global questions of control and took very little part or apparent interest in the second item of the talks – the future of atomic co-operation between their three countries. This subject was largely sub-contracted to Sir John Anderson, helped by Mr Makins of the British Embassy on the British side, and the Secretary of War, Judge Patterson, helped by General Groves on the United States side; the American State Department played a very minor role, which was, as it turned out later, unfortunate. The starting-point of the discussions was the Quebec Agreement, which had to be replaced since it was a wartime arrangement and now obsolete. Judge Patterson was prepared to recommend the President to take action so that Article 4 – whereby the British had expressly disclaimed any interest in the industrial aspects of atomic energy beyond what the President of the United States considered fair and just – no longer hampered British commercial development. But the main discussions centred round the two main fields of co-operation – raw materials for atomic energy and the exchange of information. Here the scales were evenly weighted. Collaboration over raw material supplies had brought marked benefits to the United States, and was likely to be even more advantageous to them as it now seemed probable that there were very big uranium deposits in South Africa; collaboration in the exchange of information had brought, and was likely to bring, marked benefits to the British. The British wanted 100 per cent collaboration in both fields, but while the Americans were especially anxious to continue pooling uranium through the Combined Development Trust, they were much more reluctant over the exchange of information, especially of technological information.

With some difficulty the basic principle of all-round collaboration was established. But what form should an agreement take? Should

there be a formal agreement or a less formal memorandum of agreement covered by an exchange of letters between the two sides? A
formal agreement would have to be submitted to the United States
Senate, with unpredictable results. It was hoped instead that the
President and Prime Minister would sign the less formal instrument
which would determine a working relationship. However, there was
not time to do even this before the conference ended, and an even
briefer document was prepared for Mr Truman and Mr Attlee. This
was 'a very flimsy piece of paper' signed in a great hurry on the last
morning of the conference, and later it was to become apparent that
Truman did not realise the full implications of what he was signing.
The document said:

> We desire that there should be full and effective co-operation in
> the field of atomic energy between the United States, the United
> Kingdom and Canada.
> We agree that the Combined Policy Committee and the Com-
> bined Development Trust should be continued in a suitable form.
> We request the Combined Policy Committee to consider and
> recommend to us appropriate arrangements for this purpose.

Meanwhile Anderson and Groves jointly signed a memorandum
(see Appendix 5) addressed to the chairman of the Combined Policy
Committee recommending a list of points to be considered by the
CPC in preparing a new document to replace the Quebec Agreement
and all other understandings: Canada might sign later if she wished.
There were six points. First, the three Governments would not use
atomic weapons against other parties without prior consultation
with each other; it should be noted that 'consultation' replaced the
'consent' stipulated in the wartime Quebec Agreement.* Secondly,
the Governments would not disclose any information or enter into
negotiations concerning atomic energy with other countries except
in accordance with agreed common policy or after prior consultation
with each other. Thirdly, the Governments would secure control of
all their native uranium and thorium deposits and 'use every
endeavour' to acquire all available supplies from the rest of the
British Commonwealth and other countries; supplies would be
placed under the Combined Development Trust. Fourthly, Trust
materials would be allocated to the three Governments in accordance
with 'the common interest'. Fifthly, there should be full and effec-

* See pp. 6 and 309.

tive co-operation in the field of basic scientific research among the three countries. In the field of development, design, construction and operation of plants such co-operation, 'desirable in principle', should be regulated by the CPC. Sixthly, the CPC would review the programmes of the three countries, allocate materials and settle any other matters about co-operation.

So Mr Attlee and Sir John Anderson as they went home had their brief moment of hope. Mr Attlee had found himself in agreement with Mr Truman. They had promised no 'acts of faith' and the Russians had not after all been consulted about the atomic bomb, but there was hope that the United Nations would take over the problem of control. Some Ministers in the Cabinet were, it is true, unhappy about the joint statement and felt that it would increase the difficulties of securing full co-operation between Russia and the West in establishing world organisation, but they did not press their doubts.

Meanwhile a new era of atomic collaboration with America seemed to be at hand. It was no doubt inevitable and even proper that the British Government should want to have its own three-cornered system of co-operation until the United Nations millennium dawned, or as an insurance policy in case it failed to dawn. Nevertheless, it is strange that no one pointed to the contradiction in the Washington proceedings – between the lofty protestations that the only hope for the world was to lay aside nationalist ideas, and a close three-power agreement based on the hopes of a virtual monopoly of the raw materials of atomic energy.* Indeed, the profound consequences of atomic energy made logic almost unattainable. They inspired idealism but also fear, and so the noble thoughts were accompanied by the most sober calculations of *Realpolitik*.

* There were uranium deposits in Russia and very rich uranium mines in Czechoslovakia (see Chapter 11).

LETTER FROM MR ATTLEE TO
PRESIDENT TRUMAN, 25 SEPTEMBER 1945

Dear Mr President

Ever since the USA demonstrated to the world the terrible effectiveness of the atomic bomb I have been increasingly aware of the fact that the world is now facing entirely new conditions. Never before has there been a weapon which can suddenly and without warning be employed to destroy utterly the nerve centre of a great nation. The destruction wrought by the Germans through their air fleet on Warsaw and Rotterdam was startling enough, but subsequent attempts to do the same to London were defeated, though without much to spare. Our own attacks on Berlin and the Ruhr resulted in the virtual destruction of great centres of industry. In Europe the accumulated material wealth of decades has been dissipated in a year or two, but all this is not different in kind from what was done in previous wars in Europe during the Dark Ages and the Thirty Years War, in America by your own civil war. Despite these losses civilisation continued and the general framework of human society and of relations between peoples remained. The emergence of this new weapon has meant, taking account of its potentialities, not a quantitative but a qualitative change in the nature of warfare.

Before its advent military experts still thought and planned on assumptions not essentially different from those of their predecessors. It is true that the conservative (with a small c!) mentality tended to maintain some of these although they were already out of date. For instance we found at Potsdam that we had to discuss a decision taken at the Crimea Conference as to the boundaries of Poland. These were delimited by rivers although the idea of a river as a strategic frontier has been out of date ever since the advent of air warfare. Nevertheless, it was before the coming of the atomic bomb not unreasonable to think in terms of strategic areas and bases, although here again it has seemed to me that too little account has been taken of the air weapon.

Now, however, there is in existence a weapon of small bulk

capable of being conveyed on to a distant target with inevitable catastrophic results. We can set no bounds to the possibilities of airplanes flying through the stratosphere dropping atomic bombs on great cities. There are possible developments of the rocket for a similar purpose. I understand that the power of the bombs delivered on Nagasaki may be multiplied many times as the invention develops. I have so far heard no suggestion of any possible means of defence. The only deterrent is the possibility of the victim of such an attack being able to retort on the victor. In many discussions on bombing in the days before the war it was demonstrated that the only answer to the bomber was the bomber. The war proved this to be correct. This obvious fact did not prevent bombing but resulted in the destruction of many great centres of civilisation. Similarly if mankind continues to make the atomic bomb without changing the political relationships of States sooner or later these bombs will be used for mutual annihilation.

The present position is that whilst the fundamental scientific discoveries which made possible the production of the atomic bomb are now common knowledge, the experience of the actual processes of manufacture and knowledge of the solutions which were found to the many technical problems which arose, are confined to our two countries and the actual capacity for production exists only in the United States. But the very speed and completeness of our joint achievement seems to indicate that any other country possessing the necessary scientific and industrial resources could also produce atomic bombs within a few years if it decided now to make the effort. Again, our two Governments have gone a long way in securing control of all the main known sources of uranium and thorium, the two materials at present believed to be of importance for the process. But new sources are continually coming to light and it would not be surprising if it were found that large deposits existed in parts of the world outside our direct or indirect control. Nor may it be altogether easy to defend the measures which we have already taken in this matter when they became known and are considered in the light of such principles as that of the freedom of access to raw materials.

It would thus appear that the lead which has been gained as a result of the past effort put forth in the United States may only be temporary and that we have not much time in which to decide what use is to be made of that lead. It is true that other countries, even if they succeed in producing atomic bombs, may not, at any rate at first, be able to produce them on the same scale. I am told, however, that, in future, it may be possible for the process to be developed at a far smaller cost in industrial resources than has inevitably been demanded by your pioneer production enterprise, carried through in time of war when speed was the first essential; and in any case, with a weapon of such tremendous destructive power, it is perhaps doubtful whether the advantage would lie with the possessor of the greatest number of bombs rather than with the most unscrupulous.

A further consideration which I have had in mind is that the successful manufacture of bombs from plutonium shows that the harnessing of atomic energy as a source of power cannot be achieved without the simultaneous production of material capable of being used in a bomb. This means that the possible industrial uses of atomic energy cannot be considered separately from its military and security implications.

It is clear to me, therefore, that, as never before, the responsible statesmen of the great Powers are faced with decisions vital not merely to the increase of human happiness but to the very survival of civilisation. Until decisions are taken on this vital matter, it is very difficult for any of us to plan for the future. Take the case of this country. During the war we had to shift much of our industry to the less exposed parts of our island. We had to provide shelters for our people. Now we have to restart our industries and rebuild our wrecked homes. Am I to plan for a peaceful or a warlike world? If the latter, I ought to direct all our people to live like troglodytes underground as being the only hope of survival, and that by no means certain. I have to consider the defence forces required in the future in the light of San Francisco,* but San Francisco did not envisage the atomic bomb. Its conceptions of security are based on appreciations of a situation existing in June of this year. We considered regional security and a policing of the world by the Powers with the greatest resources in the interests of all so that there should be available the forces to prevent aggression.

I have only mentioned Great Britain as an example: for every Head of Government must, in varying degree, find himself confronted with the same problems.

In these circumstances, while realising to the full the importance

---

* The international conference, 25 April–26 June 1945, at which the United Nations Charter had been agreed and signed.

of devising means to prevent as far as possible the power to produce this new weapon getting into other hands, my mind is increasingly directed to considering the kind of relationship between nations which the existence of such an instrument of destruction demands. In your country and ours resort is not had to violence not just because we have efficient police forces but because the vast majority of our citizens are law-abiding and conditions are such that men are not driven to have recourse to desperate measures. Our constitutions allow of peaceful change.

We have, it seems to me, if we are to rid ourselves of this menace, to make very far-reaching changes in the relationship between States. We have, in fact, in the light of this revolutionary development to make a fresh review of world policy and a new valuation of what are called national interests. We are ourselves attempting to undertake such a review. What was done on American initiative at San Francisco was a first step at erecting the framework of a new world society, but necessarily it could have regard only to the requirements imposed by the technical advances in methods of warfare then known. Now it seems to us that the building, the framework of which was erected at San Francisco, must be carried much further if it is to be an effective shelter for humanity. We have to secure that these new developments are turned to the benefit rather than to the destruction of mankind. We must bend our utmost energies to secure that better ordering of human affairs which so great a revolution at once renders necessary and should make possible.

I am therefore most anxious, before we proceed much further with our own deliberations, to know how your mind is moving: and it is primarily for this reason that I have set before you at such length my tentative views before they have really begun to crystallise.

Mr Byrnes has had a preliminary talk with Mr Bevin here on the matter but, later on, I think it may be essential that you and I should discuss this momentous problem together so that we may agree what the next step should be and be in a position to take it before the fears and suspicions which may be developing elsewhere have got such a firm hold as to make even more difficult any solution we may decide to aim at.

Yours sincerely,

C. R. ATTLEE

The President of the United States of America.

WASHINGTON DECLARATION 15 NOVEMBER 1945

The President of the United States, the Prime Minister of the United Kingdom and the Prime Minister of Canada have issued the following statement:

'We recognise that the application of recent scientific discoveries to the methods and practice of war has placed at the disposal of mankind means of destruction hitherto unknown against which there can be no adequate military defence, and in the employment of which no single nation can in fact have a monopoly.

2. We desire to emphasise that the responsibility for devising means to ensure that the new discoveries shall be used for the benefit of mankind, instead of as a means of destruction, rests not on our nations alone, but upon the whole civilised world. Nevertheless, the progress that we have made in the development and use of atomic energy demands that we take the initiative in the matter, and we have accordingly met together to consider the possibility of international action:

(a) To prevent the use of atomic energy for destructive purposes.
(b) To promote the use of recent and future advances in scientific knowledge particularly in the utilisation of atomic energy for peaceful and humanitarian ends.

3. We are aware that the only complete protection for the civilised world from the destructive use of scientific knowledge lies in the prevention of war. No system of safeguards that can be devised will of itself provide an effective guarantee against the production of atomic weapons by a nation bent on aggression, particularly since the military exploitation of atomic energy depends in large part upon the same methods and processes as would be required for industrial uses. Nor can we ignore the possibility of the development of other weapons or of new methods of warfare, which may constitute as great a threat to civilisation as the military use of atomic energy.

4. Representing, as we do, the three countries which possess the knowledge essential to the use of atomic energy, we declared at the

outset our willingness, as a first contribution, to proceed with the exchange of fundamental scientific information and the interchange of scientists and scientific literature for peaceful ends with any nation that will fully reciprocate.

5. We believe that the fruits of scientific research should be made available to all nations, and that freedom of investigation and free interchange of ideas are essential to the progress of knowledge. In pursuance of this policy, the basic scientific information essential to the development of atomic energy for peaceful purposes has already been made available to the world. It is our intention that all further information of this character that may become available from time to time shall be similarly treated. We trust that other nations will adopt the same policy, thereby creating an atmosphere of reciprocal confidence in which political agreement and co-operation will flourish.

6. We have considered the question of the disclosure of detailed information concerning the practical industrial application of atomic energy. The military exploitation of atomic energy depends, in large part, upon the same methods and processes as would be required for industrial uses. We are not convinced that the spreading of the specialised information regarding the practical application of atomic energy before it is possible to devise effective, reciprocal, and enforceable safeguards acceptable to all nations would contribute to a constructive solution of the problem of the atomic bomb. On the contrary we think it might have the opposite effect. We are, however, prepared to share, on a reciprocal basis with other of the United Nations, detailed information concerning the practical industrial application of atomic energy just as soon as effective enforceable safeguards against its use for destructive purposes can be devised.

7. In order to obtain the most effective means of entirely eliminating the use of atomic energy for destructive purposes and promoting its widest use for industrial and humanitarian purposes, we are of the opinion that at the earliest practicable date a Commission should be set up under the United Nations to prepare recommendations to the organisation. The Commission should be instructed to proceed with the utmost despatch and should be authorised to submit recommendations from time to time dealing with separate phases of its work.

In particular, the Commission should make specific proposals:

(*a*) For extending between all nations the exchange of basic scientific information for peaceful ends.

(*b*) For control of atomic energy to the extent necessary to ensure its use only for peaceful purposes.

(*c*) For the elimination from national armaments of atomic weapons and of all other major weapons adaptable to mass destruction.

(*d*) For effective safeguards by way of inspection and other means to protect complying states against the hazards of violations and evasions.

8. The work of the Commission should proceed by separate stages, the successful completion of each of which will develop the necessary confidence of the world before the next stage is undertaken. Specifically, it is considered that the Commission might well devote its attention first to the wide exchange of scientists and scientific information, and as a second stage to the development of full knowledge concerning natural resources of raw materials.

9. Faced with the terrible realities of the application of science to destruction, every nation will realise more urgently than before the overwhelming need to maintain the rule of law among nations and to banish the scourge of war from the earth. This can only be brought about by giving wholehearted support to the United Nations Organisation, and by consolidating and extending its authority, thus creating conditions of mutual trust in which all peoples will be free to devote themselves to the arts of peace. It is our firm resolve to work without reservation to achieve these ends.'

Appendix 5

'GROVES–ANDERSON' MEMORANDUM;
16 NOVEMBER 1945

(This memorandum was drawn up by Sir John Anderson
and Major-General L. R. Groves during the November 1945
tripartite talks in Washington and referred to the Combined Policy Committee in December 1945)

We recommend that the following points be considered by the
Combined Policy Committee in the preparation of a new document
to replace the Quebec Agreement, which should be superseded *in
toto*, together with all other understandings with the exception of
the Combined Development Trust Agreement which should be
revised in conformity with the new arrangements.

1. The three Governments, the United States, the United Kingdom, and Canada, will not use atomic weapons against other parties
without prior consultation with each other;

2. The three Governments agree not to disclose any information
or enter into negotiations concerning atomic energy with other
governments or authorities or persons in other countries except in
accordance with agreed common policy or after due prior consultation with one another;

3. The three Governments will take measures so far as practicable
to secure control and possession, by purchase or otherwise, of all
deposits of uranium or thorium situated in areas comprising the
United States, its territories or possessions, the United Kingdom,
and Canada. They will also use every endeavour with respect to the
remaining territories of the British Commonwealth and other
countries to acquire all available supplies of uranium and thorium.
All supplies acquired under the provisions of this paragraph will be
placed at the disposition of the Combined Development Trust;

4. The materials at the disposition of the Trust shall be allocated
to the three Governments in such quantities as may be needed, in
the common interest, for scientific research, military, and humanitarian purposes. Such supplies as are not allocated for these purposes
shall be held by the Combined Development Trust and their disposal

shall be determined at a later date in the light of then existing conditions and on a fair and equitable basis;

5. There shall be full and effective co-operation in the field of basic scientific research among the three countries. In the field of development, design, construction, and operation of plants such co-operation, recognised as desirable in principle, shall be regulated by such *ad hoc* arrangements as may be approved from time to time by the Combined Policy Committee as mutually advantageous;

6. The Combined Policy Committee, already established and constituted so as to provide equal representation to the United States on the one hand and to the Governments of the United Kingdom and Canada on the other, shall carry out the policies provided for, subject to the control of their respective Governments. To this end the Committee shall:

1. Review from time to time the general programme of work being carried out in the three countries.
2. Allocate materials in accordance with the principles set forth in the fourth paragraph above.
3. Settle any questions which may arise concerning the interpretation and application of arrangements regulating co-operation between the three Governments.

The above is to be understood as being without prejudice to the consideration by the Combined Policy Committee of any matters not covered in this memorandum.

4 External Policy: Hopes are Dupes

As it turned out, the hopes were very brief indeed. Within a year from the meeting of the three heads of government in November 1945 it was almost certain that the United Nations attempt to produce a scheme for the international control of atomic energy was going to fail. Within nine months from the meeting the Americans had made most forms of atomic collaboration with all other countries, including Britain and Canada, illegal. The Truman–Attlee agreement that there should be 'full and effective co-operation' had not proved worth the paper it was written on.

How did all this happen? The United Nations proceedings for control will not be described at length, for in the event they had little influence on Britain's own atomic energy plans and Britain opted out of a leading part in them. Nevertheless, there is no doubt that at the end of 1945 the British Government, like other governments, was anxious that the attempt at international control should succeed. The chain of events was broadly as follows. In December 1945 the Council of Foreign Ministers, meeting in Moscow, agreed to ask the United Nations to set up a Commission to investigate the control of atomic energy. In January 1946 the General Assembly agreed to do so: the Commission was to make proposals for exchanging basic scientific information, for confining atomic energy to peaceful purposes, for eliminating atomic and other weapons of mass destruction from national armaments, and for effectively safeguarding complying states. Meanwhile the United States Government had set up a committee under Mr Dean Acheson* to advise it on international control, and the committee in turn asked an advisory panel to produce a report on methods of control. The panel consisted of five brilliant men: David Lilienthal, head of the famous Tennessee

---

* Then Under-Secretary of State.

Valley Authority, was its chairman, while the other members were Robert Oppenheimer, scientist and wartime director of Los Alamos where the atomic bombs were made, and three of America's best industrialists.

In two months the panel produced a report in which they believed passionately; in this they differed from the authors of nearly all the other reports on control that had been drawn up. Their main proposal was for an international development authority with positive functions in the field of research, development and production. Atomic activities would be divided into 'safe' and 'dangerous'; dangerous activities would be carried out only by the international authority, which would own or control all uranium and thorium mines and all plants for the production of fissile material. These plants would be located in different countries in such a way as to maintain a strategic balance, while 'safe' activities would be permitted to individual nations under supervision. The whole plan would be put into operation by stages with adequate safeguards at each stage. As these successive stages were reached, the United States would be required to surrender to an increasing degree its lead in technical information and bomb production. The report was designed to emphasise the positive side of control – co-operative international development rather than policing by inspection.

In some ways the plan, coming at this early stage of atomic development, was not just the first but the last real opportunity for control.[1] But it never stood a chance, largely because the atmosphere of international trust essential to such self-denying ordinances was notably absent. During 1946 suspicion between Russia and the West grew, even though it had not yet erupted into the Cold War. There was increasingly bitter disagreement over reparations, the future of Germany, Eastern Europe and the Near and Middle East.

Basic mistrust gave the United Nations Atomic Energy Commission from the outset an air of unreality. There were moreover all kinds of difficulties and uncertainties. The Lilienthal Report's belief that safe and dangerous activities could be separated was based on the idea of 'de-natured plutonium' which they said would not be suitable for bombs, an idea that proved to be unrealistic. One of the complications that was to dog questions of control for evermore was that many of the activities connected with the production of atomic power were in fact 'dangerous'. Moreover it was thought, probably wrongly, that if the international authority were to own all uranium mines it would have to own most of the gold, tin and copper mines of the world and so forth. In Britain, the Advisory Committee on Atomic Energy, and the Government, were not happy about the scheme for these reasons. However, there is no doubt that some solution could have been found in scientific terms. The real difficulties were political and the British Government was apprehensive of the Lilienthal Report on political grounds. To transfer development activities to an international authority would mean in practice that atomic energy plants would be built in all the principal countries with the advice and assistance of other nations. Whether the advantages of such a scheme would justify the inherent risk depended on political judgement, and certainly no such scheme could succeed except in an atmosphere of confidence. There were, however, such wide differences of opinion and outlook and policy between the great powers that there was little prospect of general acceptance of the ideal of a supranational authority whose behests would automatically override sovereignty.

If the plan seemed full of snags to the British, it seemed positively dangerous to the Russians. After all, the Americans already possessed atomic bombs while they did not. The Americans under their plan would keep bombs for a long time while the Russians would never have a chance of acquiring them. They were asked to accept a basic inequality of power. In Britain, Professor Blackett argued that the situation might become more dangerous if Russia accepted such control, since such acceptance would be widely interpreted in the United States as an admission of great weakness and might thus encourage in the United States the idea of preventive war; Blackett and Chadwick both found this idea being expressed there at this time,* even by men of clearly liberal views. When the American plan for international control, largely based on the Lilienthal scheme, was put before the United Nations Commission in June 1946, the Russians promptly replied with their own scheme. They wanted a convention under which governments would undertake not to use atomic weapons in any circumstances, to forbid the production of such weapons, and to destroy within three months all stocks of finished or semi-finished atomic weapons. They envisaged strict supervision and control to police the agreement.

There was from the outset of the Commission's life an impasse which quickly became inescapable. Even the fervent idealism of the

* For views in Britain, see Chapter 6.

Lilienthal Committee faded away when they heard the composition
of the American delegation to the Commission. The choice of the
seventy-five-year-old Bernard Baruch as leader, as 'the vehicle of our
hopes', seemed to Lilienthal fantastic not only on account of his age
but also because of his unwillingness to work and his terrifying
vanity.² Baruch may in Chadwick's words have seen himself 'in his
sere years as Moses descending with a message for the salvation of
humanity'. But his determination to introduce from the outset subjects which were bound to terrify the Russians – such as the abolition
of the Security Council veto when atomic issues were discussed –
made the co-operation, which was unlikely, quite impossible, while
his general behaviour added a slightly farcical note to the proceedings. Even the British suspected that some members of Baruch's
team were determined that the United States should neither give up
atomic weapons nor give the know-how to Russia.

The British Government put forward no proposals and exercised
no initiative themselves. They had already, by the spring of 1946,
become increasingly apprehensive about any control schemes which
might in any way sacrifice their own national security. They felt
that the possession of atomic bombs and productive capacity by the
United States, with whom Britain was never likely to be at war,
represented the best obtainable guarantee of British security 'which
we should wish to retain until an efficient method of control had
been devised and had been seen to be working effectively'. They
could not possibly accept the Russian scheme and they supported
only reluctantly the American plan for an international authority.
As time went on, the reluctance increased, and this did not go un-
noticed in New York where it was felt Britain had not given the
United Nations Atomic Energy Commission the attention and
importance it merited. Britain's representative on the Commission,
Sir Alexander Cadogan, was considered to be an uninspired choice.
At the end of 1946 there was a query whether Britain should withhold support from Baruch because of the very unaccommodating
attitude now taken by the United States to British requests for
technological information. There were also increasing fears,
especially by Bevin, that an international authority would hamper
Britain's own national development of atomic energy for industrial
purposes. On the other hand, one or two scientists, for example Sir
George Thomson and Sir Henry Tizard, believed it would be better
if everyone abandoned large-scale development of atomic energy for

some time. They believed this would give much greater security and that the possibilities of peaceful atomic power were being much exaggerated. However, Ministers agreed at the end of 1946 that Britain's major interest was still to secure a satisfactory agreement for international control and thus that they should still support the American plan. The exiguous hopes placed on the plan's success are demonstrated by the fact that only two months later Ministers finally and explicitly decided to make not just fissile material but a British atomic bomb (see Chapter 6).

From then on the British continued to express support for international control but they became increasingly lukewarm, especially when in 1947 the Americans proposed much stronger powers for the international authority. The Americans had paid little attention to British views in the United Nations Commission, while Mr Bevin had become convinced that the Americans would like to retain a monopoly of atomic energy development as long as possible and that on security grounds they were very reluctant to see plants established in the United Kingdom. It seemed to him important therefore to avoid putting too much power in the hands of an international authority, which should certainly not be empowered to decide whether or not plants might be constructed in any given country. It was essential that any scheme should give Britain the explicit right to continue research into both warlike and peaceful uses of atomic energy and to manufacture fissile material, but Britain would admit international inspectors provided others did the same. The Chiefs of Staff, however, thought it absolutely unacceptable that Britain should place atomic weapon research under the supervision of an international authority even if other governments were ready to do so.

Ministers' apprehensions about atomic control at this time – the middle of 1947 – were rooted in general fears for national security, rather than in a specific belief in the possibility of war with Russia. The attitude of the British Government to Russia at this time was complex and changing and, especially on Mr Bevin's part, increasingly pessimistic. Nevertheless, in June 1947 the Prime Minister and the Foreign Secretary viewed with disfavour a report by the Chiefs of Staff basing British defence policy on the possibility of war with Russia; Mr Bevin thought then that a resurgent Germany would be a more serious threat to the peace of the world. At this point, scepticism about the possibility of an agreement for international control of atomic energy was universal and all three big powers doubted its desirability. Lord Hankey, the veteran ex-Cabinet Secretary and ex-Minister who was a member of a committee of the Royal Institute of International Affairs on atomic bombs, summed up the feeling of most people: 'in the world in which we live [the schemes] are unworkable, dangerous and more likely to increase international friction and the risk of war than to allay them. To my mind they are in the same category as Prohibition, the League of Nations, the Kellogg Pact, Freedom of the Seas *et hoc genus omne*.' The only practical point of debate now became whether negotiations should be ended forthwith or be continued for tactical reasons. The Americans seemed bent on both a showdown with Russia and the breakdown of the United Nations Commission, and the primary concern of the British was to avoid these.

Talks dragged on until May 1948, when the United Nations Atomic Energy Commission was wound up. By this time the British Government, shocked by Russian infiltration which culminated in the Communist take-over in Czechoslovakia, and 'fearing the piecemeal collapse of one Western bastion after another', saw Russia as a potential enemy. Atomic energy was now only one of the issues upon which the nations had divided into opposing worlds, one led by the United States and one by Russia. No tears were shed at the funeral of the United Nations Atomic Energy Commission, even though it had so recently embodied the great hopes of mankind.

Anglo-American Collaboration

In November 1945 Mr Truman, Mr Attlee and Mr Mackenzie King had agreed that there should be full and effective collaboration between their three countries in atomic energy, and negotiations between their supporting staffs at this time seemed to promise that a more detailed agreement would soon be reached. These hopes too were disappointed.

The history of Anglo-American atomic relations has to be seen against the background of Anglo-American relations as a whole. The relationship for all its imperfections had been extraordinarily close during the war and it was to become very intimate again in the late 1940s and early 1950s. But in the interim, in the two immediate post-war years, it cooled. Neither country had a really deep devotion to the other. America felt for Britain some of the contempt and irritation expressed by Charles Lamb in his essay on 'Poor Relations',* and was just not interested in the cause of her poverty, the old story of how she had stood alone against the Nazis in 1940, etc., etc., etc.

The loan of $3,750 million to Britain in December 1945 to save her from immediate insolvency was unpopular in Congress and the country, even though it was granted on fairly onerous terms. There was great bitterness in the United States over British policy in Palestine and indeed, apart from specific criticisms, Americans in general just did not like Labour, that is, Socialist Governments. Mr Byrnes, the American Secretary of State, had besides the reputation of being anti-British. For their part, Mr Attlee's Government did not share Mr Churchill's visceral love for the American people but they were surprised, hurt and resentful at the ending of the wartime special relationship. They felt that the terms of the loan showed harsh ingratitude: there was bitterness about what seemed American trouble-making in Palestine, and over other policies as well. At times the British Foreign Secretary felt like calling a plague on the houses of the United States and Russia alike as they seemed intent on dividing the world up into their own spheres of influence without regard for British interests. Nevertheless, the 'inner circle' of senior Ministers knew that Britain could not manage without the United States, not only financially, but also politically and militarily; Mr Bevin and the Foreign Office believed the Americans would appreciate their common interest in the long run and hung on to this belief throughout 1945–6.

As the Anglo-American relationship became very much less special, a good many of the co-operative exercises and organisations of the war disappeared. There was, for example, no joint Anglo-

* 'A Poor Relation – is the most irrelevant thing in nature, – a piece of impertinent correspondency, – an odious approximation, – a haunting conscience, – a preposterous shadow, lengthening in the noontide of your prosperity, – an unwelcome remembrancer, – a perpetually recurring mortification, – a drain on your purse, – a more intolerable dun upon your pride, – a drawback upon success, – a rebuke to your rising, – a stain in your blood, – a blot on your scutcheon, – a rent in your garment, – a death's head at your banquet, – Agathocles' pot, – a Mordecai in your gate, – a Lazarus at your door, – a lion in your path, – a frog in your chamber, – a fly in your ointment, – a mote in your eye, – a triumph to your enemy, an apology to your friends, – the one thing not needful, – the hail in harvest, – the ounce of sour in a pound of sweet, – the bore par excellence.'

American military planning except for the needs arising out of the military occupation of Europe. There was at this period no American commitment at all to come to the help of Britain and the other independent countries of Western Europe if they were attacked. Even the powerful Combined Chiefs of Staff organisation in Washington dwindled away. Most of the joint economic planning offices shut down. Some relics of close collaboration remained: for example, British officers were still allowed to enter many American research establishments, and in chemical and biological warfare the programmes of the two countries remained so closely in step as to be virtually integrated.

Although the Americans and British in the first post-war months kept their distance and were not inordinately fond of one another, they were still closer to each other than to any third power. America did not want bilateral understandings with Britain to cramp her multilateral style or her own bilateral negotiations with Russia. But as things turned out, the Washington lines to London were still busier than any of the other American external communications systems. The British Government was anxious to encourage America wherever possible to shoulder international responsibilities. Fears were expressed in the Cabinet about moves which tended to bring Britain more and more under the economic domination of the United States, but in any such discussion or in any proposals for British negotiations with Russia, Bevin would emphasise the importance of not estranging the United States since Britain would be 'in an impossible position if the Americans withdrew from Europe'.

So there was a nexus of common interest or mutual self-interest between the two countries even in this post-war period of relative detachment. The common interest became very much stronger as it was increasingly focused on two points – the economic reconstruction of Europe and the fear of Communism and Russia. This need and this fear had induced a gradual change in American attitudes to co-operation with Britain from the summer or autumn of 1946. In May 1946 the United States had become the main support to Iran against Russia even though that country was traditionally a British sphere of influence. At the end of 1946 the British and American zones of Germany were fused largely because this was the only way of re-establishing the economy of the British zone.* In March 1947 the Americans took over British commitments to the anti-Communist

* It was very expensive to the British in terms of dollars.

Governments in Greece and Turkey and the Truman Doctrine to aid 'free people' was announced. Then in the middle of 1947 the Americans launched the Marshall Plan for the economic reconstruction of Europe, and Britain played the leading role in organising the European response. Very soon afterwards the Cold War was generally deemed to exist between East and West; the break-up of the Council of Foreign Ministers meeting in December 1947 emphasised the iciness of the temperature. British and Americans alike now had a real fear of Russia and from now on Anglo-American military collaboration grew much closer again. As the Cold War intensified, so Anglo-American military and economic bonds were drawn more tightly.

Atomic energy relations between the two countries in the two years after the war were partly but not wholly in accord with this general basic pattern. The Americans felt untrammelled by any memories of obligations to the British in atomic as well as in financial, affairs. To them the British, who had been the wartime junior partner, were now, here too, the poor relation, although the poverty was largely reckoned in technical know-how and industrial resources. The British had, however, one redeeming asset – their apparent influence in securing the desperately needed supplies of uranium. For their part the British wished to continue the wartime atomic relationship for wider political reasons and for sheer self-interest. America after all had a stock of atomic bombs, and all the knowledge about all the methods of making fissile material as well as bombs. The British wanted the protection of the bombs and a share in the knowledge, but in the two years after the war they got the assurance of neither. The United States Act which categorically denied such assurance became law, paradoxically, in August 1946 just as the American attitude to the British began to thaw. It was not until late 1947, when common interests were much stronger again, that there seemed the chance of a return to a special relationship.

The fact that Truman and Attlee were closer together than they were with other heads of government, added to the pursuit by the British of their own interests, added to the value for the Americans of the apparent British influence on uranium supplies – all these together had led to the preliminary Anglo-American atomic energy agreements of November 1945. These agreements had augured well for future atomic collaboration between the two countries. The Groves–Anderson memorandum of November 1945 (see Appendix 5) was duly presented to the Combined Policy Committee, which set up a sub-committee consisting of General Groves, Roger Makins, still at the British Embassy in Washington, and Lester Pearson of Canada, to work out a document to replace the Quebec Agreement. The document was to be a memorandum of agreement signed by representatives of the three Governments, but it was to be an executive agreement, not a treaty, and was to be kept confidential if possible.

Business on the sub-committee went surprisingly well; Chadwick was convinced of Groves's desire for an agreement that was clear and definite and would work well in practice, even though Groves had to look up the word 'co-operation' in the dictionary and even though he insisted that the President had no power and no authority to give away military secrets. The Government in London pressed Makins very hard to go for something much more specific and unambiguous than the Groves–Anderson memorandum. They feared that the provisions for pooling raw material, where Britain appeared to have much to give, would be clear and explicit while those relating to the exchange of information on the design, development, construction and operation of plants, where America had much to give, would be too general. However, Makins advised that, apart from the notorious difficulty of drawing up a detailed document for the exchange of information, it was vitally important to get the agreements through very soon. Chadwick warned, 'the cohesive forces which held men of diverse opinions together during the war are rapidly dissolving: any thought of common effort or even common purpose with us or with other peoples is becoming both weaker in strength and rarer to meet'. Makins feared that without haste the British might 'miss the market altogether'. The sub-committee's drafts were therefore approved in London. There were three different pieces of paper: a memorandum of agreement very similar to the Groves–Anderson memorandum; a revised Declaration of Trust for the Combined Development Trust; and an exchange of letters between President and Prime Minister freeing Britain from any restrictions imposed by Clause 4 of the Quebec Agreement.

The market, if it ever really existed, was missed after all. For the doubts about the possibility of having any secret agreement, which had been so notably absent in the Truman–Attlee talks, were now raised. They were first voiced in London, where the Foreign Office pointed out that under Article 102 of the United Nations Charter every treaty and every international agreement entered into by any member of the United Nations after the Charter came into force must be registered as soon as possible with the United Nations Secretariat and published. They suggested it might be possible to have an agreement suitable for publication setting out the general principles of co-operation, though not mentioning the raw materials Trust, and a private aide-mémoire recording the interpretation which the Governments placed on the terms of agreement.

However, it became more and more apparent that the objections to publishing the agreement were overwhelming. The misgivings about the contradictions in the Truman–Attlee talks between the search for international control and the agreement on Anglo-American collaboration, which had been remarkable for their absence while the talks were in progress, now piled up. The Prime Minister and the Gen 75 Ministers saw that an agreement of the kind drawn up by the sub-committee, entered into and published so shortly before the opening of the proceedings of the United Nations Atomic Energy Commission, would be very difficult to defend. Not only would it confuse public opinion in Britain and cast doubts on British sincerity in the Commission, but it would lend force to Soviet criticisms. It was one thing to continue the close co-operation between the United Kingdom, the United States and Canada which had begun during the war. This was public knowledge, and the fact that the November discussions were held at all had demonstrated that co-operation still existed. But it would be quite different to conclude a public agreement under which the three countries agreed to share information and raw material which they were unwilling to make available to the rest of the world – provisions amounting in effect to a limited defensive alliance. The provision about consultation before using the bomb was an even more obvious target for criticism. Other nations would not believe protestations of the three that the agreement was an interim one, subject to any later scheme of the United Nations.

A public agreement was unthinkable. So was a secret agreement, which the British representatives in Washington urged. Apart from the very real objections to evading the obligations of Article 102, there was increasing alarm in Washington – in Congress, the Administration and the press – about the number of secret agreements made by President Roosevelt, and the State Department did not intend to produce another piece of dynamite. In fact, to some people in Washington the discovery of Article 102 had seemed a blessing and a deliverance. Groves had acquiesced in his subcommittee's report to the Combined Policy Committee, but he had disliked it and had alerted Byrnes that the new arrangement was in effect an outright military alliance with military, political, legal and international implications which required the closest consideration by the highest authorities in the land.[3] Byrnes was able to give full vent in this period to what Chadwick called his 'obstructive and evasive abilities'.

Meanwhile new obstacles to co-operation had arisen. In mid-February 1946 the Canadian espionage case had at last broken and this seemed bound greatly to increase American reluctance to give Britain information. About the same time the British, anxious to fulfil their obligations of frankness to the Americans, told them of their own atomic energy plans. Chadwick had constantly told Groves during the war that Britain would go in for large-scale atomic production after the war. Now, in February 1946, the British said at the Combined Policy Committee that, apart from building a research establishment, they intended to build a large-scale pile to produce plutonium for the use of the research establishment and for 'eventual industrial or military application'; the conclusions of the United Nations Commission would affect the eventual use to be made of any material produced in the United Kingdom. This announcement was coupled with a British request to Groves for some specific details about the large-scale American piles at Hanford, details additional to some which he had given earlier to Chadwick who had transmitted them to Anderson; this request was intended as a test of American willingness to exchange information.

Groves consulted General Eisenhower, then United States Chief of Staff, and the War Department. They took fright at the location of any production plants in Britain and said this was a factor which must be brought into any discussion of co-operation. They felt strongly that on grounds of strategic security British piles should be in Canada, and again Lester Pearson of Canada agreed with them. Ministers in Britain considered this whole question but decided against Canada (see Chapter 5). The Prime Minister sent a telegram to the British members of the Combined Policy Committee spelling out the reasons and emphasising that 'while the location of British large-scale production plants was a matter which could properly be brought into the discussions, His Majesty's Government could not agree that the Americans were entitled to make it a condition of the United Kingdom receiving information that they should fall in with United States views'.

The British felt their pack of hopes falling about them. 'We should be most reluctant to throw away what has been achieved', wrote the Prime Minister to Washington. 'Is there any alternative method of getting the substance?' An informal agreement seemed the only possible solution: the three Governments should individually direct their representatives on the Combined Policy Committee to secure, by decisions recorded in the Committee's minutes, the substance of the changes in the proposed new agreements. In March the British produced draft CPC conclusions which were both ingenious and ingenuous, recommending such arrangements and making it clear that the three Governments were simply providing for a continuation of the wartime collaboration until the outcome of the UNAEC discussions was apparent.

The Americans, however, were only too glad to wash their hands of the whole business. Only with great difficulty did the British manage to fix a meeting of the CPC in April 1946. At the meeting, Byrnes was ambiguous and difficult. Lord Halifax spoke at length with firmness and great dignity, but had no effect on the Americans. The United States said the British proposal was unacceptable, for such substantial amendments to the original agreement would bring it within the ambit of Article 102 of the Charter. The British pointed out that this left void the decision about full and effective cooperation agreed between the President and Prime Minister in November 1945 and asked for the United States' alternative proposals. The Americans replied they had none and could see no way out of the impasse. They felt that nothing should be done to compromise the success of the discussions within the United Nations and that assistance to the United Kingdom in building an atomic energy plant might do so. Lester Pearson of Canada supported the United States line throughout, guardedly but definitely. It seemed that the CPC had no authority to settle this matter and that it must be referred back to the three heads of government.

Many of the circumstances were distressingly similar to those of the Anglo-American atomic imbroglio of 1943* – confusion at the presidential level about agreements made and professed ignorance at the working level of all the relevant documents. For example,

* See *Britain and Atomic Energy 1939–1945*, chapter 5.

Byrnes, who was undoubtedly hostile to the British in the negotiations, told the British Ambassador that the President's recollection
of the events at the November meeting was far from clear, while he
himself had not before the April CPC meeting seen either the
November 1945 agreement about collaboration or the Anderson–
Groves memorandum. In fact, Byrnes had been chairman of the
CPC meeting in December 1945 at which both these documents
were presented and discussed. Again, before the April CPC meeting
the British had placed great hopes on the support of the scientist-
statesman, Dr Vannevar Bush. He had told Chadwick that he
believed in full collaboration and agreed with the British proposed
draft resolutions to overcome the problem of a formal agreement;*
he had said euphorically that the two countries were tying themselves together for a hundred years. As in 1943, Bush proved a
broken reed to the British: at the CPC meeting he was silent and
Chadwick could only conclude that Byrnes had given him instructions to toe the party line.

Lord Halifax, the British Ambassador, advised the Prime Minister
to send a letter immediately to the President. Attlee telegraphed the
same day urging Truman that the words 'full and effective co-
operation in the field of atomic energy between the United States,
the United Kingdom and Canada' of the November agreement
could not mean less than full interchange of information and a fair
division of raw material. He said this interchange of information
was implicit in their published Washington Declaration which had
recognised that the three countries possessed the knowledge required
for the use of atomic energy, and in their willingness, subject to
safeguards, to share with other states information about the practical
industrial applications. The Declaration contained nothing about
sharing information between the three countries, and the clear
indication was that this was already provided for. Attlee suggested
that the heads of the three Governments should issue instructions
for the interchange of information (for full text, see Appendix 6).

Lord Halifax had hoped that the Prime Minister's telegram
would reach Washington before Byrnes reported to the President
on the CPC meeting. But Byrnes got there first and the President's
reply bore his stamp. He said that he would 'regret very much' any
misunderstanding about the Truman–Attlee–King agreement. All

---

* *The New World* shows that Bush was opposed to close collaboration with
the British because it would impede international control: ibid., pp. 459, 469.

were agreed that under the Quebec Agreement the United States had not been 'obligated' to give the United Kingdom, in the post-war period, designs and assistance in the construction and operation of plants. The question was whether this situation had changed. The language 'full and effective co-operation', wrote the President, was very general and the intention of those who signed the agreement must be considered. No one at any time had informed him that it was intended that the United States should 'obligate' itself to furnish the engineering and operational assistance for another atomic energy plant. 'Had that been done I would not have signed the memorandum.' The President admitted he had not been aware of the existence of the Groves–Anderson paper but believed it showed that, even in the minds of the gentlemen who had prepared the Truman–Attlee–King agreement, the words 'full and effective co-operation' applied only to the field of basic scientific information. He thought an arrangement at this time to assist Britain to build an atomic energy plant would be exceedingly unwise for the United Kingdom as well as for the United States. For on 15 November, the day before the signing of the agreement, the three Governments had jointly declared their intention to request the United Nations to establish a Commission to control production of atomic energy and prevent its use for military purposes. Mr Truman wrote:

> I would not want to have it said that on the morning following the issuance of our declaration to bring about international control we entered into a new agreement, the purpose of which was to have the United States furnish the information as to construction and operation of plants which would enable the United Kingdom to construct another atomic energy plant. No such purpose was suggested by you or thought by me.

In view of the Declaration's advocacy of international control, public sentiment in the United States would not permit the construction of another plant there until the United Nations Commission had had an opportunity to report on the subject. It would be even more critical of any arrangement to help the United Kingdom with a plant.

This telegram, or 'solicitor's letter' as the Canadians called it, seemed to the British to deny all meaning to the simple words 'full and effective co-operation', even as defined in the Groves–Anderson memorandum of November 1945 (see Appendix 5), while there was great resentment of what seemed 'monstrous intrusion' by the United States Government in seeking to put a veto on United Kingdom atomic energy development.

A further reply to this telegram was delayed pending two developments. One was a forthcoming visit by Lord Portal to America and the other was the outcome of some crucial negotiations on raw material allocations. Anglo-American collaboration on uranium procurement had been very close indeed and the buying from third countries, in particular from the immensely rich mines of the Belgian Congo, was handled by a joint organisation, the Combined Development Trust. During the war uranium allocations had not mattered very much, because the British were not likely to have research or production piles in operation for some time, and all supplies had gone to the United States. But suddenly, in March 1946, there was a probability that supplies of Congo uranium would diminish very sharply before the end of 1947 and that there would then be a serious shortage. It therefore seemed essential for the United Kingdom to secure a substantial share of the only large tonnages which could be relied upon – that is, those being mined in 1946 or 1947. The British felt they had an unanswerable case. But for British efforts the Americans might have got no material at all from the Belgian Congo, while all material captured in Germany had gone to the United States, though much of it had come into British hands in the first place. In addition all the Canadian material, apart from supplies to Chalk River, had gone to the United States.

The difficulty was to decide a fair basis for allocation now that uranium was the limiting factor on programmes. The question was raised at the same April 1946 CPC meeting which had killed British hopes of technical collaboration, and the outcome of this discussion was almost equally gloomy. The Americans proposed that the principle of allocation should be based on current requirements of the three Governments for their respective programmes. This was intolerable to the British as it would perpetuate in peacetime an American advantage arising out of an agreed division of the war effort. The British wanted to divide raw material supplies on a 50:50 basis between the United States on the one hand and the United Kingdom and Canada on the other, and the supplies to be so divided should, they said, include not only 1946 and 1947 production but also all 1945 supplies after the end of the war with Japan, and all stocks unused at the end of the war including material captured in Germany. General Groves said that this suggestion would mean that the United States would soon have to start shutting down plants for lack of material.

In practice, Chadwick and Groves were left to sort out these irreconcilable views. Chadwick put forward a compromise whereby all material captured from Germany and all material from the Belgian Congo which was delivered in New York by the end of March 1946 should be allocated to the United States, but all further Congo material delivered in 1946 should go in half shares to the United States and the United Kingdom, while the United States would supply to Britain in addition 50 tons of special oxide and 15 tons of uranium metal. Groves adamantly opposed this solution on two points. Firstly, he said it would lead in a few years' time to the curtailment of production in the United States plants. Secondly, he reiterated that material should not be supplied for the construction of a plant in the United Kingdom because of its vulnerability, and that any British plant should be built in a safe place such as Canada. Lord Halifax fought vehemently against these views with Mr Acheson and found it irritating, almost painful, to hear him reproducing the exaggerated argument of Groves who, he said, 'evidently intimidated the rest of the American side'. Halifax said that Groves's first argument represented an outrageous claim to the whole of the CDT material, while the second raised questions about the national defence and security of the United Kingdom of which the British Government must be the final judge. Halifax told the Government in London that if Acheson did not agree to the compromise within five days, he himself would formally say that His Majesty's Government could no longer acquiesce in the continued shipment of Trust material to the United States, and the consequences of liquidating the CDT should be reviewed.

In the end the Chadwick compromise won the day, although the actual formula was rather more complicated.* Chadwick's triumph was of the greatest importance to the British, because it secured

* Subsequently, at a CPC meeting on 31 July 1946, the financial arrangements of the CDT were revised. Hitherto the UK and USA had paid for CDT material on a 50:50 basis irrespective of its destination. Now each Government was to pay for the material it received and this was to be retrospective to VJ Day. The continuing dollar advantages which the British gained from the financial arrangements are described in Chapter 11.

uranium supplies which, far more than technical information, were indispensable to the British project; shipments received in 1946 and 1947 as a result of the agreement sufficed to keep the project going to the end of 1952, and they consisted moreover entirely of high-grade Congo ores purchased at a most advantageous price.

The solution of the raw material allocation question in May 1946 seemed to have saved the last link of United States–United Kingdom co-operation. Lord Portal was at about the same time being received with great friendliness by Groves and others in the United States, but it was made clear to him that it would be useless to attempt to enter into further negotiations with the American authorities on technical collaboration at this stage.

Technical collaboration between the two countries was at this moment on the way to becoming not simply administratively inconvenient to the United States Government but legally impossible, under the McMahon Bill which was passing through Congress. Political controversy raged round atomic energy legislation in the United States in the year after the end of the war. Early in October 1945 President Truman sent Congress a message about the domestic and international aspects of atomic energy. He treated these subjects separately and urged Congress to enact legislation for the control of activities connected with the development and use of atomic energy in the United States.[4] The subsequent legislation was thus always viewed primarily as legislation for domestic control and not for the regulation of relations between the United States and other countries. It became, however, almost inadvertently but nonetheless relentlessly, the instrument for regulating atomic relations between the United States and its closest allies, Britain and Canada, for the next ten years or more.

The first Bill to be introduced in Congress for the domestic control of atomic energy, the May–Johnson Bill,[5] did not severely impede international arrangements or the interchange of information. But the Bill produced a torrent of protest on other grounds,* The scientists were especially vehement; they swarmed down from

* The scientists detested it because it permitted military officers to hold key positions and because it seemed to think of atomic energy primarily in terms of military applications. Scientists and many others believed the relations between the proposed Commission and the Executive to be undemocratic and the penalties for infringements of security to be vicious. In addition there was mistrust of the secrecy with which the Bill was prepared and the arbitrary manner of its promotion.

their ivory towers and played a large part in consigning the Bill to limbo.[6]

It was succeeded by the McMahon Bill, which pleased those who had so disliked the May–Johnson Bill. Among other apparent advantages it emphasised international control and placed a minimum of restriction on the flow of information. The first draft of the Bill in December 1945 drew a distinction between 'basic scientific' and 'related technical' information: the former would be completely public while the Commission was to disseminate as much of the latter as was consistent with national security. The only sanction restricting the circulation of technical data was the Espionage Act. But as the Bill went through its Congressional career, attitudes towards the dissemination of information hardened. The main issue in the Bill on which battle was fought was whether the proposed Atomic Energy Commission should be wholly civilian or whether the military should play a major part in it. One of the chief reasons why some members of Congress wanted the military to have a larger role than the first draft of the Bill proposed was because they believed that the military would be much more reliable than civilians in keeping 'the secret' of the bomb. In spite of more and more attempts at public education in the meaning of atomic energy, more and more people had come to believe that here was a secret which lay at the very heart of the security of the American state. The incipient hysteria over secrecy was intensified when news broke in February 1946 of the Canadian spy ring, including the treachery of Dr Nunn May, one of the British atomic scientists in the Canadian project. In these circumstances, far stricter provisions in the Bill about the dissemination of information were to some extent the price for retaining the principle of civilian control.

It is impossible to follow the progress of the McMahon Bill in detail because most of the amendments were made in executive session of the Special Senate Committee. But it seems likely that evidence given by the Secretary of War, growing fears on security, plus a growing concern at what some members of Congress regarded as the irresponsibility of the young scientists, led to a much more stringent redrafting of the provisions dealing with dissemination of information. When the Bill reappeared in the open in April 1946,[7] 'the common defense and security' of the state was included for the first time in the preamble as the prime objective of policy. A new clause ($10(a)$) introduced a new concept of 'restricted data' which

covered all data about the manufacture or utilisation of atomic
weapons, the production of fissionable material or its use in the
production of power. The Atomic Energy Commission was to
control the dissemination of these data in such a manner as to assure
'the common defense and security', but it could also decide that
certain restricted data could be published without adversely affecting
the common defence and security. There should be exchange of
information on the use of atomic energy for industrial purposes with
other countries as soon as Congress declared that effective safeguards
against the use of atomic energy for destructive purposes had been
established. Draconian penalties – a fine of up to $20,000 or im-
prisonment of up to twenty years, or both – were prescribed for
anyone conveying restricted data with intent 'to secure an advantage
to any foreign nation'.

In the subsequent Congressional debates this clause was tightened
still further.[8] The House of Representatives would have liked to
strike out altogether the clause which envisaged sharing industrial
information with other nations when safeguards against destructive
use had been erected. Instead a more negative form was adopted.
The final Act said, as far as interchange of information with foreign
countries was concerned, that until Congress declared by joint resolution that effective and enforceable international safeguards against
the use of atomic energy for destructive purposes had been established, there must be no exchange of information with other nations
with respect to the use of atomic energy for industrial purposes. The
penalties for transmitting information now included, in certain
circumstances, life imprisonment or death.[9]

The Combined Policy Committee meeting of 16 April 1946, and
President Truman's telegram of 20 April to the Prime Minister, had
almost killed British hopes of a new arrangement for technical
collaboration. The McMahon Act provided the death blow. The
redrafted Bill had not been mentioned at the CPC meeting nor in
the President's telegram, and it is impossible to know whether the
United States representatives at the CPC had grasped the implications of the Bill for relations with the United Kingdom and Canada
or whether, if they did, they cared. Indeed the McMahon Bill, if
they understood its terms, may have seemed to them to provide a
comfortable clothing of legal and political respectability as they shed
their embarrassing commitments to the British.

In retrospect it seems extraordinary that the McMahon Bill, with its complete disregard for solemn commitments to the British and Canadians, both in writing and in spirit, should have been allowed to reach the statute book without, as it seems, a murmur from the Administration. The commitments – the Quebec Agreement of 1943, the Hyde Park Memorandum of 1944, and the Truman–Attlee–King concordat of November 1945 – were secret and their disclosure even in the confidential surroundings of a Senate committee would have been difficult. But much secret information was imparted now and later to Senate committees and leakages were rare. However, there is no evidence that anyone from the War Department or the State Department even asked himself whether this was something which should be discussed. When the House of Representatives debated the Bill in July 1946, one member did specifically ask: 'Are there any international agreements in respect to atomic matters that are now in existence? I would appreciate a yes or no answer.'[10] Another Representative said: 'If my understanding is correct, we have agreements with Great Britain and Canada. Is that not true?' The chairman of the House Military Affairs Committee, Mr May, replied: 'That is my understanding, but I do not know what they are.' A third Representative said Mr May knew that while this matter was being considered by the Military Affairs Committee, 'we made special enquiries of the State Department as to whether or not there were any secret agreements affecting the atomic bomb that had not been published in any respect and we received definite and positive word without qualification to the effect that there was nothing affecting this legislation that had not been completely published and publicised'. It was pointed out that this assurance contradicted Mr May's belief that there were some agreements of some kind with Britain and Canada, and one Representative urged that if there were agreements or promises it was highly important to find out all about them. However, the discussion petered out and the information was not forthcoming.*

In 1949 Senator McMahon told A. V. Alexander, Labour Minister of Defence, that if he had been given all the information which he requested from the authorities about the history of co-operation with the United Kingdom and Canada there would probably have been

* Dean Acheson writes of his knowledge of the Quebec Agreement and his embarrassment about it and the imputation of bad faith. However, he writes of the McMahon Act as 'a domestic control' Act and does not seem to appreciate that it made any Quebec-type agreement potentially illegal.[11]

no need for his Act to have been passed on such restrictive lines. He said much the same later to Mr Churchill. Although this information was not given by the Administration, it is curious that the McMahon Committee did not appreciate that Britain had a special atomic relationship with the United States which might conceivably merit special treatment. The two British statements (see Appendix 1) about the atomic bomb setting out the British contribution to the wartime project, which had been published in August 1945, were included in a booklet specially produced for the Committee and also in Senator McMahon's April 1946 report on the redrafted Bill. In the hearings before the Committee Leo Szilard, the scientist, had emphasised that the early British work had given the main impetus to the American project.[12] Above all, the nature of Britain's and Canada's relationships with the United States was both implicit and explicit in the Truman–Attlee–King November talks. So the outline of the relationship, though not the specific agreements, must have been known to Congress.

The McMahon Act was passed. It was regarded as a great and liberal Act in American political annals, but Clause 10(a) seemed for Britain, America's wartime ally, a disaster. The Bill's threat had not at first been appreciated. In March 1946, when, admittedly, the draft Bill was fairly innocuous, the British Embassy in Washington had written to London that there was no need to worry about it; the Americans were a long way from agreement among themselves about the best form of control and legislation and there would be many changes before any measure received Congressional approval.*

When the April draft of the Bill appeared almost simultaneously with the distressing meeting of the Combined Policy Committee, it was Chadwick who immediately realised its significance; the Embassy seemed unmoved by it. Chadwick wrote to Anderson full of foreboding. To him the April CPC meeting had shown 'a feeling which goes beyond a mere reluctance to conclude an agreement or a desire to strike a hard bargain' and the new draft of the McMahon Bill confirmed this, since it seemed to exclude the possibility of collaboration with Britain. The Foreign Office Legal Adviser confirmed Chadwick's view and for a time it seemed that another clause in the Bill might prevent the raw materials arrangements from operating. However, the Americans gave specific assurances that the

* The Embassy sent London contents of the revised Bill on 13 Apr 1946 without comment.

Combined Development Trust, which was of course helpful to the Americans, would not be affected.

In London, officials took their time since they thought the Bill might be delayed, and they waited to get the raw material negotiations out of the way and to see the outcome of Lord Portal's forthcoming visit to America (pp. 104, 109). Chadwick wanted to talk privately to Senator McMahon, but the Embassy in Washington was conscious that lobbying Congress was a notoriously risky tactic and advised that any such action by Britain would not affect the Bill since the Senate Committee was 'quite unamenable to official promptings'. This was probably right, but even if such a talk had done no good it would at least have avoided later pleas of ignorance. There was sudden panic in London on 2 June 1946, when word came from Washington that the Bill had been brought up unexpectedly in the Senate and passed through almost unamended, and was on its way to the House of Representatives. Sir John Anderson rushed to the Prime Minister who felt that it was essential that he should make one further and final appeal to the President before the Bill became law. Perhaps such an appeal might fall on receptive, if confused, ears. Lord Halifax had recently made a farewell visit to Mr Truman on relinquishing his post as Ambassador and had raised the question of atomic co-operation. The President had said that his main preoccupation was to secure the passage through Congress of atomic energy control legislation and he could do nothing to jeopardise this, but thereafter all would be well between the United States, the United Kingdom and Canada. He seemed unaware that the legislation as it stood would prevent effective co-operation, while he appeared to agree that the argument that exchanges between the three countries were contrary to United Nations obligations was pretty thin. It was clear, said Halifax, 'that the President is not very well-informed on the whole matter and that his telegrams on the subject were probably drafted for him by others'.

The chances that any appeal would succeed were small in any case, but the long delay in London until the Senate had passed the Bill made them absolutely nil. Nevertheless, however slender the chances, it seemed in London essential that Britain should not allow her case to go by default. It was easier to state a case than to suggest what action the British were asking the President to take. The British Embassy emphasised that there was no hope of intervention by the

Executive to delay the Bill and no other step would have practical effect. They believed a telegram would be inopportune: if it was simply a question of going on the record this was as likely to impair as to assist any possibilities of favourable action in future. A long telegram did go from the Prime Minister on 6 June 1946, replying to the President's seven-week-old April telegram (see Appendix 7). It was essentially a historical justification of Britain's case and urged in general terms that, notwithstanding the McMahon Bill, co-operation on uranium should be balanced by an exchange of information. No reply, not even an acknowledgement, to this telegram was ever received.

The wartime special Anglo-American relationship had almost petered out in atomic energy just as it had petered out in many other areas of economic and military collaboration. The November 1945 discussions had, it is true, failed to recognise the apparent cynicism in the simultaneous signing of a public call for international control and a secret bilateral agreement, even though in terms of hard national interest such a dual approach was intelligible. Early in 1946, amidst the euphoria generated by the discussions and reports of the Acheson and Lilienthal committees, some powerful Americans in the Administration enthusiastically favoured an international approach to atomic energy and did not want a bilateral approach to prejudice it.[13] Yet even the internationally-minded were ambivalent. They might be high-minded about the bilateral exchange of technical information, but they were very anxious to maintain the Anglo-American arrangements for procuring an effective monopoly of the uranium supplies of the non-Communist world – arrangements quite contrary to some of the main American proposals for an international atomic energy authority.

Thus the British had good cause for suspecting less high-minded reasons for American attitudes. They had scant sympathy with the other main American argument against technical collaboration – the strategic vulnerability of the British Isles (see p. 98). They realised that the Administration had serious political difficulties over agreements, but noted again that they were not embarrassed by the raw material agreement. The British concluded that at heart America simply wanted to retain her existing atomic monopoly.[14] Certainly the Americans never gave any sign of regret at going back on the undertakings given by two successive Presidents, in the Hyde Park Agreement of September 1944 and in November 1945. For example,

Mr Acheson, who was more friendly to the British than many of the Administration, told them in March 1946 that they must resign themselves to the fact that, 'although we made the agreement, we simply couldn't carry it out, that things like that happen in the Government of the United States due to the loose way things are handled, and they would have to face the problem of their own country's feelings of being let down, just as we would have to face our problems'.* It merely irritated the American Administration when the British harped on the past – their services, their sacrifices and their rights.

The fact was that the British had no lobby for their atomic interests in Washington. At this stage Britain's affairs as a whole were only of marginal importance to the Americans, and in atomic energy she counted for nothing provided she played the game with raw materials. She was squeezed between the multilaterally-minded internationalists and the nationalists. Even the American atomic scientists, who had close and friendly relationships with the British and who had fought for the passage of the McMahon Bill, did not interest themselves in its effects on Britain. Only afterwards were they sad to discover 'that it was impossible to talk with British friends and associates even about these subjects on which they had worked together during the war'.[15]

The coming into force of the McMahon Act destroyed hopes of improved collaboration but did not make much difference to the immediate situation because there had been so little exchange of information ever since the end of the war. Chadwick had occasionally got useful scraps of information from scientists in the American plants and had received answers to some specific questions he put to Groves about, for example, the thickness of fuel cans or about cooling tubes in nuclear piles, but practically all other questions had been unanswered. No information was forthcoming on questions that were important for the British piles – for example, about expansion of graphite and the release of stored energy in graphite. Lord Portal had visited the main American plants, including Hanford and the gaseous diffusion plant, but as he had no technical knowledge he was unable to bring back anything very useful, although he was

* Lilienthal, *Journals*, p. 26. It is not stated to whom Acheson said this. However, Mr Acheson himself says in his memoirs, *Present at the Creation*, p. 164, that during the winter of 1945–6 he learned about the matter and adds it 'was to disturb me for some years to come for with the knowledge came the

able to comprehend the sheer size of the plants.* Indeed he would probably not have been allowed to make the visit if he had been technically qualified. The British derived some valuable information through the Canadian project which the United States were still supporting with heavy water and uranium metal. This traffic was two-way: there was full exchange of almost all material, classified or not, between Harwell and the Canadian project, and reports sent from England were available to the United States liaison officer in Canada if he asked for them. There would, however, be little from Harwell that would interest the Americans until 1948.

The only significant remnants of direct collaboration in 1946 and 1947 were those concerning raw materials, cyclotrons, medical affairs and declassification policy, together with retention by the United States of the services of some of the wartime British team. The raw materials collaboration covered not only procurement but also the treatment of ores and geological research and exploration: nothing was barred here, though the flow of information was often sluggish. In the case of the cyclotron, drawings that were valuable to Harwell were supplied from Berkeley. In medical affairs United Kingdom visitors discussed the use of tracer isotopes in the United States, but only from mid-1947 did further consultation begin about medical and public health matters. Full tripartite declassification conferences were to begin in November 1947 and they provided one of the rare forums where British and American nuclear scientists could meet, while discussions about whether certain items should still be regarded as secret inevitably gave some scientific clues to the British. The continued service of certain Britons in the American project was more strange. Chadwick had been anxious to make the transition of the British teams back to Britain as smooth as possible for both the Americans and the British, and they had only trickled back. Klaus Fuchs left Los Alamos as late as June 1946. When the McMahon Act was passed into law, four members of the British

---

belief that a Government, having made an agreement from which it had gained immeasurably, was not keeping its word and performing its obligations'.

* The scientists and engineers remember today their disappointment over this. Lord Portal's main impression of the diffusion plant was that people had to ride round it on bicycles because it was so big. However, no other result could have been expected. Any informed questions would undoubtedly have been evaded.

team were still at Los Alamos – E. Bretscher, A. P. French, E. Titterton and J. L. Tuck.* The British all now left except for one of them – Ernest Titterton, instrumentation group leader at Los Alamos. The director of Los Alamos begged to keep him and was allowed to do so on the grounds of his irreplaceability until the spring of 1947, when Congressional witch-hunting about the members of the new United States Atomic Energy Commission was in full swing and it seemed more sensible to let him go, since he refused to become an American citizen.

There were six British scientists with the teams which conducted the first American post-war atomic bomb tests at Bikini in July 1946. They included Tuck and Titterton (both still employed at Los Alamos), William Penney, and five other 'British missionaries'.† Titterton gave the countdown and the detonation order for the tests. Care was taken in all the publicity to avoid saying who he was or where he came from: the radio commentator at the second test after naming 'everybody and his uncle' referred to Titterton as 'the Voice of Abraham', Abraham being the code radio call sign. Penney had already returned to England and was Chief Superintendent of Armament Research in the Ministry of Supply when the Americans asked for him to come back to take part in the Bikini tests. He was needed for blast measurements; after his report on the Japanese bombs, Groves felt he was the one man on whom he could rely. The full results of the trials would clearly contain much top secret information of prime military importance, so much so that permission to attend had not been granted to many United States scientists whom the Navy Department wanted. However, the United States Navy persisted in their demands for Penney and he was eventually allowed to take part on the grounds that his presence was in the interests of the defence of the United States, which the preamble to the McMahon Act laid down as its criterion. He played a very important part in the trials, and was subsequently invited back to America for highly secret discussions of the trial.

* Dr Tuck returned to the USA (University of Chicago) in 1949 and became an American citizen.

† These five were R. Pilgrim (of the Armaments Research Department), two Admiralty representatives, Dr J. H. Powell and Lt-Cdr R. J. Daniels, and two medical experts, Drs E. E. Pochin and F. C. MacIntosh. Their participation in the test was kept secret. Besides the scientists the British Government were invited to send two official observers; these were Mr F. Beswick, MP, and Commander A. H. P. Noble, MP.

Apart from these important but isolated personal experiences, and apart from raw material affairs, Anglo-American atomic collaboration was minimal. This was properly a matter of the greatest political and strategic concern. However, some people in the project believed that the absence of technical collaboration was much less important than London assumed. For example, Chadwick reiterated time and time again that the British knew enough to get along on their own: 'Are we so helpless', he would ask, 'that we can do nothing without the United States?' Hinton took the same line. Indeed, when Portal told him of the McMahon Act, he expressed the view that it was the best thing that could possibly happen because it would make the British think for themselves.[16] He believed that with full access to American information the British would inevitably feel constrained to copy plants which the Americans had built hastily and therefore clumsily. He always felt afterwards that Portal regarded him with suspicion from the time he uttered this apparent heresy.

The British project could and did succeed without American help. One most important and difficult plant – the chemical plant which separated the plutonium, uranium and fission products in the fuel rods irradiated in the pile – was much better than the American plant which was being planned and which the British might have copied if they had been given information about it (see Chapter 22). Britain built air-cooled piles rather than American-type water-cooled piles primarily because of the difficulty of finding a suitable site, but if there had been access to American information, Lord Portal might well have insisted on a water-cooled pile. Nevertheless, technological independence brought, besides some real benefits, some disadvantages. There were some areas – for example, knowledge about graphite or about particle emissions from pile chimneys – where early and adequate knowledge of American experiences would have saved the expenditure of scientific and engineering effort when British resources were heavily overstrained. Irritating obstacles in the British programme could have been quickly removed by minor help from the Americans. American export of certain materials which would have been very useful was refused. Meanwhile, in the post-war Canadian project, when the first sizeable pile was soon to be commissioned, the American stationed there was said to sit by and watch the Canadians make mistakes which he could have forestalled. There was general agreement at the time that full co-operation from the United States might reduce the time required for the British programme by a year. If there had been such co-operation the British might have been able to acquire relatively cheap uranium-235 when the Americans could spare it in later years, and this might possibly have influenced the course of her reactor development (see Chapter 19).

Even after the McMahon Act was passed, the British were determined to renew the struggle for Anglo-American atomic collaboration once the moment seemed propitious. There was, it seems, only one dissenting voice to this policy: that of Professor Blackett, who was still on the Advisory Committee on Atomic Energy. He returned from a visit to America after the mid-term elections at the end of 1946 deeply concerned about the extremely conservative United States that was emerging and by the talk there of preventive war – though he did not believe such a war would in fact be launched. He thought that close co-operation with such an America would become increasingly difficult for a Labour Government and he therefore favoured a neutralist policy in atomic energy as part and parcel of a neutralist foreign and defence policy; he also felt, as we shall see later, that the British should not make atomic bombs (see Chapter 6 and Appendix 8). He submitted a paper to the Gen 75 Committee at the beginning of 1947 and saw Mr Attlee on two occasions, but his views had no influence at all on the Government. The Foreign Office found Blackett's views 'dangerous and misleading rubbish', based as they seemed to be on the assumption that Russia was a peaceable state harbouring no expansionist designs, thrown on to the defensive by an aggressive and warmongering United States. Officials thought the idea of the United States waging preventive war almost too ludicrous to entertain.* They could not accept Blackett's belief that Britain as an important power could remain neutral in a major war, grounding her policy on the narrowest possible basis of material self-interest and regarding the fate of democratic countries elsewhere as a matter of indifference.

---

* But David Lilienthal, *Change, Hope and the Bomb* (Princeton UP, 1963) p. 143, refers to an entry in his diary for 1 Nov 1949 about a talk with Senator McMahon: 'Pretty discouraging. What he is talking about is the inevitability of war with the Russians, and what he says adds up to one thing: blow them off the face of the earth, quick, before they do the same to us – and we haven't much time.... The whole world revolves round the exploding atom as he sees it – that's the whole of it and there is no hope.'

If a great power wished to attack Britain to gain bases or other resources, 'are we to ensure that we are imperfectly equipped for self-defence or counter-attack?' There were some uncomplimentary remarks about the author of the memorandum. Bevin pencilled 'he ought to stick to science',* and the Minister of State thought the only point calling for action was whether or not Blackett should remain on the Anderson Advisory Committee.

In Government circles the question was not whether, but when, by what channel and in what form a new approach should be made to the United States. The British would not appear as 'impotent suppliants' who could not get along without the Americans, and the view of most people was that timing and tactics should be cautious. 'To achieve the best results in this matter', wrote the British Embassy in Washington, 'I fear we shall have to exercise an almost biblical patience. It is a mistake to flog a dead horse especially when a new one is about to emerge from the stable.' Not until December 1946 did the Prime Minister send a brief message to the President asking how the understanding reached a year ago in Washington could be put into effect. This time the President replied, saying he was giving the message careful consideration.

By then the new horse had emerged. In November 1946 the first United States Atomic Energy Commission had been appointed and on 1 January 1947 it took over the United States project. This civilian body was the creation of the McMahon Act and the British could not be sure of its friendliness. At first the British Embassy found the new Commission 'rather disorganised and very nervous', clinging strictly to the letter of the Act. But it was soon clear that key members of the Commission were well disposed to Britain, notably the Chairman, David Lilienthal, and the young General Manager, Carroll Wilson, as well as the scientist Commissioner, R. F. Bacher, and the Director of Research, J. B. Fisk. They were concerned that the McMahon Act had been drafted in ignorance of the United States' international undertakings and that it conflicted with them. They appreciated the importance of co-operation with the British not merely for its own sake but for the wider implications.

* In fact, one of Blackett's main contributions to the war effort had been not so much in science as in the development of operational research, that is, the application of scientific method and analytical techniques to strategic and tactical problems.[17]

Nevertheless, there were serious difficulties. The Commission found themselves tightly tied by the Act in many directions even though their legal advisers were doing all they could to stretch it. The elasticity was limited and it was obviously impossible to ask Congress to ease the restrictions in the near future. The Commission had concluded they could participate in the raw materials Trust because it was an arrangement in the interests of the United States. But they felt that the Combined Policy Committee and all the other implications of the Quebec Agreement were foreign relations and a matter for the State Department.

However, here too the outlook was brighter, for in January 1947 Mr Byrnes was succeeded as Secretary of State by General Marshall, the wartime Chairman of the Combined Chiefs of Staff and a friend and close colleague of the British. He was prepared to continue the Combined Policy Committee. Moreover another wartime friend, General Eisenhower, who was United States Chief of Staff, was interesting himself in what seemed to him the unfair treatment of the British.

The prospects of Anglo-American atomic co-operation seemed to improve as the general international situation darkened and the possibilities of agreement in the United Nations Atomic Energy Commission grew dim. America and Britain seemed to be drawing more closely together again, and in December 1946 the Co-ordinating Committee of the United States War and Navy Departments had issued a new directive about the disclosure of United States military information to the British. All classified military information, including the United States order of battle, and all information about combined research and development projects to which the United Kingdom had contributed or was contributing, and United States research and development projects, could be released to the United Kingdom. The release was subject to conditions, for example that the United Kingdom must not pass on the information to third parties without specific approval. The directive did not cover atomic energy but it covered a very wide range of other military information – intelligence, technical and scientific information on weapons and methods of manufacture, and non-technical information about United States forces. As such it was symptomatic of a renewed desire by the United States forces to collaborate with the British. A good deal of informal collaboration developed in the standardisation of equipment and tactics and in some forms of research and development, even though some important weapons, notably guided missiles, were for a long time excluded.

However, even if the omens seemed auspicious there was not much hope of any quick answer to Britain's renewed requests for atomic collaboration. In January 1947 the new Congressional Joint Committee on Atomic Energy, which was set up under the McMahon Act with greater powers than those of any other Congressional committee, began hearings to confirm the suitability of Lilienthal as chairman of the new Commission. He had been chairman of the famous – to many Congressmen and businessmen, infamous – Tennessee Valley Authority, pride of Roosevelt's New Deal. The confirmation hearings were vicious and lasted well into April, and though Lilienthal was confirmed, the struggle took up much time and effort of the Commission[18] and made it impolitic for them to embark on contentious issues like relations with the British.

Moreover it became clear that, notwithstanding Generals Marshall and Eisenhower, the United States Chiefs of Staff felt no happier than before about the prospect of atomic piles in Britain. Eisenhower had wanted the American Chiefs of Staff to discuss the location of plants in the United Kingdom, confident they would deny any objection, but he did not want to raise the matter with them himself. The Prime Minister was willing that the British military representative in Washington, Field-Marshal Lord Wilson, should discuss the matter with the US Chiefs of Staff in the hope that they would not merely disavow their former views but would actually admit that they saw advantage in plants in the United Kingdom which would strengthen United Kingdom defence potential. Since exchange of information would then be in the interests of the defence of the United States, it should be possible under the McMahon Act. The Prime Minister emphasised that the decision to construct plants in the United Kingdom was not negotiable.

The joint talks were never held. At the beginning of March 1947 General Eisenhower told Field-Marshal Lord Wilson that his Chiefs of Staff had sent the State Department a paper which stressed the risk of locating any atomic plant or store of uranium on the periphery of the Anglo-American zone of defence, and the need to use available supplies of uranium for United States production of fissile material in order to create a large stockpile of bombs for defence purposes. In short, they thought it unwise to place atomic plants as close to a European enemy as the British Isles. Eisenhower said the decision was not due to doubts about the adequacy of British military precautions but to a study of the difficulties and conditions Britain and Western Europe were facing, and might be facing some ten years hence. Situations could be envisaged, he said, where Britain might be subject to pressure from a major power offering conditions which she might be unable to resist. Eisenhower said this opinion was very strong in Washington and that the risk was considered to be more political than military.

In reporting this to the Prime Minister, the British Ambassador and Field-Marshal Wilson said 'the questioning of our reliability in future years will be as unpalatable to you as it is to us'. It seemed peculiar that this conclusion had been reached so soon after the military had agreed to make available to Britain all classified and military intelligence with the sole exception of atomic energy intelligence. There were two likely explanations. Firstly, atomic energy, because of its particular role in the recent war and its current political implications in the United States, was still placed in a niche entirely of its own. Secondly, recent events in the domestic and foreign affairs of the United Kingdom had caused a wave of doubt about her ability to survive as a first-class power. At home the cold weather in the early months of 1947 had brought a disastrous fuel crisis and the shut-down of factories. Abroad, Britain gave up her military role in Greece and in Turkey. These doubts were not so strong at the time when the general directive on military information was being worked out.

The advice of the Ambassador and Field-Marshal was that London should not be discouraged by this development, 'which marks the failure of only one move in the game'. Gradually the British attitude to American co-operation was changing. At the beginning of 1947 they had felt they would be satisfied with nothing less than the fullest possible collaboration over the whole field with complete exchange of information and visits. But the emphasis changed to establishing a firm and long-term basis of collaboration, if necessary on limited terms. Roger Makins, back in London at the Foreign Office from the British Embassy, and now chairman of the Atomic Energy Official Committee, suggested that it was desirable to find a *modus vivendi* or working relationship between the United States, Britain and Canada which would give the maximum that the United States Administration could politically agree to at the moment. Apart from improving the exchange of information, such a working arrangement would supersede the Quebec Agreement.

And so, accepting this limited objective and the American political difficulties, the British pressed less hard, and agreed that the Americans must be left to make the next move. The British were still anxious to get technical information from the Americans, especially about plutonium separation and the handling of plutonium, but now that they had decided not to build American-type piles (see p. 190) their needs seemed rather less urgent. There was besides practical evidence of the willingness of the United States Atomic Energy Commission to co-operate in admittedly small ways – for example, in sending declassified reports quickly, in supplying cyclotron drawings and arranging a visit to the Berkeley cyclotron, and in arranging co-operation on declassified medical and public health affairs.

On their side the Commission felt that one preliminary was essential to any further international negotiation. This was the disclosure to the Joint Congressional Atomic Energy Committee of all the secret wartime and post-war international agreements on atomic energy. Something about them was already known or guessed by members of Congress and responsible American journalists, but there would be an uproar if a major leak occurred and Congress knew nothing officially. The question of publicly releasing this embarrassing cat – or rather collection of cats – was considered on both sides of the Atlantic, but London was as anxious as Washington to keep them secret. The wartime raw material agreements would be considered provocative and inconsistent with the Atlantic Charter, while questions would be asked about the secret collaboration agreement of November 1945. Why had the agreement been necessary once hostilities were over? Why had it been kept secret? Why had it been signed just when the same individuals were proposing publicly that the whole subject of atomic energy should be handled by the United Nations? Had the intentions of the signatories been implemented, and if not, why not? In Britain there would be dismay about the article in the Quebec Agreement which had subordinated British commercial atomic development to United States wishes. All in all, the political storms that would be raised by an announcement seemed unthinkable, especially when the Foreign Secretaries were about to meet in Moscow. More important still, it seemed likely that irresistible pressure would be exerted on the

Belgian Government to denounce their agreement to supply Congo uranium. So publication was out of the question.

The United States Atomic Energy Commission, however, decided that a full factual statement of all agreements and negotiations must be made to the Joint Congressional Committee, and this was duly carried out by Mr Acheson on 12 May 1947.* It was reported to the British† that oral summaries were given of the Quebec and Hyde Park Agreements,‡ the Trust's terms of reference, and the personnel of the Combined Policy Committee. The outline of all the raw materials agreements was given. The Committee was completely surprised and betrayed an ignorance about Britain's wartime role[19] which was unwarranted in the light of information given to Congressional committees in 1946 (see p. 108). They were alarmed that Britain was getting half of the Congo uranium and extremely vexed that the Quebec Agreement had laid down that her consent was needed before the atomic bomb could be used. There was, however, no general outcry against the Administration and its predecessor such as had been feared. The need for extreme secrecy was impressed on the Committee and to most people's surprise the secrets were closely kept and did not leak to the press.

The response to this dreaded disclosure makes the failure to reveal the agreements to the McMahon Committee early in 1946 the more inexplicable, especially since the 1946 Congress was more favourable to the Administration than the 1947 Congress. The incident also emphasises the inequality of the Anglo-American relationship and the different legal and constitutional procedures in the two countries, which resulted in different standards of disclosure. Britain was told of the forthcoming revelation of the agreements, but in spite of promises that her consent would be sought, it does not seem that it was. There is no evidence that anyone in London suggested that any of Britain's elected representatives in Parliament should receive this same information, even though several MPs were constantly trying to get information about the Quebec Agreement. The status of the Joint Committee on Atomic

* In his *Present at the Creation*, p. 167, Acheson implies that the revelations were made in 1946.

† The British were not made aware at the time how very angry some of the Senators were about the Quebec provision for consultation on the use of the bomb.

‡ No mention was made in the communication to the British of the Attlee–Truman November 1945 agreement.

Energy gave Congress an informed interest in, and control over, atomic energy, whereas Parliament had virtually none. The disparity was to be underlined on other occasions in the future.

However, for the United States Atomic Energy Commission the disclosure meant that they were safely over a major hurdle and could begin to think seriously about ways of improving Anglo-American collaboration. At last the log-jam was showing signs of breaking.

The British had seen the McMahon Act as a reverse, not as a defeat. There had been no break in the policy of pursuing indefatigably the atomic connection with the United States; indeed the Ministerial Committee Gen 75 had not discussed the breakdown of collaboration in this period. The reasons for this pursuit are occasionally explicit but more often implicit. Underlying it was the consciousness of the enormous power of the United States on which Britain and the non-Communist world must rely for defence, and above all the consciousness that the United States alone possessed atomic bombs. The Government's conviction grew that the economic and political destiny of Britain and of Europe depended on the fullest possible alliance with the United States – however unpalatable the conclusion might be to some individual Ministers. A secondary reason for the pertinacity was born of grievance, of the feeling that the Americans were treating the British unjustly and must not be allowed to get away with it.

American technical knowledge was vast. In 1946 Britain wanted to share it in order to assist her own research and technology for the manufacture of fissile material. No requests had been made in 1946 for information about weapon development because, as we shall see, the decision to make a British bomb had not yet been taken. The need for information about the industrial plants may well have been, as Chadwick and Hinton believed, exaggerated. In 1947, however, Britain was firmly launched on the manufacture of an atomic bomb, and weapons questions began to loom large. It was not yet realised how rapidly weapon technology would develop, but now that the military objective of the British project had been made clear and explicit, the need for collaboration with the United States had intensified. It might be impolitic to ask too soon for weapon information, but the desire for it became increasingly a spur to continued negotiation.

Once it had been decided that the objective of Britain's atomic energy project was first and foremost a military one, perseverance with the American atomic connection was inevitable. The only valid alternative was abdication from the military aspects – a policy suggested, as we shall see, by Professor Blackett and at times by Sir Henry Tizard but never seriously contemplated by the Government.

The need for renewed collaboration with the United States was not paramount with the Government; Britain's inviolable right to construct plants in the United Kingdom took precedence. Such collaboration, however, came next in the order of priorities whether of the Prime Minister, the Chiefs of Staff, the Foreign Office, the Ministry of Supply or the Official Atomic Energy Committee. The pursuit of this collaboration carried one penalty – the denial of atomic collaboration with the countries of the Commonwealth (other than Canada) and the countries of Europe.

Appendix 6

TELEGRAM FROM MR ATTLEE TO
PRESIDENT TRUMAN, 16 APRIL 1946

Lord Halifax has reported to me what happened at the meeting of the Atomic Energy Combined Policy Committee on 15th April and Mr Byrnes has no doubt made a report to you.

I am gravely disturbed at the turn which the Combined Policy Committee's discussions have taken over the implementation of the second and third paragraphs of the short document which you, Mr Mackenzie King and I signed on 16 November last. I feel that unless you and we and the Canadian Government can reach a satisfactory working basis of co-operation, at least to cover the period until we see the outcome of the discussions in the United Nations Commission on Atomic Energy, we in this country shall be placed in a position which, I am sure you will agree, is inconsistent with that document.

As you know, the document stated that it was our desire that there should be 'full and effective co-operation in the field of atomic energy between the United States, the United Kingdom and Canada'; and it seems to me that this cannot mean less than full interchange of information and a fair division of the material. Moreover, the interchange of information was implicit in the Washington Declaration, paragraph 4 of which recognised as a matter of principle that our three countries possessed the knowledge required for the use of atomic energy, and paragraph 6 of which stated our willingness, subject to suitable safeguards, to share with other States information about the practical industrial applications. The Declaration contained nothing about the sharing of information among ourselves and the clear indication is that this was already provided for. The war-time arrangements under which the major share of the development work and the construction and operation of full-scale plants were carried out in the United States have naturally meant that technological and engineering information has accumulated in your hands, and if there is to be full and effective co-operation between us it seems essential that this information should be shared. I would therefore urge most strongly that the Combined Policy Committee should make a further attempt to work out a satisfactory basis of co-operation. In the last resort a solution might be that the heads of the three Governments should each issue instructions for the interchange of information, including, in particular, the technical information which each of us requires for the implementation of immediate programmes.

Appendix 7

TELEGRAM FROM MR ATTLEE TO PRESIDENT TRUMAN, 6 JUNE 1946

Your telegram of the 20th April (see pp. 100–1) about the exchange of information on atomic energy.

I have held back my reply until I had been able to discuss the matter with Halifax and with Mackenzie King.

I should like first to go back a little over past history. In the early years of the war, in 1940 and 1941, our scientists were amongst the first to become convinced of the enormous military possibilities of the atomic energy project, and it will not, I think, be denied that both then and later, if we had been willing to face the diversion of industrial effort that would have been needed, we had the resources and the scientific and technical skill that would have enabled us to embark on the development of the project in this country. But to do that we should have had to reduce our efforts in other directions in which we were already heavily engaged, both in comparatively new but highly important fields of development such as radar and jet propulsion, and in the more established forms of war production. To do so at that time would not have been opportune, particularly so long as the threat of invasion lasted and while our principal centres of production were subject to air attack. Nevertheless, if we had continued to stand alone, I do not believe that we could have afforded to neglect so revolutionary a development and to gamble on the chance that the war would end without our enemies succeeding in developing it. At whatever cost we should have been bound to make the attempt to develop it in this country. Whether or not we should have succeeded before the war ended, we should certainly have gained much knowledge and experience.

Fortunately, however, it was not necessary to make the choice. President Roosevelt had become interested in the idea of an atomic weapon and had decided to engage upon it all the vast resources of the United States. In October 1941 he wrote to Mr Churchill and proposed that any extended efforts in this field should be co-ordinated or even jointly conducted. It was thus possible for us to decide that we would concentrate on assisting to the best of our ability the developing of the enterprise in the United States. It is not for me to try to assess what that assistance was worth, but we gave it in the confident belief that the experience and knowledge gained in America would be made freely available to us, just as we made freely available to you the results of research in other fields such as radar and jet propulsion, on which, as a result of this decision, we were able to concentrate. It was part of that wise division of effort and pooling of resources which was made possible by the system of reciprocal aid which, without attempting to compare and measure the aggregate contribution on each side, enabled both countries to concentrate their efforts on those fields where they seemed likely to be most productive. I must repeat that but for that system, we should have been forced to adopt a different distribution of our resources in this country, which would not have been so advantageous to the common interest.

As I said, we entered on these arrangements in a spirit of partnership and in the belief that both countries would pool the experience which they gained. It was, in fact, later expressly provided in the Quebec Agreement that there should be complete interchange of ideas and information on all sections of the project between members of the Policy Committee and their immediate technical advisers, and, at the lower level, interchange of information in the field of design and construction of large-scale plants was not ruled out but was made subject to *ad hoc* arrangements to be approved by the Combined Policy Committee. At the same time it was left to the President of the United States to specify the terms on which any post-war advantages of an industrial or a commercial character should be dealt with as between the United States and Great Britain.

In the latter days of the war, we considered more than once whether, under the existing arrangements, we were making the best use of our resources and whether the time had not come when we ought to undertake a policy of more active development in this country if we were not to fall too far behind in a field of development in which we had, but a short time before, been in the forefront. But, on each occasion, after full deliberation, we came back to the principle of the Quebec Agreement – that the earliest .possible realisation of the project must come first and before any separate national advantage, and that, while our scientists could still contribute anything to the work in the United States, they should not be withdrawn. We felt that we could rely on the provisions of the Agreement to ensure that we should not suffer, that we should be given full access at the highest level to the knowledge of all sections of the project, and that the dissemination of such information to lower levels would be limited only by considerations of security.

This situation continued until the goal had been reached and the first bomb dropped. At that point, we considered, we might reasonably prepare to undertake a more active programme of development in this country and might expect to be able to make use of the experience which had been gained up to that point in the joint enterprise.

Almost immediately the war came to an end, and we were told that until new arrangements could be concluded the supply of information must be stopped. When I visited Washington, therefore, in November, it was an important part of my purpose to secure that, as President Roosevelt had promised Mr Churchill at Hyde Park in September 1944, the co-operation which had existed during the war should be continued and that it should be full and effective. I was very much reassured, therefore, when you agreed that this should be so and that the Combined Policy Committee should be asked to recommend arrangements to that end. It seemed a natural and a logical continuation of the previous agreement that the arrangements for peace-time collaboration would cover at least the same ground as before and would take account of the fact that this country was now free to devote a substantial industrial effort to the atomic energy project. The matter was discussed, in the first instance, at a conference held in Judge Patterson's room at the War Department and afterwards in greater detail by Sir John Anderson with General Groves and Mr George Harrison, and together they drew up the memorandum to which you refer. I can find no support in the paragraph of that document which you quote for the view that there was no obligation to exchange information about the construction of large-scale plants. It is indeed clearly laid down that, while the principle was not in doubt, the best means of giving effect to it should be considered further by the Combined Policy Committee.

Such discussions did, in fact, take place and lasted many weeks. Finally a unanimous report was submitted to the Combined Policy Committee by a sub-committee on which your Government was represented by General Groves. The draft agreement which the sub-committee drew up provided that there was to be full and effective co-operation in the exchange of information required for the development programmes of the two countries. We made it clear in the discussions that our own programme would include the construction of large-scale plants in this country.

When the sub-committee's report was considered by the Combined Policy Committee, it came as a surprise to us to find that your Government was not prepared to enter into any agreement, nor to proceed on the basis of the agreements previously reached between us, nor yet to agree that co-operation should, in fact, continue by administrative action. The clause of our Agreement, signed in November, by which the Combined Policy Committee was to recommend the arrangements required for continued co-operation has thus remained a dead letter.

I cannot agree with the argument that to continue such co-operation would be inconsistent with the public declaration on the control of atomic energy which you and Mackenzie King and I issued in November. That our three Governments stand in a special relationship to one another in this field is a matter of record and was, in fact, the reason why we took the initiative in issuing the declaration. It is surely not inconsistent with its purpose that the co-operation begun during the war should continue during the peace unless and until it can be replaced by a wider system. And until recently, at any rate, I think it is fair to say that it was generally assumed in both our countries that this co-operation was continuing. And, indeed, in one important part of the field it is: I am referring to our joint control of raw materials. We have not thought it necessary to abandon that – in my opinion, quite rightly. Why then should we abandon all further pooling of information?

You evidently feel that it would be inconsistent with the declaration issued at Washington that another atomic energy plant should be constructed and that the United States should assist in its construction. The purpose of the Washington Declaration was to promote the development of atomic energy for peaceful ends and to ensure that it should not be used as a means of destruction. It was certainly not intended to stifle all further development in other countries, any more than it was suggested that the development which has already taken place in the United States should be abandoned. We have made no secret of the fact that we intend to produce fissile material, though naturally the use which we shall make of it will be much affected by the deliberations of the Atomic Energy Commission.

In the meantime, I can see nothing in the Washington Declaration, or in the Assembly Resolution, which requires us to dissolve our partnership, either in the exchange of information or in the control of raw materials, until it can be merged in a wider partnership. I should be sorry to think that you did not agree with this view.

I have set out the position fully and frankly as I am sure you would have wished me to do. I realise that an additional complication may arise from the fact that the McMahon Bill containing stringent provisions about the disclosure of information has within the last few days been passed by the Senate.

I would nevertheless most strongly urge that for the reasons I have given our continuing co-operation over raw materials shall be balanced by an exchange of information which will give us, with all proper precautions in regard to security, that full information to which we believe that we are entitled, both by the documents and by the history of our common efforts in the past.

5

External Policy: The Commonwealth and Europe

Canada

To Britain, atomic relations with the United States seemed far more important than relations with any other country and indeed governed them. For one clause of the Quebec Agreement of 1943 had said that the signatories would not communicate any atomic information to third parties except by mutual consent. The agreement was obsolete, having referred to the war, but it had never been abrogated and the British still regarded themselves as bound by this particular clause. The Prime Minister himself specifically endorsed this view. Only one country, Canada, was exempt from these restrictions for she was a third, if subsidiary, party in Anglo-American atomic affairs. This special triangular relationship was not confined to atomic energy, for Canada played a more important role than any of the other British Dominions* in the Marshall Plan and the subsequent organisation for implementing it and also in NATO; her status as a power in the atomic world no doubt influenced her role in these other spheres. Meanwhile, quite apart from the atomic triangle, Britain and Canada also had their own very strong bilateral links.

Canada had been persuaded to establish an atomic energy project by the British in 1942 because this seemed the most suitable lodgement for the Anglo-French slow neutron team from Cambridge. The Americans would not have the team in their project but seemed willing to co-operate if it settled nearby in Canada.[1] The Montreal Laboratory was therefore established but soon came to a standstill in default of American co-operation. After the Quebec Agreement Chadwick had succeeded in persuading Groves to help the project and to make it an officially approved Anglo-Canadian-United States

* The terms 'Dominions' and 'Colonies', though now obsolete, are retained as they represent the Commonwealth situation in the period of this book and to change them would be anachronistic.

affair. Canada provided all the buildings and equipment and many of the staff; Britain provided and paid the majority of the staff; the United States provided essential materials and some technical help. It was possible to go ahead with the design and construction of a heavy-water pile at Chalk River. It should be noted that the team also included five French scientists and a group of young New Zealanders. After a bad start the project had flourished from 1944 onwards with John Cockcroft as its director. Canada had also become involved in atomic energy during the war because she possessed rich uranium deposits. For these reasons Canada had been kept fully in touch with all the Anglo-American negotiations which led up to the Quebec Agreement. Canada was not a signatory of the agreement, but her part in the project was recognised by Canadian membership of the Combined Policy Committee. Similarly, she did not sign the declaration establishing the Combined Development Trust for raw materials, but again one of the six trustees was Canadian.[2]

During the last year of the war Canada's association with the project was happy and fruitful, but until then relations between Britain and Canada had often been strained.[3] In particular, Canada could always appreciate much better than the British the viewpoint of her next-door neighbour, the United States. When she sold her uranium to the United States or when occasionally she took their side in disagreements, the British were irate and aggrieved by what appeared to them disloyalty. The Canadians on their side had resented some tactless British actions which had seemed to emphasise that British rather than Canadian authority ruled the Montreal Laboratory.[4] Sir John Anderson's high-handed proconsular attitude had made his wartime dealings with the Canadians especially unfortunate. Canada had not been adequately and fully consulted, although Chadwick, who got on extremely well with the Canadians, had quite often found that they did not wish to be brought into negotiations between the United States and Britain even though their interests were involved. With this past history, post-war relations with the Canadians needed very delicate handling. Once more there were two interconnected but distinct aspects to the relationship. Firstly, there was the Anglo-Canadian relationship within the triangular negotiations for collaboration with the United States. Secondly, there was the need to determine the relationship between the wartime Anglo-Canadian atomic project in Canada and Britain's post-war native project.

Canada played a full part in the post-war negotiations with the Americans. Although she had no intention of making atomic bombs, her Prime Minister, Mr Mackenzie King, had been an equal participant with Mr Truman and Mr Attlee at the Washington discussions in November 1945, and had signed the public declaration and the secret agreement on collaboration. He had originally intended not to sign the secret agreement but agreed to do so on the advice of C. D. Howe, the Minister who had long dealt with atomic affairs, on the grounds that it did not seem to commit Canada to anything very much and particularly not to any expense. Subsequently Lester Pearson, then Canadian Ambassador in Washington, had been an equal member with General Groves and Mr Makins of the sub-committee of the Combined Policy Committee which had been appointed to work out a document to replace the Quebec Agreement.

In the subsequent debate this document, and indeed any technical collaboration, had, it will be recalled, been repudiated on two grounds – chiefly because it conflicted with Article 102 of the United Nations Charter and also because the United States disliked the idea of production plants in the United Kingdom. It was here that the two aspects of Anglo-Canadian atomic relations came together. The United States suggested that Britain should build her plants in Canada for reasons of security, while, as we shall see, Canada had hoped, whether justifiably or not, that the British would build production plants in Canada after the war as part of a joint project. Cockcroft and Chadwick both at that time wanted the first British production pile to be built in Canada and so did the British members of the Combined Policy Committee. We shall take up this point in discussing Britain's atomic production plans (see p. 172). Briefly, everyone in London was determined to build a first pile in the United Kingdom on the grounds of control and availability of industrial capacity. The Chancellor of the Exchequer supported them, saying that Britain could finance a pile in Canada only by borrowing additional dollars from the Canadian Government, which was, in her financial circumstances, quite impracticable. The Prime Minister had put all this in a telegram to the British Ambassador in Washington:

We consider it essential if this country is to make its proper contribution to progress in this new field and to enjoy its share in

the development of the benefits of atomic energy that we should
have a large-scale plant in this country, where we have the necessary industrial, scientific and technical resources readily at hand.
We feel that it would be quite wrong for the United Kingdom to
be dependent on an outside (even though a Dominion) source for
the supplies of fissile material which will be required for the
research and development work to be conducted at Harwell and
for the application of atomic energy to other needs. . . . If the pile
is to be built and paid for by the Canadian Government it becomes
a Canadian enterprise, and even though we might be ready to help
by lending staff, the plant would necessarily be owned and to a
large extent controlled by the Canadian Government.

On both the main issues of the Anglo-American-Canadian
negotiations – the international aspect and the location of the British
plants – the Canadians sympathised much more with the Americans
than with the British. They appreciated that Britain must be able
to make up for lost time, especially in view of her great contribution
to the wartime project, but they believed that co-operation between
the three powers might militate against the chance of an international
solution. Apart from their own doubts about the vulnerability of
plants in the United Kingdom, most of the Canadians were already
disappointed, as we shall see, to find that Britain was not to make
her main post-war production effort in Canada.*

Here too the situation of 1943 seemed to be repeating itself. The
difficulties between the United Kingdom and the United States
increased the existing acerbity in Anglo-Canadian atomic relations,
and Britain did not welcome Canadian attempts to act as a go-
between if they showed excessive sympathy with the American point
of view. In 1946 they seemed to show just this. Lester Pearson felt
that the whole atomic business had gone sour and said unjustifiably
that co-operation even in the past was rather a misnomer even
between Britain and Canada. He thought that the American attitude
was neither very surprising nor even very unreasonable: they had
the plant, the material and the knowledge; they did not intend at
this stage that Britain or anyone else should have them; they considered that they were a peace-loving people and that Britain ought

* See p. 137 below. Mr Howe and Dr Mackenzie of the National Research
Council wanted Britain to build big piles in Canada, but apparently the
Prime Minister, Mr Mackenzie King, did not.

to be glad that all this was in their hands. Mr Pearson agreed that Britain 'as a peace-loving people with a public opinion' could not really leave the United States and Canada alone in the atomic production field. Nevertheless, the Canadians felt that Britain would be well advised not to press the question of exchange of information for the present. Even though they were shocked by President Truman's letter of April 1946 to Mr Attlee, they felt that it was all-important that this serious divergence between Britain and the United States should be covered up, if it could not be patched up, for it would have a disastrous effect on world opinion. It seemed likely that if Britain did break completely with the United States on atomic affairs, Canada would negotiate her own two-party agreement with the Americans and this might make it very difficult to keep British staff in Canada. Britain would then lose experience which was essential to the success of the United Kingdom project.

The Anglo-American rift did not burst open: the Combined Policy Committee and the Combined Development Trust remained in existence. But as we saw, the Americans remained adamantly opposed to the building of plants in the United Kingdom (see p. 118). Continued Canadian doubts about the wisdom of Britain's firm decision to build plants in the United Kingdom seemed ammunition for the Americans. At the end of 1946 the United Kingdom High Commissioner tackled Mr Mackenzie King, who described the allegation that Canada was opposed to the building of a plant in the United Kingdom as 'sheer nonsense'. Canada, he said, had neither the right nor the wish to oppose any development in the United Kingdom which the United Kingdom thought desirable. However, when the High Commissioner asked for a short written statement to this effect it was very brief and cautious: it merely said that the Canadian Government had expressed no opinion to the United States Government on this matter.

Britain's decision to build the first pile in the United Kingdom was irrevocable. However, Field-Marshal Lord Wilson, the chief British military representative in Washington, suggested at the end of 1946 that a second pile should be built in Canada not in substitution for, but in addition to, the British pile; it might be a co-operative venture with all the Dominions. Mr Attlee pointed out that the British contribution would be limited by the demands of the existing United Kingdom atomic programme and by dollar difficulties. If the British contribution was limited to the loan of technical staff plus the supply of a few components, the chief burden would fall on Canada. There were already indications that Canada was worried about the extent of her financial commitments for defence and she seemed very unlikely to favour a proposal involving heavy extra expenditure. The project only seemed worthwhile if the Americans themselves put forward proposals for an enterprise in Canada on the grounds that it would be a pretext for them to pass on the fullest possible technical information. Of this there was no sign and the discussion went no further.

When, in December 1946, the British told the Canadians that they were going to return to the charge over collaboration with the United States Government, Mr Howe was not prepared to join in. It was true, he said, that Canada had received very little information from the United States and this had delayed by some months the operation of her pile, but she was prepared to accept the position.

The triangular atomic relationship between the United States, Canada and Britain remained uneasy throughout the period up to the end of 1947. The same could be said about the dual relationship between Canada and Britain as they tried to settle the future of collaboration in the joint project they had built up during the war. The project was, as we have seen, a combined one, and indeed its main outline had been specifically authorised during the war by the Combined Policy Committee. But Canada was clearly far more concerned in it than anyone else. Almost accidentally, and in order to render a favour to the United Kingdom, Canada, a rich but small nation, had become the second power in the world to sponsor an atomic project – the most costly and complicated scientific and technological operation then devised by man. The project by the end of the war was more expensive than all the other research activities of the Canadian Government combined. A large organisation was in being and excavators and cranes were busy preparing a large site at Chalk River, 150 miles from Ottawa. A small research reactor was finished and the 10,000-kW NRX reactor was halfway to completion. What was to be the future of the project? The predominance of military aspects over all other atomic developments made the project distasteful to a large body of Canadian opinion. Canada in any case had no intention of making atomic bombs. As for atomic power, it belonged to the more distant future, and Canada, with her great hydroelectric resources, seemed to be the last country to need it. Supplies of radioactive isotopes would be obtainable from the United States. Was Canada therefore simply encumbered, largely at British behest, with a very costly research establishment that was not likely to result in serious development? Furthermore, Canada at that stage did not seem to possess the native scientific resources to staff the project.

These questions had not been thrashed out directly during the war. In 1944 the Canadians had expressed their anxiety about the future, and their fears that the British contribution of skilled men, without whom the project could not continue, might be withdrawn at the end of the war. Sir John Anderson had assured them that the British would continue to support the project, second staff, and do everything possible to ensure its success.[5] But the detailed terms of post-war collaboration were not discussed. Such conversations allayed the Canadian fears but bequeathed a legacy of misunderstanding. The British had no doubt at all, even then, that they were going to start a project in the United Kingdom and part of the work at Montreal was preparatory work for it. However, the planning in this period was directed to a British research establishment and not to large-scale production. Here was the focus for misunderstanding: the Canadians had got the impression, whether rightly or wrongly, that the location of British large-scale production was still a subject for discussion.

Bitterness flared up in November 1945 when the British told the Canadians that Professor Cockcroft had been appointed head of the British research establishment. No one had thought of consulting the Canadians in advance about the British plans or about the proposal to offer the appointment to Cockcroft. They were now told that Britain would arrange matters so that the work at Montreal would not be prejudiced, and that her wish to recapture Cockcroft was not to be taken as loss of interest in the Canadian project; indeed she would help to find a suitable successor. C. D. Howe listened more in sorrow than in anger and complained that to take Cockcroft away at this crucial moment before the NRX reactor was finished was contrary to the general understanding that the British would help with staff. He had always hoped that the Canadian project would be regarded as the nucleus of the Empire's future atomic effort. Was it now proposed that the two countries should each go their separate ways, the British with a large project of their own in the United Kingdom, and the Canadians, bereft of the

United Kingdom contribution by way of staff, left to their own devices with Chalk River?*

It was a sorry business, badly handled, but even now the British had not learned their lesson about the need for the fullest possible consultation with Canada. They announced their plans for research and production, including the construction of a large-scale graphite pile for producing plutonium, at the Combined Policy Committee in February 1946 without previous consultation with Canada. Mr Howe was so angry that he instructed Lester Pearson to say at the Committee that, in view of the British statement about the United Kingdom programme and the withdrawal of British scientists from Chalk River, the Canadian Government considered the arrangements for co-operation between the two Governments in the project to be at an end. Pearson did not make the public statement, but the British were left in no doubt about Canadian feelings.

The Canadians never wavered in their belief that they were given cast-iron assurances during the war that Chalk River would be the preliminary to a large joint enterprise in Canada, and that the major British atomic energy development would take place there. The unilateral British decision to build plants in the United Kingdom seemed to them not merely a reversal of policy but a flagrant breach of faith carrying most damaging consequences for Canada. The British felt that the Canadians were being most unfair. They were quite sure they had given no such assurances and there were very good reasons why Britain wished to have a pile in the United Kingdom to meet her own requirements. This did not imply the rejection of the idea of a similar development, possibly on a Commonwealth basis, in Canada, but the dollar shortage made it impossible for Britain to take a strong initiative herself in building a pile in Canada.

As for the assertions about the removal of staff, Cockcroft had not yet returned to Britain, even though the time when he should have left had been overstepped,† and almost no other scientists had been withdrawn by the British Government. Some men who had been secured with great difficulty for Canada had completed their agreed terms of service and had gone back to their ordinary jobs, but they could not be compelled to remain. The Government had done their best to find suitable substitutes and would continue to do so.

* Mr Howe had, by May 1946, visited the project only once.
† He left Canada in September 1946.

There was no doubt that an earlier visit by Sir John Anderson had been too late and that once more his manner had offended Mr Howe. When Ministers discussed in March 1946 what seemed to be a grave turn in relationships with Canada, they fortunately agreed that Malcolm MacDonald, the United Kingdom High Commissioner in Canada, together with Cockcroft and Chadwick – all of whom had good relationships with the Canadians – should discuss future Anglo-Canadian atomic co-operation with Mr Howe and Dr Mackenzie who, as head of the National Research Council, was in charge of the atomic energy project. They should repeat the assurances that Cockcroft's appointment and plans for large-scale production in the United Kingdom in no way implied a lessening of British interest in the Canadian plant. Meanwhile a great deal hinged on the choice of Cockcroft's successor. The British had already suggested W. B. Lewis, a member of the great team of nuclear physicists at the Cavendish Laboratory in the 1930s, and during the war one of the foremost men in the British radar establishment. However, Mr Howe now seemed unwilling to appoint anyone from Britain.

The subsequent meeting of Howe and Mackenzie with the three Britons in March 1946 seemed to restore goodwill, although the Canadians still felt considerable resentment against London. The High Commissioner assured the Canadians that the British desired to do their utmost, consistent with their obligations in the United Kingdom, to bring the Canadian project to fruition and maintain the closest co-operation on the general development of atomic energy. Although many of the British team at present in Canada would soon be required for work in England, a substantial team would remain in Canada and would contain senior men of experience as well as younger men. The British hoped that Canada would send a team to Harwell. The discussion brought out the apprehension in the minds of Howe and Mackenzie that Britain wanted some control over the Canadian project. The British disclaimed this, agreeing that Chalk River was essentially a Canadian undertaking even though it had taken shape from a joint wartime endeavour.

It was accordingly agreed that Canada alone should be responsible for appointing a new director to replace Cockcroft, and that the director should henceforth be employed directly by the Canadian Government. The British emphasised that in bringing forward the name of W. B. Lewis they were not attempting to force the

Canadians' hand but were simply offering help by finding the most suitable available man in England. It was also agreed that arrangements for the secondment of United Kingdom staff to the Canadian project should be agreed upon by both parties. They should come for agreed periods and not be withdrawn without consultation with Howe and Mackenzie. They would be employed and paid by the British Government but should conform to the rules and general discipline of the Canadian project. Finally, discussions should take place later on the co-ordination of the British and Canadian programmes.

After the meeting Howe wrote to MacDonald to say that there seemed no room for further misunderstanding over the business. Chadwick, in a letter to London, confirmed the atmosphere of restored goodwill – Howe, who had always been friendly and helpful to him, had invited him to go salmon-fishing – but was more cautious. He believed Cockcroft's departure still rankled but that Howe and Mackenzie accepted the inevitable and were 'no longer pulling such a disagreeable face over it'. Chadwick had emphasised that the programmes of Chalk River and Harwell had a great deal to gain from close collaboration. Britain, for example, would depend on Chalk River for supplies of plutonium and other materials to be made in the pile there.

But Chadwick foresaw dangers. He was anxious to cover two possibilities which would arise unless Anglo-Canadian affairs were very carefully handled. The first possibility was that Canada might be pushed 'into the arms of the American octopus'. The Canadians by themselves could undoubtedly get closer collaboration than the British with the United States project, but they would become a very subordinate part of the United States project and be more or less absorbed. 'They would not object strongly to this', wrote Chadwick, 'but I am convinced they would prefer to work with us so long as we treat them as partners and so long as we maintain friendly relations with the United States. The danger is a very real one.' The second possibility was that Chalk River might develop into a combined project of the Dominions in rivalry to a British project at Harwell. This could be averted if Britain maintained the closest co-operation with Canada and invited the other Dominions to send teams to Harwell. Meanwhile Chadwick had advised Howe that it would be a wise precaution for the future if the Canadians took over from the Americans the heavy water plant in British Columbia.

The prospects of Anglo-Canadian collaboration seemed more promising when, in the summer of 1946, the Canadians after all appointed W. B. Lewis as director. Their first choice had been Dr Zinn, a Canadian-born scientist who had been a member of the United States project, but he did not accept. In September 1946 Cockcroft left Canada and Lewis took over, becoming one of Britain's most valuable exports to Canada. With the change of director the Canadian project was no longer a joint one but wholly Canadian. At that time there were 67 United Kingdom staff in Canada, but the number was expected to fall to 15–20 within a year; they were engaged partly on the Canadian plants but their main effort was for the British programme. Close co-operation was certainly envisaged in terms of co-ordination of the experimental research programmes at Chalk River and Harwell and the interchange of information, small items of equipment, uranium metal and fissile materials. Cockcroft also suggested that the programmes being planned in the two establishments for building different types of piles should be divided between them according to facilities and resources. Nothing was said about co-ordinated planning of large-scale production, which was now assumed to be a matter for each nation separately.

The Canadians were dissatisfied with this pattern of collaboration and in the course of 1947 it became clear that the misunderstandings which were supposed to have been cured a year earlier still festered; the British High Commissioner in Ottawa wrote of a 'smouldering resentment' beneath the outwardly excellent relations. Mackenzie and even Lewis were apparently referring to 'the break' with the United Kingdom. When meetings were arranged to sort matters out, it was clear that day-to-day collaboration and exchange of information between Harwell and Chalk River were excellent. But Mackenzie felt that the British were using Chalk River mainly for their own purposes. For example, the Chemical Group at Chalk River was almost wholly engaged in working out a process for separating plutonium and uranium from the fission products in irradiated fuel rods from a pile. This work was entirely in the interests of the United Kingdom, since Canada had no intention of producing plutonium in large quantities and present methods met her needs. Mackenzie was embarrassed by carrying out such work, essentially for the United Kingdom project, for he had no formal authority for the continuation of collaboration since Chalk River ceased to be a joint project in September 1946. Mackenzie also pointed out that few of the United Kingdom group were senior men and the Canadians feared that, as Harwell facilities developed, there would be fewer still.

Mackenzie's chief complaint went further than this; he deplored the lack of exchange of information at a high level on atomic policy matters – on general policy about long-term aims and projects and also on technical policy for pile development and so forth. As the British High Commissioner in Ottawa said, 'occasional crumbs from the master's table are simply not good enough for a genuine partnership'. It was clear that by 'the break' with Britain the Canadians meant the British decision to erect their main plants in the United Kingdom so that Chalk River became a purely Canadian concern instead of a joint project. Even if Canada had not realised the British intention to abandon major operations in Canada through a misunderstanding, nevertheless the news had come as a shock from which Canada had not yet recovered. Mackenzie and Howe both felt that Britain at bottom had little interest in Canadian developments: her policy was to make use of Canada when in difficulty and ignore her as soon as other possibilities opened up. They were moreover very irritated by the lack of collaboration with the United States, which they attributed partly to the British decision to build piles in the United Kingdom. Added to this, the Canadian venture was becoming more and more difficult to explain in Parliament. Canada was feeling her isolation in atomic energy most acutely; she had been left out on a limb by the British withdrawal on one hand and the refusal of the Americans to give information on the other. There was great anxiety about the future of Chalk River for Canada seemed too small to proceed independently.

There was distress among the British about Canada's feelings. Sir John Anderson might take his usual lofty view about them, suggesting that Dr Mackenzie was 'at the bottom of the trouble' and pointing out unfairly that Canada had taken the first step towards independence when, without saying anything to Britain, she abandoned 'the partnership arrangement' over Eldorado uranium back in 1943. (No actual arrangement had existed.) Others too would not accept that Canada had been left in the lurch: Britain maintained a considerable and effective team at Chalk River in spite of her great need for these men in the United Kingdom. There had moreover been occasions in 1946 when the British felt the Canadians had not played fair over raw material questions. But most people also realised that Howe and Mackenzie were good friends of Britain who deserved well of her. There was agreement that Canada must be treated with the utmost consideration, as far as possible as an equal partner, and that she must be taken into British confidence.

In May 1947, therefore, Cockcroft visited Canada and brought the Canadians fully up to date about British plans, and this in itself did much good. He also hoped to take collaboration further and drafted a document which might form the basis for a formal agreement. The draft was prefaced by the remark that the development of atomic energy required a scientific and industrial effort likely to strain the resources of any nation other than the United States. Since the future of collaboration between the United States, Canada and the United Kingdom was uncertain, it was, the draft said, all the more important to establish the fullest collaboration between Canada and the United Kingdom and later to draw on the scientific and technical resources of other parts of the Commonwealth. The paper described the contributions of Canada and Britain to a co-ordinated programme for the various facilities being built or planned, and it also set out the extent of the programmes that were desirable, the measures of mutual assistance that existed and the possible interchange of basic materials. All this was in effect confirmation of existing practices or expectations. But Cockcroft added something more fundamental – co-operation in a power development programme. He outlined the stages such a development would follow, and suggested that it should be decided which parts of the programme Canada would be interested to take up in the light of resources of basic materials.

This draft agreement was left with Mackenzie for submission to Canada's Energy Board. Meanwhile Lord Portal had been corresponding with his opposite number, the chairman of the Canadian Board. They both agreed there should be the fullest possible liaison through reports, visits and exchange of staff, but they also emphasised the need to co-ordinate British and Canadian programmes to avoid duplication and to co-operate even at this early stage in the development of atomic energy for industrial purposes. Christopher Hinton, who was in charge of building the British large-scale plants, would have liked to go further and have Canadian representation on all British committees which considered forward atomic energy policy; the Canadian representatives should not only receive minutes and papers but ought to attend whenever business was of direct interest to them and in any case not less than once every six months.

Was all this presaging a further move towards what the Canadians had originally wanted – not just co-operation but a joint programme? It was still uncertain how far the British as a whole wanted to go. Portal set down the advantages and disadvantages of a closer relationship. On the credit side were advantages to the British programme from Canadian facilities: at present the British depended on Chalk River for the solution of certain technical problems but had no voice in apportioning resources or priorities.* There were also the possibilities of exchanging raw materials, while one remote possibility of integration, offering strategic and other advantages, would be the development in Canada, as the result of bilateral or multilateral Empire agreement, of large-scale production of fissile material. On the debit side would be the increased risk of security leakages. The United States might go further with Britain if she was independent than if she was tied very closely with Canada, especially as, said Portal, they probably had a higher opinion of British than of Canadian security – an ironic touch in view of later developments. More importantly, cession by Britain even of part control over her own project, together with the danger of disagreement, delays and obstruction, might outweigh Canadian assistance. There seemed no point in discussing the whole question further until Canadian comments on the Cockcroft memorandum were received, and these never came. As the weeks went by there were signs of the reopening of negotiations for collaboration with the Americans; Anglo-Canadian affairs seemed once more inextricably mixed up with these.

Relations between Canada and Britain, even if they did not advance, now seemed cordial, although one cynic suggested that though 'hatchets were now buried their handles were only thinly covered'. Meanwhile the work at Chalk River continued to be of the utmost importance to the British programme. In the late summer of 1947 there would still be no facilities at Harwell for 'hot' chemistry for about nine months. British chemists in Canada were doing research and development work that was essential for Hinton's programme. The Americans also allowed the British to receive milligrams of plutonium and millicuries of fission products

---

* The British scientists 'on the spot' in Chalk River did have a voice in these matters – through the courtesy of the Canadians.

extracted from American uranium slugs at Chalk River. Later it was agreed that Chalk River would provide Britain with gram quantities of plutonium in the form of plutonium nitrate much earlier than Harwell could produce them; this would be essential for the metallurgical programme. Meanwhile the NRX pile, which went critical in July 1947, had a neutron intensity ten times that of the Harwell experimental pile; the Canadians allowed the British to carry out experiments in it which were important for the future of their piles, whether for producing plutonium or power.

Anglo-Canadian co-operation was essential in this period for both sides – absolutely essential to the British for their research and development programme and essential to the Canadians to keep Chalk River going at this critical stage in its history. But did the British miss a great opportunity for something much more than this – for a joint project jointly controlled, just as they had misguidedly chosen co-operation rather than the joint project the Americans had offered in 1941? Twenty-five years later, different people give different answers to this question. There would undoubtedly have been difficulties. One was that Canada did not intend to mount a weapons programme, but this need not have prevented a joint project to produce fissile material, for the Canadian Government had no basic conscientious objections; they gladly sold plutonium to the United States and co-operated in vital aspects of the British plutonium programme. Another difficulty was the dollar shortage, but Canada might well have been ready to solve this as she had done during the war. To be sure, joint technological programmes, which sound so attractive, have often generated friction and failed. Nevertheless, the wartime project at Montreal and then Chalk River had been a genuinely joint, and remarkably successful, international project. There was already a very sound foundation on which to build.

As it was, the international aspect of Chalk River was allowed to die soon after the war without any compunction or real sorrow in London. The British were determined to have at long last their own independent project, and suggestions for joining in large-scale operations in Canada were seen as diversions of effort and capacity away from their native production plans. It was reasonable enough for Britain to want a research establishment and some plants in the United Kingdom to form the nucleus there for scientific and industrial interest in atomic energy. Moreover there would probably not have been the industrial capacity in Canada in the late 1940s to cope with the first stage of a large production programme. But it is unfortunate that in 1945 and 1946 British eyes were not lifted to a rather further horizon. Britain could in due course have contributed manpower to a joint programme, while Canada possessed uranium, and manufactured very pure graphite and heavy water. She had the cheap power which makes gaseous diffusion and enriched uranium an economic possibility. She had an abundance of remote sites for experimental plants. The two countries were, as we shall see, to achieve some co-operation and some division of labour, but this fell far short of a real joint programme and it may even have had disadvantages for the British power programme. Might not Britain and Canada, planning and using their resources jointly, have been able to mount a more varied and successful atomic power programme than either was to achieve separately, a programme that might have led to resounding success in reactor markets? In 1946 the British had chosen independence with collaboration rather than a joint programme, and although they seemed anxious later to change their minds they were not given the opportunity to do so. By mid-1947 people in the British atomic project wanted to revise the choice and return to much closer co-ordination and planning. But it was already too late.

The Rest of the Commonwealth

Apart from Canada, the countries of the Commonwealth had had no official connection with the wartime atomic energy project; in accordance with the Quebec Agreement no information was divulged to them. Only the Prime Minister of South Africa, Field-Marshal Smuts, with his special personal status, had been told about the project, since by the end of the war it seemed possible that South Africa would be a rich source of uranium. The Australian and New Zealand Governments knew nothing, but three Australian-born scientists – M. L. Oliphant, H. S. Massey and E. H. Burhop – had been members of the British team in North America while New Zealand engineers had made valuable contributions to the Anglo-Canadian project. Soon after the war, the immediate feeling about co-operation with the Dominions was that neither Australia nor New Zealand was likely to be of any consequence either industrially or as a source of raw material, but that they would 'presumably'

1 Mr Attlee flew to Washington in December 1950 to make urgent representations about the Korean War and the atomic bomb. Standing behind President Truman and Mr Attlee are (left) Secretary of State Dean Acheson and (right) Secretary of Defense General George Marshall.

2 King George VI with the Chiefs of Staff — Sir Andrew Cunningham, Sir
Charles Portal and Lord Alanbrooke — at Buckingham Palace in 1945.

3 Mr Churchill and Lord Cherwell visit Harwell in 1948. Lord Cherwell is sitting on Mr Churchill's left. Standing, from left to right, are Sir Edwin Plowden; Mr Christopher Soames, M.P.; D. R. Willson; Sir John Cockcroft; Mr Churchill's detective; L. F. Potter (deputy security officer); H. Arnold (security officer); Dr B. J. F. Schonland; R. F. Jackson (holding monitor); Dr H. Seligman.

4 Lord Cherwell.

5 Sir Henry Tizard.

6 Sir James Chadwick.

7 Sir Roger Makins at his desk in the Foreign Office (1950).

8 M. W. Perrin.

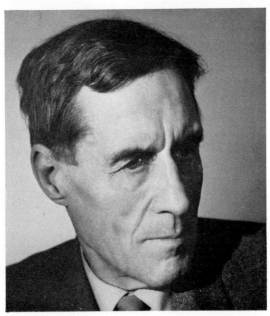

9 Professor P. M. S. Blackett.

have to be kept informed about the development of the project. On the other hand it seemed desirable to associate South Africa more clearly with the project than hitherto, because of her uranium.

New Zealand made it clear that for the time being she was only interested in fundamental atomic research. Dr Evatt, Australia's Minister of External Affairs, however, emphasised that his country was vitally interested in atomic energy, not only because of its military applications but because of the vast industrial possibilities, so important to a country which was believed to have no indigenous oil and limited coal.* Australia was determined to keep abreast of the world in industrial atomic development. Evatt asked for copies of the British report which had led to the setting-up of the research establishment and for enough technical information to enable Australia to assess the possibilities. The Australian Government wanted to see a Commonwealth atomic project and make their own significant contributions to it; the primary research and development might best be carried out in Britain, but Australia could send skilled scientists to help. For later development, Australia had large open spaces and was developing hydroelectric power which would be useful for full-scale plants. She might possibly also possess uranium deposits.

It is not clear what reply was sent to this request. However, Commonwealth atomic co-operation was ventilated at the Conference of Dominion Prime Ministers in May 1946. It was acknowledged within British Government circles that since Dominion co-operation was one of the cardinal principles of British defence policy, close co-operation in the development of atomic energy logically followed. Independent plans in the United Kingdom and the Dominions would lead to much duplication and loss of time; a co-ordinated effort, based upon the plans approved for Britain and Canada, would be sensible. There was one big snag in all this: if Britain was known to be engaged in far-reaching discussions with the Dominions, envisaging the automatic sharing of any information received from American sources, this would finally wreck any possibility of atomic agreement with the United States; Commonwealth co-operation came lower in the order of priorities. The Dominion Prime Ministers were therefore told at the May 1946 Conference about the importance of United States co-operation, and

---

* Exploration changed the position and up to 1973 Australia had not found a nuclear power programme necessary.

were given information about the British programmes. They were also asked to help in finding and developing raw material supplies and in seconding scientists to Harwell. Otherwise collaboration went no further. There was no apparent discontent and the whole business was left for another year.

In the summer of 1947 Ernest Bevin resurrected a suggestion he had first mooted a year earlier – that Britain might build a pile, on a Commonwealth basis, in Rhodesia. The idea of using the water-power in the Victoria Nyanza area appealed to him: there would be abundant water for cooling the pile and for electric power; uranium supplies would be near; the site would be safe. There was a suggestion of approaching South Africa to sponsor the scheme, but the Secretary of State for the Colonies quickly pointed out that anything that gave South Africa – or Southern Rhodesia – a major say in a colonial territory would be politically dangerous. Sir Henry Tizard was enthusiastic about the strategic advantages of such a plan because he believed in the dispersal of war industry to the Dominions. Lord Portal, however, showed that there was a very strong case against trying to spread more widely the resources available for producing fissile material. Moreover by this time it had been decided to build air-cooled, not water-cooled, piles, so the curious suggestion was abandoned.

However, in the course of the irritated, if cursory, examination which Portal and his staff gave the suggestion, it was acknowledged that the whole question of Commonwealth co-operation in atomic energy would have to be thrashed out again at some stage. Portal himself was very doubtful whether the time was ripe. Even if the Dominion Governments were ready for discussions – which he doubted – the tendency for the United States to extend collaboration with Britain as the prospects of international control receded might well be checked by any separate British commitments to other nations of the Commonwealth, and even perhaps by the knowledge that the Governments were in consultation on the subject. Portal agreed nevertheless with Tizard that the Official Atomic Energy Committee might begin to consider the basis of a Commonwealth plan for atomic energy.

Very soon after this, in July 1947, the question was forced on the Official Committee by a request from Australia and New Zealand for information about the low-energy pile at Harwell, Gleep, as they were jointly considering a policy for developing atomic energy.

South Africa would probably also soon want to discuss her plans. The present state of co-operation was that five scientists from New Zealand, one from Australia and one from South Africa were working at Harwell on the British payroll and more Australians were to come soon; otherwise co-operation with the Dominions had been limited to raw material information and no other documents, secret or declassified, had been sent to them. While none of the information about a low-power pile which Australia and New Zealand wanted came from United States sources, and while most of it could almost certainly be declassified, one or two crucial items might still be secret. Moreover the Dominions would need supplies of graphite and uranium metal for the pile from Britain.

The Official Committee decided to agree in principle to assist the two Dominions – after informing the United States and Canada – provided their Governments had made satisfactory security arrangements. It was known that the Americans were especially dubious about Australian security. When Cockcroft wrote to Sir David Rivett, Secretary of the Australian Council for Scientific and Industrial Research, asking for security guarantees, Rivett did not conceal his impatience:

> As to all this business about classified information, security, secrecy and the rest of it I just loathe it. Of course we shall be prepared to give whatever guarantees may be required if that is the only way we can engage in research work of any value. I have however the utmost distrust of secrecy practices particularly when they are influenced by military people.

This heartfelt outburst could hardly be taken as an assurance of security, but while London was wondering what to do about it the Australian programme went back into the melting-pot and no agreement was reached by the end of 1947.

Meanwhile the Atomic Energy Official Committee had gone on to consider the broader issue raised by Portal and Tizard: would it be wise to initiate now a movement towards an integrated Commonweath project of atomic energy development or should efforts still be concentrated in Britain? The arguments for an integrated project were the desirability of strategic dispersal and co-ordination of research and development. The arguments against were the dissipation of resources needed for the British project and the effects on the possibility of co-operation with America. The dissipation of the

United Kingdom effort seemed to rule out co-operation with the Dominions leading to an early large-scale effort, while the position vis-à-vis the United States suggested that Britain should step warily in Commonwealth co-operation even in scientific research and small-scale development. The time would come when the whole question of the co-operation of the Commonwealth in a co-ordinated atomic energy programme would have to be thrashed out, and Britain might then have to choose between co-operation with the United States or with the Commonwealth countries. But should this issue be forced now? By waiting until events forced the issue, the door might be kept open to eventual effective collaboration between the United States and Britain and, in an idyllic future, such co-operation might perhaps be combined with full Commonwealth co-operation. Coming down to earth, it seemed that there was little prospect of full co-operation unless and until the United Nations discussions broke down, which might not happen for another year, and even then the possibilities were very uncertain. Yet to defer even the beginnings of inter-Commonwealth planning was to postpone the time when the full benefits could be reaped of such material resources and manpower as the Dominions could contribute and the orderly planning of advantageous sites for further plants. Remaining aloof from the Dominions might be too high a price to pay for preserving the hope of American technical assistance which might never come – or might come in any event.

Sir John Anderson felt very strongly that the chances of getting full co-operation with the United States would be gravely jeopardised if Britain embarked just then (in 1947) on a joint Commonwealth programme for the development of atomic energy, except possibly in the case of South Africa. On reflection, the Foreign Office and the Embassy in Washington did not agree. They believed that American apprehensions about future uranium supplies were a good reason for embarking on a Commonwealth programme. Moreover the present time, when Commonwealth co-operation in general matters was so much to the fore, seemed a good opportunity to develop co-operation in atomic energy as well. This might conceivably prove a lasting and important bond between Commonwealth countries.

In September 1947, accordingly, the Official Committee was all set to recommend a co-ordinated Commonwealth programme unfolding in several phases: first an approach to the Canadians, followed by discussions with the Dominions on security, then a scheme for training Dominion scientists and engineers, then exchange of information, then a long-range programme of research and development. However, the Chiefs of Staff, while agreeing with the ultimate objective of full collaboration with the Dominions, believed the present time to be inopportune. It might frighten the Americans and it was premature to contemplate full collaboration with the Dominions when no precise programme had been worked out for the development of atomic energy in Britain, especially in relation to defence. On further reflection the Official Committee agreed that it would be necessary, if only because of the Quebec Agreement, to consult the United States Government before any proposals were put to the Dominions for general collaboration on atomic energy. A senior official of the Ministry of Defence minuted his Minister bitterly: 'It is unfortunate that we can't discuss these matters with our sister countries in the Commonwealth without first asking leave of a foreign nation but there it is.'

Ministers agreed* with the final conclusions of the Official Committee: that the ultimate objective should be full Dominion collaboration in atomic energy and the gradual evolution of a Commonwealth programme; that the immediate practical objectives should be the introduction of adequate security in the Dominions and the extension of the scheme for training scientists; but that first Canada's views and then United States views should be sought.

Cockcroft was just about to go to the United States and it was agreed that he should talk to the Canadians. These talks took an unexpected turn. Mr Howe and Dr Mackenzie had hitherto been sympathetic to the idea of wider Dominion collaboration, but now they were convinced that it was the wrong time to press it; they could not be shaken by arguments to the contrary. Mackenzie, on a recent visit to Washington, had been so impressed by the deter-

---

* One subsidiary question considered was whether, for the purpose of atomic collaboration, the Dominions included India and Pakistan. Officials and Ministers felt the time was not ripe to include them, even though India controlled the world's largest supply of monazite for thorium, because rigorous security could not at present be created there, nor was their official scientific activity 'sufficiently settled to enable them to take part'. The Commonwealth Relations Secretary disliked this as he felt that two classes of Dominions were developing. Moreover it was already apparent that Professor Bhabha, an extremely able theoretical physicist with wide contacts, was thinking of a pile programme for India.

mination of the United States atomic authorities to seize any opportunity of closer co-operation with Canada and Britain that they were
convinced it would be wrong to risk disturbing the promising
atmosphere. They emphasised that for Canada – and presumably for
Britain – the objective of full co-operation with the United States
must take priority over all other considerations. It might be difficult
to return a blunt negative to inquiries for help from Commonwealth
countries, but surely it should be possible to prevent demands for
classified information from being pressed. 'Otherwise', said the
Canadians, 'we might be risking the substance for the shadow.'

Almost immediately after these talks in Canada, discussions began
for a new Anglo-Canadian agreement for atomic collaboration, the
modus vivendi. This, as we shall see, was to define carefully certain
limited areas of co-operation with members of the Commonwealth;
within these areas, the criterion for transmission of information was
to be, subject to satisfactory security, the principle of 'current
usability'. And so the co-ordinated Commonwealth programme was
stillborn and 'the lasting and important bond' was not forged. The
special relationship with the United States proved a far more compelling link.

Europe

The end of the war had left Britain with atomic relationships, both
contractual and sentimental, with two countries in Europe – Belgium
and France. At the end of 1944 the Belgian Government had, somewhat reluctantly, given the United States and Britain the option on
all the Belgian Congo uranium ore for ten years ahead.[6] The output
of these immensely rich mines was the foundation of the American
and British atomic energy programmes in the early post-war years.
The only concession to the Belgians in the 1944 agreement lay in
Clause 9(*a*), which said that if the United States and Britain decided
to use the ores obtained under the agreement as a source of energy
for commercial purposes, the Belgian Government would be admitted to participation on equitable terms.

After the war Belgium fulfilled fautlessly her obligations to supply
uranium (see Chapter 11). The main difficulty that arose between
her, the United States and Britain in the first two post-war years
concerned the secrecy of the 1944 agreement. M. Spaak, the Belgian
Prime Minister, was constantly harried by Communists in the

Assembly about the agreement, and he would have liked to publish it, but the Americans and British wanted the details to remain secret. With difficulty Spaak held back the inquirers, and gave the barest outline of the arrangements.

As 1947 wore on, the Belgian Government became increasingly conscious of their vulnerability on the whole uranium question. They could not lightly expose themselves to a campaign that they were selling all the Congo uranium to the Anglo-Saxons at much too low a price and getting absolutely nothing in return. In return for the agreement which they had signed more or less blind in 1944, the Belgians had the assurance that when the time came for them to share in the commercial exploitation of atomic energy their claim would be honoured. The Belgians began to ask for some token that Article 9(*a*) would be put into effect, and they would not be put off by assurances that commercial exploitation of atomic energy was not yet a practical or commercial proposition. However, the main negotiations to give some reality to the promise, made in Clause 9(*a*) in return for Belgium's great services to the United States' and, to a lesser extent, Britain's projects, were to take place in 1948 and 1949. The prologue in 1947 made it clear that neither of these two countries was going to rush to fulfil the joint obligation.

The Anglo-Saxon atomic obligations to and from France were not tripartite as in the case of Belgium. They existed solely between Britain and France, and in 1944 and 1945 the United States had made it abundantly clear that they disliked these obligations and had no part whatever in them. Mistrust of the French atomic scientists ran deep in Washington. The last vestige of participation by French scientists in the wartime project was removed when, in January 1946 (at General Groves's insistence), Bertrand Goldschmidt, the French chemist who had led the important early work on the separation of plutonium, left the Montreal Laboratory. When he left to return to France, Sir John Anderson wrote to thank him and to remind him of his undertaking not to disclose any information he had obtained through his association with the project.

The feeling of obligation towards the French, which had been important in some British minds in 1944 and 1945, had by now largely evaporated. There remained only the links of friendship, centred in particular on Harwell, since Cockcroft had worked closely with the five Frenchmen who had been members of the Canadian project. The precious stock of heavy water – some 150 kilos – which Halban and Kowarski had brought with them in their flight to England in 1940 was still being used by the British and Canadians.[7] There was also that troublesome legacy from the past, the French patents. In particular, there was the 1942 agreement between the British Government and the two French scientists, Halban and Kowarski,[8] which had included a provisional scheme for carving up the rights in the eleven patent applications with which the French had been concerned. Of these, five had covered inventions made in Paris before France fell in 1940, while six covered inventions made by Halban and Kowarski jointly with British scientists after they had fled to England. The British Tube Alloys officials had believed that these patents would be extremely valuable in a post-war nuclear world.

The question of possible Anglo-French atomic collaboration after the war therefore seemed to hinge on the final decision about the ownership and prosecution of these patent applications. In the spring of 1946 Kowarski and Goldschmidt, both now members of the new French Commissariat à l'Énergie Atomique, came to London bearing an invitation to the British Government to discuss atomic energy patents with the French Government. In May, Joliot-Curie – who had been the leader of the French scientists, had stayed in France during the German occupation, and was now High Commissioner of the CEA – came to official meetings in London. He said that the French Government were not prepared to enter into any specific interchange of rights such as the 1942 agreement had envisaged. They believed that the inventions made in France and at Cambridge formed an interlocking bloc, that there should be common United Kingdom and French action to exploit the inventions *en bloc* in all countries, and that there should be complete pooling of all Anglo-French patents. Joliot suggested alternatively an even bigger, if improbable, pool, bringing in the United States as well as France and Britain.

The French had already begun to pursue patent applications vigorously all over the world on the five inventions that had originated on French soil. A particularly delicate situation arose over two of these inventions for which patent applications in England had been made not by the French team collectively but by Halban and Kowarski as individuals after their flight from France in 1940. In the 1942 agreement the two men had specifically assigned to the British Government these two inventions and all patents,

British and foreign, for them. Now, in 1946, the French Government was applying for patents on the same two inventions in fifty countries, including Britain. The embarrassment to Anglo-French relations of a lawsuit on the subject was unthinkable and a compromise was reached whereby Britain was to have all rights in the inventions in the British Empire, and France all other rights in the world.

These questions of detail were relatively minor. The far more important problem raised by Joliot's proposal for a patents pool was the whole future of the Anglo-French atomic relationship. In practice the British could not accept complete pooling of patents because their freedom of action was already limited by their agreement with the United States and Canada, for secrecy reasons, not to file atomic energy patent applications except in the United States, Canada and Britain. In spite of this limitation, Joliot urged that the idea should at least be explored. He clearly had in mind the possibility of pooling not so much patents but rather the two countries' efforts in the whole field of atomic energy. The idea was therefore a starting-point for the consideration by the Official Atomic Energy Committee in December 1946 of the balance of advantage to be gained by collaboration with the French.

The fundamental bargaining point of the French was their belief that they would hold master patents which would entitle them to royalties from any country using a nuclear energy pile. However, though patents had already been granted in some countries, others, notably America, had refused the applications on the ground that they were too general and theoretical and not accompanied by details of practical application. Even if patents should issue in Britain for two of these master patents, the royalty cost to the British Government would be a very minor element in the cost of an atomic pile. But if the British Government decided to join the French Government in world exploitation for profit of the original patents bloc mentioned in the 1942 agreement,* the financial gain might be very large.

In the wider field of co-operation the principal French asset was the possession of a number of able scientists. Their help was by no means essential but they could be of substantial assistance, for

---

* A bloc covering these patents alone would not infringe the US–UK–Canadian patents agreement. This was of course different from the pooling of *all* patents, past and future.

example to Russia, and there was always the risk that an outright rejection of their offer might drive the French into the arms of the Russians. Finally, there was the lingering recognition of some obligation to France for their help in the early development of the British project. Chadwick believed that even these French assets were exaggerated. He emphasised that the French owed far more to Britain, since their men had gained practically all their knowledge and experience through being taken into the British project and this had been of enormous help in setting up the French establishment and directing their efforts on the right lines. He thought they had few good men and that the advantage from co-operation with France was imponderable rather than tangible, more political than scientific.

Chadwick's remarks were intended to induce caution in dealing with co-operation with France, not to argue against it under any circumstances. He would be very happy to see Britain reach an understanding with them, but not at the cost of ruining relations with the United States. This indeed was the familiar counterweight in balancing the advantages of atomic co-operation with other countries, and to the Official Committee it weighed very heavily.

There was the familiar hope that if the United Nations atomic discussions broke down, the United States might be persuaded to restore full co-operation with Britain and Canada. And there was the inevitable conclusion: that this outcome was far less likely if the United States regarded Britain as closely linked with France in atomic energy matters. They would assume that information would be passed on from Britain to France, whose leading atomic scientist had political sympathies to the far left. The Foreign Office represented the general view: that while the French were 'quite important in atomic energy (as in other things)', the Americans came first. The Official Committee concluded that Britain should not at present accept French proposals for co-operation either in the wider field of exchange of information or in the more limited matter of patents and inventions. However, it would be unwise to reject the proposals outright. The oral reply to Joliot should be that while Britain was anxious in principle to see co-operation, the time was not ripe for such an agreement, which should be considered later in the light of the results of discussion in the United Nations Commission.

Should the Americans be told about these French proposals? The Official Committee was tempted by the prospect of letting it be understood in Washington that in default of American co-operation Britain would be obliged to consider entering into some closer arrangement with the French, but, perhaps regretfully, it was realised that this course might defeat its own object and set back collaboration. So it was agreed that the Americans should be told what had happened only as evidence of British virtue in adhering closely to past understandings with them. All these proposals were approved not by the Ministerial Committee but by the Foreign Secretary and the Prime Minister. Joliot for his part expressed understanding of the reasons for Britain's inability to accept his proposals and her need to put her commitments to the Americans first; he emphasised his anxiety to avoid any action which would embarrass Britain. He was reported to hope merely that Britain's links with the United States would be weakened to such an extent that she would be able to reconcile them with atomic co-operation with France and Western Europe. He was also reported to have egged on those in Belgium who would like to bring the Congo ore contracts into the light and cancel the existing agreement. His thoughts were turning to the prospects of co-operation in other European directions – possibly with Norway, Belgium and Holland.

Here matters rested so far as general co-operation was concerned. In September 1947, however, the French asked for two specific measures of assistance from Britain. One was discussion on electronic equipment used for pile control: this was easy since it was declassified. Secondly, the French asked whether Harwell would test the nuclear properties of a sample of graphite produced in France. This raised much greater difficulties. From their work in the Canadian project the French had very full knowledge of the factors entering into the production of pure graphite, but they had no absolute standards against which to check the graphite they were producing. The British could refer their own graphite to United States standards because of tests of Canadian graphite carried out at the US laboratory at Argonne in 1945. The French were therefore in effect asking the British to state the purity of French graphite in terms of Argonne standards. It would be possible to do less than this and tell them whether or not the proposed French pile would work with graphite of the proposed purity. There was no doubt that ultimately, by trial and error, the French would produce satisfactory graphite, but without comparison with American standards they might build a pile which would not work, thus incurring a setback of two to three years in their programme. There were also fears of leakage of this information to other, possibly unfriendly, countries.*

The British felt that 'it would not be wise' to pass on information of such direct technological value to the French. They consulted the Americans who predictably hoped that the French request would be turned down; the request was just left to die. Sir John Anderson alone voiced disquiet:

> It seems to me very hard [he wrote] that we should not be free to help the French to this small extent. . . . There is little we can offer France in the way of collaboration and to refuse this small measure of assistance seems to me very short-sighted. We don't want to drive them into the arms of Russia. I agree we can't go against America at this juncture but I would like to temporise.

Anderson felt the argument that it was an important technological contribution was outweighed by the very material help the French gave to the whole atomic energy project at the beginning and by the long-term considerations. Finally, at the end of 1947, the French asked somewhat diffidently for the return of at least some of their 1940 heavy water. Earlier when the problem of its ownership had arisen there had been a suggestion that the British might offer to pay the French for it, but this was turned down on the grounds that the French would almost certainly refuse to accept payment, which would be embarrassing. Now it was agreed that the water should be brought back from Canada, where most of it was, and returned to France.

In the formative period covered by this chapter – from the end of the war to the end of 1947 – we see a descent from the joint wartime project with Canada to close, but loose, collaboration with her; no co-ordinated development plans, except in raw material affairs, with the rest of the Commonwealth; the rupture of the wartime atomic bonds that had existed between the British and the Canadians on one hand and the French on the other; and finally a reluctance to embark on any other schemes of technical co-operation with Europe, even in the case of Belgium where there was a debt, in writing and in honour, to be paid. Atomic technological collaboration with the Commonwealth (outside Canada) and with Europe could not have

---

* In the event there was no evidence of leakage of atomic information from France to Russia.

amounted to anything much in this period: there was nothing to collaborate with except in France. However, these countries were asking for very little indeed, and the case for providing it lay in the wider political considerations of the future – technical leadership and goodwill in Europe and closer Commonwealth ties. The very little asked for was denied.

This denial was due partly to security. The British Government itself was imbued with strong convictions about the necessity for keeping the whole atomic business, other than the declassified areas, highly secret. They were, on this account alone, loath to pass on information to the Australians, who then had the reputation for not being sufficiently security-minded, or to the French because Joliot-Curie, the High Commissioner of the French project, was an out-spoken and much publicised member of the French Communist Party. But the overwhelmingly important reasons why Britain dragged her feet even in such limited areas of atomic collaboration with the Commonwealth or Europe were her legacy of obligations to the United States under the Quebec Agreement, her perpetual hope that renewed Anglo-American-Canadian atomic co-operation was round the next corner, and her anxiety to do nothing to frighten it away. Her eyes were firmly fixed across the Atlantic on North America, and even there she was preoccupied above all with her relationship with the United States and allowed the full wartime collaboration with Canada to decline. If, when a specific decision about overseas co-operation came before any committee, there was the possibility of conflict with United States co-operation, the United States interest always won. Similarly, it is safe to say that almost all the scientists who were in the project full-time or as consultants – except Professor Blackett – would have put a much higher priority on collaboration with the United States than with any other country; there was a real consensus on this point. In the absence of American willingness to co-operate, Britain was committed to an essentially independent atomic project.

6 Deterrence

Programme and Purpose

THE brief hope of international control of atomic energy which would prevent an atomic arms race had foundered by early 1947. The brief hope of atomic co-operation with the United States had already run on to the rocks by the spring of 1946, and yet the possibility that it might be refloated prevented for years effective co-operation with the Commonwealth and Europe. The only collaboration manifestly open to Britain was with Canada, and here Britain had chosen loose co-operation rather than the integration which the Canadians had at first desired. So partly voluntarily, but mainly involuntarily, Britain built up her atomic project in near independence.

What shape did the project take and what purposes was it intended to serve? Logically, it might be expected that decisions on purposes would be taken first and that decisions about the size and type of programme would follow in their wake. The thoughts of some people, notably Chadwick, ran in this sequence, but the Government decisions, as we shall see, did not. There were four possible purposes of an atomic project. Firstly, there was research and development in the broadest sense, including both pure science which would roll back the frontiers of knowledge in the several disciplines involved in atomic energy, and the application of this science for practical purposes.* Secondly, there was the production of atomic weapons. Thirdly, there was the production of electric power. Fourthly, there was the production of radioactive isotopes for medical and industrial purposes. In Britain, in August 1945, the first and fourth purposes were generally accepted and they could be fitted together in the same establishment. The real dilemma concerned the second and third purposes, and their relative importance. The chief dilemma over atomic weapons was political, but there was also a technological choice. Their production meant the large-

* The categories of research are defined in more detail in Chapter 18.

scale production of fissile material – that is, either plutonium or uranium-235. At the end of the war there was no immediate likelihood of generating electricity from nuclear power, but everyone had this purpose very much in mind as a goal for the years ahead. For the present, work on nuclear power would come under the heading of research and development, but the type of research and development that could be done would depend on the type of fissile material available from large-scale production. Moreover, if bombs were to be made and plutonium were chosen as the fissile material for them, its large-scale production would be in large-scale nuclear reactors. These reactors would produce heat as well as plutonium and it was therefore likely that the pattern for the future development of nuclear power would be influenced by any early decisions to make plutonium bombs.

Thus the decisions about both the purposes of the atomic energy project and the shape of the programme were complicated and interwoven. One decision, as we have already seen, was simple and overdue: the decision to set up a research establishment. In September 1945 Sir John Anderson, as chairman of the Advisory Committee on Atomic Energy, submitted to the Government the same memorandum advocating such an establishment which he had submitted as Chancellor of the Exchequer to Mr Churchill in June;[1] the Gen 75 Ministers now duly approved it.

When the research establishment was approved, its location was still undecided. The listed specifications were exacting. It had to be not less than 10 miles from a large town, partly so that no large population could be affected by radioactive gaseous effluent from the chimney of a pilot-sized air-cooled pile, and partly so that the establishment would work in clean undisturbed surroundings; it had to be near a large university for the benefit of the scientific staff so that they did not become mentally inbred. It had to be reasonably close to light engineering capacity; have good access to London and other big cities; be near open, sparsely inhabited country suitable for non-atomic ordnance explosions;* have an area of at least 100 acres; be able to obtain large supplies of electricity and water; have a suitable soil for heavy load-bearing, and a low water-table so that underground tanks could be built for radioactive liquids; have some buildings already, easily convertible into laboratories, and some houses. The only existing type of establishment likely to be suitable

---

* A separate weapons establishment was not then foreseen.

was an airfield, and the small committee which had been touring possible sites had concluded that Harwell, 13 miles south of Oxford, was by far the most suitable in every way. The disadvantage of location in the Thames catchment area was apparently not thought to outweigh the advantages, but strangely enough this point was not discussed by the Advisory Committee. The Air Ministry was very loath to release this site, for it was one of the most modern airfields in the country with long runways, it had cost £1 million and was badly needed for the current trooping programme. However, they surrendered after the Prime Minister had intervened.

The research establishment had only vague terms of reference (see Chapter 18) – 'all aspects of the use of atomic energy'; in effect it was intended to investigate all problems concerning the theory and practice of the utilisation of atomic energy, from fundamental nuclear physics and chemistry to metallurgy and electronics and instrumentation. Initially it was expected to cover new methods of producing atomic energy and the rapid application of existing methods to the generation of power and other industrial and scientific ends, and also experimental work on bombs: in fact, it was expected to do everything short of large-scale production. It seemed that much of the country's research in nuclear physics might tend to concentrate at Harwell, but the Anderson Advisory Committee was very anxious that nuclear physics in the universities should not be starved and a sub-committee was set up to be responsible for recommending grants to them for equipment (see Chapter 18).

Not long after the decision to proceed with the research establishment was taken, it was agreed that Harwell should be responsible for the production in its experimental pile of most of the radioactive isotopes to be used for research in physics, chemistry and biology. Harwell, it was thought, would simply produce the radioactive material while all the processing and distribution would be done by the National Radon Filling Centre* (probably run by Thorium Ltd on behalf of the Government). As we shall see, however (in Chapter 20), this agreement did not operate as expected.

There remained the problem of large-scale atomic production. During the war there had been a great deal of discussion about this but no decisions had been taken, partly because of fears of American

---

* This was the beginning of what was to become the highly successful Radiochemical Centre at Amersham (see Chapter 20).

reactions and partly because it was not certain which of the various possibilities was the right one for Britain.[2] Once the war was over the scruples about the United States lingered a while because the military and industrial aspects of the process could not be separated and under the Quebec Agreement Britain's use of atomic energy for industrial purposes was restricted. But they were soon forgotten. Indeed there was a feeling that the extent to which Britain would be able to influence decisions of the United States Government about international atomic collaboration generally would depend very much on the speed with which she began a major programme. The uncertainties about the right programme persisted longer, in relation to purpose, technological preference and economics.

Above all, was Britain going to make bombs? In the wartime discussions all the chief scientists and statesmen connected with the project, except Sir Henry Dale, the President of the Royal Society, accepted it as axiomatic that Britain would wish to make bombs after the war.[3] In 1945, before Hiroshima, a committee of scientists under Sir Henry Tizard had been compiling a report for the Chiefs of Staff on future technical developments in warfare, but by Mr Churchill's express command they had been allowed no access to information about the atomic bomb project.* Nevertheless, since the eminent committee members were J. D. Bernal, P. M. S. Blackett, C. D. Ellis and G. P. Thompson,† they had known enough about the business to conclude, in June 1945, that if the atomic bomb could be made, the only answer they could see to it was 'to be prepared to use it ourselves in retaliation'. A knowledge that Britain was prepared in the last resort to do this might well deter an aggressive nation:

> Duelling [said the committee] was a recognised method of settling quarrels between men of high social standing so long as the duellists stood 20 paces apart and fired at each other with pistols of a primitive type. If the rule had been that they should stand a yard apart with pistols at each other's hearts we doubt whether it would long have remained a recognised method of settling affairs of honour. . . . On the assumption that the atomic bomb

---

* Churchill had written testily in answer to Tizard's request for information: 'He surely has lots of things to get on with without plunging into this exceptionally secret matter'.

† Thomson had been chairman, and Blackett and Ellis members, of the Maud Committee.

materialises we are unable to be sure that there is any defence on which a country could rely. We are convinced no such defence is possible without a drastic alteration to civilian life in peacetime. In our opinion it would be necessary to house a large percentage of the urban population in deep dwellings such as provide reasonable living conditions. . . . Carried to the limit such measures would produce a troglodyte existence and the refinements of modern technology would be needed to make such an existence tolerable.

Such views, expressed by scientists some of whom were later to oppose the British atomic bomb, were the kernel of the doctrine of deterrence that was to govern Britain's atomic weapons policy for many years. In the last few months of 1945, after the war ended, it constantly recurred. In September, Chadwick sent a telegram from the United States saying that the military applications of atomic energy obviously made a production plant 'of our own' essential for the defence of the United Kingdom and the Commonwealth. 'I believe', he wrote, 'there can be only one opinion on this question.' In October the Chiefs of Staff said emphatically that the best method of defence against the new weapons was likely to be the deterrent effect that the possession of the means of retaliation would have on a potential aggressor. They thought British production of atomic weapons should start as soon as possible and that 'to delay production pending the outcome of negotiations regarding international control might well prove fatal to the security of the British Commonwealth'. (As Mr Bevin was reported to have said more colloquially: 'Let's forget about the Baroosh* and get on with making the fissle.') When, soon after this, Ministers asked a group of officials to produce proposals for international control, they too reported that, whatever arrangements might be made in the international field, Britain should undertake production of bombs on a large scale for her own defence as soon as possible; the Prime Minister should issue a directive to this effect.

It was in this atmosphere that the Anderson Advisory Committee planned the main outlines of the large-scale production programme. No one at these meetings uttered any protest against the idea that Britain might make bombs, though by September 1945 Professor Blackett was suggesting that the interests of atomic research and

---

* i.e. the Baruch plan for international control (see Chapter 3).

production were to some extent competitive, and that it might be a greater advantage to Britain in the long run to regain her lead in fundamental physics research, rather than expend a disproportionate effort in building up a stock of atomic bombs which might not be large enough to be of military value. The likelihood that Britain would want to make bombs undoubtedly had a considerable influence on the shape of the large-scale programme, and in particular on the decision to produce plutonium first rather than uranium-235. Of course everyone would have liked to follow the United States example and develop both the two main processes from the outset; the Technical Committee (see p. 45) believed in October 1945 that the national importance of the project was so overwhelming that it would justify such a decision. But it seemed doubtful whether Britain, in her economic straits, could afford the skilled manpower – especially the design engineers and draughtsmen and, to a lesser extent, the building labour – for this.

So a choice had to be made. Some of the Tube Alloys staff who had remained in England – Sir Wallace Akers, for example – remained dedicated to uranium-235 on the grounds that the British already had enough knowledge to start at once on a detailed design of a gaseous diffusion plant which would increase the concentration of U-235 in uranium from the naturally occuring 0·7 per cent to 3·5 per cent. Material enriched to this extent was likely to be of great value for development work, while the design work for an electro-magnetic plant to carry the concentration up to 90 per cent could be carried out fairly quickly. By contrast, the British had no knowledge at all of the design of large-scale reactors to produce plutonium, which would therefore take longer to produce than U-235.

However, the British scientists in America had no doubts at all that plutonium must come first, and their chief reason was its superiority over U-235 for use in atomic weapons, so recently proved in Japan. The critical size of plutonium was much less than that of U-235 while its efficiency of utilisation in an explosion was, weight for weight, much greater than that of U-235. They calculated that a bomb would need ten times as much U-235 as plutonium to produce half the TNT equivalent. This meant the country must have a plant to produce plutonium. 'If it is desirable to conserve our resources in men and materials', wrote Chadwick, 'we can't afford to shoot all over the target and we must concentrate on making

[plutonium] so as to produce atomic weapons as soon as possible.'
At present U-235 was not needed for defence purposes, although
Chadwick and several others emphasised that the position might
change as the super- or hydrogen-bomb was developed. There were
also possibilities that U-235 plus plutonium might become more
efficient than plutonium alone in ordinary bombs. Meanwhile, if
U-235 was needed for experimental purposes and could not be
obtained from the United States, a small plant might be built. By
the time the first pile was in production, the right course might be
different, but, urged Chadwick, it could not be wrong to start
production of plutonium.

The main point in the emphasis on plutonium was military
efficiency, but most other factors also argued in its favour. It was
true that in the initial stages plutonium production was less economical than U-235 in the use of the raw material uranium. On the
other hand, although estimates of the capital cost of a plutonium
reactor plus its auxiliary plant varied greatly – by a factor of 2 – it
seemed almost certain to be less than the capital cost for an equivalent output of U-235. Allowing for the lower military efficiency of
U-235, the capital cost of U-235 plants was ten times or more that
required to build piles for the production of the same number of
bombs a year. As for nuclear power, reactors using uranium enriched with U-235 together with ordinary water were a possibility.*
On the other hand, plutonium might also be used in the future as a
reactor fuel; if so, this might increase the likelihood of economical
atomic power because a far higher proportion of the natural uranium
could be burnt up. In any case, production of plutonium would be
accompanied by production of heat; in itself this would lead into the
industrial use of atomic energy. The general opinion was that the
balance of advantage between the two materials for industrial
development was close, with a little extra weight on the side of
plutonium. The British scientists in America felt that the difficulties
of building large-scale reactors because the British lacked knowledge of them were exaggerated. The design of the reactor itself
was, relatively speaking, a simple matter. The knowledge obtained
about pilot reactors in North America should obviate serious teething
troubles and design problems; the Montreal work on the separation

---

* With natural uranium, ordinary 'light' water could not be used as a
moderator because it absorbed too many neutrons, and heavy water, which
was expensive and difficult to obtain, was necessary.

of plutonium was very successful; uranium metal was being produced in Britain which was substantially purer than American metal.

At first it had seemed that decisions on the relative importance of (i) the production of bombs, (ii) the development of atomic energy for industrial purposes, and (iii) research and development beyond (i) and (ii) – that is, on new methods of releasing atomic energy – would affect the choice of fissile material to be produced. When the officials studying international control of atomic energy recommended giving top priority to atomic bombs, Ministers asked about the effect of such a directive. Now, however, it was concluded that for the time being both bomb production and development for industrial purposes could best be satisfied by producing plutonium, although the Government should keep in mind the possibility of building a U-235 plant later in the light of technical developments. There was thus no competition between the three objectives above except in so far as the amount of plutonium production had to be divided between them: the problem was not which fissile material should be produced, but what should be the size and output of the plutonium project.

These decisions had to be taken in terms of number of piles. At first it was decided for reasons of speed to stick to the American Hanford-style design of pile rather than try alternative designs, and therefore the type and size of a single pile were assumed to match those of Hanford – that is, a 300,000-kw water-cooled graphite-moderated pile. Should the British build one or two piles? For research and development for industrial power, up to and including large pilot plants, 100 kilograms of fissile material might be required. But it would be consumed only slowly and would not be a recurring demand. It was impossible to forecast at present the design of a large-scale industrial nuclear power station and the quantity of fissile material needed to start and replenish it. In any case, it had yet to be shown that nuclear power would be cheaper than conventional power, so that it seemed better to think only of research and development needs at present.

It was clear that a decision on the number of piles needed depended on the output of bombs the Government wanted. The needs of research and development would be met after a single pile had been in full-time production for a year – possibly by January 1951. Thereafter its whole output would be available for bombs at the rate of

15 per year. With two piles, either a larger output of bombs could be available or material could be diverted to the production of industrial power if developments there were promising. Even if it were decided that two piles should ultimately be built, would it be better to concentrate on a single pile and get that finished first, in case important advances in knowledge affecting pile design were made in the next five years? The Anderson Advisory Committee concluded surprisingly that 'our knowledge of the subject has now reached a stage at which the likelihood of any novel advance of this sort is so remote that it can be disregarded for this purpose'. Moreover the building of a pile would fall into distinct stages employing different types of labour. If two piles were ultimately required, the Advisory Committee thought their construction should be undertaken simultaneously on the same site. The total cost of one pile, including site, housing, metal plant and chemical separation plant, was now put very tentatively at £20 million and of two piles at £30–35 million. The requirements of design engineers and draughtsmen would not be much more for two piles than for one. Two 300,000-kW piles would on present methods require less than half the current United States consumption of uranium ore and, allowing for increased efficiency in the use of uranium, it should be possible to meet these requirements.

The basic decision about the number of piles was submitted to the Gen 75 group of Ministers.* There it was pointed out that the construction of two piles would make heavy demands on the capacity of the chemical engineering and heavy electrical industries which were of great importance to the revival of the export trade, and on building labour and machinery for heavy excavating which were very scarce. Ministers felt that it was not essential to take a decision about the second pile immediately. They therefore approved in December 1945 the building of one pile to produce plutonium as a matter of the highest urgency and importance.† The work undertaken should include the provision of the common services and facilities that would be needed should it be decided later to build a second pile, together with capacity, in oxide purification and metal

* Ernest Bevin and the Minister of Defence were absent, but Hugh Dalton (Chancellor of the Exchequer) and Sir Stafford Cripps (President of the Board of Trade) were present (18 Dec 1945).

† A small number of electromagnetic units for separating U-235 were also to be built at Harwell.

and graphite production, sufficient for two piles.* But the decision about the second pile should be postponed until the Chiefs of Staff had reported on their atomic bomb requirements and the possibility of consequential reductions in other forms of armaments, and until the Minister of Supply had shown what demands the pile would make on industrial capacity that would otherwise be available for reconstruction or the export trade. He should also say what special forms of priority would be needed to complete the piles within three years.

The three Chiefs of Staff sent their report to the Prime Minister on New Year's Day 1946. They repeated their conviction that the best method of defence against atomic bombs was likely to be the deterrent effect of retaliation:

> We must be prepared [they wrote] for aggressors who have widely dispersed industries and populations. This means that in order to be effective as a deterrent we must have a considerable number of bombs at our disposal. It is not possible now to assess the precise number which we might require but we are convinced we should aim to have as soon as possible a stock in the order of hundreds rather than scores.

The output of one pile would be comparatively insignificant against a determined aggressor. Although the Chiefs of Staff could not say that two piles would produce enough bombs at an early date, 'clearly two piles are better than one and in the number of bombs we have will lie our strength'. Since a potential aggressor would not know exactly the number of bombs the pile would produce, the known existence of two might act as a powerful deterrent to a would-be aggressor, especially if he credited Britain with new techniques in production.

The Chiefs of Staff said that since it would take five years before material for bombs became available, it was impossible to wait to begin production until the outcome of the United Nations negotiations was clear. If these failed, five years would follow when Britain would have no bomb capacity and therefore no insurance against war. However, they emphasised, Britain was in no way committed to the manufacture of atomic bombs by beginning the construction of two piles now. The decision whether to devote their output to

* Lord Hinton has told the author that he is sure he was never given any such direction.

industrial development or to bombs could await the actual production of fissile material, in the fifth year after pile construction started. Meanwhile, said the Chiefs of Staff, Britain required, as quickly as possible, the greatest atomic bomb capacity that economic factors and raw material supplies would allow, and they recommended proceeding with the construction of 'at least two' atomic piles. The Minister of Supply did not produce his estimate of the cost of the piles in terms of industrial capacity and priorities. He said that even if an immediate decision were taken to build two piles, no action could give effect to the decision for another three to four weeks. The decision about a second pile was therefore postponed – as it turned out, for good.

The Chiefs of Staff memorandum was extremely vague on the question to which Ministers had wanted a specific answer – what output of bombs was necessary? A clear answer would have required a careful analysis of the probable advantages and disadvantages of the use of the atomic bomb by Britain in given tactical and strategical circumstances. The Chiefs of Staff organisation did not attempt this and was, indeed, still ill-equipped to do so. At the beginning of 1945 Mr Churchill had agreed that the three Chiefs of Staff and his own Chief Staff Officer, General Ismay, should be told about the atomic bomb but had added 'there is surely no necessity for them to go into technical details which are a life study in themselves'. In the aftermath of war, when there was a host of immediate military problems to be dealt with, the Chiefs of Staff had to be briefed by the Tube Alloys organisation with the most simple basic information about atomic energy. The limitation of their knowledge is apparent in their assertion that it was unnecessary to decide whether fissile material should be devoted to bombs or power until production had begun; they did not seem to realise the great effort required for the development of the bomb device itself. Moreover little thought was yet being given to the defence problems of the middle or long-term distance. The identity of the possible 'aggressor with widely dispersed industries and populations' did not require many guesses, but no potential wars or enemies had been officially defined. The Chiefs of Staff, moving away from their earlier unqualified plea for the manufacture of atomic bombs, reflected the uncertainties of the moment: the brief hope of international cooperation and the desire to cover Britain's atomic options. They did not ask themselves one question implicit in their paper and its reference to the need for hundreds of bombs – the question at which Blackett had already hinted. Was Britain going to spend a disproportionate effort in building up a stock of bombs too small to be of military value?

Blackett was now, in November 1945, asking this question more earnestly.* He went carefully over a number of assumptions about possible wars between Britain, the United States and Russia and a number of alternative technical assumptions about bomb development. Taking into account the peculiarities of Britain's geographical position, the actual military strengths of the great powers, the actual political situation within the great powers and the particular properties of atomic bombs, he believed a decision by Britain to manufacture or acquire atomic bombs now would tend to decrease rather than increase long-term security. For the use of these bombs as a threat was very likely to stimulate Russia to aggressive military reaction, not directly against the United Kingdom but elsewhere in Europe. The decision not to manufacture bombs would allow the greatest possible progress in Britain in the industrial application of atomic energy as well as her retrieval of her once leading position in nuclear physics:

> To dissipate our limited nuclear physics resources in copying American techniques of bomb production would be as mistaken as to dissipate our aerodynamic resources on building Super-Fortresses, unless it can be shown that the immediate acquirement of a few atomic bombs is essential to our security. If this latter was held to be the case, then clearly we should ask the United States for a supply.

If Britain decided not to make bombs it was, Blackett said, clearly essential to announce this publicly. Otherwise other countries would be encouraged to start also. If Britain announced she was not going to make bombs it was equally essential to make sure she was believed. This should be done by requesting inspection by representatives of the United Nations Security Council, irrespective of whether other countries did the same. Other countries than the United States and Russia might then follow suit, for it was difficult to see any possible advantage – and many grave disadvantages were obvious – for any small country participating in an atomic bomb armament race. Such

---

* His memorandum is reproduced at the end of this chapter as Appendix 8.

a policy would also involve a reappraisal of Britain's nuclear relations with the United States.

This memorandum by Blackett inevitably included some mistakes of fact* and some debatable hypotheses, but it was on a different intellectual plane from the Chiefs of Staff memorandum about atomic policy produced in this period. It merited an answer on the same plane, but did not get it. The Prime Minister said, 'The author, a distinguished scientist, speaks on political and military problems on which he is a layman', and sent the papers to the Chiefs of Staff. The Chiefs of Staff found themselves in complete disagreement with the paper from the military point of view. They simply said curtly that they did not accept its conclusions, nor agree with the assumptions on which these were based. The Prime Minister concurred.

So by the beginning of 1946 the programme for large-scale plutonium production had been fixed as one pile, capable at full output of providing the material for 15 bombs a year. During the discussions another point had come up: the location of the large-scale pile and ancillary plants. When in September 1945 Chadwick had advised the construction of a large water-cooled reactor, he had said that in his opinion this first pile should be located in Canada, without any commitments about subsequent piles or plants. There would be great technical advantages in Canada – a prepared site and ample water – and even greater political advantages vis-à-vis the Americans. Cockcroft took the same view. Other members of the Technical Committee, however, strongly opposed the suggestion that the first stage of the plans for large-scale production of explosive material should take place in Canada, and at the Advisory Committee it was argued that Britain could not find the dollars to finance Canadian construction themselves. If Canada financed it, it would not be fully under British control; there might be difficulty in getting a large enough share of the final product. In the report that finally went to, and was agreed by, Ministers, it was proposed that any pile built in Canada as part of a Commonwealth enterprise should be in addition to, and not part of, the programme of large-scale production to be undertaken to meet Britain's own needs. Thereafter the decision to keep production for British needs within the British Isles

* e.g. it assumed that Britain would accumulate a stock of bombs before Russia. It also over-emphasised the role of nuclear physics in an atomic project.

was defended as an article of faith against all North American attacks on it (see Chapters 4 and 5).

Field-Marshal Lord Wilson, chief British military representative in Washington, remained unconvinced by these arguments and later in 1946 he was to return to the attack. He thought the prospect of increased efficiency of atomic bombs, and of the development of hydrogen bombs and guided missiles, together with the progressive deterioration of relations with Russia, made Britain especially vulnerable. He was also convinced that collaboration with the United States would not be possible except on the basis of a strategic plan acceptable to the United States. While he agreed there were cogent reasons – political, industrial, psychological, and perhaps strategic – for building the first pile in the United Kingdom, he urged that any second pile should be built in Canada and regarded as a Commonwealth pile. This would have the advantage of cementing the Anglo-Canadian partnership, so strained by atomic diagreements. Nevertheless, the Chiefs of Staff and Lord Portal still felt that the suggestion was wholly unacceptable, indeed dangerous. It would, they felt, encourage the United States belief that an atomic energy plant in Britain was vulnerable and be seized as a means to persuade the British not to build the first pile in the United Kingdom. The Chiefs of Staff were perfectly confident in their ability to defeat security risks to atomic energy plants in the United Kingdom from third powers, whether through sabotage and leakage of information or through the possibility that plants might fall into enemy hands through airborne or seaborne raids.

Decisions had been taken which enabled work on large-scale production of fissile material – plutonium – to begin. Was it to be used for atomic bombs? Here there was what can only be called a non-decision: the Government had not said 'yes' and had not said 'no', nor even clearly and emphatically 'we shall wait and see'. The scale of production decided upon had certainly not been related to strategic policy, as Lord Portal himself admitted later, although the confusion of the decision-making process was such that a secretary of the Chiefs of Staff Committee believed it had been. On various occasions at ministerial level the statement was made that the use to be made of the fissile material would depend on 'circumstances' and in particular on the conclusions reached by the United Nations Commission on Atomic Energy. This was the formula in the preparation of notes for supplementary questions in connection with the announcement in the House of Commons in January about the setting-up of the production organisation,* at the Combined Policy Committee meeting in Washington in February 1946 and the Dominion Prime Ministers' Conference in April 1946, and in the Prime Minister's telegram to President Truman in June 1946.

Yet the general assumption was that Britain was going to make atomic weapons. Chadwick thought so (see p. 164) and the men in charge of the new production organisation had no doubt whatsoever that this was the destination of the plutonium they had been told to make with all haste.[4] In November 1945 Mr Churchill had said in the House of Commons: 'This I take it is already agreed, we should make atomic bombs.'[5] A Labour Member of Parliament (Mr Percy Morris)[6] said that this assumption gave him 'a sinking feeling', but in the course of a long foreign affairs debate, no Minister or MP made any other reference at all to Britain's manufacture of the bomb. In August 1946 the Chief of the Air Staff put to the Ministry of Supply through the normal channels the first requisition for an atomic bomb.† Soon afterwards the Ministry of Supply added a token figure for research on atomic weapons in the budget which the Deputy Chiefs of Staff Committee were then reviewing. At about the same time the Air Ministry issued the first operational requirement for a new medium bomber that would fly sufficiently fast, high and far with a heavy load; it was clearly intended to carry atomic bombs even though they were not mentioned. The requirement was followed by a specification which was issued to the aircraft industry at the beginning of 1947.

It is possible that the inner group of Ministers may themselves have believed by the summer of 1946 that the decision to make bombs had been taken, for otherwise one of them would surely have remarked on this gap when in July the Cabinet's Defence Committee considered and approved a report by the Joint Technical Warfare Committee of the Chiefs of Staff (see also Chapter 2). This report said that there was no firm basis for assessing the quantity of atomic and biological weapons required by any nation to bring

* The notes said, *inter alia*: 'The fact we are setting up this organisation and that the first head (Portal) is a man who has done so much in organising and developing one of the Services in no way implies the Government are looking at this matter primarily from the standpoint of military preparations.'

† Unfortunately the actual requisition document seems to have been destroyed. But it is referred to with date and number by the revised requisition in August 1948 (OR 1001 (issue 2)).

about the collapse of another. Russia had not been confirmed as a possible enemy, but the report said its best estimate was that 30 to 120 atomic bombs accurately delivered by Russia might cause the collapse of the United Kingdom, whereas several hundred bombs might be required to bring about the collapse of Russia. It believed that within five to ten years the United States with or without the help of Britain might possess enough atomic bombs to devastate a large percentage of the cities in Russia, though not necessarily to secure its collapse. The uncertainty surrounding the effects of atomic and biological weapons and the difficulties in the precise assessment of the chances of success should be a deterrent to aggression, while deception would have an important part to play in maintaining uncertainty. Meanwhile the development of high-performance long-range bombers must proceed on the highest priority.* Supersonic pilotless aircraft and/or rockets might well replace manned aircraft, but this was not likely within ten years.

The Chiefs of Staff conclusion was that the main emphasis in military development must now be laid on the new weapons and on the means of delivery and countering them. The overall national effort involved in the successful delivery of atomic bombs was very considerably less than that required to produce the same effect by normal bombs. Atomic and biological weapons and defence against them, plus the aircraft or rockets to carry atomic weapons, came first among the problems of defence research. In all this there was no shadow of a doubt that atomic bombs were going to be made in Britain.

That atomic bombs would be made was also generally assumed during discussions in the summer and autumn of 1946 about an addition to the programme for large-scale production of fissile material. These discussions were prolonged and involved, and Lord Portal's reconstituted Technical Committee of scientists took part in them as well as Anderson's Advisory Committee. They were concerned with the need to proceed with the construction of a gaseous diffusion plant for producing uranium enriched in U-235. It will be remembered that there had originally been some dispute as to whether Britain should begin by producing plutonium or U-235 as a fissile material and it had been agreed, largely but not wholly because of its superiority for bombs, that plutonium should be the first

---

* For the varying priority status of the bomber programme, see pp. 234-5.

priority but that it might be desirable later to build a U-235 plant as well.

In the spring of 1946 there was a desire in some quarters to review this policy. In particular, Lord Portal, who was new in office as Controller of Production, Atomic Energy,* was frantically worried by the prospects of building a graphite pile in the present state of ignorance about its design and operation, especially as unpleasant pieces of information filtered through from Hanford – for example, tales about troubles due to expansion of the graphite or to blistering of the cans holding the uranium, and about the difficulties caused by corrosion by cooling water or 'poisoning' by fission products. Portal's gloom increased when he visited the United States project in May 1946 and General Groves told him that the best advice he could give about building a pile was not to build it at all. The General's dissatisfaction with the permanent safety of the piles was such that he would not be at all surprised to be called to the telephone one morning to hear the news that one of the piles had 'gone up'. Portal, sure that the Government's policy was to get atomic bombs as quickly as possible, wondered whether this would not be achieved by the more straightforward U-235 process instead of plutonium. Chadwick's short answer was: 'The decision has been taken to make bombs and therefore we must make plutonium.' If it were not for the military needs, he agreed that it would now be best to begin with a U-235 plant. He also did his best to be reassuring. 'We in the United Kingdom don't know everything about piles', he wrote, 'but we know a good deal. I don't wish to under-estimate the difficulties arising from our lack of technical information on some points but I think they are being exaggerated. There is no need to be afraid of them.' Portal added in the margin: 'We are not but it would be sad if our pile didn't work.' In fact, the engineers were on Chadwick's side. Christopher Hinton was confident by June 1946 that, provided a suitable water supply for cooling was found, he would be able to satisfy the engineering and nuclear physics requirements.

However, by now there seemed to be a pressing need for U-235 for other reasons. In the short term the need arose because the prospects of the supply of uranium ore were worsening so that it was essential that it should be used economically. The existing method of pro-

* He had not been appointed when the decision about production policy was taken at the end of 1945.

ducing plutonium for weapons meant that the uranium could stay in the pile for only a relatively short time.* When the rods were removed for the separation of the plutonium the uranium could not be recycled until it had been re-enriched with U-235. This meant that only a small amount of plutonium was produced from the uranium, and on the present allocation of uranium to Britain the number of bombs produced might therefore be very small. If, however, the used uranium were reinforced with extra fissile atoms to replace those used up in the first cycle, it might be reused in the pile. This recycling could be done either by mixing the depleted uranium recovered from the irradiated fuel elements with uranium which had been enriched in the gaseous diffusion plant, or else by 'seeding' the fuel elements with fissionable material. Seeding could be done by incorporating in the fuel elements some of the plutonium produced in earlier cycles. But if plutonium were fed back and locked up in the pile, there would again be little left for weapons. If U-235 were used for re-enrichment, the amount of military plutonium finally produced from a pile would be nearly three times as much as the amount produced after seeding with plutonium. Moreover, re-enrichment in this way would be an insurance against the unavoidable use of graphite which was not pure enough, which might absorb too many neutrons and make the neutron multiplication rate too low for the efficient operation of the pile.

On a long-term view the main argument for U-235 was that it was needed for research and development on the most promising future nuclear power development – that is, fast neutron reactors with no moderator operating with concentrated fissile material instead of natural uranium.† These reactors would produce power and also produce more fissile material than they consumed. Any large-scale exploitation of atomic energy must, it was thought, ultimately depend on this breeding. Development in this field would involve a considerable research programme which would be dependent on the possession of an appreciable amount of fissile material in rather concentrated form. If plutonium were used for this programme it would interfere with supplies for atomic weapons.

* Otherwise an excessive proportion of plutonium-240, which is liable to spontaneous fission, would be produced.

† The Americans already had a small experimental fast reactor at Los Alamos. The first reactor to be connected to a turbine and electric generator was a fast reactor, the American EBR1, completed in 1951 at Arco in Idaho.

Moreover it might be better to start such a reactor research programme with U-235, which presented fewer health and safety hazards than plutonium.

From this the Ministry of Supply, all the various scientists and subsequently the Anderson Committee concluded in 1946 that a gaseous diffusion plant providing uranium enriched twentyfold in U-235 should be built. The cost of the plant could not be accurately estimated but might well be £30–40 million, and it would take four to five years to design and construct. It would need a substantial team of design engineers, and a large force of civil, electrical and mechanical engineering workers. The power consumption would be 100,000–150,000 kW – ½ per cent of the existing fuel consumption of the country or 15 per cent of the planned yearly increase in installed electricity capacity. This task would put a very heavy additional load on to Hinton's design staff, but no other organisation could be found to do it (see Chapter 21), and so they shouldered it. The essential immediate step was to recruit as rapidly as possible the necessary engineering and design staff. No heavy capital expenditure would be needed for at least two years and the business could be reviewed again before a major financial commitment was assumed (see pp. 217–18 below).

In the summer of 1946 the Ministry of Supply and Anderson's Advisory Committee enlarged on the technical merits of the proposal which appealed both to military needs and to the nuclear power enthusiasts. The Chiefs of Staff spokesman, for example, found the number of plutonium bombs that would be produced from the available allocation of uranium, after the needs of research and development were met and without recycling, derisorily small – only 15 to 18 a year. It was becoming only too apparent, as Portal had concluded after his visit to America, that if Britain was not to lag hopelessly behind the United States for an indefinite number of years in practical achievement in this field, she would have to 'think big, take chances and above all translate into reality the priority which HMG have accorded to the project'.

The financial and economic problems which all these people had brushed aside as beyond their competence were left to the hapless Gen 75 Ministers. In their discussions in October 1946 it was urged: 'We must consider seriously whether we could afford to divert from civilian consumption and restoration of the balance of payments the economic resources required for a project on this scale.... We might find ourselves faced with an extremely serious economic and financial situation in 2/3 years.' On the other hand it was argued that Britain could not afford to be left behind in a field of such revolutionary importance from the industrial no less than the military point of view. Britain's prestige in the world as well as her chances of securing United States co-operation would both suffer if she did not exploit to the full a discovery in which she had played a leading part at the outset. The development of a new source of industrial power might strengthen her industrial position very considerably in the future, especially since it was becoming more and more difficult to find labour for coal-mining. It was asked whether the gaseous diffusion plant could not be built in Canada, but it was pointed out that without the extensive help of United States or United Kingdom organisations, Canada probably could not carry through such an elaborate engineering project. Moreover the plant, which was necessary to the success of Britain's own programme, would not be under her control if it were built in another country. Ministers therefore authorised the design and construction of the gaseous diffusion plant to go ahead on the understanding that the project would be reviewed before any unescapable commitment was undertaken for expenditure above £500,000.

Again the need for atomic bombs went unquestioned in all these discussions, and again no one pointed out that a decision to make them had never been taken. The moment, however, had come when a decision was imminent.

The Decision to Make a Bomb

This decision was not taken casually as a simple acceptance of an assured fact. Far from it: it was taken most deliberately and under cover of the greatest possible secrecy. The whole question cropped up because no provision was apparently being made for research into the purely military application of atomic energy – that is, the ordnance side. It had been vaguely assumed that this would come under Cockcroft's research establishment, even if not at Harwell. In 1946 it was certainly not within Lord Portal's orbit, which only covered large-scale production of fissile material. All those who had been connected with United States work on bomb design and production had emphasised the novelty and technical difficulty in the use of fissile material as a bomb. Yet the Englishman who had

become one of the chief Anglo-American experts on the weapon
side, the brilliant mathematician W. G. Penney, now had no part in
the atomic energy business. He had played a leading part in the
Bikini trials as a member of the American team and had then
returned home to take up the post of Chief Superintendent of
Armament Research in the Ministry of Supply. Chadwick had,
however, spoken about atomic explosives work to Portal during the
latter's May 1946 visit to the United States and thereafter wrote to
Penney: 'He seems to be very willing it should be put in your
charge with final responsibility devolving on him [Portal].'

The two men later got together in England and Penney began to
plan an Atomic Weapons Section in his Armaments Research
Department. On 1 November 1946 he sent his scheme, typed by
himself because of the extreme secrecy, to Portal. He said that the
manufacture of an atomic bomb of present design fell naturally into
two parts: firstly the production of the active material and secondly
the ordnance part, that is, the manufacture and assembly of the
components causing the explosion of the active material. The second
part of the work could be begun and completed without the need to
use fissile material at any stage. Formally, but not with a clear
conscience, he wrote, it could be maintained that the whole of the
second part of the work was conventional armaments research. The
implications of this for international control were profound, but
Penney's immediate purpose was to suggest how the job should be
done in Britain 'if it was decided in the national interest that such
work should proceed'. He assumed that the ordnance parts of the
weapon must be completed a year before the fissile material was
produced and that the highest priority would be given to certain
modest building requirements. Penney said the work could suitably
be done within the Armaments Research Department, using for the
present the sites at Woolwich, Fort Halstead and Shoeburyness. He
produced an organisation chart, an estimate of staff requirements
and a list of eighteen individuals whom he would want very soon.
Very stringent secrecy arrangements would be needed.

Soon after this, according to some euphemistic minutes which
never mentioned the words 'atomic bomb', the Ministry of Supply's
Scientific Co-ordinating Board agreed that Penney should have
technical responsibility in this affair to Lord Portal, although his
existing Controller in the Ministry would retain full administrative
control. Penney remained in addition in full charge of the normal

armaments research work. The talks and plans about how the weapons research was to be organised brought home to Lord Portal and Michael Perrin, his deputy for technical policy, that although there was a tacit assumption that the bomb would be made in Britain, and not the slightest doubt that it should be, no mandate, either official or unofficial, existed for developing it. The Prime Minister had refused to be drawn into saying that the Government intended to develop a bomb. Portal talked off the record to the Chiefs of Staff, who agreed that he should take the responsibility for this weapons research. He proposed to see the Prime Minister and ask him whether he wished the whole question to be referred formally to him for a mandate; whether he, Portal, should go ahead and accept the responsibility without a formal mandate; or whether he wanted the whole matter to find its way into the ordinary machine with the inevitable result that a very large number of people would know what was happening.

Portal felt that secrecy was the overriding consideration. It was not only a question of keeping the technical secrets from other nations, though that was very important. There was also the general political aspect. Was there, for national or international reasons, any object in conceding the fact that Britain was working on the development of the atomic bomb? Finally, there was the Anglo-American aspect. Hopes of getting help from the United States 'under the counter' might depend on their assessment of British secrecy arrangements. If, as it seemed, the whole business was thrice secret it would be unwise to throw the bomb requirements into the normal departmental machinery for weapons development. Hence the proposal for the Portal–Penney arrangement, with Portal as the channel for communication for the Chiefs of Staff and Penney's work camouflaged under a misleading name such as 'basic high explosive research'. The Chiefs of Staff agreed to suppress any reference in their Ministries to details of manufacture, though Tizard would have to be informed of the background to these arrangements.*

Portal saw the Prime Minister who said he wished to discuss the question with one or two of his colleagues. Portal wrote a memorandum which he regarded as so secret that he did not show it to anyone in the Ministry of Supply, although he discussed its essence with the

---

* See above, Chapter 2. It seemed probable that Tizard did not in fact know of the decision to make an atomic weapon.

Permanent Secretary and the two Controllers of Supplies. He hoped particularly to avoid consulting his Minister or having to report to him on this; he proposed to explain, if asked, that he thought it might save the Minister some embarrassment if the paper were cleared direct with the Prime Minister to whom in a sense he, Portal, was responsible. However, although the Prime Minister did not want the matter to go to the full Gen 75 Committee, he signified that the Minister of Supply should come to the ministerial meeting.*

This *ad hoc* gathering awaited the Foreign Secretary's return to London; it took place early in January 1947 and was called Gen 163. Although the meeting was being held when Britain was almost at her darkest economic hour with factories closing down for lack of coal, neither the Chancellor of the Exchequer nor the President of the Board of Trade was present. Portal's paper was circulated in the utmost secrecy to the Ministers attending the meeting and was withdrawn afterwards. Only three copies of the minutes of the meeting were made. Portal's paper opened: 'I submit that a decision is required about the development of atomic weapons in this country.' He suggested that there were three courses: (*a*) not to develop atomic weapons at all; (*b*) to develop the weapon by means of ordinary agencies in the Ministry of Supply and Service departments; and (*c*) to develop the weapon under special arrangements conducive to the utmost secrecy. He imagined (*a*) would not be favoured by the Government in the absence of international agreement, while if (*b*) were adopted it would be impossible to conceal for long the fact that the development was taking place. Moreover it would certainly not be long before the United States authorities heard that Britain was developing the weapon, and this might seem to them another reason for reticence over technical matters not only in the field of military uses of atomic energy but also in the general knowledge of production of fissile material. If for national or international reasons the special arrangements at (*c*) were required, they could well be made through the Portal–Penney organisation

---

* The three Gen 75 Ministers who did not go to the Gen 163 meeting were the Chancellor of the Exchequer (Hugh Dalton), the Lord Privy Seal (Arthur Greenwood) and the President of the Board of Trade (Sir Stafford Cripps). Ministers present were the Prime Minister, Foreign Secretary (Ernest Bevin), Lord President (Herbert Morrison), Minister of Defence (A. V. Alexander), Dominions Secretary (Lord Addison) and Minister of Supply (John Wilmot).

described above. Under this, only five or six senior officials outside Portal's organisation need know of the arrangement. Portal therefore asked for directions on two points – whether research and development on atomic weapons were to be undertaken and, if so, whether the special arrangements were to be adopted.

The Secretary of the Cabinet noted that a report of the United Nations Atomic Energy Commission recommended that the exclusive right to carry on atomic research for destructive purposes should be vested in an international authority. The British representative had supported the various proposals as a general statement of principles, but in further discussion it seemed desirable that he should call attention to the difficulty of giving practical effect to the prohibition of research into atomic weapons. If so, it was 'inevitable' that Britain should undertake such research.

At the single Gen 163 meeting early in January 1947 the Foreign Secretary said it was important that Britain should press on with the study of all aspects of atomic energy. 'We could not afford to acquiesce in an American monopoly of this new development.' Other countries might also develop it and unless there was an effective international system prohibiting the production and use of the weapon, Britain too must do so. The meeting agreed that work on atomic weapons should be undertaken and approved the special administrative arrangements Lord Portal proposed. Most curiously, Dr Penney did not know of this ministerial meeting in January 1947 and was not told to go ahead until the following May (see Chapter 23). Then a third and largely independent kingdom was added to the atomic empire, under the loose suzerainty of Lord Portal, as Dr Penney took up office alongside Dr Cockcroft and Mr Hinton. Britain was now going in for independent deterrence in earnest.

The only document the author has found in the Government archives of this period suggesting that Britain should not produce atomic weapons was a second paper of February 1947 by Professor Blackett, which was circulated as a Gen 75 paper. There is no evidence that he knew that a decision to make bombs had already been taken and, as we have seen (in Chapter 4), the paper was largely a plea for a complete reappraisal of Britain's foreign and defence policy in the shadow of the almost certain breakdown of the negotiations for international control of atomic energy. Blackett proposed as a basis for discussion a British defence policy which would renounce atomic bombs and weapons of mass destruction, design forces on defensive lines and in effect adopt a policy of neutrality between America and Russia. Blackett had two conversations with the Prime Minister at this time about his proposals, but Mr Attlee wrote no comments after them. There was no discussion of his paper at any ministerial meeting.

At this time there was much unrest in the Labour Party about the Government's foreign policy, and this was strongly voiced in Parliament, but the atomic bomb was kept out of the discussions. It was the big unmentionable subject, but in the circles where its possibilities were discussed – for example, the Technical and Advisory Committees – Blackett's voice was the only one of dissent. There was ignorance, deliberately encouraged by the Government, about the independent deterrent, but even where there was knowledge or a good guess, the deterrent was accepted almost without opposition. In the *Atomic Scientists' News* of the time the only vociferous opponents of the bomb were Dr Kathleen Lonsdale (a lifelong pacifist) and Professor N. F. Mott.* Few awkward questions were asked.

The British decision to make an atomic bomb had 'emerged' from a body of general assumptions. It had not been a response to an immediate military threat but rather something fundamentalist and almost instinctive – a feeling that Britain must possess so climacteric a weapon in order to deter an atomically armed enemy, a feeling that Britain as a great power must acquire all major new weapons, a feeling that atomic weapons were a manifestation of the scientific and technological superiority on which Britain's strength, so deficient if measured in sheer numbers of men, must depend. A bomb would not be ready in any case for five years, so that the decision was of the variety that was impossible *not* to take rather than of the type that must be taken for urgent and immediate purposes.

The decision was also a symbol of independence. It had not been taken as a result of the breakdown in 1946 of Anglo-American atomic co-operation. The decision to produce fissile material in the United Kingdom had been taken before this breakdown and was regarded as non-negotiable in any circumstances. If the Anglo-American atomic agreements drafted early in 1946 had been en-

* The Association of Scientific Workers opposed Britain's manufacture of a bomb but they were believed to be far left, politically speaking.

dorsed they would in no way have altered the decision to produce plutonium, though it is possible that they would have made it unnecessary for Britain to plan her own gaseous diffusion plant. The agreements in themselves had no provisions which would have assured a supply of American atomic bombs to Britain, thus removing the need for Britain to fabricate them herself. It is conceivable that if the agreement had been signed and if henceforth Anglo-American relations had been bathed in sweetness and light, arrangements might have been made for the pooling of atomic weapons production. But in view of the actual American mood at this time, such a possibility is not worth even a cursory exploration. As it was, American atomic attitudes in this period hardened Britain's resolution not to be bullied out of the business and not to acquiesce in an American monopoly; it encouraged her determination to be a nuclear power for the sake of the influence this was expected to give her in Washington.

If America adopted these attitudes, as has sometimes been suggested, in the pure and altruistic pursuit of non-proliferation of atomic weapons, her tactics could hardly have been less suited to the purpose. Late in 1947, when it was suggested that Britain might rely on the United States for the maintenance of her nuclear striking force, Lord Tedder, Chief of the Air Staff, voiced a general feeling when he replied that this would involve a close military alliance with the United States in which Britain would be merely a temporary advance base, would involve complete subservience to United States policy and would render Britain completely impotent in negotiations with Russia or any other nation.

In fact, as we have seen, there were at this time – in 1946 and 1947 – no United States military commitments to come to Britain's help in war. If Britain wanted to be sure of being covered by an atomic deterrent, she had no option but to make it herself.

Mainly Military

Once a clear decision to make the bomb had been taken, the whole atomic project took on a new urgency. Hitherto it had been assumed that the project had a strong military flavour, but now there was no doubt that military needs were its chief, indeed for a time almost its exclusive, purpose. The belief that the Government considered the national security depended on producing atomic bombs as soon as possible – a belief accentuated by the extreme secrecy – gave those working in the project an obsession with the need to execute the programme faultlessly and to time.

Soon after the decision was taken, the Prime Minister bestowed his own priority on the project. Up till then the project was supposed to have a high priority, but there had been no system for dealing specially with its needs and in practice it was subordinate to three other categories – housing, coal-mining and exports – and equal to many others. Lord Portal asked the Minister of Supply to bid for first and overriding priority for the programme's requirements of labour, raw materials and industrial capacity. In February 1947 the Prime Minister accordingly sent personal minutes to the Ministers concerned saying that everything must be done to avoid delay in meeting the atomic energy programme. If any conflict arose which could not be resolved, it was to be reported to him.*

All this new urgency was not in itself evidence of new strategic pressures, nor did it reflect sudden new alarms about the world situation at the end of 1946, however gloomily Professor Blackett had surveyed it. Ministers still had a desire not to offend the Russians unnecessarily. Early in 1947 Mr Bevin had an eye on their feelings over the arrangements with the United States for military standardi-sation; the Americans abolished the Combined Chiefs of Staff mainly for the same reason. The possibility of an Anglo-Soviet military alliance was discussed only to be discarded because it would prejudice Anglo-American exchange of military information. Ministers were certainly not yet prepared to accept that Russia was in effect an enemy, albeit undeclared. The Chiefs of Staff, in an aide-mémoire on future defence policy in January 1947, had assumed there was at present only one foreseeable enemy, but the Prime Minister had struck out this assumption. Again in June 1947 the Chiefs of Staff proposed that defence policy should be based on the possibility of war with Russia. Attlee and Bevin thought this was dangerous: even to circulate such a report would tend to bias Britain's outlook in international affairs and would probably lead her to take steps which Russia would see to be directed against her, steps which might conceivably precipitate war. Bevin still believed that Germany in time might well once more become the chief threat to the peace of the world. Russia might be in a position to threaten

* For a discussion of this priority, see Chapter 14.

world peace rather earlier, but Bevin thought that provided Britain and the United States presented a strong enough front, Russia would not pursue her policy beyond the point at which war could be prevented. The Chiefs of Staff report was circulated no further.

No one believed in 1947 that war was imminent. In August 1947 the Minister of Defence issued a directive that the risk of a major war could be ruled out during the next five years, and that the risk would increase only gradually during the following five years.[7] The risk would vary directly with Britain's offensive strength. 'If attacked we must fight with what we have.' It had become a major tenet of faith among Chiefs of Staff and Ministers alike that the United Kingdom was peculiarly vulnerable to attack with atomic bombs, rockets and biological weapons, that a third major war would be utterly disastrous, and that the supreme object of British policy must be to prevent war, in particular by deterring aggression which might lead to war.

Some thought that even so the Government was exaggerating the dangers. Some Ministers in 1947 hotly disputed the estimates for the size of the forces. Sir Henry Tizard felt strongly on the subject. 'For what war are we supposed to be preparing?' he asked. 'For war with Russia. There is no other conceivable risk of major conflict. But in spite of aggressive words in public, there is no indication the Russian rulers have any intention of risking a major war in the near future.' The real danger to the Western democracies, he said, was not war but economic collapse and disorder, and Russia would do, and was doing, all she could to cause such a collapse. That was why she was pursuing a policy calculated to induce Britain to maintain forces at a cost she could not afford. Every single man taken away from productive work in industry to join the Services was a loss to the nation. It would tax British strength and determination to the utmost to provide for necessary imports by exports, and if the country did not succeed 'we shall go down for ever as a first-class nation'.

As we shall see, Tizard subsequently became a strong opponent of Britain's independent nuclear deterrent. But in 1947, while there was great controversy in deciding the total size of the Services and the division of men and resources between them, the argument raged largely over their shape and size in the period of conventional war before weapons of mass destruction were available. The atomic bomb itself fitted uncontroversially into the ideas of all the Chiefs of

Staff. No one doubted that long-term scientific research and development, including atomic research, should have a high, even the highest, priority in defence expenditure. Atomic bombs would not be ready in the next five years, the period when no war was expected, but thereafter an air striking force equipped with the bomb would be the chief tangible evidence of the intention and ability to retaliate immediately, the chief deterrent to aggression, and the only effective backing for foreign policy. The question was asked whether Britain would in fact use weapons of mass destruction: if a potential enemy did not use mass weapons at the outset of a war, the political objections against Britain's initiating their use might be insuperable. The Chiefs of Staff agreed that it would be a cardinal principle of policy to be prepared to use such weapons immediately, but no hypothetical sequence of events was established.

At first the possession of atomic weapons had seemed so remote and their possibilities so daunting that they had entered very little into the military planners' reckonings. By 1947 they were becoming firmly embedded there but they had still been related to strategy only in the very vaguest terms and no attempt had been made to calculate how many atomic bombs were needed for the deterrent purposes they were supposed to serve. When an estimate was at last made, the methodology was so ridiculous that its conclusions seemed worthless. In July 1947 Tizard's Defence Research Policy Committee made its first comprehensive survey of defence research. Reasonably enough, it felt obliged to comment on atomic weapons even though it kept away from research and development in the production of fissile material, for which it was not responsible. It pronounced that for atomic weapons to be a useful deterrent, a stock of the order of 1,000 bombs must be held 'involving the production of about 1 per day', and there must be the means of delivering them immediately on the outbreak of war. The Committee admitted it had no reliable figures on the cost or time factor involved in the manufacture and storage of atomic bombs, but it made some estimates of its own. The exclusion of Tizard from knowledge of the decision to make a bomb is apparent in the Committee's belief that the research on atomic weapons was largely confined to their effects and to protection against them; it did not go into the question of the use of American bombs.

The figures in the report had been inserted without any reference at all to the Ministry of Supply, and a frigid correspondence ensued.

Lord Portal pointed out that the production of one bomb a day would involve multiplying the production of plutonium by a factor of 24 and the intake of ore by a very large factor.* The order of magnitude was entirely different from that planned and far above present prospects of uranium supply. If these figures were indeed grossly inflated, they should not be left to scare Ministers. If they represented the considered view of the Chiefs of Staff about the size of stockpile necessary, it would become a matter of high policy to consider whether heavy expenditure should continue on a pro-gramme which could not possibly achieve more than a small fraction of what was necessary. It transpired that the figure of 1,000 had been based on a conclusion by the Home Defence Committee that 25 bombs would be required to knock out Britain. The geographical area 'we have in mind' was 40 times the size of the United Kingdom and $25 \times 40 = 1,000$.

This simple arithmetical approach was naïve, but it raised again doubts about the atomic energy programme. Firstly, the programme had originally been fixed in relation to the availability of raw materials and scientific and engineering effort; it had never been properly related to strategic and tactical needs and probabilities. Secondly, there were doubts about the machinery for managing the business. Atomic energy had been taken out of the machinery of government and placed in a holy of holies on its own. How, in these circumstances, could it be rationally related to other parts of the country's defence research and development? At the end of 1947 it was clear that these questions must be cleared up.

A Hope for Nuclear Power

The atomic energy project was now so predominantly military that industrial power was only a gleam for the future in the eyes of the scientists and engineers (see Chapter 19). Nevertheless, they turned to thinking of it when they could, even though they varied in their optimism about the possibilities. In the discussions about programmes for large-scale production of fissile material, questions of nuclear power did, as we have seen, play some part, though a subsidiary one. The chief reason for the decision to begin the design of a gaseous diffusion plant had been the need for economy in raw

* A well-informed observer, the late Leonard Beaton, in a 1964 pamphlet, estimated the current stockpile of British nuclear weapons as 1,000–1,500.[8]

materials, but the scientists had also clearly longed to get their hands on some U-235 so that they could experiment with other types of reactors and, in particular, with fast breeder reactors where the real hope for economic nuclear power seemed to lie.

During 1946 and 1947 scientists and engineers were identifying the various technological problems that must be solved by extensive and expensive research and development in order to make power generation feasible. The possibilities were governed by nuclear properties, by chemical engineering difficulties, by the radiations from radioactive fission products, by the available resources of fissile material, by engineering, structural and heat-exchange limits and, of course, by economics. In the autumn of 1946 a member of the Economic Section of the Cabinet Office studied some of the economic possibilities and consequences. As a piece of technological and cost forecasting it was in most ways quite wrong and much too optimistic,* but its conclusion was that there should be a continuing study of the technical, cost and economic implications of a nuclear electricity system.

A change in the large-scale production programme in May 1947 brought the prospects of nuclear power a little nearer (see Chapter 22). The original plan for the pile to produce plutonium was for one 300,000-kW water-cooled pile like those at Hanford. During the war the Americans had considered building piles cooled by gas (helium) under pressure, but had decided not to proceed because of technical and supply difficulties. A water-cooled pile also had its difficulties, however, notably its complexity and the danger of corrosion. But to the British the main disadvantage of a water-cooled pile was the problem of finding a suitable site. A large supply of very pure water was needed, the site had to be on the sea coast to enable effluent to be discharged into tidal water, while for reasons of safety the pile had to be well away from large centres of population. The only suitable site found in Britain was near the mouth of the river Morar in Inverness-shire. It was very remote and completely underdeveloped with poor transport, and all construction labour would have to be imported and a new town built there. Even then the water available had a chlorine content four times higher than that recommended by the American project.

While the work of designing the water-cooled pile had been going

* For example, it largely concentrated on the possibilities of U-233 from thorium (see Chapter 19).

ahead, the scientists and engineers at Harwell and Risley had been thinking of designing gas-cooled piles to give the same output of plutonium. A technical solution was devised by the engineers which made it possible to contemplate a 'super-Harwell' pile – that is, a scaled-up design of the 6,000-kW experimental pile, Bepo, which was cooled by air drawn through the pile and discharged through the chimney (see Chapter 22). The new proposal removed most of the disadvantages of the pressurised gas system which the Americans had rejected during the war* and its advantages were very great. Two or three of these piles would be built instead of the one water-cooled pile in order to produce the required plutonium, and this in itself would spread the risk of failure. Most important of all, site selection became infinitely easier because large supplies of pure water were not required and there was a much smaller risk of the pile over-heating (see Chapter 22), leading to the dispersal of radioactive fission products; the pile could therefore be located nearer to centres of population and water catchment areas. The time taken to build the pile would be substantially less and plutonium might be available two years earlier than previously forecast,† while the total cost would be reduced by at least 40 per cent. The design was also much simpler and there was greater certainty that it would operate without trouble and with more efficient conversion of uranium. For a given power level, plutonium production would be about 12 per cent higher, while twice as much plutonium would be obtained from a given quantity of natural uranium metal without re-enrichment of the fuel being necessary.‡ There were technical difficulties and un-certainties over the air-cooled pile and also a possible health hazard. Air blown through the pile would become slightly radioactive, but being dispersed from 400-ft stacks it would be substantially diluted before reaching the ground. The levels would be only one-tenth of the tolerances fixed by the Medical Research Council.

There appeared to be one other great advantage of the air-cooled pile. It seemed that it was a step in the direction of power production because it would make possible higher outlet temperatures compared

* The Americans had built an experimental air-cooled pile at Oak Ridge during the war.

† In fact it was not, but if a water-cooled pile had been built, the time taken would have greatly exceeded the first estimates.

‡ This argument made the need for U-235 rather less urgent, but the other reasons for producing U-235 still stood.

with the water-cooled pile, which was thought to be obsolescent and not in the line of future development. Hinton was especially anxious to lose no time in designing and building a dual-purpose pile for plutonium production with power as a by-product. His engineers had already been thinking out their plans for this: instead of the air-cooled pile there would be a pile enclosed in a pressure shell which would make the use of pressurised gas as a coolant safe and practicable. Such a pile could be run at high enough temperatures to raise steam and generate useful power as well as produce plutonium. Hinton proposed to Lord Portal that the total plutonium requirements should be met by building one air-cooled pile and then a second pressurised gas-cooled pile. This pile would take longer but would be a better design in every way; it would be better for plutonium production and would open up entirely new power possibilities. Portal, fearful of the risks in an untried system, replied crushingly. He rebuked Hinton for considering the gas-cooled pile at the expense of the design of the water-cooled one without raising as a major question of policy whether such interference with the project was acceptable:

> I came into this work [he wrote] knowing full well that one of our greatest difficulties would be to judge how far to allow the best to be the enemy of the good. But I did expect that in whatever decision I was called on to make I should have either the engineers or scientists on my side. To find myself in the position where the scientists and engineers are apparently at one in their desire to stake everything on the timely solution of problems on which little or no practical work has been done would be a very unexpected experience. I should be very much happier if I felt that the whole of the production side under me was animated by a single purpose, namely to produce fissile material in substantial quantities at the earliest possible date.

Three months later, supported by Cockcroft and members of the Technical Committee, Hinton again wrote to Portal who still, however, refused to consider any modification to the new plan for two or three air-cooled piles. Neither the Chiefs of Staff nor Ministers were consulted as to whether the urgency of the demand for plutonium for bombs could be relaxed sufficiently to allow this modification, which would have hastened Britain's progress in nuclear power technology. Military needs had given atomic energy its great push forwards but they were now twisting its development.

As it was, Ministers agreed to the plan to substitute air-cooled piles for the single water-cooled pile. It had been proposed that the piles and ancillary plants should be built on the site of the old Royal Ordnance Factory at Drigg in Cumberland. However, a difficulty arose because Courtaulds had already agreed to use the Royal Ordnance Factory next door at Sellafield for rayon production and they claimed that the area could not cope with both organisations. Courtaulds withdrew and the piles then went to the more suitable site at Sellafield, or Windscale as it was called. The refusal to permit a more advanced design for the second pile meant that two 'monuments to our initial ignorance', as Hinton called them, were erected against the Windscale skyline, rather than one.

However, once all these decisions had been reached, Hinton could plan his production schedule in detail. The programme was settled; so now without doubt was the purpose. The plutonium would be used for a bomb.

Appendix 8

ATOMIC ENERGY: AN IMMEDIATE POLICY
FOR GREAT BRITAIN

Memorandum by P. M. S. Blackett

1.1. *Introduction*

In ACAE (45)20, the arguments in favour of Great Britain pressing for some form of full international control of atomic energy are presented forcibly. In the last paragraph of the above paper, the difficulties in the way of attaining this major objective are stressed and the possibility of proceeding by stages is raised.

The object of the following paper is the formulation of a policy for Great Britain, which can be put in operation, in the not unlikely event of failure to attain the major objective at an early date.

Such an interim policy must be based on an analysis, as objective as possible, of the actual political, military and industrial situation in the world at present and as it is likely to develop in the next few years. The essence of the argument presented below is that it is not a foregone conclusion that it is in the interest of Britain to start the manufacture of atomic bombs now, but that this is a proposition to be established by detailed analysis. The arguments presented lead to the conclusion that there is an alternative policy which is likely to lead to more satisfactory results.

1.2. Some of the factors of chief importance for British Policy are the following:

(a) For some years the United States alone will possess a stock of bombs. The outstanding problem is the possible uses to which this stock might be put. The question of disclosure of secrets is of far smaller importance. There is a very understandable pride in the USA in this great technical achievement, and a natural reluctance to dispose of this assumed national asset, particularly in view of their alarm at certain aspects of Soviet policy.

(b) The USSR, though fully appreciating the good intention of the present US Government, must be also well aware of groups in the United States who wish to use these bombs to coerce or to liquidate the Soviet Union (ACAE (45)11, paragraph 23; F.O. Press Summary; *New Times*,* 1st September 1945). They certainly must consider the circumstances of the first use of the bomb, and the fact that no statement was made at the Foreign Secretaries' conference in London about the future of the bomb, as symptoms to be noted with uneasiness.

(c) Looked at through Soviet eyes, the war just concluded has been very profitable to the United States, in that unemployment was abolished, a rise of civilian consumption of 16% achieved, at a loss in killed of $\frac{1}{4}$% of the population.

In contrast, the USSR must consider the war to have been an unmitigated disaster to the Soviet Union, having cost them a very large fall in living standards and a loss in killed of 5% of their population, and a reconstruction problem which will absorb all their industrial effort for many years.

(d) As a consequence of holding these views, the USSR will inevitably take every possible step to avoid another major war. She will certainly strengthen herself against any possible attack and will most likely attempt to produce bombs at the earliest possible date.

(e) Great Britain is not in a power position to exert a very decisive direct influence on this situation, but is in a position to exert a decisive indirect influence, e.g. by adopting a policy such as that advocated in Section 9.

It is in the light of these facts that Britain must formulate a policy, and in particular answer the question; should Britain manufacture atomic bombs for war purposes, and if so on what scale?

1.3. It is essential that Britain's foreign policy be based on a realistic appreciation of our actual military and strategic position. Now it is generally recognised that British Sea Power is now and probably will be permanently very much weaker than American Sea Power, and consequently that British interests, say, in the Pacific, would be defenceless against American attack. Further, there are not now, nor cannot be for many years, any possible allies for Britain strong enough to change this situation.

Similarly, it is equally impossible for Britain alone to defend her

* *New York Times.*

interests in Europe by force against the Soviet land forces; nor are there likely to be any potential allies in Europe strong enough to allow her to do so within the next ten years. Only a full participation by America in a large-scale land war in Europe might be effective. (See Sections 4 and 6.)

In these circumstances, it is essential for Britain to formulate a realistic defence policy. In particular, the value of atomic bombs for the defence of the United Kingdom must be carefully assessed. Clearly to have some, but too few to be effective in case of war, might lead the country into great dangers. Assuming the number necessary for an adequate defence to have been estimated, it is essential to proceed to estimate what additional measures are required to make the United Kingdom secure enough as a base from which the bombs can be launched.

2. *Assumptions as to rate of Production of Bombs*
Many detailed questions on the use of these bombs will have to await the report from the Chiefs of Staff. But it is not possible to wait for their report to discuss the general problem and to outline an interim policy.

For concreteness the discussion will be based on the following assumptions:

(*a*) The United States produce atomic bombs at the rate of some 80 a year, starting in July 1945, and will continue to do so. (Table I)

(*b*) Great Britain could start producing at the rate of 40 a year starting in January 1949. This would imply piles dissipating nearly 800,000 kW, reserved exclusively for weapon production. This seems to be about the minimum which could be held to have any decisive military value in a major war.

(*c*) The USSR will produce at the rate of 40 a year starting in January 1952.

(*d*) No other power will produce for ten years.

The present types of bombs are assumed. The effects of technical improvement are discussed in paragraph 6. It will be assumed that each bomb has the same lethal effect as 30,000 tons of normal bombs (15,000 ton TNT). Thus the assumed production of bombs in the United Kingdom is the equivalent of 1·2 million tons of ordinary bombs a year.

3. *Consequences of these Assumptions*

Since atomic bombs are not required for police measures or minor wars, in fact are peculiarly unsuitable for this purpose (as in Greece, Palestine, India, Java, etc.) it is only necessary to consider the effect of their use in the next decade in a war or threat of war between two or all of the Big Three, US, USSR and Great Britain.

3.1. *War between Great Britain and the United States*

For very good reasons it is usual, and correct, to dismiss such a war as 'unthinkable'. However it is worth considering the purely military aspects of such an imaginary war.

Our assumed permanent inferiority in supply (Table I), combined with our much greater vulnerability makes any production of bombs by us militarily useless, as a *defence measure against the US*.

The fact that the coastal cities of the United States are very vulnerable to atomic bombs launched, say, from submarines can by no means offset the general disparity in supply and vulnerability.

The argument is sometimes used, that the possession of a few bombs, which could be used for retaliation against a much stronger power, would make this country safer. It can as plausibly be argued that the knowledge that a few bombs were being produced would be just as likely to stimulate attack to prevent more being made, as to ward it off.

3.2. *War between Great Britain and the USSR*

Between 1949 and 1952 the United Kingdom would have a moderate stock while the USSR had none; thus Britain could certainly cause heavy destruction of Soviet cities. But Britain alone could not effectively oppose the Soviet land forces. Nor is it hardly conceivable that a group of Western powers could be built up before 1952 which would be able to do so. France is the only potentially strong ally and any attempt by her to engage in such a conflict would be likely to lead to civil war.

After 1952, Britain would become extremely vulnerable to attack by atomic bombs from Soviet occupied territory and from the sea.

If war under these conditions is contemplated, it would be essential to take drastic defensive steps. Since the United Kingdom is too small for effective dispersal, these steps might have to include the housing deep underground of a large fraction of the population and the dispersal of much production and population to the Dominions. Even if realisable in the time available, these measures would mean an expense far greater than the cost of the bombs.

The chief military advantage to Britain of the possession of a hundred or so atomic bombs in the event of war with the USSR would be as a counter to a sea-borne invasion threat. However, it is by no means certain that this would be the most severe threat the United Kingdom would have to face. In fact the only serious possibility of the United Kingdom fighting the USSR is as an ally of the United States. This case is considered below.

4. *War between the United States and the USSR*

After say 1952, when it is assumed that the USSR will have appreciable stocks, the outcome of a war with the United States is difficult to predict, as it will depend on the balance between the greater stock of bombs of the United States and the smaller vulnerability of the USSR.

In the event of the USSR being aggressively minded, she would tend to wait as long as possible, in fact until she had produced at least some bombs, that is, on the assumption of Table I, certainly till 1953.

In the event of the United States wishing to check possible Soviet expansionism in Europe, she would seek to choose a time, say between 1948 and 1951, when she had accumulated a large stock, but before there was much chance that the USSR would have produced any.

That the USSR would capitulate before a threat alone can be excluded as not remotely probable. On the contrary, the reaction of the USSR to the serious use by the United States of the threat of atomic bombs would be in the following directions:

(a) To accelerate to the limit her research into nuclear physics with the object of the rapid production of bombs.

(b) To strengthen her air defence organisation.

(c) To consolidate her influence in all semi-satellite countries from which attack by aircraft or rockets could be made.

(d) To prepare to adopt at the outbreak of war a policy of expanding her effective frontiers to include all possible potential bases from where such attacks might be launched.

The outcome of such a war would depend to a large degree on the

bases available to the United States from which to launch an attack
with atomic bombs, and on the degree to which the USSR can make
her economy less dependent on Baku oil and other vulnerable areas.

It is, however, difficult to suppose that the destruction of many
Soviet towns and factories would prevent the mobilisation of the
Soviet Army and of its advance over most neighbouring territories
on the continent of Europe and in the Near East, and possibly the
Far East also. This could only be prevented if the attack with
atomic bombs were accompanied by the staging of a full-scale
military campaign in Europe with at least 200 divisions. Since
preparations for such a campaign could not be concealed, it is likely
that the USSR would move first, and would attempt to seize the
land areas which might be the base for such a campaign.

Further, any European country, which was faced by the unpleasant choice between occupation by the Soviet force and being
fought over by both Soviet and American forces, might decide that
the former was the lesser of two evils.

Thus the probable outcome of a war between the USSR and the
United States in which the latter used atomic bombs would be to
destroy much of the Soviet homeland, but also to extend Soviet
power over nearly the whole of the European mainland, much of the
Near and possibly also the Far East.

Now the object for which the United States might engage in such
a war would presumably be to prevent the spread of the Soviet
system and to retain as much of the world as possible under the
system of Western Democracy. The probable outcome would be just
the opposite of what was desired.

5. *Possible attitude of United Kingdom in case of War between the
US and the USSR*

Nothing that Great Britain could do to aid the United States by
giving air bases, sending an expeditionary force for Europe, etc., is
likely to prevent the above probable outcome. Great Britain would
quite likely then find herself with Russian forces on the Channel
coast, and it would only be a matter of time before the United
Kingdom would be forced to cease effective military operations.
Much further consideration will need to be given to the military
situation of the United Kingdom, considered as a forward base and
an advanced airfield in a war between the USSR and the United
States, in which atomic bombs were used by either or both sides.

But simple arguments would seem to show that the United Kingdom would suffer far more than either of the two main contestants.

6. *Effect of alternative technical assumptions*
In general, the above conclusions are not very dependent on the precise assumptions about bomb production made in Section 2. However, it is desirable to consider the following alternative hypotheses.

6.1. *The United States predominance is greatly enhanced by one or more of the following developments:*

  (*a*) increased production;
  (*b*) the invention of super-bombs;
  (*c*) by the Soviet production being slower than assumed.

Even under these conditions the possibility that the USSR would capitulate under threats alone can be dismissed. The reaction to the threat could still only be an acceleration of the steps outlined in paragraph 4.
Prediction in the case of actual war is difficult, but it is not unreasonable to assume that the necessary conditions for the *final* defeat of the USSR would be two-fold:

  (*a*) The widespread use of atomic bombs (e.g. a thousand) in a tactical as well as a strategic role, as part of a full-scale military campaign.
  (*b*) The possession of bases from which aircraft would obliterate a large number of cities and factory areas east as well as west of the Urals.

In the next five years or so, the USSR is not in fact likely to be defeated by atomic bombs alone.
The USSR are certainly aware that the dropping of 1·5 million tons of ordinary bombs on Germany was by no means decisive. The equivalent number of the present types of atomic bombs is about 50. The USSR will certainly estimate that her greater area and so her dispersal possibilities, combined with the larger depth for fighter defence, would mean that an enemy would need something of the order of 500 atomic bombs to affect the USSR decisively, without in addition a full-scale military campaign.

6.2. *Russia reduces or cancels American superiority by speeding up production or by some new discovery*

In this case, the United Kingdom is clearly undefendable against the USSR, even with full American help. Further, Great Britain could do little decisive to aid or impede either side, whether she had supplies of bombs or not.

7.   *Should Britain Manufacture Atomic Bombs for War Purposes?*

7.1. *Reaction of the USSR*

If Britain announces that she intends to manufacture atomic bombs, the Soviet Government will certainly assume that they are intended for use against her, probably in alliance with the United States. If Britain makes no announcement as to whether she is or is not intending to manufacture, the USSR will certainly assume that she is, and that they are directed against her.

In both cases, the USSR will inevitably accelerate the steps outlined in 4, i.e. will prepare to adopt an expansionist policy.

7.2. *Reaction of the United States*

If America intends to attempt to use her present superiority to coerce the USSR, then she would be likely to take objection to Britain manufacturing in the United Kingdom, since she might, with whatever little reason, fear a Russian invasion or raid to capture the plants.

The objection would not hold if we manufactured in Canada. However the advantages of doing so seem small, for we become as effectively dependent on the United States as if we did not manufacture at all, but asked for a supply of bombs from American production. If increased production on the American continent is required, this would be much more efficiently done in the United States than in Canada.

7.3. *Reaction of Other Countries*

Most countries other than the United States and USSR are in a somewhat similar position to Britain, in that they are relatively very vulnerable, are in various degrees deficient in industrial resources and have no assured home supplies of uranium. Thus their interests are closely like our own.

It will be readily agreed that it would certainly not be in the interest of a small country near the Soviet Union (e.g. Sweden) to manufacture bombs. It would be very difficult to find convincing arguments that France should do so at the present time. Thus there certainly are some countries which in their own interests should not manufacture bombs; hence there can be no general proposition that atomic bombs are good things for a country to have. The argument for and against must be a detailed one, specific for each country.

8. *Internal Consequences of Manufacturing Bombs in the United Kingdom*

The general effect must be inevitably to retard the application of atomic energy for industrial and other purposes. This will result from a combination in various degrees of shortages of the following factors:

Overall industrial resources
Scientific and technical personnel
Uranium
Dollars to purchase materials, e.g. graphite

It is not possible yet to predict how soon the use of atomic power will be turned to industrial and other non-military uses, nor when its use will become economic. However, the potentialities are so great that in the interests of world prosperity every effort should be made in all countries that have the resources to develop atomic energy for peaceful uses.

To justify delaying the industrial application by manufacturing bombs now, it must be shown that the possession of a supply of bombs of existing types manufactured in the United Kingdom would be of decisive military importance to this country in the next few years.

9. *Conclusions*

From the above analysis we can come to the following conclusions:

9.1. Taking into account, (*a*) the peculiarities of Britain's geographical position, (*b*) the actual military strengths of the Great Powers, (*c*) the actual political situation within the Great Powers, and (*d*) the particular properties of atomic bombs, it is probable that the decision to manufacture or to acquire atomic bombs now would tend to decrease rather than to increase our long-term security.

For the object of having bombs could only be interpreted as a defence against the USSR. Now the special property of the bombs is that they are very efficient for the destruction of cities and civilian lives but relatively ineffective against deployed armies. Their use as a threat is therefore very likely to stimulate the USSR to an aggressive military reaction, not directly against the United Kingdom but elsewhere in Europe. The use of atomic bombs could do little to impede this. The final situation may well be to leave the United Kingdom more vulnerable than before.

9.2. The decision not to manufacture bombs will allow the greatest possible progress in Great Britain in the industrial application of atomic energy. Only if we can retrieve our once leading position in nuclear physics, are we likely to take an important part in these industrial developments. To dissipate our limited nuclear physics resources in copying American techniques of bomb production would be as mistaken as to dissipate our aerodynamic resources on building Super-Fortresses, unless it can be shown that the immediate acquirement of a few atomic bombs (or Super-Fortresses) is essential to our security. If this latter was held to be the case, then clearly we should ask the United States for a supply.

9.3. If we decide not to manufacture bombs, e.g. for a specified term of years at any rate, it is clearly essential to announce it publicly. Otherwise it will be believed that we are doing so, and other countries will be encouraged to start also. If we announce that we do not intend to make bombs, it is equally essential that we make sure that we are believed. This would be best done by requesting inspection by representatives of the United Nations Security Council, irrespective of whether other countries did the same. It is highly probable that nearly all countries other than the United States and the USSR with its satellites, would immediately follow suit, as it is difficult to see any possible advantage, and many grave disadvantages, to any small country participating in an atomic bomb armament race.

If this prognosis is correct, we would soon have set up a system of inspection and control over a considerable part of the world. When this control system was in existence, the groups within the United

States which are in favour of a similar policy would be greatly strengthened, while the groups which wish to use the bomb for coercive purposes would be correspondingly weakened.

9.4. The above policy of inviting inspection implies opening our research and development establishments to inspection by the United Nations [i.e. including the USSR]. This implies that the work of the Research and Development Establishment must be essentially non-secret. But this is just the condition for the most rapid development of our scientific and technical knowledge, and is probably also the only condition on which adequate numbers of first-class scientific personnel would join the establishment.

10. *Future Co-operation with America*

There are two opposed policies which we might adopt with regard to our relations with the United States:

10.1. We might ask to be allowed to continue complete co-operation on all atomic energy projects, including all the most secret aspects of the bombs, and to keep British scientists, as at present, in secret American establishments. In the first place, it seems rather unlikely that the United States would agree to this. And it is certain that we ought not to ask for it, unless as part of a complete pooling of all war secrets, naval, army, air force, biological warfare, etc. To be in one set of secrets but not in another would be dangerous. Militarily, this proposal would mean the close integration of British and American military forces. If carried over into Foreign Policy, this integration might bring great danger to Britain, owing to the totally different geographical and strategic positions of the two countries. Whenever atomic energy impinges on world affairs, we would find our initiative limited, as it is now, and we might well find ourselves tied to policies which we might consider disastrous to our own interests.

10.2. The alternative policy would be to co-operate with the United States to the same degree as with other nations. We would then initiate negotiations with the United States to secure that as much of the scientific and technical work already done should be published. In the event of the policy suggested in Section 9 being adopted, that of inviting inspection, we would base the work of our research and development establishments only on what was published. Full reciprocal scientific co-operation in nuclear physics would then be possible with all countries which came into the system of inspection and control, and full one-way co-operation with the rest.

11. *Recommendations*

It is recommended that, failing a more comprehensive international agreement, His Majesty's Government take the following steps, either immediately or at the latest at the first meeting of the United Nations:

(*a*) Announce that we do not intend to manufacture atomic bombs for war purposes for a specified period of say 5 or 10 years; nor to ask the United States to supply us with any.

(*b*) Announce that we intend to push ahead as rapidly as possible with research and development work towards the industrial uses of atomic energy.

(*c*) Offer unilaterally inspection and control facilities in the United Kingdom and Crown Colonies to inspectors appointed by the Security Council of the United Nations. [For possible control procedures see ACAE (45)20, paragraph 6.]

(*d*) Invite the Dominions and all other countries with similar interests to our own to subscribe to (*a*) and (*c*); our action under (*c*) to be unilateral, i.e. to be independent of how many countries adopt the same policy.

(*e*) Negotiate with the United States as to what information can be published, and base the work of the Research and Development Establishment on what is agreed.

(*f*) State that all future development in the field of atomic energy will be published, but where applicable, will be covered by patents in the normal way.

(*g*) Announce that when the experimental production of a bomb is considered necessary as a part of a general experimental programme, the Security Council will be notified and observers requested.

(*h*) Negotiate with the US as to the distribution of uranium and thorium to countries which (*a*) accept control as outlined above, and (*b*) are considered by a technical panel to be set up by the United Nations as being competent to make use of it.

TABLE I Cumulative Stocks of Bombs assumed in January of each year

	1946	1947	1948	1949	1950	1951	1952	1953	1954	1955
US	40	120	200	280	300*	440	520	600	680	760
UK	0	0	0	40	80	120	160	200	240	280
USSR	0	0	0	0	0	0	40	80	120	160

* 300 in the original document. This must be a misprint for 360.

1947-1951

7 Deterrence Recalculated

The Size and Shape of the Programme

THE British post-war atomic energy programme had begun with the assumption that Britain would want both to make some atomic bombs and also to pursue a broadly based research and development programme with an eye on the future – probably the far future – possibilities of nuclear power. A programme for the production of fissile material had been fixed soon after the war which was in effect a minimum programme for these purposes, but which was also for some time an open-ended programme. Britain was determined to have a native atomic energy programme, but the Government had not decided to go ahead with the actual fabrication of atomic bombs until nearly eighteen months after the war was over.

This decision was not the result of careful strategic calculation but rather the reflex action of a still great power with great military commitments. The atomic bomb was the last word in weapons so Britain must have it, the more so since the only defence anyone could see against an enemy's bombs was the threat to retaliate in kind. At the time the decision was taken, at the beginning of 1947, there was, as we saw, no real fear of war in the next decade at least, and the British Government did not believe that Russia was necessarily a potential enemy. Moreover at the time the decision was taken it seemed enough simply to have a small supply of the primitive type of bomb dropped on Japan, which would for many years to come be carried, it was thought, in aeroplanes.* The remorseless logic of future advances in atomic bomb technology – including the technology of delivering these horrific weapons – was not foreseen at the

---

* Immediately after his return from the Nagasaki operation, Group Captain Cheshire wrote a perspicacious paper on the effects of the atomic bomb on future military planning. He said the critical factor henceforward was not so much the possession of atomic power but rather the ability to guarantee accurate delivery of the bomb; the only foreseeable means of doing this was by space projectile.

time or, if it was, it was not discussed in high quarters. No one except Professor Blackett had seriously questioned whether Britain could in the future expect to keep in the technological race. No one had yet foreseen that the future in such weaponry lay with a new category of super-powers to which Britain could not aspire. Russia was generally believed to be technologically and scientifically behind Britain and was not expected to begin producing atomic bombs until considerably later.

The decision of January 1947 to pursue research and development work for the fabrication of atomic weapons had been taken in the darkest secrecy. Ministers had approved special arrangements with the object of concealing not only the technical details of the weapon and the organisation and methods by which it was to be produced but also the fact that work was being done on it at all. Subsequently a cover plan had been devised to enable action to be set in train without allowing the many people who had to contribute to know the real object of their activities. The work had been put under Lord Portal and under the immediate control of Dr Penney, the Chief Superintendent of Armament Research, and was called High Explosive Research, which sounded a fairly ordinary activity. A special officer had been appointed to Lord Portal's staff with non-secret responsibilities as a cover, whose real job was to act as a focal point for this work. All contacts between Penney's team and the outside world took place through him, and the connection between Penney's work and the Atomic Energy Division in the Ministry of Supply was hidden.

A year later the Minister of Supply – now G. R. Strauss – reported to his colleagues that this arrangement was becoming increasingly ineffective, an impediment to progress and a possible source of embarrassment or even of danger. More and more people had to know about the business and it was becoming unreal to regard as so specially secret, a matter within the official knowledge or well-founded speculation of a large number of people. It was now necessary to enlist the help not just of individuals in various Government research establishments but of whole teams. Moreover problems of location of sites, storage, carriage, and handling and arming of the bomb would now involve much detailed study by the Services. Excessive secrecy was delaying progress since it was difficult for officers, who could not be given an inkling of the real nature of the job they were asked to do, to understand its importance and urgency.

There was a danger that sooner or later some journalist would become aware of the connection between atomic energy and the so-called high explosive research and publish something most embarrassing because of its content or timing. This could not be prevented by issuing a D-notice because it was forbidden to mention the subject to the Services' Press Committee which issued such notices.*

The Minister therefore suggested that a suitable opportunity should be taken for letting it be known that the Government was developing all types of modern weapons, including atomic weapons. He thought that the announcement should be made casually and incidentally and not as a separate and formal statement calculated to attract attention, and that it should be covered by a D-notice to prevent press speculation about the organisation and location of the work, or the individuals, establishments or firms concerned. There was no intention of relaxing any of the security restrictions on information about details of the work. At the Atomic Energy Ministerial Committee, the Foreign Secretary said he had hitherto been anxious to maintain secrecy for political reasons and he wanted to be quite sure no difficulties would arise with the United States if the announcement was made. The Chancellor of the Exchequer suggested it was widely assumed that Britain was making atomic bombs and that there was little point in trying to keep the fact secret. It was therefore agreed that, subject to consultation with the United States authorities, a suitable opportunity should be taken to let it be known Britain was making atomic weapons.

The Ministry of Supply secured the agreement of the Services' Press Committee to the D-notice.† This said that it was important in the interests of national security that there should be no disclosure of information about, or reference to, the following matters relating to the development and production of atomic weapons: the location or progress of work in the United Kingdom on the development or production of atomic weapons; the design, methods of construction, weight and size of atomic weapons which were being developed in

---

* D-notices are explained in Chapter 16. Briefly they are a self-denying ordinance not to publish certain information of military importance. A committee of the press decides whether to accept requests for D-notices from the Service departments.

† This was D-notice No. 25. D-notice No. 12 already banned disclosure of information about the import, export or movement within Britain of uranium or thorium or their ores.

the United Kingdom and the materials being used; the place or places where such weapons were stored; the identification of individuals with work on atomic weapons. It was made clear that the ban was not intended to prevent the publication of statements imputing lack of progress on atomic weapons: the Press Committee would in no circumstances surrender their right to comment on instances of inefficiency or disorganisation they might detect. It was also emphasised that the notice was concerned solely with work on atomic weapons, and that information about general atomic energy research or the programme of production of fissile material were not affected because these were thought to be sufficiently covered by the Official Secrets Act and the Atomic Energy Act.

The Ministry of Defence was irritated by the Ministry of Supply's insistence on a public announcement which amounted to using a very large sledgehammer to crack a not very difficult nut. Their main object was to be able to tell people engaged on research into atomic weapons what they were doing, and this, they thought, could be done by administrative action without any special public announcement. It was after all common practice in Government service for staff to deal with matters of the highest secrecy about which there was no publicity of any kind. The whole atomic energy organisation, said the Ministry of Defence bitterly, 'has a curious "barbed wire" mentality of which this is only one example'. If a statement was really necessary it would be better to let it slip casually rather than by a prearranged question in the House of Commons. However, the Press Committee would only accept the proposed D-notice on the clear understanding that an official pronouncement was made in Parliament and that the Government's attitude on this matter should not be allowed to leak out in an informal way. The Minister of Defence therefore duly conveyed the important piece of information as unostentatiously as possible in a Parliamentary question of 12 May 1948.* These few lines of print were the only inti-

---

* HOC Deb., vol. 450, col. 2117:

    Mr George Jeger asked the Minister of Defence whether he is satisfied that adequate progress is being made in the development of the most modern types of weapon.

    The Minister of Defence (Mr A. V. Alexander): Yes, Sir. As was made clear in the Statement relating to Defence 1948 (Command 7327), research and development continue to receive the highest priority in the defence field, and all types of weapons, including atomic weapons, are being developed.

mation vouchsafed to the public in four years that Britain was on her way to becoming a nuclear military power.

Since the decision at the beginning of 1947 to fabricate bombs, the British atomic energy project had become unquestionably a primarily military affair. As we have seen, many of the scientists and engineers and indeed some officials and Ministers were very conscious of the industrial and power possibilities and already research was going ahead. But this was a diversion, albeit an important one. The leaders of the project – Cockcroft as well as Portal, Hinton and Penney – believed that it was a matter of supreme importance to the nation that it should possess atomic bombs, however few, at the earliest possible moment. This view derived from the Chiefs of Staff, and if the project had not been primarily for defence it would, as the Ministry of Supply said, not have got the steel needed for the plutonium piles.

In 1947 the current strategic outlook had not really supported such extreme urgency. The haste had an element of general national prestige in it and a reluctance to concede atomic monopoly to the United States, besides a professional determination on the part of everyone concerned to succeed in this very difficult job – in producing atomic bombs and producing them to a very tight timetable. In 1947 the international situation was dark but the risk was not so much war as a collapse of Western Europe through economic failure which would leave the way open for the Communists without any need to fight. In 1948 the situation deteriorated. The Marshall Plan and the adverse Russian reaction to it in the summer of 1947 had finally signalised the separation of Eastern and Western Europe. The Cominform Declaration published in October 1947 had proclaimed the doctrine of a world divided into two opposing and conflicting camps. In December the meeting of the Council of Foreign Ministers had broken down. The forebodings of Mr Bevin, the Foreign Secretary, had been growing throughout 1947, and after the Communist coup in Czechoslovakia early in 1948 he finally decided that there was no hope of reaching a satisfactory settlement by agreement among the Big Four or through the United Nations.

Mr Jeger: Can the Minister give any further information on the development of atomic weapons?

Mr Alexander: No. I do not think it would be in the public interest to do that.

The reluctance which still existed in the summer of 1947 to name Russia as a political enemy had vanished. Bevin told his Cabinet colleagues in March 1948:

> It has really become a matter of the defence of Western civilisation or everyone will be swamped by this Soviet method of infiltration. Unless positive and vigorous steps are taken it may well be that within the next few months, or even weeks, the Soviet Union will gain political and strategic advantages which will set the great Communist machine in action, leading to the establishment of World Dictatorship or to the collapse of organised society over great stretches of the globe.

He did not believe the danger of war was imminent provided the opponents of dictatorship could present a really united front and provided the necessary economic means were made available by 'those who have them'.

In June 1948 Russia blockaded West Berlin and for the first time there seemed a real possibility of war in the near, rather than the more distant, future. Hitherto defence needs had come second to the overriding need to restore economic stability, but rearmament now began and defence needs were higher in the order of priority. This in itself did not directly affect Britain's atomic programme because no British bombs could be ready to influence the immediate dangers in Europe. Indeed, even when the Defence Committee itself discussed reports on defence research and production programmes, atomic weapons were hardly ever mentioned in the reports or the meetings.

Nevertheless, as the East–West disagreements and disputes of 1946 and 1947 hardened into the Cold War of 1948, the production of atomic bombs by Britain inevitably took on military urgency. Moreover the Chiefs of Staff apparatus had begun to think in more detailed terms about why they wanted atomic bombs and how many they wanted. Towards the end of 1947 it had been recognised that the atomic programme must now be related to specific and quantitative requirements from the Chiefs of Staff rather than to a general belief in deterrence. The existing atomic bomb programme had been the consequence of a decision to build atomic piles of a certain size. Now it was necessary to change the sequence of reasoning and ask how many bombs were wanted by the military and therefore how much fissile material was required and by what date.

In the general reorganisation of atomic energy committees at the beginning of 1948, a committee had been set up under Lord Portal 'to review the scale of atomic energy production in relation to the requirements of defence' (see pp. 35–7). The first stage in this review was the calculation of the requirements. This process again had two stages. First there was a long factual report based on experts' authoritative statements on the nature of atomic weapons present and future, their potentialities, the effort involved in their manufacture, the means of delivery, their estimated effects on various types of target, and the likelihood of other countries making them and the possible dates. This report was then sent to an inter-Services sub-committee which was asked to estimate the strategic requirements of the number and type of atomic weapons desirable from United Kingdom production. The Chiefs of Staff directed the sub-committee to assume (1) that defence policies were those the Chiefs of Staff had defined in 1947;* (2) Russia and her satellites should be taken as potential enemies; (3) the United States stockpile of atomic weapons would be used in the common effort, but Britain could not count on being allowed to carry United States bombs in British aircraft; (4) in view of the vulnerability of the United Kingdom to air attack, it would be wise to depend more on the accumulation in peacetime of a stock of atomic weapons than on subsequent production in war.

The defence policy as defined by the Chiefs of Staff in 1947 had laid great emphasis on the conclusion that the only means by which Russia could be prevented from using atomic bombs when she had them – assumed to be 1956–7 onwards – was by facing her with the threat of large-scale damage from similar weapons. 'We believe', the Chiefs of Staff had said, 'the knowledge that we possessed weapons of mass destruction and were prepared to use them would be the most effective deterrent to war itself.' The decision whether or not to use these weapons could not be taken now, but it must be a cardinal principle of British policy to be prepared, equipped and able to use them immediately. Thus a high priority was given to the air offensive and to weapons of mass destruction. It was this policy which the inter-Services sub-committee attempted to quantify. They calculated the stockpile of atomic bombs that must be accumulated before 1957 in order to attack simultaneously those targets whose

* See Chapter 6. This policy had been discussed by, but not confirmed by, Ministers.

destruction would have the most rapid and decisive effects on Russia's ability to wage war. A wide range of estimates could be given according to different assumptions about bombing accuracy, loss of bombs before attacking the target, size of reserve stocks and so forth. Tizard thought the whole problem – the selection of target systems for attack and the assessment of the actual number of bombs required – should be further considered by a fresh set of individuals. But he, along with the Chiefs of Staff, was prepared to put an absolute minimum figure on total strategic requirements by 1957, that is, 600 bombs. Then, however, the third assumption which the Chiefs of Staff had given came into the reckoning. What proportion of this total was to be met from the United States stockpile of bombs? The answer, admittedly quite arbitrary, was two-thirds, leaving 200 atomic bombs to be made in the United Kingdom before 1957.

The whole calculation was obviously and unavoidably extremely speculative in the estimates of date, total number and the proportion to come from the United States; and ridiculous as it seemed, the Americans could not utter a single word on the subject. But believing that the figure could not be too large, the Chiefs of Staff asked Lord Portal's Review of Production Committee to take it as the defence requirement. The chief importance was to be attached to production of the required number of bombs by the date specified; the subsequent rate of production was less important.

The review of production was again purely factual. It discussed various practicable methods of increasing production and gave estimates of the financial and economic cost. But its conclusion was daunting: it was regretted that there was no practicable means of producing the number of atomic bombs required by the Chiefs of Staff by the date indicated, and in view of this the Committee itself felt unable to make a specific recommendation. The present production programme was confined to the plant for processing uranium metal, two air-cooled piles, and a chemical separation plant for isolating plutonium and fission products. Approval had been given in principle for a low-separation gaseous diffusion plant subject to confirmation before more than limited expenditure had been incurred (see p. 179). The function of this plant was primarily to economise in the use of uranium and secondarily to help with research into nuclear-powered submarines and industrial power, so that it would not contribute to increasing the number of bombs. This present programme would produce less than half the bombs the Chiefs of Staff wanted by 1957.

How could the supply of fissile material be increased? Bombs could be made of pure plutonium, plutonium mixed with uranium-235, or pure U-235. In practice, the pure U-235 bomb did not seem to have much future because, although less bulky than a plutonium bomb, it required a much larger weight of fissile material and its explosive effect was much smaller. On the other hand a mixed bomb would be equally effective as an explosive and would make a given supply of plutonium go much further. This meant that the supply of fissile material for bombs could be increased by building additional plutonium-producing piles and/or building a high-separation plant to produce highly concentrated U-235.

The most obvious course was to build more piles. A third pile could easily be built on the existing Windscale site and could be producing plutonium by mid-1952. This would make it the more essential to build the low-separation plant in order to economise in raw material by re-enriching the depleted uranium with U-235. The production from three piles would, however, still fall far short of the Chiefs of Staff requirements. The time factor ruled out a fourth pile because the Windscale site could not accommodate it and the ancillary plant and a new factory site would have to be developed. A high-separation plant would mean adding additional stages to the low-separation plant which was already being designed. If a high-separation plant were built instead of a third pile and all the output put into mixed bombs, the stock of bombs by 1957 would be about the same as with a third pile – that is, about half the Chiefs of Staff requirement – but thereafter the rate of production would be 50 per cent higher. 200 bombs would be ready by 1960 instead of 1961. The largest practicable increase in the number of atomic bombs could be obtained by building a third pile and a high-separation plant. The 1957 stockpile would still be only two-thirds of the required number, but this figure would be reached by 1959.

The difference in estimated capital expenditure for the three courses was considerable. A low-separation plant (LSD) would be some £9 million, and a third pile and an LSD £19 million; a high-separation plant (HSD), £33 million; or the whole lot* £41–43 million (since HSD would include LSD costs). All the programmes

---

* In the event the third pile was not built (see p. 291). The LSD cost £13.9 million. The £33.5 million for an HSD was sanctioned by Ministers in July 1951.

would make heavy demands on the labour force, building materials, engineering equipment and electric power. For example, a low-separation plant would place a load of 60,000 kW on the electricity supply system; a high-separation plant a load of 120,000 kW which would necessitate a new electricity station (see p. 178 above).

The Review of Production Committee made no recommendations, although it pointed out that the big combined programme, which would come nearest to meeting the stated requirements by the stated date and would give a much higher production rate thereafter, would also give the country the best equipment for the future development of industrial as well as military uses of atomic energy. However, the cost of deterrence was threatening to become very large. These estimates of the cost of expanding the atomic energy project (and a good many items were left out, as the report said), on top of the existing £41 million programme, looked large compared with a ceiling for defence expenditure fixed at the beginning of 1948 at £600 million.*

The Chiefs of Staff, when presented with these facts and figures, realised that the effect of not reaching the target figure in 1957 could not be assessed since the requirements had been estimated from a number of uncertain factors. But there seemed some evidence that the Americans thought the British estimates of Soviet atomic energy capabilities, which had governed the target date, were too low. In spite of the lack of firm data, the Chiefs of Staff thought it vitally important to increase the size of the overall programme which was so very far short of their admittedly imperfect estimate. 'The bomb', they said, 'is incomparably the most powerful weapon in the world today and its possession in adequate numbers provides the only means in the military sphere of offsetting the enormous Russian preponderance in conventional armaments.' The Chiefs of Staff had always maintained that Britain would have to depend on her lead in science and technique in a war against a country so vast in size and population as Russia. The atomic bomb was the supreme example of this technical and scientific superiority which it was so necessary to maintain, and it was no good relying on the effectiveness of bombs unless there were enough of them. It was essential to go as far towards meeting the stated requirements as was practicable without disrupting other United Kingdom production programmes.

The Chiefs of Staff had economic costs very much in mind, and it

* Atomic energy did not come into the Defence Estimates.

was largely for this reason that they advocated the third pile plus the low-separation plant. The latter was essential for raw material economy and for the future development of power for industrial purposes and ship propulsion. Moreover it would give the essential basic stages for a high-separation plant which might be required later. Nevertheless, even this least expensive method of expanding production would demand 26,000 tons of structural steel, 1,600 tons of precious stainless steel, £1½ million worth of electrical equipment, continuing electrical power consumption corresponding to half the output of a modern power station, and a constructional labour force of 2,500 men employed for five years. Such demands would inevitably adversely affect the export trade. Apart from the capital cost of £19 million, operating costs would be £3 million in 1952, rising to £5 million in 1954 and thereafter. Nevertheless, the Chiefs of Staff believed and assumed that these demands of the atomic energy project on manpower, materials and housing would continue to receive the highest priority.

Ministers were thus asked to agree that one extra pile should be built, that the financial limit of £500,000 should be removed from expenditure on a low-separation gaseous diffusion plant, which had already been agreed upon in principle (see Chapter 6), and that research and development for a high-separation plant should continue. The proposals were considered not by the Ministerial Atomic Energy Committee but by an almost identical Gen meeting with yet another new number.* Ministers were concerned about the demands of the programme, especially upon skilled men, but although they would affect other activities they were not impossibly heavy. The Chancellor of the Exchequer was prepared to accept them on the assumption that the atomic weapon should be given high priority. So the programme was accepted and the highest priority was to be given to its needs.

A good deal of effort had gone into the attempt to reconcile strategic needs and production, but the outcome was not much more rational than the previous situation, if only because of the absolute refusal of the Americans to collaborate in any planning. Lord Portal had argued against Sir Henry Tizard's seemingly crazy

---

* The Committee held only one meeting. Those present were the Prime Minister, Lord President, Minister of Defence, Minister of Supply, Chiefs of Staff, Permanent Secretary to the Treasury (for the Chancellor), Lord Portal, Mr Roger Makins, Mr Michael Perrin.

estimate of atomic bomb requirements in 1947. 'A statement show-ing the production of a certain number of atomic bombs was stra-tegically essential and which was beyond our capacity to produce or finance might lead to the argument that no production should be undertaken since the minimum thought necessary was beyond our means.' The logic was still applicable.

When the decisions about expanding Britain's atomic energy programme were taken at the beginning of 1949, there was great emphasis on the need for exchange of atomic information with the United States. As we shall see, the Minister of Defence had recently sent a formal request to the United States Secretary of Defense for exchange of information about atomic weapons (see p. 259). Now the discussions about strategic requirements of atomic weapons reminded the Chiefs of Staff more strongly than ever that above all they needed information about American plans for the strategic employ-ment of atomic bombs; this subject, the most important military subject of all, had been strictly excluded from the talks that were now being held at intervals between the military planners of the two countries.

Although the exchange of information on atomic weapons and on their strategic use might lead to a reconsideration of the emphasis and size of Britain's atomic energy programme, the Chiefs of Staff were at this stage absolutely clear that Britain could in no circum-stances forgo the right to produce fissile material or atomic weapons and rely instead on the United States to supply them. They suspected that the United States might argue that such reliance would be in accordance with the principles of the Marshall Plan or the new Atlantic security concept. But the Chiefs of Staff were certain that it would be ill-advised to rely on an American assurance of this nature which could be terminated or repudiated at any time. Moreover, said the Chiefs of Staff, it would not 'appear compatible with our status as a first-class Power to depend on others for a weapon of this supreme importance'.

As we shall see, America was about to deploy just such argu-ments, and by October 1949 the Chiefs of Staff were prepared to go much further to meet them than they themselves would have thought credible in January 1949. Britain's belief in independent deterrence as an inherent part of first-class power status had by then been smitten from two sides: firstly by the discovery of the huge strides the United States had made in weapons manufacture, and secondly by Russia's first atomic explosion. The second piece of news was profoundly disturbing. Tizard was one of the many who, reeling from the shock, thought the Russians' explosion must be largely due to spies, and he could only believe that they had stolen some plutonium. He wrote:

> I find it extremely difficult to believe that in the time available the Russians have not only solved the technical problems but have been able to build and operate a plant on a sufficient scale to give them material for a full-scale trial. To make this at all possible they must have been able to acquire absolutely full details of the whole US process. Even though they managed to acquire these details I still find it difficult to believe they have built and operated a plant. We should ask the Ministry of Supply whether they would guarantee to have done so much had they had the fullest information from USA.

Tizard's colleague, the Chief Staff Officer to the Minister of Defence, asked: 'How does it come about that, knowing all we did in 1945, we are still without the atomic bomb by contrast with Russia who starting from scratch have apparently already passed us?'

This amazement was not wholly rational. Estimates of the time Russia would take to make a bomb had varied widely.* General Groves had told a Senate committee soon after the war that if a country worked in secrecy and obtained no aid from the United States, Britain or Switzerland,† it might produce the bomb in fifteen to twenty years. With such aid, it might produce a bomb in five to seven years. In 1944 he had said in a discussion with Professor Oliphant that he thought the United States and Britain could hope to retain ascendancy in nuclear weapons for about ten years following the collapse of Germany. He believed that Russia would have full information about the project, as soon as normal communications between America and Europe were resumed, either through her agents or 'through Communist sympathisers among the American and British scientists on the project'. Given the information, the Russian scientists were fully capable of seeing it through, but he

---

* An explanation was given by the Nobel Prize winner, I. Rabi, when he said how astonished he had been that the Russian bomb came so soon. 'I tell you this was a peculiar kind of psychology. If you had asked anybody in 1944 or 1945 when would the Russians have it, it would have been five years. But every year that went by you kept on saying five years.'[1]

† Sic.

thought that they would be handicapped by the deficiencies of the Russian engineers and technologists, by welding, metallurgy, etc. Scientists had been more realistic. Dr I. Langmuir, a Nobel Prize winner who worked in American industry and knew Russia, gave an estimate of three years, and Hans Bethe, the eminent physicist, gave three to six years. The British committee which had considered the matter just after the war had given three years as a possibility (see Chapter 3) and Field-Marshal Lord Wilson had said 'say five years'. In the following years, different estimates seemed to be in circulation. One in official circles at the end of 1947 said 'a minimum of five years, more likely ten', but a month later January 1951 was given as the earliest date, with 1954 more likely. Yet at much the same time the Ministerial Defence Committee was told that no probable enemy would possess weapons of mass destruction within the next seven, or perhaps ten, years. By the beginning of 1949 there were reports that a minimum of one bomb by mid-1950 was likely, which was not after all far out. When the news of the bomb test was heard, however, David Lilienthal, chairman of the US Atomic Energy Commission, noted that it was much earlier than even the 'most pessimistic' had recently been expecting:[2] the Russians seemed to be two years further ahead than was thought. In this period intelligence methods were still primitive compared with later years, so much so that Lilienthal wrote in 1949: 'in my opinion our sources of information about Russian progress are so poor as to be actually merely arbitrary assumptions'.[3] In Britain, throughout 1947, no Minister or adviser appeared to have had a shadow of doubt that she was ahead of any potential enemy in the development of atomic energy and in science and technology generally. Even though later estimates suggested that Russia might produce a bomb before Britain, the full import of this does not seem to have sunk in. Hence the shock, shared of course with the United States.

When the first explosion came in August 1949 it blew up many illusions about the technical backwardness of Russia. The mid-twentieth-century technological revolution had remorselessly demoted Britain in power ranking, though the graduations between 'first-class' and 'great' were nebulous and not clearly defined. By the autumn of 1949, as we shall see, the British Government were prepared to integrate their atomic weapons production with that of the United States in return for American commitments to supply a certain number of bombs to Britain under her own control. In demonstration of their eagerness and in order not to absorb uranium that the United States needed, the British agreed to drop their third pile and they did not resuscitate it when the negotiations broke down. They insisted on keeping their low-separation gaseous diffusion plant throughout, but they had hoped that if an agreement had been reached they might be able to acquire pure uranium-235 from the United States instead of building a high-separation plant themselves.

The low-separation plant, which was built at Capenhurst in Cheshire, was thus the only addition to the original, 1946, British programme. In 1949, it is true, the decision was taken to establish an atomic weapons research establishment at Aldermaston, but this was simply a re-siting and expansion of Dr Penney's work. Henceforth he was to be split not only nominally but also physically from the Armaments Research Establishment at Woolwich and Fort Halstead in Kent.

Thus the British programme was largely static, and the only point of reference for strategic requirements remained the report produced at the end of 1948 to guide the Review of Production Committee. In the summer of 1951 it was this report which was used as part justification of the proposal to go ahead and build a high-separation plant, which would also involve doubling the low-separation plant. But there were other reasons. Research and development on the high-separation plant had reached the stage where a decision had to be taken whether to build a full-scale plant or not. It was clear that there was now very little chance of getting any U-235 from the United States. Moreover Britain, having committed herself to an atomic weapons programme, was concerned as much with future types of weapons as with quantities, and recent weapons development suggested that U-235 was going to become more important for bombs not only when mixed with plutonium but also on its own. A high-separation plant was an essential part of the atomic energy programme of any first-class power, it was said, since without it half the potential field of development would be closed. The doubling of the low-separation plant would make it possible to produce, in addition, the enriched material needed for developing industrial power and submarine propulsion.

There was some concern that the new plant, estimated to cost £33½ million, would interfere with the rest of the defence and investment programmes. A working party, however, foresaw no major adverse effect, though some existing difficulties, especially with the supply of professional and technical works staff, would be aggravated. The large demand for electricity – 83,000 kW in 1957 – would only be about 0·4 per cent of the capacity likely to be available in that year. Ministers therefore allowed the proposal to go ahead.

Questions of Priority

In 1947 the Prime Minister had issued instructions that everything should be done to avoid delay in meeting the atomic energy programme and any conflicts with other high-priority programmes were to be reported to him.* A year later the Chancellor of the Exchequer had aired his doubts about this priority. Since it was instituted, he said, the balance of payments crisis had become more acute and he thought it wrong that all atomic energy work should continue to get automatic top priority if the country's dollar-saving or food-importing capacity was reduced in the process. The steel requirements of the programme were involving heavy diversion from other vital and more immediate uses. However, the Prime Minister said the priority must remain, although the Ministry of Supply must ensure that demands based on it were not inflated. After the decisions were taken on the revised production programme at the beginning of 1949 – the addition of a third pile and low-separation plant – the Prime Minister issued a new directive:

> I attach to this expanded programme the same high degree of importance and urgency as I attached to the original. . . . I hope nothing will be allowed to interfere with its realisation and that you will let me know at once if any difficulties are encountered. . . . With the sole exception of some scientists, engineers and technicians who will have to be withdrawn from other important projects the effects of demand on other high priority programmes should not be serious.

Nevertheless, in spite of this emphatic endorsement of the atomic project's priority, from now on it was constantly disputed. The protagonist was Sir Henry Tizard, still Chief Scientific Adviser to the Minister of Defence. It may be recalled that he had, back in 1947, felt very strongly about the fact that his Defence Research Policy Committee, which was supposed to advise the Minister of Defence

* Priorities are discussed in more detail in Chapter 14.

and Chiefs of Staff on matters connected with the formulation of scientific policy in the defence field, had no jurisdiction whatsoever over the atomic project. It seemed that he had won a victory when, in the committee reorganisation at the end of 1947, an Atomic Energy (Defence Research) Committee had been set up under his chairmanship to keep under review, and report on, the relation between defence research programmes as a whole and atomic energy defence research. But it was a hollow victory, for it was made quite clear that the only function allowed to this committee was to do everything it could to help supply scientific and technical staff for Dr Penney's establishment. This 'cake-cutting' committee, as it was called, became in practice a recruiting agent on a small scale for Penney and a progress-chaser for housing accommodation. It met rarely, and though the heads of the Service scientific departments complained bitterly about its depredations, its performance did not satisfy Portal, who complained that Penney's requirements had not been met, even though the Chiefs of Staff had told him that they were prepared if necessary to see other work slowed down or stopped.

A letter to this effect was sent just after the Prime Minister had issued his new priority directive in February 1949. Tizard had been in no way consulted about this but he said: 'an order is an order and if it is claimed this order gives Portal the right to demand selected scientists from other branches of defence research I could not dispute it'. But, he said, it would be for the Defence Research Policy Committee to put on record for the benefit of the Chiefs of Staff what effect this would have on progress in other directions. Quite recently, at a conference of Service and Supply Ministers, Tizard's point had got across: a great and increasing proportion of the country's research effort was being devoted to the atomic project and this could only be done at the expense of other vital projects such as aircraft, radar and guided missiles. Yet there was no machinery for looking at all of them together. The Minister of Supply himself had agreed that it was open to question whether atomic energy should continue to have overriding priority.

Tizard was successful in causing alarm among the Chiefs of Staff about the many research and development projects that were held up for lack of resources, and surprise that there was still no machinery for ensuring that these projects and the atomic project were properly related. They realised, seemingly for the first time, that the recent major decisions to increase the atomic programme had been taken by Ministers without full knowledge of their implications for other crucial defence programmes. Or perhaps they had forgotten that at the meeting with Ministers they themselves had said the programme would make unpalatable inroads on other important activities but that this must be accepted.

The Defence Research Policy Committee prepared a strong memorandum for the Minister of Defence. They had long maintained, they said, that it would be futile to attempt to be strong everywhere and that it was essential to determine which were the important projects vital to survival and then concentrate on them. In the non-atomic field the effort available for even these selected projects was wholly inadequate, and there was no hope of all the projects in the highest category of importance being completed by the time they were needed to implement the accepted defence policy. The Committee felt it their duty to point out the facts about this non-atomic research and development – facts which had not been given to Ministers when they made their recent priority ruling. It was clear that Britain might well have atomic weapons before she had either the aircraft to carry them or aids to ensure that the aircraft could reach their target and drop the weapons accurately. Air defence was imperilled because the guided weapons programme was inadequate. There were still vital problems unsolved about the defence of sea communications. Chemical and biological warfare must not be neglected, because of their offensive potentialities and because they might be used against Britain. There was no serious clash with atomic energy in demands for labour and raw materials: the real problem was in the competition for the very scarce high-grade scientists, especially in electronics where atomic energy made particularly heavy demands.

The Prime Minister, the Minister of Defence and the Minister of Supply met with Tizard in May 1949 in yet another Gen combination to consider this. They decided that the Chiefs of Staff must review the whole defence field, atomic and non-atomic, and advise where the nation's effort should be directed. They also agreed that the decision-making machinery should be reconsidered, since the present division of responsibility for advising on defence research and production was so patently unsatisfactory. They thought there was a great deal to be said for ceasing to treat atomic energy as a special subject distinct from all other top-secret defence projects.

In the ensuing review, the views of the Chiefs of Staff fluctuated.

They kept to their basic list of strategic objectives if war should come: to defend the United Kingdom; to take offensive air action with the Allies at the outset; to safeguard essential communications; to hold the Middle East; to assist the Allies to hold Europe as far east as possible. They began by reaffirming their previous opinion on the strategical importance of atomic weapons, and the desirability of giving them the highest possible priority, but they realised the same priority should be given to the means of delivering the weapons, including aircraft and aids to accuracy. Tizard, however, urged very strongly that it was quite wrong to select one particular group of projects such as those connected with atomic weapons and give them overriding priority. He expressed alarm at the lack of progress in many other projects which might well be vital to the survival of the nation, and he believed that equal priority should go to all major defence, research and development projects. The First Sea Lord agreed and the other Chiefs of Staff were for a time inclined to follow suit. They showed a lack of understanding of the atomic programme when they suggested that Harwell alone should be in a special category because the delays in finishing the 'hot' laboratories there were holding up the plans for the vital chemical separation plant. Lord Portal had to point out that the work at Risley and in Penney's establishments was equally important.

Finally, the Chiefs of Staff decided that 'for political and strategic reasons' it was essential to press on with the production of atomic energy and atomic weapons in the United Kingdom. They advised Ministers that the work of Harwell and of the atomic production organisation should continue to enjoy overriding priority. Research and development of the atomic weapon and the means of delivering it (aircraft to carry it and aids to enable aircraft to deliver it with accuracy on a given target), although of the highest importance, must be considered alongside other vital defence research and development projects, but their needs should be met unless the effort required gravely imperilled any of the other projects. It would be necessary to keep the balance of effort between atomic and non-atomic projects constantly under review, and this would be the responsibility of 'Tizard's Committees'. Tizard said at the ministerial meeting that the new policy would make the task of the Defence Research Policy Committee much clearer and much easier. He took the opportunity of mentioning that the Committee at present saw no prospect of adequately meeting air attack on this country by fighters or guns. The only hope lay in the successful development of guided weapons and the Committee was most unhappy about the rate of progress in that field, which called for effort of the same kind as the atomic weapon programme. If the Committee had any difficulty over the balance of effort they would refer back to Ministers.

A revised priority directive was issued. A few days later, however, the first Russian bomb explosion occurred. This, and the arrest in February 1950 of Klaus Fuchs,* the Harwell atomic spy, who had worked at Los Alamos during the war and who had given a vast amount of information to the Russians, led to new heart-searchings about priorities.† Overriding or very high priority had been given to the atomic project in the belief that Britain had a lead over Russia which it was of the utmost importance to maintain. In advocating maximum production of atomic weapons since the war, the Chiefs of Staff had been working on two assumptions. The first was that Russia would be unable to develop such weapons for some years and for that and other reasons was unlikely to embark on premeditated war before about 1957. The second was that Britain therefore had time to develop and produce other weapons vital to her defence as well as atomic bombs. She could therefore give high priority to what was primarily an offensive weapon. What now? There might, the Chiefs of Staff reflected, be a good deal to be said for continuing to give the bomb its present priority. If Russia had the bomb, the greater the lead the West could keep the greater would be Anglo-American ability to deter Russia from starting war, and the greater their ability to win it if it came. Even if the Fuchs case had ended all chances of collaboration with the United States, could Britain afford to abandon the attempt to possess herself of so powerful a weapon when she might one day again find herself fighting alone? This question forgot the long-accepted axiom that Britain could never again fight a major war alone. But in any case, the Chiefs of Staff could find compelling enough arguments on the other side. If Russia had atomic bombs, might not a serious risk of war develop earlier than 1957? If so, Britain had less time to develop defensive

---

* The Fuchs case is dealt with in some detail in Chapter 16.

† The terms of reference of the AE (DR) Committee became 'to keep under review and report to the DRPC on the balance of research and development between the strategic bomber force (including atomic weapons) and other strategic fields'.

weapons on which her survival might depend. At the present rate of progress, was there any chance of Britain being able, in time and on her own, to make a contribution to the Anglo-American pool of bombs such as would enable her to exercise any influence on a war or its conduct? Would she just be making a relatively insignificant number of powerful but obsolete bombs? If so, might it not be better for Britain to concentrate her resources on vital projects to which she was more suited and which were already behindhand – guided weapons, for example?

One person, Sir Henry Tizard, was absolutely clear about his answer to these questions. He had not apparently dissented from the calculations of strategic requirements of atomic bombs made for the Chiefs of Staff at the end of 1948. But during 1949 he had become increasingly anxious, not simply about the machinery for comparing the level of atomic and non-atomic defence efforts and about their relative priority: more and more he was convinced that Britain should not be making atomic weapons at all. The basis of his thought was a realistic appraisal of Britain's position:

> We persist in regarding ourselves as a Great Power, capable of everything and only temporarily handicapped by economic difficulties. We are not a Great Power and never will be again. We are a great nation, but if we continue to behave like a Great Power we shall soon cease to be a great nation. Let us take warning from the fate of the Great Powers of the past and not burst ourselves with pride (see Aesop's fable of the frog).

Tizard was convinced that the economic reconstruction of the country must come before all else.

He disagreed moreover with the general balance of Western strategy. He had formed the impression by the end of 1949 that the Chiefs of Staff could see no way of winning a war against Russia except by the use of atomic weapons. He doubted whether this was a practicable way of defeating her and felt that the attitude to Europe was defeatist. He wrote at the end of 1949 that it was assumed that Russian armies would occupy the whole of Europe in a few months or even weeks, and he thought that such an assumption was intolerable: there must be much more serious planning for land battles and the aim must be to hold Russia on land, not further west than the Rhine. Tizard certainly saw an important place for a strategic atomic air offensive, but he was quite sure that it must be left to the Americans not just in the short term, which was inevitable, but in the long term as well. Britain must opt out of it and concentrate, apart from land forces, on the defence of the United Kingdom; this meant keeping alive research and development on long-range aircraft and atomic weapons but abandoning production of both. The primary objective, he emphasised, was not to win the next war but to prevent it. The real issue was not the race between the scientific and technological resources of different powers but a test of the ability of the democratic nations to work together and plan to spend their resources wisely. It was foolish for Britain to do things that America could do so much better. The Americans' large and increasing stock of atomic bombs, said Tizard, might well cause the Soviet rulers to hesitate to provoke open conflict. 'But how, I ask, do we add to that deterrent effect by letting it be known that we have none but hope to make a few later on' – when moreover the few would be obsolete? Meanwhile, Tizard added, Britain was diverting badly needed capital resources and a high proportion of her most highly skilled manpower to the task. The figures for atomic energy expenditure that were produced appalled him. He disputed the idea that the development of atomic energy on a large scale was going to yield results of first-class importance to industry: to him the chance of doing so within twenty years was extremely remote.

During the early part of 1949 Tizard had been conscious that suggestions for the concentration of atomic weapon production in North America had been greeted 'with the kind of horror one would expect if one made a disrespectful remark about the King'. Before the 1949 tripartite discussions on collaboration began, discussed in Chapter 9, he would have been glad to shut down the project in the United Kingdom and start again in Canada in order to get full co-operation with the United States. He welcomed eagerly, therefore, the United States proposals in the autumn of 1949 for integration of production, and even when they fell through he still felt that manufacture of atomic bombs in Britain was a mistake and that she must rely on the United States capacity for any air offensive. Of the British project only Harwell, he thought, should be kept.

Tizard's views had a good deal of support in the Ministry of Defence, but he did not win over the Chiefs of Staff or indeed other friends. Cockcroft probably represented the views of many of them when he wrote to Tizard: 'I feel that as leader of Western Europe and the British Commonwealth we ought to have some independent power.' Nevertheless, early in 1950 the Chiefs of Staff did hold their agonising reappraisal as to whether, following the Russian explosion, Britain should continue to make atomic weapons. Lord Portal joined in the discussions. The amount of money likely to be spent on the British atomic programme up to the end of 1955 was £154 million and it would employ about 1,500 scientists and engineers. Portal said that in practice a decision to abandon work on atomic weapons would save very little money, since most of the work at Harwell would have to continue and one pile and the low-separation plant would have to be kept on for industrial applications. If scientists and engineers were released from bomb work, the United States would certainly try to skim the cream; some of the key men like Penney might be persuaded to go to the United States if they thought the Government regarded the British programme as of little importance. There was also the question of co-operation with the United States: any further indication of Russian progress would tend to promote collaboration, but the United States desire for collaboration would ebb if British enthusiasm for their own programme receded.

The Chiefs of Staff accordingly agreed it would be wrong to recommend to Ministers that work be stopped on the atomic weapons programme or that the planned scale of production be reduced to a trickle. While the stockpile Britain could accumulate by, say, 1954 was tiny compared with the number of atomic bombs the United States would have, there were strong military reasons, they said, in favour of Britain having a small stockpile of her own. There were also 'strong political reasons', notably the fear that prospects of ever getting an agreement with the Americans would fade as they came to see that Britain had less and less to contribute. However, the Chiefs of Staff agreed that the United States stock of bombs was probably so big that some delay in the British programme could, and should, be accepted in the interests of speeding up work on other vital projects.

They reported to the Defence Committee to this effect in April 1950 and said they did so in the hope of ultimate agreement with the United States to pool resources. Without such an agreement the case for continuing the British atomic weapons programme would be even stronger. This recommendation coincided with a new Chiefs

of Staff review of global strategy, the first since 1947. The keynote
was the interdependence of the Western Allies. The review rejected
any idea that the West could contemplate preventive war and said it
was important not to give the Russians grounds for a degree of
apprehension that might drive them to preventive war. A shooting
war was not regarded as inevitable, or even as likely, provided the
Allies maintained their resolution and built up their military
strength. But the enemy's aim was quite clear, it was asserted: that
is, a Communist world dominated by Moscow. It was essential to
the West's ability to win the Cold War that Allied foreign policy
should not be cramped by the fear that if they went too far they
could not defend themselves against armed attack: an increasingly
offensive strategy in the political and economic fields was needed. In
this respect, Western superiority in atomic air power and the
security of the United Kingdom against air attack were vital. The
Allies should concentrate research and development on defensive
weapons to ensure survival, and on offensive weapons to carry the
war into the interior of Russia. The ability to achieve Allied aims
without active hostilities depended, it was said, largely on the threat
of atomic weapons, which would also be of decisive importance in a
shooting war. As far as the British share in the military side of this
strategy was concerned, the top priorities were her own air defence,
security of North Atlantic sea routes and her commitments to
Western Europe land defence. In research and development terms
this meant that the first priority would go to guided missiles, aids
to improve tactical aircraft, sea defence and anti-tank defence:
atomic energy would be downgraded to a second priority.

The Minister of Supply did not dissent from the strategy but he
dissented from the alteration in priorities which, he said, would be
more harmful to atomic energy than the Chiefs of Staff realised.
The classes to have A priority were very wide, so that atomic energy
would be bottom of the list. It was, the Minister said, a fallacy to
suppose that work on atomic weapons could be slowed down by loss
of priority without wrecking the programme. The real experts in
atomic weapons were few, and if it was known the Government no
longer regarded the work as of supreme importance the staff would
drain away and the programme be ruined. The loss of these men
would make agreement with the United States impossible. Moreover, if the United States knew the atomic project had low priority
they would not agree to allocate raw material for it.

At the Defence Committee, Tizard urged again the reduction not of the research side of the atomic project but of production, whether of fissile material or weapons. The Minister of Supply pointed out that if basic research and development, including the first bombs, were maintained, the release of resources would be small, and it would take perhaps two years to re-expand the programme if this became necessary later. The Prime Minister himself said the question of priority for the atomic weapons programme was not entirely a military problem and that it would be a mistake to make any change in the existing arrangements without the most careful consideration. Ernest Bevin wished to make it quite clear that he would not be a party to any change which would lead to a slowing-up in the development of atomic energy in the United Kingdom. He spoke not only of the production of weapons. He saw atomic energy as the foundation on which the future industrial strength of the country might well depend. He was sure that it would not be good for the world if Britain surrendered to the United States the monopoly of so great a source of power. The Minister of Defence insisted, however, that because of the paramount strategic objective of defending Britain from atomic air attacks, the guided weapons programme must have the maximum boost, if necessary at the expense of the atomic energy programme. In the end, guided weapons and the atomic project received joint overriding priority and a new directive was issued.

Lord Portal had in effect won, and he withstood new attacks on his project in 1951. In February of that year the Chiefs of Staff had suggested in a report on the new defence programme that work on the development of the atomic bomb might have to be slowed down so that some of the staff could be transferred to other more immediate defence work. Portal immediately asked them to reaffirm unequivocally atomic energy's top priority. This was done, with the qualification that it would continue 'so long as conditions remained the same'. The staff in the atomic energy project had not found Lord Portal dynamic in his role as their controller, but in his own former citadel, the Chiefs of Staff Committee, he was imperious and triumphant. There were political and military arguments for a British atomic project, but it is doubtful that they would have justified the high priority they got, especially against the vehement advocacy of Tizard, if it had not been for Portal. The political and military arguments mattered to him, but his project, this extraordinary collection of gifted scientists and engineers, had developed its own momentum and its very existence had almost become the reason for its existence. Portal was determined to defend it to the limits of his considerable capacity.

One of the strangest elements in this story is that although the Chiefs of Staff visualised atomic bombs as part of the air striking force, they did not, except briefly in 1946, invest the development of the aircraft to deliver them with the same overriding, almost mystical, priority. Nor indeed is there any evidence that Lord Portal, ex-Chief of the Air Staff as he was, pressed them to do so. The 1946 report of the Joint Technical Warfare Committee of the Chiefs of Staff had included a recommendation that the development of high-performance long-range bombers must proceed on the highest priority, and the Cabinet's Defence Committee had approved the report (see Chapter 6). But the Prime Minister did not suggest the inclusion of these aircraft in his first priority directive. In 1947 the only priorities meted out, apart from the overriding priority for atomic energy, were for civilian items, and at the beginning of 1949 the Prime Minister reaffirmed the supreme importance of atomic energy, mentioning no other competitors for priority (see Chapter 14). The Air Ministry had specified in 1946 the new high-performance bomber – later to be called the V-bomber – and development contracts for three different models were let to three different firms between the last months of 1947 and the spring of 1948. However, economies were being sought in defence expenditure while current defence needs all over the world were pressing. In the circumstances the new bombers, which were essentially long-term, did not enjoy a high priority even within the RAF's own immediate plans.

We have seen that, as 1949 drew on, Tizard in particular had pointed out the absurdity of having different priorities for atomic bombs and their delivery systems. Finally, in September 1949, the Prime Minister had issued the directive giving the topmost priority to Harwell and Risley and equal importance just below that to research and development on the atomic weapon and the means of delivering it. Thereafter aircraft disappeared again from the top-priority class, for in the summer of 1950 the Defence Committee had decided simply that guided missiles should have priority equal to all aspects of the atomic energy project, a ruling that lasted for the rest of the life of the Labour Government.

Partly because of the lack of priority and the overload on the aircraft industry, none of the three prototype V-bombers was ready at the end of 1950, while the plans for the next three years' expenditure on the forces still included no provision for the build-up of the effective bomber force which Britain did not possess. It was only at the end of December 1950 that the first production order was placed for 25 Valiants, the most orthodox model of the three aircraft. The first Valiant prototype did not fly until May 1951 and crashed in January 1952. The second prototype flew in April 1952 and was grounded six months later after an accident. All three V-bombers suffered the delays and postponements invariably associated with new aircraft. It had been hoped that the first Valiant production delivery to the RAF would be in 1953–4, but the first aircraft did not go into service until January 1955 and the first squadron was not operational until 1957, the year when the delivery of the first production aircraft of the two other V-bombers began.*

The first production model atomic bomb had been delivered to the RAF in November 1953. This gave time to build up a stock of bombs for equipping full squadrons with them. However, enormous pressure had been exerted to produce the first bombs and the fissile material for them as soon as possible, both as a deterrent and as a symbol of power status: the inability to deliver them must have diminished this effect. If the bombers had been ready first they could still have served a potentially useful military purpose, armed with conventional bombs. Atomic bombs without aircraft suitable to carry them could serve no immediate purpose. The atomic project had enjoyed higher, longer and more consistent priority than the aircraft, while modern aircraft design – the problems of the engine, the airframe and the equipment – is notoriously uncertain. Nevertheless, the task of developing the production of fissile material and the bomb itself was also fraught with many and great complexities, and the hiatus between the delivery of the first bombs and the first aircraft to carry them emphasises the successful execution of the atomic project.†

---

* Development of smaller atomic bombs meant that the Canberra, which was not designed as an atomic bomber, could also carry them. From March 1950 the British received American B-29 (Washington) bombers, but these did not carry atomic bombs.

† See Chapter 14 for figures of costs.

Towards Nuclear Power

So the atomic project went ahead and received its overriding priority and its immediate impetus because of the need, military and political, for atomic bombs. It would not have got anything like this priority simply for its as yet unproven potential as a source of industrial power. But as we have seen, the industrial possibilities were very much in the minds of Ministers and officials and even the Chiefs of Staff; Ernest Bevin was especially impressed by them. It was clearly understood that much atomic research and the processes for producing fissile material were common to both the military and industrial uses of atomic energy. When in 1950 and 1951 the question was seriously asked whether Britain should continue to make atomic bombs, no one, except possibly Tizard, doubted that whatever happened she must keep not only Harwell going but one pile and the low-separation plant as well, because of the power possibilities.

Already research into these possibilities was being pursued with as much vigour as military needs and the availability of equipment and materials allowed. As we have seen, Hinton was very anxious in 1947 that he should be allowed to design one of the Windscale piles for the production of power as well as plutonium. When this was denied, Hinton was somewhat reluctantly allowed by Lord Portal to continue the theoretical work already done on such a design; perhaps Portal did not realise how small was the effort devoted to the work. The first design study of a natural uranium power reactor was done under the guidance of two or three men in the Risley Technical Section who had the Parolle Electrical Plant Company* working with them under contract and supplying most of the manpower and the know-how on the power plant side. This work continued during 1948 and 1949, but when the programme for the production of fissile material was increased in 1949, following the report of Portal's Review of Production Committee, Risley were unable to take the work any further and the whole business was put into cold storage. Meanwhile Harwell had been separately pursuing their interests in nuclear power, and by the end of 1949 they were reporting on design studies of four main types of power piles all with a variety of coolants, moderators and fuel cans. These discus-

---

* A subsidiary owned jointly by C. A. Parsons Ltd and A. Reyrolle Ltd. See Chapter 19 on nuclear power schemes.

sions are dealt with at length in Chapter 19. The only high-level review of nuclear power in this period was one in 1950 from a special committee of the Advisory Council on Scientific Policy (see Chapter 2). This committee had been set up at the beginning of 1948 under Chadwick's chairmanship, in the course of the Prime Minister's reorganisation of atomic energy committees, and was to advise on the civil uses of atomic energy; at the end of 1949 the Lord President of the Council had asked it to report on the possible uses of atomic energy and its economic importance.

The material for the paper was provided by Harwell and the Technical Committee. The report said that the most promising line of development for power was a natural uranium high-temperature reactor. A system of this type feeding the country's total current electricity requirements would need 800 tons of uranium a year,* and this meant that there would have to be intensive development of new ore supplies. On the basis of estimates of the cost of low-grade South African ore, and assuming the reactor could run for twelve years on one fuel charge, the net cost of the electricity generated should be about the same as that from coal-fired stations.† Many technical problems remained to be solved, but a small experimental reactor ought to be working in about five years, full-scale experiments might begin in ten years and a number of power stations might be completed in fifteen years.

The second line of development described in the report was the fast breeder reactor, which was attractive because of its very efficient consumption of nuclear fuel and its possible use of thorium, cheaper and more abundant than uranium. Breeder reactors could supply the total United Kingdom power requirement from about only 80 tons of uranium a year, but the cost of power would probably be high. There were greater technical difficulties to solve than with natural uranium power reactors and safety risks were far higher. Development of this type of reactor would probably take some twenty to thirty years. Immediately after the war, hopes of nuclear power had been pinned primarily on fast breeders. Now the

---

* Assuming a 'burn-up' of 1 per cent of the uranium and 25 per cent efficiency in converting heat to electricity.

† Allowing for the amortisation of the whole cost of the reactor plus the fuel, but excluding the amortisation and operating costs of the conventional parts of a power station (and presumably excluding extra transmission costs from remote sites).

development period was likely to be so long that attention was increasingly swinging to the intermediate generation of natural uranium power reactors.

In general, unless there was the prospect that atomic energy might ultimately be capable of satisfying an appreciable part of the country's heat and power requirements, it would not be worth developing on an industrial scale. Atomic energy seemed to promise no revolution in the cost of power even if it was likely to be competitive with coal. Its value as an alternative source of power seemed to hinge largely on the availability of supplies of other fuels. One of the Labour Government's most intractable problems throughout its term of office had been inadequate coal production, and official estimates were that Britain's coal reserves would not last more than two hundred years. Oil was not even mentioned: petrol was still rationed and here too world supplies seemed exhaustible.* It was not surprising that the prospect of atomic energy for power seemed attractive even though its immediate advantages in terms of cost could not justify the huge capital investment that would be needed to develop it.

There were some complaints that the report of Chadwick's committee had dealt with the subject too much in technical rather than in economic terms. In fact its forecast of the time scale for power development and its order of magnitude of relative costs was to prove remarkably good. Nevertheless, it was Sir Henry Tizard who, as chairman of the main Advisory Council on Scientific Policy, sent the report forward to the Lord President. He had for long been almost as sceptical about British atomic power as about British atomic bombs and felt that its importance as a source of heat and power in the next twenty to thirty years was very much exaggerated. Could Britain, he asked, afford to put all this money and effort into it in view of the needs of other branches of industry and defence? Now he emphasised to the Minister that while costs might compare favourably with coal, the initial capital cost was very heavy and atomic power stations did not seem a very attractive proposition in a

---

* The Ridley Committee Report in 1952 (Cmd 8647) doubted whether oil supplies could expand to meet the energy shortage foreseen. It was unlikely that oil would be competitive in price with coal, except in a limited number of cases, and also uncertain whether the oil companies would be willing to expand production to meet what might well be a demand created by short-term coal shortages.

country with abundant coal supplies. However, they could be useful in some areas overseas where fuel was scarce and expensive. In any case, they would be developed in the United States and elsewhere; Britain ought not to be left behind in this important field of technical and economic progress.

In September 1950, soon after this report was passed on by the Advisory Council on Scientific Policy, there was the first important conference at Harwell to discuss natural uranium power reactors with representatives of the Ministry of Fuel and Power, the British Electricity Authority and industry. The main paper at the conference was a report (see Appendix 23 and Chapter 19) on the economics of such a proposition by a Harwell engineer, R. V. Moore. He compared generating costs in an average coal-fired station and in a natural uranium power station and described the part which nuclear power could play as an alternative source of energy taking effect in the last quarter of the century. A scheme of combined power and plutonium production seemed feasible, in which the power system would be financially self-supporting and plutonium could be carried forward free of cost to provide fissile material for more advanced breeder reactors. Moore pointed out, however, that even if generation cost nothing, the price per unit could not be reduced by more than 40 per cent because of transmission and distribution costs. The conference concluded that there was every possibility that natural uranium power would be no more costly than coal power and that there was a strong case for further investigation with a view to building a pilot plant.

Hitherto the natural uranium reactor had been low down on Harwell's list of priorities. Their chief concern had been the fast fission breeder reactor because of its long-term promise. Another project with high priority had been a submarine reactor, that is, a small reactor using enriched uranium; in 1950 a one-year contract for a design study was given to Metropolitan-Vickers, but this project was discontinued as the design study resulted in a reactor which would be impracticably large. The Harwell Power Conference had brought gas-cooled natural uranium power reactors to the forefront as an immediate focus of study. As we shall see, in 1952, after the Labour Government had left office, the whole power business was to go forwards on these lines.

The spade-work, the clearing of minds about nuclear power, had been done in the first five post-war years at a time when military objectives were supreme in atomic energy. At the same time, the military programme was providing the basic requirements for atomic development in terms of fissile material. It had distorted the power programme, but when the Labour Government left office the first lump of British plutonium was near to being made and plants for separating uranium-235 were being built. The first stage of Britain's atomic project was almost complete and her first atomic bomb was soon to be exploded.

8 The Anglo-American *Modus Vivendi*

In January 1947 the British Government had finally embarked on manufacturing its own nuclear deterrent. It had done so at a time when Anglo-American collaboration had broken down completely except in raw material procurement and when Anglo-American relationships in general seemed at their nadir. As we have seen, the question whether Britain would have been so determined to make bombs if she had been offered American bombs under her own control is too hypothetical to be worth an answer. Failure to secure American collaboration ensured that Britain's deterrent would be independent, but it was not the reason why Britain was determined to possess it.

Britain remained resolved, however, to work for a resumption of Anglo-American atomic collaboration and was prepared to forswear any co-operation, however small, with the Dominions (other than Canada) or any European country as part of its price. However, in the years 1947 to 1951 such collaboration never reached a point where it radically affected Britain's policy of an independent deterrent. British production plans had gone ahead on the assumption that the British deterrent would be only very minor compared with the United States strategic air offensive, but Britain was not even given enough information about this strategic plan to calculate rationally her own nuclear role. How had this come about? What had happened to Anglo-American atomic collaboration between 1947 and 1951? This chapter and the next are concerned with this question.

Between the middle of 1947 and 1951 the Anglo-American special relationship, which had wasted away after the war, was renewed. In January 1947 General Marshall, a good friend of Britain, had become Secretary of State instead of the hostile Mr Byrnes. In June 1947 the Marshall Plan had been launched and Britain had played a major part in organising the European response; and as East–West tension grew, America and Britain drew still closer together. Ernest Bevin's hopes of sustaining Western Europe against Russian pressure had fastened on a Western European system organised by Britain and backed by the material aid of the United States, a system which should develop a power and influence equal to that of the United States and Russia. Bevin believed strongly that it was for the British as Europeans to give the lead, spiritually, morally and politically, in Western Europe, to help in forming what he himself called a Third Force. The Western European Union remained a dominant theme of Bevin's policy, but he always saw it within the framework of an alliance with the United States. As military requirements became more compelling, the importance of this alliance grew and Britain's relations with the United States took increasing rather than diminishing precedence over relations with Europe. In June 1948, as Berlin was blockaded and the airlift began, the United States was allowed to station strategic bombers in the United Kingdom. The pact establishing the North Atlantic Treaty Organisation was signed in April 1949. In economic, military and foreign affairs there was again much Anglo-American collaboration and much joint planning. The collaboration and planning were sometimes as great as they had been during the war – for example in foreign affairs – sometimes imperfect and in some cases, for example research and development in guided missiles, positively bad. But nowhere was the failure of collaboration as complete as in the field of atomic energy.

Why did atomic energy remain the big exception to this new intimacy? For a time it had looked as if the new spirit in Anglo-American affairs was going to produce a new era of atomic collaboration. As we saw, the men now at the head of the US Atomic Energy Commission and the State Department were friendly to Britain. During 1947 cheering news had filtered through that they were seeking an interpretation of the McMahon Act which would permit co-operation. Since the preamble to the Act emphasised that its purpose was the defence of the United States, could not information be passed to the United Kingdom if this was in the interests of American defence and security? The idea was promising, but the American who had told the British about it warned that 'this egg would have to be sat on by a good many more senior and responsible hens before it could hatch and even then it might prove to be addled'. Meanwhile one obstacle to co-operation with America was cleared away: the Joint Congressional Committee on Atomic Energy had been told in secrecy about the existing Anglo-American-Canadian agreements. Thereafter the possibility of new agreements could be discussed less surreptitiously in Washington.

The first major step forwards came in November 1947, when Carroll Wilson, General Manager of the USAEC, suggested to Cockcroft, who was visiting America, that they should run over various areas of mutual interest to particularise the sort of information Britain needed: 'the log-jam might break' in the next week, he said. It appeared that after long weeks of discussions about new collaboration arrangements, the business had come to the crunch because some Congressional leaders were asking embarrassing questions about the supply of uranium in the context of the Marshall Plan. The British did not realise that the main reason for the American anxiety for talks was their determination to get their hands on the uranium which Britain could claim under present arrangements. It is true that General Marshall, who was in London in December 1947, wrote a cryptic note to Mr Bevin referring to the stockpiles of ores in the British Isles, saying 'what we need urgently in *the near future* is more of such which you have'. At the same time Roger Makins felt bound to warn the American Ambassador, who was saying that the British would be asked to transfer part of their stockpile of uranium to the United States. 'Any suggestion that valuables were not safe in this island', he stated, 'was one we could not for a moment admit.' In Washington the American authorities were talking in far stronger terms. They had apparently agreed that they would 'strive to abrogate the wartime agreements, to acquire British ore stocks, to get a much greater share of Congo production, to restrict the storage of raw material in Britain to a minimum and to obtain British and Canadian support for ore negotiations with South Africa. In return the United States would give some information.'[1]

The British saw a warmer, less calculating side of the Americans. Their probings in Washington revealed that the State Department was also relating atomic energy to its general political strategy towards the Russians. It seemed that the State Department, the Defense Department, the USAEC and the members of Congress who were consulted all favoured a new and more liberal construction of the McMahon Act in which Britain and Canada might not be the sole beneficiaries. The presence of a strong Communist element among the French scientists made it unlikely that co-operative arrangements could be expanded to include France, but they might well cover Belgium. It was not contemplated that henceforth the tripartite relationship should be exclusive.

Again the constitutional difference between the United States and Britain was apparent. Just as the Joint Congressional Committee on Atomic Energy had been told of the tripartite agreements, about which Parliament had no information at all, so now it was this committee that agreed in December 1947 to the opening of discussions with Britain and Canada: no back-bench Member of Parliament and very few Front Bench Ministers knew anything of the business. After the long delays the Americans now showed frantic haste to begin the discussions, and the British Embassy urgently called for representatives and instructions to be sent to Washington. London replied that they must get ministerial approval for the conduct of the discussions and added they were sure 'the Americans will understand that we are not (repeat not) hanging back but that they must give us at least two days to consider issues which they have been milling over for two years'. Officials quickly drew up a brief which Ministers accepted. Everything was to be done in the greatest secrecy,* for in the present state of international tension it was most undesirable that there should be any suggestion that the United States, Canada and Britain were ganging up in atomic energy.

The secrecy was so great that Lord Portal was not allowed to go to the Washington talks lest his visit arouse comments. In view of the emphasis on technical information for the production of fissile material, it is surprising that nobody from Hinton's organisation was asked to go to America.† John Cockcroft, Roger Makins of the Foreign Office, and David Peirson of the Ministry of Supply were rushed there under various cover stories. They had been briefed to work for a general settlement on the lines of the draft agreements proposed in February 1946 by the Groves–Makins–Pearson committee (see p. 96). The British negotiators were to be accommodating over raw materials while insisting on an allocation that would enable Britain to build up a stock of material. But no agreement on

---

* At this time, however, Donald Maclean, who later defected to Russia, was on the staff of the British Embassy in Washington, dealing with atomic energy affairs.

† There was moreover very little consultation with Hinton about the items to be included.

the allocation of materials or anything else could be signed unless it included satisfactory arrangements for the exchange of technical information; exchange of information about weapons was desirable as well as about production of fissile material if the possibility arose. Meanwhile, remembering earlier exchanges with the Americans, officials and Ministers were adamant that their representatives must resist any suggestion that might directly or indirectly limit freedom of action to construct plants, or accumulate uranium or weapons, in the United Kingdom. The British must remain the sole judges of what was, and was not, in the interests of their national security. Meanwhile it was hoped that a settlement would provide for limited atomic co-operation with the Dominions and with Belgium.

The talks were launched at a meeting of the Combined Policy Committee on 10 December 1947, where Mr Lovett, the Acting US Secretary of State, and indeed his whole team seemed to show every sign of wanting to reach a fresh and fair understanding. They wanted a document to replace the wartime agreements of Quebec and Hyde Park which had no agreed interpretation and were a source of friction. They wanted to put on a single piece of paper a new understanding covering exchange of information, raw materials and political aspects so that in future all three Governments would 'play from the same score'.

Makins was especially struck by the forthcoming and friendly spirit of the Combined Policy Committee compared with the atmosphere at the time of his own departure from Washington ten months earlier. He attributed the improvement to a variety of causes. The friends of Britain were, he confirmed, in the ascendant in Washington while the USAEC itself was now firmly in the saddle and self-confident. The United States wanted to draw closer to Britain and Canada in defence as the international outlook darkened and as their anxiety about raw materials for their atomic weapons programme increased. There also seemed to be a genuine desire to pool information and technical experience; for example, the report of a small team of American scientists that had seen the Medical Research Council's work on biological effects of radiation in England had hastened the United States' wish to collaborate.

In this generally favourable atmosphere, working parties were set up to settle the details about the exchange of information and the allocation of raw materials. John Cockcroft worked with the scientists Vannevar Bush and James Fisk from the United States

and with Dr Mackenzie from Canada on the exchange of information. The British had understood that the Americans had hoped
to get over their legal difficulties by defining areas of collaboration
where it could be shown to be in the United States' interest to exchange information. Cockcroft had therefore brought with him a
tentative list of fourteen topics for technical collaboration, and in the
course of three meetings held in two days after his arrival the group
reached agreement. Officials in London, meeting on a Sunday to
discuss the details, were not very happy. Two new topics had, it was
true, been added, including one that was to be important – the long-
range detection of atomic explosions. But other topics had been
excluded. The final list did not appear to meet any clear criteria; it
simply comprised all those topics which the Americans thought they
could justify to the Joint Congressional Committee in terms of the
McMahon Act, that is, items where the British had something to
contribute immediately. There was thus no possibility at present of
information exchanges about gaseous diffusion, or future reactor
systems, or thermonuclear reactions, or basic operating experience in
production piles, or plutonium metallurgy. It was intended that the
exchange of information should be a continuing process of interpretation with new topics introduced from time to time, but there
were no specific promises. However, since Cockcroft believed that
the British would now get everything that would be of real practical
value to them in the next twelve months, officials in London
reluctantly accepted the list.

Sir Henry Tizard called a meeting of his own because he felt
strongly that the list was inadequate. He pointed out that there
would be exchange of information only on matters of fundamental
science, where the British might have as much to give as to receive,
and on a few matters of technology not of the highest importance
for defence nor indeed for possible civilian uses. He wanted the list
extended to include information about atomic weapons, bomb
mechanisms, and bomb storage and use. Portal re-emphasised, however, that if the negotiations were not to be fatally prejudiced, the
exchange of such purely military information must be discussed
separately with the Americans.

The list of topics for technical collaboration endorsed by the
Combined Policy Committee thus comprised the following (all
subject to the general principle that classified information should be
given only when it was currently usable by the recipient):

1. Topics listed in the proposed declassification guide as being suitable for immediate declassification. For the most part these topics were either basic studies and general theory or peripheral. The topics were carefully defined and hedged by warnings against giving information which could lead to further disclosures of secret information.

2. The entire field of health and safety, including work on radiation tolerances, genetics, therapy of over-exposures, reactor health hazards including effluents and toxic materials, and instrumentation.

3. Research use of isotopes; this covered mutual exchange of isotopes for general research purposes.

4. Fundamental nuclear and extra-nuclear properties of all the elements, including experimental methods and instruments, e.g. particle accelerators, detection devices.

5. Detection of a distant nuclear explosion, including meteorological and geophysical data, instruments, air-sampling techniques and analysis.

6. Fundamental properties of reactor materials, including moderators, fuel elements, structural materials, liquid metal and other coolants, the reactions of materials to radiations, and the preparation of moderator materials such as graphite and heavy water.

7. Extraction chemistry, including the basic chemistry of processes, problems of scaling-up laboratory methods, techniques of remote control, and concentration and storage of fission products.

8. Design of natural uranium reactors in which the power generated is not wasted, and the economy of operation including schemes for enrichment of depleted fuel for reuse.

9. General research experience with low-power reactors (at Clinton, Argonne, Chalk River and Harwell).

Since definite arrangements for information exchange had been fixed only on a short-term basis, it seemed all the more important that Britain should make only short-term commitments about raw material allocations. The British negotiators in Washington were told to stand firm on the original formula. This was that Britain should keep all the stocks of Congo uranium that were actually in the United Kingdom, whether already allocated to Britain or not, and simply promise the United States the total 1948 supply of Congo ore plus the 700 tons in course of shipment – the latter in exchange for some fissile material which would enable Britain to study plutonium metallurgy herself, since exchange of information here was being denied.

The Americans contested this proposal vehemently on grounds of sheer military need. With worsening international relations, the Department of Defense was increasing its requirements for atomic bombs, but the USAEC was facing an acute raw materials shortage which would restrict production: according to detailed figures given to the British, net uranium stocks in their pipeline were down to danger level, and must be reinforced. The Americans insisted on some principle of allocation which would assure the minimum operating level of United States plants in 1948 and perhaps 1949, with an adequate cushion of reserves. They felt that in these circumstances horse-trading was inappropriate.

The business was so important that Cockcroft, Makins and Peirson all recrossed the Atlantic for a meeting of the Official Atomic Energy Committee two days before Christmas. The cordial atmosphere in Washington and the successful negotiation of the agreement on exchanging information had put the Committee in a more generous mood on raw materials. They attached major importance to the statement at the Combined Policy Committee by the US Secretary of Defense, Mr Forrestal, affirming that the United States regarded Britain and Canada as partners in a common defence policy. Moreover in these negotiations the Americans had for the first time been completely frank, producing detailed figures about their programme, their stocks of raw material, their future needs and the purposes to which they were related. The British had done the same and had found that the Americans no longer questioned the existence of a British production programme and the location in Britain of plants and stocks of material. This seemed a great step forwards. The Americans might be no more than resigned to these facts of life, but they were now prepared in effect to assist and underwrite the British programme and to accept the target dates for the stages of its implementation. In the raw material negotiations the Americans had made no attempt to use Marshall Aid as a bargaining counter, although they emphasised that as the Joint Congressional Committee saw the connection only too well, the Administration must be able to defend the allocations. They would be unable to defend the British proposals, which would mean that United States stocks would be down to three weeks' supply at the end of 1949 while British stocks would be enough for five years' production. Moreover the stocks of material in Britain, which she claimed, did not belong to her but were held on joint account. The Canadians on their side had said categorically that they regarded the British raw materials proposals as untenable and inequitable.

Clearly, no agreement on anything at all could be reached unless His Majesty's Government were prepared to concede in principle that some of the material in Britain could be released to the United States. The basic principle of the formula proposed in Washington was mutual support of the agreed minimum programmes of the two countries with pipeline stocks and reserves calculated on an identical basis. The requirements of each country would be set down for 1948 and 1949. If in these years current deliveries from existing sources of supply were insufficient to maintain the minimum United States programme, they would be supplemented from the unallocated supplies at present in Britain. At the end of each quarter a balance of supply and requirements would be struck and submitted to the Combined Policy Committee, and if United States reserve stocks were below the agreed minimum, the deficit would be covered from stocks in Britain. The practical result of this would be that two-thirds of the unallocated stocks in Britain would become available to support the American minimum programme during 1948 and 1949 in case of need, while the United States would draw the whole of the Congo production.

Raw material allocations and exchange of technical information had been regarded as quids and quos in the negotiations. But when Mr Makins, fresh from Washington, presented officials and Ministers with the contentious uranium allocation formula, he put forward with it the third part of the package deal. This was a general political agreement which would be brought into effect by the method considered so unthinkable in 1946, that is, formal statements of interest would be written into the record by the chief representative of each country at the Combined Policy Committee. For this overall agreement the draft agreement (see p. 96) of February 1946 had been taken as the model, with two main changes. Since it was intended to nullify the Quebec Agreement there was really no point in exchanging letters about the Quebec Clause 4 (see p. 6), which restricted British industrial exploitation of atomic energy; this would simply die. Much more important was the elimination of Clause 2 of Quebec, which had laid down that neither the United States nor Britain would use atomic weapons against third parties without the other's consent. A similar clause, covering Canada as well as the other two countries, had been prominently re-embodied in the abortive February 1946 document except that the word 'consultation' had replaced 'consent'. The discovery of the 'consent' clause had caused something of a furore when the Quebec Agreement had been revealed in May 1947 to the Joint Congressional Committee; they were shocked to find that Britain could veto the use of atomic weapons by the United States. The Administration wanted to drop this provision, and in the December 1947 negotiations the British Embassy in Washington had assumed in a cable to London that there would be no objection since, so long as present collaboration between the two countries continued, the clause was otiose. Now in the submission to Ministers it was suggested that this was a political clause 'which was perhaps out of place in a working arrangement of the kind proposed'. There was one other item in the political part of the package: the British hoped to persuade the reluctant Americans to modify the original provisions about giving no information to other countries to the extent of agreeing to some exchange of information with Commonwealth countries.*

The advantages of the three-part package deal seemed great: mutual agreement and support by the United Kingdom and United States of each other's atomic energy programmes; no more talk of the strategic vulnerability of United Kingdom stocks and plants; the exchange of technical information; the beginning of atomic co-operation with the Dominions; getting rid of Clause 4 of Quebec; setting up a working partnership with the United States and Canada which would have beneficial effects beyond atomic energy. The major disadvantage weighed in the balance was the surrender of Britain's uranium claims. Moreover the proposed arrangements for uranium allocations for the next two years were quite definite, whereas the United States' obligation to share their information was not equally precise. Nor had the United States promised to provide the fissile material Britain needed for research and development. Most curiously, in view of the potential issues of life and death that

* There were also provisions in the general political agreement that in accordance with British wishes the UNAEC should continue and not be broken up as the Americans wanted.

were involved, neither officials nor Ministers showed any concern or interest in the surrender of Britain's veto, or right to consultation on the use of the bomb. The one person to question it was the Vice-Chief of the Air Staff, Sir William Dickson. He thought the inclusion of the veto clause might enable Britain to exercise some restraining influence on the United States in the event of a sudden alarm. The Chiefs of Staff argued, however, that since there was little real value in a clause of this nature there was little point in advocating it, especially since it was embarrassing to the United States Administration.

Ministers and officials supported the package deal. They simply insisted that it be made clear that the agreement was to be treated as a whole and that the United Kingdom could reopen the whole business, including uranium allocations, if the flow of information was unsatisfactory. The Minister of Defence expressed concern that the proposed agreement gave no assurance that atomic weapons would be made available for British use in a sudden emergency, but his colleagues believed that to discuss this point now with the United States would make any early atomic energy agreement impossible.

Cockcroft, Makins and Peirson rushed back once more across the Atlantic to clinch the agreements. It was decided that there should be a general declaration of intent which should be called a *modus vivendi*. This was a form of agreement which the President could conclude without reference to Congress and which would not come within Article 102 of the United Nations Charter. It was essentially a temporary or working arrangement, a means of coexistence pending a permanent settlement such as was foreshadowed in the Truman–Attlee–King declaration of November 1945. There was no suggestion that the document was temporary in any other sense.

The *modus vivendi* was not signed. Instead, amidst great solemnity at a Combined Policy Committee meeting on 7 January 1948, the representative of each of the three countries declared its intention to proceed on the basis of the document (reproduced in Appendix 9). The CPC agreed separately that the reports on the material allocations and technical co-operation should come into effect and also the recommendations they had just drawn up for very limited co-operation with British Commonwealth countries. In addition, they set up a standing group of scientific advisers to implement the report on technical co-operation and keep other possible topics under review.

The negotiations for the *modus vivendi* had taken less than a calendar month from start to finish. The pace had been set largely by the timetable of the legislation for the Marshall Plan and the desire to avoid mixing questions of uranium supplies with it. On the British side there was also anxiety to take full advantage of the apparent overwhelming victory of the Anglophiles in the Administration, a victory ostensibly supported at the moment by the military authorities and even by some of the less friendly Republican senators on the Joint Congressional Committee. Here was an agreement which would, according to Makins, 'wipe out the misunderstanding and bitterness of the past and put our relationship on a solid basis'. It would, he added, be wise to settle the problem 'before the rats can get at it'.

In the general relief, and belief in American goodwill, there was little disposition to inspect the *modus vivendi* more minutely. If there had been, flaws might have been seen. The partnership was, in spite of hopes to the contrary, to be an exclusive one. Commonwealth countries might be given only innocuous technical information so that any real co-operative atomic venture with them was out of the question. There seemed no intention of giving any information at all to any European countries, whether to Belgium – whose uranium was to feed the American and British plants and who had been mentioned in December as a possible beneficiary of a new agreement – or to France, to whom Britain had some moral obligations. At a time when the Foreign Secretary himself was wanting Britain to be the leader of Europe she was deliberately closing the door even to very limited co-operation in this important field. However, in the end these disadvantages did not prove as heavy as might have been expected.

A more serious flaw was the surrender of the British veto on the American use of the atomic bomb, without even substituting the word 'consultation' for the word 'consent', as had been proposed in 1946. At the time, American use of the bomb may have seemed improbable or hypothetical in Whitehall. But international stormclouds were gathering quickly and within a few months American bombers were to be stationed in England (see Chapter 9). Three years later there was to be the danger that the atomic bomb might be used in the Korean War. The surrender of this clause of the Quebec Agreement, a clause which was intolerable to the Americans, was seen in part as a reciprocal exchange for the surrender of Clause 4, which restricted British industrial exploitation and was intolerable to the British. Nevertheless, the exchange was scarcely a fair one for by the force of events Clause 4 was already dead and the British were building production plants; the Americans had made no attempt to enforce it. Clause 2 or a modified form of it, on the other hand, might be of momentous importance. The original power of veto might be illusory and might never bind the United States if they thought their security was threatened. But until it was formally abrogated, it gave Britain at least a contingent right to consultation before action was taken that might lead to her own annihilation. Now Britain had no claim whatever even to consultation of the kind which had been included in the abortive February 1946 document. As we shall see, attempts had to be made later to re-establish such a claim and they were only partially successful.

There were other peculiarities. Firstly, the *modus vivendi* had no set term; the uncertainties of the status of the wartime Quebec Agreement had been replaced by uncertainties about the status of the *modus vivendi*. The raw material allocations had been made for a specific period, but all the other provisions were very vague about time so that for some years to come officials on both sides of the Atlantic were never sure whether they were still in force or not. Secondly, the rationale of the *modus vivendi* was so tortuous that it was bound to lead to misunderstanding, especially when new men were in office in Washington. The aim of the agreement was the greater defence and security of the United States. It is true that the Americans thought they were achieving this aim by acquiring additional uranium through the *modus vivendi* and by burying the agreement for consultation on the use of the bomb. They may have regarded the exchange of information simply as the price to be paid for these gains. Nevertheless, the British were entitled to believe that if the exchange of information was to promote American defence and security, it would do so by helping the British production of plutonium for weapons. Moreover the British programme for plutonium production in the quantities which had been underwritten by the Americans in the agreement could not possibly have any other purpose than weapons. Certainly, no one could say that American defence would be strengthened by helping the British to develop industrial power stations. Indeed in the McMahon Act the restrictions on the exchange of information for industrial purposes were paradoxically much more rigid than those for military purposes. Yet the agreement itself of set purpose omitted all direct mention of atomic weapons, and in a few months the Americans were to reel with shock at the news that the British were making material for bombs and to use it as a reason for limiting technical collaboration.

In the long history of strange atomic energy agreements, the *modus vivendi* emerges as the strangest of them all. Makins, the leader of the British negotiators, knew America extremely well and was realistic about Washington moods. Yet even he had been impressed by the new, understanding, attitude of the Americans. The men most prominent round the tables – George Kennan, David Lilienthal, Carroll Wilson – had this deeper desire for friendship in full measure, so much so that the British did not realise how unrepresentative they were. Nor did they know that the main reason for the talks had been to buy British accommodation in uranium at a rock-bottom price. This was not necessarily an unworthy aim on the part of the Americans. Nevertheless, once the deal was made, the British were entitled to expect that it would be honoured, and as we shall see it was not. The British also gave the United States negotiators credit for understanding what they were doing, and again it was to transpire that they did not. These unpleasant revelations lay in the future. In the New Year of 1948 no one seriously doubted that the egg was a good one. Only later did the British find that it was addled after all.

For a few weeks all seemed to go well. In February 1948 a first list of subjects under four of the topics in the *modus vivendi* was agreed for the immediate exchange of information: the medical side of health and safety (topic 2), extraction chemistry (topic 7), natural uranium reactors in which power was not wasted (topic 8), and general research experience with low-power reactors (topic 9). The amount of detail varied. In the case of topic 7 it was considerable and included basic chemistry of the elements and fission products involved, the chemical and physical behaviour of materials used in the extraction processes, the theory and application of process methods, the behaviour of chemical systems in high radiation fields, and process technology. In the case of topic 9 it only included subjects relating to the Canadian NRX pile.

There were some very useful visits to the United States, by a British medical group, a chemical extraction group and a reactor physicist. The medical mission obtained the essential information over the whole field of health and safety apart from effluents. The chemical extraction team, composed of scientists and engineers, had a genuine exchange of information with their opposite numbers. The American pilot plant for the separation of plutonium, uranium and fission products by solvent extraction was broadly similar to the process developed quite independently at Chalk River by the British chemist, Robert Spence, except that a different chemical was to be used. Each side was able to make some contribution to the other, but in general, British work on solvent extraction was further advanced than American work (see Chapter 22); the most valuable result of this particular mission had been to give the British engineers confirmation of their approach, and confidence that the process at Chalk River would work.

Americans visited Britain for exchanges on topic 8 – the natural uranium reactors in which the heat of fission was not wasted – and here too the transmission of information from Britain to the United States exceeded that in the other direction. The American team – W. H. Zinn and G. L. Weil of Argonne and C. W. J. Wende of Hanford – came to Britain at the beginning of June 1948 and were given very full information about the design for air-cooled production piles at Windscale and also about the ideas then being considered for a gas-cooled pile to produce power. They also heard about the British progress in producing very pure graphite, and about the process for getting heat out of uranium by multiple finning of the cans; in both these fields the British seemed well ahead. Zinn and Weil described no similar United States projects, so that the British got the impression, rightly or wrongly, that United Kingdom technology and thinking on gas-cooled piles seemed in advance of the United States. The British obtained some valuable incidental information from their visitors, supporting that brought back by the British physicist, C. A. Rennie, after a visit to Brookhaven – information on the effects of irradiation of graphite and carbon dioxide, on the oxidation of graphite by air, on the effect of pile radiations in producing blistering and warping of uranium metal slugs, and also on the change of reactivity of piles with time. In general, however, the British were left with the impression that the American experimental work was surprisingly thin in relation to their resources and that many of the data, though stimulating, were so fragmentary as to be unreliable.

Exchange of information on topic 9 – research experience with low-power reactors – was confined to the operation of heavy water reactors and little information of importance was obtained from the United States: it appeared that Canadian technology in this field was now substantially ahead of the United States. However, further visits to other types of United States low-power reactors lay ahead.

Although a useful beginning had been made with exchanges of information, the British were not altogether happy. The small quantities of fissile material they had expected to get were not forthcoming. Above all, what had for so long seemed a touchstone of true co-operation – visits to the production plants at Hanford – still eluded them. Excuses were made, one after the other, for postponing any such visits, even by a medical team to study effluents. Equally disquieting was the extraordinary slowness of the administrative machine at the American end. Minutes went unapproved so that further meetings were held up, letters making various requests or asking for further visits went unanswered, or the people whom the British wished to see were 'too busy' to come. It was the old story: adapting the words of the learned judge in Bardell *v*. Pickwick, if the Americans wanted to give the British the information they would find a reason for doing so, and if they didn't, why then they wouldn't!

The British did not doubt the desire to co-operate of some of the chief people in the Commission, notably David Lilienthal and Carroll Wilson. But the self-confidence which the British had observed in the Commission in December 1947 was waning by April 1948. Partly because of this, the Commission felt it must be extremely cautious in these early days of collaboration and details had to go through the overworked senior executives and all the Commissioners. The British in their innocence had believed that the 'common defense and security' clause of the McMahon Act had been invoked to make possible the *modus vivendi* as a whole and that once invoked it covered the whole technical collaboration programme written into the agreement. The lawyers of the USAEC, however, had ruled that the common defence and security criterion must be applied to each individual request, so that if exchange of information was not to the advantage of the defence of the United States it could not be approved. The lawyers were more than ably backed by one of the Commissioners, Lewis Strauss, who was reputed to be anti-British. Sir Gordon Munro of the British Embassy decided to 'carry the war into the enemy's territory' and invited him to lunch. There Strauss admitted that he might fairly have been described as 'the nigger in the woodpile', but said he had become convinced that co-operation was desirable for the United States and that they had something to receive as well as to give.

Nevertheless, the picture remained patchy. In some of the topics collaboration remained close and fruitful. This was especially true of medical affairs and extraction chemistry and of research and development of radioactive and stable isotopes. On this last topic visits and reports were freely exchanged, and isotopes were made mutually available on a non-reimbursable basis for research programmes, but they were not to be transferred outside the atomic energy projects of the three countries. The Americans specifically excluded from this exchange fissionable materials and materials for weapons use or weapons research.

On other topics there were disappointments. One was over plutonium metallurgy. The British were specially anxious to discuss this under topic 6 (fundamental properties of reactor materials) during a visit to England by Cyril Smith, head of the Chicago Institute of Metals and formerly chief metallurgist at Los Alamos, who was, ironically, British by birth and education. After clearing the subject, the USAEC countermanded the permission and said there must be no discussions on it; the incident became a *cause célèbre* in the annals of the American project. Then the USAEC told the British they had somewhat belatedly concluded that topic 8 as at present worded – 'natural uranium reactors where power is not wasted' – covered no single item of mutual interest since neither the United States nor the United Kingdom had such reactors, and there could be no more discussions on the subject. It appeared that the slow rate of American research and development in this field, which had seemed to be one of the conclusions of the Zinn–Weil visit to England, reflected rather the two Americans' embarrassment at their false position. They had felt unavoidably unable to do justice to themselves.

The British remembered the promise that the exchange of information was to be a continuing process related to circumstances as they developed, and they planned to ask, in the autumn review of collaboration, for an extension or redefinition of the existing topics, and some quite new ones. They also felt that the time was ripe to discuss collaboration on atomic weapons. This item had been excluded on American advice from the *modus vivendi* discussions, but the illogicality of the position had been highlighted by the fact that there had been no British representatives at all at the recent Eniwetok trials, in contrast to the Bikini trials in 1946. Lord Tedder emphasised in mid-1948 that it was becoming a matter of urgent necessity to discuss atomic weapons freely with the United States. National defence policy was being based on the use of a weapon 'about which we in fact know very little'. The official Atomic Energy Committee decided that the first step should be to approach Mr Forrestal, the Secretary of Defense, to get his agreement in principle to an exchange of information on weapons and an assurance of his support at the Combined Policy Committee. If he was sympathetic, a formal proposal would then be tabled at the Committee at the same time as the other proposals for extending the list of topics.

Before any documents were prepared in London, a bombshell exploded in Washington. In August 1948 Dr Woodward, head of the British Scientific Mission there, conversed with Carroll Wilson and Donald Carpenter who, since March 1948 (that is, after the *modus vivendi* was signed), had been Forrestal's atomic energy deputy. Carpenter said that Zinn and Weil had reported on their return from Britain that her greatest effort was being put into plutonium production and that only relatively minor interest was being shown in the potential industrial applications of nuclear energy. This, Woodward was told, had shaken everyone in the USAEC and had caused a terrific sensation in the Joint Congressional Committee. Carpenter asked whether it was the British intention to make bombs; if so, where were they going to be manufactured and stored?

Carroll Wilson admitted that he should not have been surprised by the Zinn–Weil report, but in fact during the discussions leading to the *modus vivendi* neither he nor any of his colleagues had considered what the next stage of British development would be. Soon after this Gordon Arneson, who was in charge of atomic energy in the State Department, added that when the Department had originally explained the general object of the *modus vivendi* to the Joint Congressional Committee, they thought the Committee had understood United Kingdom intentions about plutonium and weapons production; if they had not, the British were in no way to blame. The fact which the *modus vivendi* had not stated explicitly –

that Britain would be making atomic weapons – could be deduced from the agreement on uranium allocations, but some people had been misled. Meanwhile it became apparent that there were real political difficulties. Carroll Wilson emphasised that there were still many Republicans in the United States who were just as isolationist as in 1940, and indicated that one of the five Commissioners fell in this category; although obviously sincere and consistent, he had strenuously opposed and was continuing to oppose any move towards further collaboration with foreign countries, however friendly. Moreover a presidential election was looming with a possibility of a Republican victory. In that case, as the British Ambassador reported, the Administration feared the newcomers might abuse their predecessors for laxity over safeguarding atomic secrets.

By the time the disturbing accounts of Woodward's conversations arrived in London, instructions were already on their way from the Chiefs of Staff to Admiral Sir Henry Moore, the head of the British military mission in Washington, accompanying a memorandum from the British Minister of Defence, Mr A. V. Alexander, to the United States Secretary of Defense, Mr Forrestal. Mr Alexander wrote that now the British production programme was well launched and Britain was in a position to make an increasing contribution to the common effort, he would like to propose that United States/United Kingdom collaboration on atomic energy be extended to include exchange of information on atomic weapons. He made his proposal in the sincere belief that United States and British strategic interests and national defence policies were fundamentally identical and that frank exchange of information on this vital matter would be in the common interest. He said: 'In particular I believe

(*a*) our national defence policies are directed to the prevention of war and the best way to do this is for both of us to be strong. The atomic weapon is the greatest single source of military strength in the world at present and it is in the interests of the security of the US as well as the UK that both countries should develop it to the maximum of their ability and with all possible speed. The closer we can work together on its development therefore the greater will be our combined strength;

(*b*) the atomic weapon which the US already have and the UK will have in the not too distant future is likely to be the greatest single factor in deciding the outcome of any future world conflict. It must therefore play a vital part in all US and British strategic meetings, in the framing of defence policy, in the shaping of strategical and tactical plans, in the planning of war potential, in the design of equipment, in the training of the men who will use it and in planning the protection of those who may have to withstand the weight of its attack from the enemy. If we fail to prevent war and are to make the best use of the atomic weapon in war it is vital we should share our knowledge of it, and concert our thinking on every aspect of its development;

(c) in a future world conflict, US and British forces will find themselves fighting side by side and the principle of standardisation has already been accepted in other fields. It is commonsense that it should be extended to cover the most vital field of all so that the design of US and British equipment and the technique of US and British production and tactics can proceed as far as possible in step;

(d) as the UK programme develops we feel sure that the contribution we can make will not be inconsiderable.'

The Minister attached a first list of topics which would be of great and immediate assistance to the British programme and said that any information received would be subject to special standards of security to be agreed. The topics covered those of great and immediate assistance to the programme for the design and manufacture of the atomic bomb;* those of great and immediate assistance to operational requirements; those of great assistance in the long-term design of aircraft; those of immediate assistance in planning the protection of personnel in fighting and civil defence services.

When Forrestal was handed the memorandum he made a variety of points in a talk that was 'very frank'. He said that the chief possibility of differences of opinion concerned the building of a bomb-production plant in Britain. Could this be justified in the light of the danger of having a plant in the United Kingdom in case it was overrun, and the cost in relation to Marshall Aid? Could Britain, said Forrestal, not be satisfied with a supply of bombs from

---

* This list included plutonium metallurgy and devices in aircraft to permit the carriage of US bombs in British aircraft and vice versa if this was ever necessary.

the United States in case of need or, alternatively, with siting the plant in Canada? He said that when the Combined Policy Committee held their meetings the previous autumn, stress had been laid on the general humanitarian aspect of the use of atomic power rather than on the military side. The accent had recently shifted in the United States to the military angle, but some members of the Combined Policy Committee 'would be more difficult as a result'. Admiral Moore replied that questions of siting the British plant had been fully considered by the Government, who had decided to go ahead in the United Kingdom. Even if Britain did not get the information asked for she would go ahead and make the best weapon she could, but naturally she wished, and presumably the United States also, that she should have the most efficient one possible as a result of a combined effort. Forrestal agreed orally.

In London this conversation, added to the Carpenter one, had the familiar undertones of the last five years of Anglo-American atomic negotiations – promises forgotten, former discussions misinterpreted, facts stood on their head, sheer administrative muddle with departments pulling in different directions. The irrationality of the *modus vivendi* was becoming only too apparent. It was certainly not true that in the CPC *modus vivendi* discussions stress had been laid on humanitarian uses rather than on military uses of atomic energy. In all the disputes over plutonium metallurgy no one seems to have pointed out that extraction chemistry, where exchange of information was very full, was largely a military business: it happened to be one where the British had a good deal to offer. Moreover very recently – in March 1948 – when the British Government had consulted the United States Government about their announcement that they were engaged on atomic weapons research (see Chapter 6), Forrestal was surprised only that this was not already publicly known. As for Marshall Aid, one of the objects of the *modus vivendi* was to keep atomic energy entirely separate from it.

In January 1948, when the *modus vivendi* was joyfully concluded, Kennan of the State Department who had led the American team had expressly urged the British Government to bring forward any doubts which might arise about the way the agreement was working. It was therefore small comfort to be told by the British Embassy in Washington that the Americans were caught up in their own security machine and that many of them knew neither what the others were doing nor what had been agreed with the United

Kingdom. As evidence of this, Dr Woodward cabled that in another talk Mr Carpenter had said the USAEC, the Joint Congressional Committee and the military were working on a blanket instruction to all United States representatives in any tripartite talks:

> While recognising that a distinction between atomic energy mat-
> ters of military significance and of non-military significance cannot
> be clearly made, all exchanges shall be further governed by the
> general criterion that information specifically relating to weapons
> or the design or operation of present plants for the production of
> atomic weapon materials or parts is not a subject for discussion.

This criterion became firmly embedded in the USAEC rules for implementing the technical co-operation programme.*

When Sir Oliver Franks, the British Ambassador, tackled the Acting Secretary of State, Mr Lovett, the latter was reassuring and said he could give a 'clear, definite and complete answer' that there was no basis for misunderstandings about the British atom bomb. Yet even he stood quite firm in refusing exchanges on the specific issue which the British were pressing, under the original agreed topics, that is, plutonium metallurgy; he did so on the grounds that this undoubtedly came under the heading of military use. He also said that if the British pressed for an early reply to Mr Alexander's memorandum the answer could only be 'no' and that he himself was very anxious not to crystallise the position in this way. For the time being, he added, the only course was for the British to play things along and get information under the topics where co-opera-tion existed.

The British felt that with the 1948 presidential election so close, they had no choice. Makins, who knew Washington so well, voiced the general speculation about American policy: 'Have they changed their minds about our programme and is it their purpose to hinder and delay it as much as possible and restrict the information they give to the minimum necessary to secure our combined co-operation over raw materials?' The Franks talk with Lovett was to Makins 'a disagreeable reminder of those I used to have with Acheson when the US Government under War Department pressure were refusing to observe the obligations of the Quebec Agreement'.

---

* Cockcroft said that he was 'completely at a loss' to understand how interchange of information on chemistry and chemical engineering – which continued – satisfied this criterion.

Franks replied that there were two main arguments in the American mind – one about vulnerability and one about the division of labour. Without assuming that Britain would be overrun by Russia in a war, the United States thought this was a possibility which their strategic planning and policy must take into account. If it happened, the loss of atomic material and information might endanger United States security. Even if Britain was not overrun, her atomic plants were considered vulnerable to the fifth column. Other observers, apart from the Ambassador, pointed to the attitude of some parties in the United States to the British Labour Government, to the fear that it might move further to the left, thus jeopardising security, and indeed to general United States doubts about British security standards.

The second argument, according to the Ambassador, was that the strategic interests of the two countries would best be served if their military production programmes were fully co-ordinated and if the United States concentrated on atomic weapons and Britain on other military equipment such as aircraft. It was clear that the exchange of information on military weapons could not be pursued at present, but when it was taken up again, the main British effort would have to be directed to persuading the Americans that it would serve their strategic interest, no less than that of the British. Meanwhile the more the British could show that they were giving the Americans useful information, thus emphasising the two-way nature of co-operation, the easier it would be for the United States Government to carry the Congressional Committee with them. Franks did not mention the important contribution of Britain, Canada and the Commonwealth in raw materials. But he did not believe that it would be worth following up the provisions of the *modus vivendi* and threatening to withhold uranium shipments because of dissatisfaction over certain items in technical collaboration.*

Valuable technical information was after all still forthcoming, as Cockcroft found on a visit to the United States in the autumn of 1948. He found the USAEC staff in particular extremely friendly. Arrangements were made for developing still further co-operation on the original topics 1–7 (apart from the disputed plutonium metallurgy under topic 6). Topic 8, which had caused difficulties because it overlapped production reactors, was withdrawn, but it was hoped

* In fact, according to the *modus vivendi* formula, no shipments from Britain were needed.

to expand topic 9 to include the design, operation and use of research-type reactors, including the Brookhaven reactor whose operating conditions were very similar to Windscale's. Formal proposals for new topics – plutonium metallurgy, diffusion plant, methods of economising in the use of uranium, new reactors including breeders, and the exchange of small quantities of fissile material – would be tabled after the presidential election.

Meanwhile Cockcroft prepared for Franks a paper on the advantages to the United States of collaboration with Britain and Canada. He said that although the British atomic scientists and engineers were fewer in number, their standard was high; that Chalk River, which the British helped to staff, had radiation intensities at least twenty times greater than those available in the United States; that the Medical Research Council Unit had an international reputation; that the British had equalled United States results in the detection of atomic explosions and in atomic piles and had made important contributions with only a very small fraction of their effort; that the British had made or initiated more intensive and systematic studies than the United States of the behaviour of graphite under irradiation, the canning of uranium and the use of beryllium; that British graphite was now thought to be superior in quality to United States graphite; that swapping of experience in extraction chemistry where the two countries were working on parallel lines was mutually advantageous; that Britain now had considerable experience of the Windscale design which might help Brookhaven. Finally, said Cockcroft,

> perhaps the greatest advantage of co-operation comes from the interchange of ideas with an independent group of scientists. The development of science depends on the free exchange of ideas and competition among scientists. There is a great danger that a secret project interchanging no ideas with the outside world will inbreed and become sterile. Collaboration and mutual discussion and criticism between our three groups should be of great value in preventing this situation arising.

And so even if the egg of the *modus vivendi* was addled, it was, like the curate's, 'good in parts', and had yielded some valuable results for both sides. But it is doubtful whether the good parts were ever worth what had been given up for them, in particular Britain's surrender of any right to consultation on the use of the bomb and of her atomic co-operation with the Dominions and Europe. And even if some parts were good, the agreement had certainly not fulfilled its purpose, briefly avowed by the Americans and enthusiastically supported by the British, of opening a new era of tripartite partnership in atomic energy. This was inevitable because the central question – the interrelationship of America and Britain as possessors of nuclear weapons – had been evaded and thus confused by concentration on the first stage of the business – technical collaboration in some scientific aspects of the production of fissile material.

The British were making atomic bombs, because to their Government this seemed inevitable for a country with her role and commitments in the post-war world. The Americans did not want Britain to make atomic bombs for a variety of reasons, varying from old-fashioned isolationism and a feeling that the atomic bomb was God's sacred trust to the American people, to the merits of using resources with maximum efficiency and avoiding proliferation of weapons. It can only be emphasised that the last of these reasons was not made manifest to the British in 1947 or 1948 any more than in 1946 (see Chapter 4).

If non-proliferation had been an earnest policy it would surely have included frank talks on the place of the American atomic bomb in the strategy with which Britain was to defend herself. The Americans were extraordinarily lacking in sensitivity to ascribe Britain's nuclear programme simply to 'national pride'. This was an element, but the strategic necessities as interpreted by the British, whether rightly or wrongly, were more compelling. As it was, no specific offers of American atomic bombs were ever made. In 1948, as the British and Americans were drawn closer together by the Berlin airlift and by the presence of American bombers in Britain – even though Britain had surrendered her right to consultation on the dropping of the atomic bomb from them – atomic energy remained something apart from all the other strands that were weaving a new and stronger special relationship. In the last days of 1948, the British Ambassador wrote, 'the whole question of our relations with the Americans on atomic energy questions seems to me to be becoming increasingly bound up with the larger issue of the extent to which the Americans are prepared to treat us on more or less equal terms as a first-class power'.

Appendix 9

THE *MODUS VIVENDI*

1. All agreements between the three governments or any two of them in the field of atomic energy shall be regarded as null and of no effect, with the following exceptions:

(a) The Patent Memorandum of 1 October 1943 as modified by subsequent agreement on 19 September 1944 and 8 March 1945.

(b) The Agreement and Declaration of Trust dated 13 June 1944.

(c) The exchange of letters between the Acting Secretary of State and the British Ambassador of 19 and 24 September 1945, concerning Brazil.

(d) The agreed public Declaration by the President of the United States, the Prime Minister of the United Kingdom, and the Prime Minister of Canada of 15 November 1945.

2. The Combined Policy Committee, already established, and subject to the control of the three governments, shall continue as an organ for dealing with atomic energy problems of common concern. The Committee shall consist of three representatives of the United States, two of the United Kingdom, and one of Canada, unless otherwise agreed.

3. The Committee shall *inter alia*:

(a) Allocate raw materials in accordance with such principles as may be determined from time to time by the Committee, taking into account all supplies available to any of the three governments.

(b) Consider general questions arising with respect to co-operation among the three governments.

(c) Supervise the operations and policies of the Combined Development Agency referred to in paragraph 4 below.

4. The Combined Development Trust, created on the thirteenth of June 1944 by the Agreement and Declaration of Trust signed by President Roosevelt and Mr Winston Churchill, shall continue in effect except that it shall henceforward be known as the Combined

Development Agency. Of the six persons provided for in Clause 1(2) of the Declaration of Trust, three shall represent the United States, two the United Kingdom, and one Canada.

5. The United States, the United Kingdom and Canada will, within the limits of their respective constitutions and statutes, use every effort to acquire control of supplies of uranium and thorium situated within their respective territories. The United Kingdom will, in so far as need exists, communicate with the governments of the British Commonwealth for the purpose of ensuring that such governments exercise control of supplies of uranium and thorium situated in their respective territories. The United Kingdom will consult with the Commonwealth Governments concerned with a view to encouraging the greatest possible production of uranium and thorium in the British Commonwealth, and with a view to ensuring that as large a quantity as possible of such supplies is made available to the United States, United Kingdom and Canada.

6. It is recognised that there are areas of information and experience in which co-operation would be mutually beneficial to the three countries. They will therefore co-operate in respect of such areas as may from time to time be agreed upon by the CPC and in so far as this is permitted by the laws of the respective countries.

7. In the interests of mutual security, classified information in the field of atomic energy will not be disclosed to other governments or authorities or persons in other countries without due prior consultation.

8. Policy with respect to international control of atomic energy remains that set forth in the Three-Nations Agreed Declaration of 15 November 1945. Whenever a plan for the international control of atomic energy with appropriate safeguards which would ensure use of atomic energy for peaceful purposes only shall be agreed upon, and shall become fully effective, the relationship of these countries in atomic energy matters will have to be reconsidered in the light thereof.

ANNEX I

Allocations

1. The agreed objective is the maintenance of the United States, United Kingdom and Canadian minimum programmes with reasonable pipeline and reserve stocks.

2. In 1948 and 1949 all supplies available from the Belgian Congo will be allocated to the United States, subject to para. 4 below.

3. In 1948 and 1949, if supplies additional to those which will flow from existing sources are required to maintain the United States minimum programme, they will be provided, subject to para. 4 below, from the unprocessed and presently unallocated supplies now in the United Kingdom, according to the following arrangements:

(a) The United States requirement is 2547 tons in 1948 and 2547 in 1949, including capital charge of 370 tons for one pile in each year, a pipeline stock of 2800 tons and a reserve stock of 2547 tons throughout 1948, diminishing to 2176 tons at the end of 1949.

(b) The United Kingdom requirement to the end of 1949 is as follows: capital charge for two piles 600 tons, pipeline stock of 770 tons, reserve stock of 660 tons.

(c) At the end of each quarter a balance will be struck and submitted to the CPC. If the reserve stock in the USA is below the agreed minimum, an amount equivalent to the deficit will be ear-marked from the unallocated and unprocessed stocks in the United Kingdom. At the end of the third quarter in 1948 and 1949, a review of the situation will be made by the CPC in the light of the current position and the prospective shipments in the fourth quarter of each year. In striking this balance supplies will be taken into account which are in transit from the port of shipment. Should stocks at any time before the end of the third quarter fall below seven months' supply, emergency shipments to safeguard continued operation will be made.

(d) According to the result of this review a shipment will be made or ear-marked supplies will be released as the case may be. A similar arrangement will apply in due course in respect of the United Kingdom programme.

(e) From its allocation during 1948 and 1949, the United States will furnish metal to Canada as required for the Canadian programme in amounts not to exceed the equivalent of 20 tons of U_3O_8 per year.

(f) It is understood that when depleted sludges are available for re-use the quantities thrown up should be taken into account.

4. An immediate review of these arrangements may be requested by any of the three governments:

(*a*) If the total unallocated supplies seem likely to be insufficient to support the agreed programme or alternatively to be materially in excess of the estimates* contained in Tab. CCC annexed to the minutes of the CPC meeting of 15 December 1947; or

(*b*) in the event of a state of emergency; or

(*c*) in the event of a change of circumstances bringing about a substantial alteration in the relationships established at this time by the CPC.

*Estimates of Uranium Ore Production 1948–52
(Dated 12 December 1947)

	1948	*1949*	*1950*	*1951*	*1952*	*Total*
Congo	2,200	1,200	1,200	1,200	1,200	7,000
United States	100	200	200	200	200	900
Canada	150	150	150	150	150	750
South Africa	–	–	125	320	825	1,270
Portugal	–	–	–	50	50	100
Total	2,450	1,550	1,675	1,920	2,425	10,020

(All in short tons U_3O_8)

ANNEX 2

*Areas of Co-operation between Members of the
British Commonwealth*
(Approved by the Combined Policy Committee
at its meeting on 7 January 1948)

Apart from the arrangements which already exist between the United Kingdom and Canada, the question has arisen of co-operation between the United Kingdom and other members of the British Commonwealth.

As a part of the combined effort during the war years, assistance to the British atomic energy project was given by scientists from New Zealand, Australia and South Africa. Some of these have worked in Canada and some in United States and from there have moved to Harwell. Several of them will shortly be returning to

New Zealand and at a later stage – one year or more – there will be a similar return to Australia. It is intended to admit further scientists from these Dominions to work at Harwell.

The three CPC governments are also actively co-operating with the Dominions in the field of raw materials. South Africa in particular is likely to become an important source of raw materials and is carrying out active work on benefication of ores. In due course South African interests may be expected to extend.

With a view particularly to making secure the information held by Dominion scientists on their return to their respective countries, and of furthering full co-operation in the field of raw material investigation and supply, it is recommended that the areas of co-operation outlined below should be recognised:

(a) The subjects covered in Sections I and II of the proposed Declassification Guide and which are listed as 'Topics for immediate declassification'.

(b) *The field of health and safety*, including
   1. Experimental work from which radiation tolerances may be established.
   2. Genetics.
   3. General medical and biological studies.
   4. Instruments, laboratory design and techniques of this field.

(c) *Research uses of radioactive isotopes and stable isotopes, including*
   preparation, techniques for handling, instruments, mutual availability for research purposes.

(d) *Detection of a distant nuclear explosion*
   Operation of recording stations.

(e) Survey methods for source materials.

(f) Benefication of ores – co-operation with South Africa and with other Dominions of (*sic*) the work developed there.

(g) Extraction of low-grade ores – within the fields defined by the ores locally available.

(h) *Design information on research reactors*
   Design information on the low-power graphite reactor build at Harwell (Gleep) to be communicated by United Kingdom to New Zealand. It is recognised that this information will be effectively available to the New Zealand Government on the return of its staff in early 1948.

(*i*) *General research experience* with the following reactors
Harwell, Gleep, to be communicated by United Kingdom
to New Zealand.

Co-operation within the above classified fields will be subject to
an understanding between Governments to adopt common standards
in holding information secure. Transmission would also be subject
to the principle of current usability.

ANNEX 3

Technical Co-operation
(Memorandum to Combined Policy Committee, approved at the
meeting on 7 January 1948 as the basis of co-operation)

The sub-group has considered a wide range of subjects of common
interest within the field of atomic energy and from among these has
selected certain topics which were agreed upon for presentation to
the Combined Policy Committee as suitable subjects in which co-
operation and the exchange of information, at the present time,
would be mutually advantageous.

1. Those subjects covered in Sections I and II of the 'Proposed
Declassification Guide' which are listed as 'Topics for immediate
declassification'.

2. *The entire field of health and safety*, including

(*a*) experimental work from which radiation tolerances may be
established;
(*b*) genetics;
(*c*) general medical and biological studies; therapy of over-
exposure to radiation;
(*d*) health hazards associated with reactors, such as effluent gases
and their ecological effects, disposal of wastes, toxic effects of
reactor materials including Be and Pu; tolerances for the
various toxic substances and the various radiations;
(*e*) instruments, laboratory design and techniques of this field.

3. *Research uses of radio-isotopes and stable isotopes* including
preparation, techniques for handling instruments; mutual availability for general research purposes.

4. *Fundamental nuclear and extra-nuclear properties of all the*

elements including experimental methods and instruments (e.g. particle accelerators, detection devices).

5. *Detection of a distant nuclear explosion*, including meteorological and geophysical data; instruments (e.g. seismographs, microbarographs); air sampling techniques and analysis; new methods of possible detection.

6. *Fundamental properties of reactor materials (i.e. solid state physics, basic metallurgy)* including moderators, fuel elements, structural materials, also liquid metal and other coolants; the reactions of materials to radiations; the preparation of moderator materials, e.g. graphite, heavy water.

7. *Extraction chemistry* including basic chemistry of processes, problems of 'scale up' of laboratory methods, techniques of remote control, concentration and storage of fission products.

8. *The design of natural uranium reactors* in which the power generated is not wasted. The economy of operation of such reactors, e.g. preferred schemes for enrichment of depleted fuel for re-use.

9. *General research experience with the following (low power) reactors*: Clinton (graphite), Argonne (graphite, heavy water), Chalk River (heavy water), Harwell (graphite).

In furthering these objectives it is considered desirable to encourage the exchange of technical experience and information in these fields. Administrative arrangements should be followed which apply the general principle that classified information shall be currently usable by the recipient.

United Kingdom:	J. D. COCKCROFT	F. N. WOODWARD
Canada:	C. J. MACKENZIE	GEORGE IGNATIEFF
United States:	V. BUSH	J. B. FISK

9 Independence Reconsidered: I

New Hope of Anglo-American Integration

AT the end of 1948 the British requests for the extension of atomic energy collaboration – for the inclusion of new areas for technical interchange and for the exchange of information on atomic weapons – were in the familiar state of suspended animation in Washington, where they lay unanswered. Nothing could be done until the Administration and Congress had settled down after the elections. At the elections not only was President Truman returned but the Democrats won control over both the Senate and the House of Representatives; those in the Administration who advocated greater atomic co-operation with Britain could now expect greater Congressional support.

Nevertheless, the British realised that there were still fundamental differences of opinion in Washington on the subject. They knew that the differences arose largely between the military and the US Atomic Energy Commission or the Joint Congressional Committee and USAEC. They did not, however, realise the seriousness of the split within the Commission itself. Lewis Strauss, the Commissioner who had opposed the limited co-operation of the *modus vivendi*, now opposed its further expansion in spite of his lunch-time remarks to Sir Gordon Munro.[1] Someone of this mind had 'got at' the President, who was saying early in February 1949: 'We have got to protect our information and we certainly must try to see that the British do not have information with which to build atomic weapons in England because they might be captured.'[2] Those sympathetic to the British in the Administration regarded the *modus vivendi* as increasingly out of date; as Lilienthal, chairman of the USAEC, put it, 'It is clear that the kind of in-between world in which we are living is a source of irritation to our friends and to us and worsens rather than improves relations with the United Kingdom and

Canada.'³ The hallmark of the new American approach was a laudable desire to integrate atomic energy more closely with foreign policy, and thus with British–American relations. Its advocates were determined not to have another haggling match about swapping uranium for 'secrets', with bludgeons exhibited on both sides.⁴ Such integration was overdue. As we have seen, from 1947 onwards world events had pushed Britain and America much closer together again. It was largely due to the initiative of Ernest Bevin that the countries of Western Europe had collaborated first in economic reconstruction and then in foreign affairs and military defence, with the United States as support and partner. Britain had acted as the leader of Europe, and could no longer be regarded in the American Administration as a tiresome mendicant or political 'has-been'. The Anglo-American relationship in this new phase was still based not on deep mutual love but on common political and military interests, and it therefore embodied a good deal of cold calculation on both sides. But whatever its roots, it had changed so greatly since 1946 that the principles of American atomic energy policy enshrined in the McMahon Act were wholly inappropriate by 1949. When the United States was engaged in forming what amounted to several military alliances with Britain it was absurd that the one topic which could not be discussed together was the most powerful weapon in the Allied armoury – atomic bombs and atomic strategy. Moreover, if collective defence was to include the Western European countries and the British Dominions, was it not also irrational to prohibit discussions with them about atomic affairs?

So the British welcomed the American suggestion for a general review of atomic energy policy. By early 1949 Ministers believed that the United States authorities were beginning to realise that Britain was their most reliable ally and that the review might therefore settle the outstanding questions which the British had been pressing to no avail. In any case, the raw material allocations of the *modus vivendi* would have to be reconsidered soon as they only ran to the end of 1949. However, the welcome to the United States suggestion was cautious; the British were especially apprehensive that the premises on which the *modus vivendi* rested, notably the recognition of their own atomic energy programme, might be called in question. They agreed that they would not seek discussions themselves but would join in, if officially invited, and insist that the Canadians be invited too.

Meanwhile in the United States, Robert Oppenheimer, the former head of Los Alamos and a member of the USAEC's General Advisory Council, unofficially gathered together at Princeton a group of people mainly from the USAEC and the State Department who were anxious 'to get things going'.* Hitherto some of them, including Oppenheimer himself and Dr Conant, who was also in the party, had concentrated on the possibilities of international control. Now they all agreed that it was essential that co-operation with Britain and Canada, the two great strategic and economic allies of the United States, should be clarified, fostered and developed in all fields of atomic energy development. They also urged that if atomic energy policy was to be adequately co-ordinated with overall foreign policy, ultimate responsibility must lie with the Secretary of State. Other interested parties – the AEC and the military – would act in an advisory rather than executive capacity. The top-level atomic energy authority reporting direct to the President should be a committee composed of the Secretary of State (chairman), the Secretary of Defense and the chairman of the AEC: major questions should be referred to, policy decided by, and directives and instructions issued from, that committee and not be dealt with by individual departments or agencies. Presumably this was designed to prevent the divisions which had bedevilled policy in the past. The British heard that the Administration had approved the recommendation of the Princeton group, that the proposed committee had been set up and that a sub-committee – in effect the Princeton group minus Oppenheimer and Conant – was already doing spade-work on proposals for co-operation with the British.

All this sounded promising, but the British were alarmed lest the United States proposals should crystallise before the British were given any indication of what was in them and could tell whether they were acceptable in principle. They were apprehensive when they heard that General Eisenhower, as chairman of the US Chiefs of Staff, was suggesting to the chief British military representative in Washington that if only Britain would agree not to store any finished bombs in the United Kingdom, his Government would probably agree to the fullest atomic co-operation, including the supply of bombs to Britain 'on call'. This was a development of the US

---

* One of the members of the group was W. Webster, who had succeeded Donald Carpenter (see p. 258) in charge of atomic energy affairs in the Defense Department. He was much more sympathetic to the British case.

military line which Britain had often rejected in the past; she was still not prepared to discuss any suggestion which involved interference with, or freezing of, her own programme.

Hearing that certain proposals had been agreed by the top American committee and were now with the President, the British urged the Americans to let them know the general lines of their thoughts. They realised only too well that if, after extensive clearance within the United States Administration and Congress, Britain rejected the proposals, the situation might be even worse than if no improvement had been attempted. For weeks Makins and Cockcroft held themselves ready to fly to Washington for informal talks, which were time and time again postponed. First the President was away, then he had more urgent affairs to settle on his return. Then, when he looked at the atomic energy proposals with Dean Acheson, now Secretary of State, they agreed that the proposals were so far-reaching that they must be discussed in a general way with Congressional leaders before talks with the British could even begin. Then it was unwise to approach Congressional leaders just as they were debating the North Atlantic Treaty and military assistance to Western Europe. Then, the final blow, a major row blew up between the USAEC and the Joint Congressional Committee on Atomic Energy when the latter's ex-chairman, Senator Hickenlooper, charged the Commission with 'incredible mismanagement'. The keynote of the charges was lax security, and although specific cases were at issue there were also implications that the Commission had given away to other countries more information on atomic energy than the JCAE thought desirable. This new witch-hunt would obviously make the Administration hesitant in approaching the JCAE about the tripartite talks and would not predispose the JCAE to favour the Administration's proposals for sharing information. The whole subject of co-operation had become inflammable and a further cooling-off period was necessary.

It now seemed that talks with Britain would have to be postponed until the autumn of 1949, even though, as the Americans admitted, 'concrete was being poured and hardened with time'. Even if the proposals were not ostensibly fixed, it was clear that after so long some US representatives would come to the discussion with their ideas solidified. Yet still during all these weeks and months the British had no clue at all about the nature of the proposals that were brewing. Britain's friends in the Administration – men such as

Carroll Wilson of the USAEC and George Kennan and Gordon Arneson of the State Department – made kind and encouraging noises but remained impeccably reticent about the proposals.

Meanwhile there were rumours that some members of the JCAE were suggesting that Britain was spending astronomical sums on atomic energy, that she should not be spending so much in her economic difficulties, that her programme conflicted with the principles of Marshall Aid, that she had been using US dollars for the purpose and so on and so on. Figures were sent off from London to show that the sums being bandied about were wildly exaggerated: the percentage of total UK capital investment programmes represented by atomic energy was less than 0·5 per cent.* The figures were highly confidential† and were not available to Parliament; it was agreed, however, that they might be given, orally, to the Congressional Committee.

The moment did not seem very propitious for the Administration's overtures to the JCAE. Indeed, when in July the Committee's chairman, Senator McMahon, was asked what he thought about putting the proposals to the JCAE, he replied that the Committee's 'temperature was about 106 degrees and the present was not a good time to trouble the patient'. In spite of this, the Administration took the plunge and the President explained the new proposals to a few top Congressmen‡ on 14 July 1949.

The British were told that at this famous Blair House§ meeting the Administration had explained the whole background of cooperation and had outlined the US proposals for its extension. The Administration had said they would hold talks with the British and refer back to the Congressional Committee[6] any agreement they reached. They had emphasised that one of the main questions was whether to give Britain information about production of fissile material for military purposes. According to all reports, the President, Mr Acheson and General Eisenhower had stated the case for increased collaboration very well and Senator McMahon had

* This figure does not appear to be directly comparable with the figures in Chapter 14 (which exclude capital investment in housing).

† Ministers had said that no information might be divulged about the size in terms of money or manpower of the UK research and production programme.

‡ i.e. some but not all of the JCAE and some other Congressional leaders.[5]

§ The house in Washington where the President was living while the White House was being restored.

been helpful. On the other hand, Senator Hickenlooper had apparently spoken entirely in a spirit of isolationism. Senator Vandenberg had said that the United States was continually being asked to 'bail out' Britain and they were already doing enough for them in the economic sphere, but the President had reminded him of the great help the United States had received from Britain in the early days of atomic energy. Vandenberg then argued that Britain should be told she must leave the job of making bombs entirely to the United States, whereupon Acheson had replied that Vandenberg must remember they were dealing with a sovereign nation and not a satellite. In recent years Lilienthal's *Journals* have given us a more graphic picture of the meeting,[7] with Eisenhower emphasising Britain's importance to the United States and making a blistering attack on isolationism, Vandenberg and Hickenlooper insisting that the United States must keep 'the vital secret' to themselves, and Lilienthal trying to convince the Congressmen that they were deluded if they thought that Britain, who had contributed to the know-how, could not make atomic bombs.

Lilienthal writes:

> It was asked: What about asking Britain to stop [their plan to make their own weapons] and we give them no information or partnership, but hold some of our weapons and earmark them for them? I said (as did Acheson) this would be so humiliating a proposal, considering their place in the world and their contribution to this enterprise, that it would do more harm to make the offer than just to ride along; and I added, if the alternative were full partnership or continuing the limited area-by-area arrangement under the *modus vivendi*, my personal view would be to drop the whole thing and each go it alone, because the present arrangement leads to friction because it is almost impossible to administer, since the facts don't come in these neat little compartments of the agreement, so we have increased ill-will against us, and the creation of goodwill and mutual confidence and trust is defeated rather than furthered; that whether the British were justified or not in their view, they did feel they'd been badly dealt with from the end of the war.[8]

A few days later Dean Acheson explained the proposal to a full meeting of the Joint Congressional Atomic Energy Committee. The British were told that the Committee had been difficult on the constitutional question but much less so on the general question of extending co-operation. The British did not feel reassured: still quite ignorant of the US proposals, they feared JCAE compliance meant the proposals carried unacceptable strings. It now appears that the meeting was stormy and that Eisenhower on this second appearance was a broken reed. Yet another meeting had to be held with the Committee, at which the Administration took 'a very, very conciliatory position'. The conversations with the British would go forward, looking towards broader arrangements, but no commitment would be made without consultation with the Committee, who would determine whether legislation was necessary. Even this was opposed, though unsuccessfully.[9]

The talks with Britain and Canada, so long delayed, could begin and Pandora's box of proposals at last be opened. Before considering them it is worth drawing four morals from the July Congressional talks. One is now clear: the supporters of Britain in the Administration were still contending with very strong opposition in Congress and their freedom of manoeuvre was correspondingly limited. Secondly, the talks with Congress show the disadvantages to the British case of inadequate publicity. Britain was paying a heavy price for her reluctance to publicise her part in the project from 1946 onwards. To be sure, the facts had been put before the original committee which drafted the McMahon Act in 1946 (see p. 105), the Joint Committee had been told about the wartime Anglo-American agreements in May 1947 (see p. 121) and further background information about past collaboration had been given to the Committee at the time of the *modus vivendi* negotiations. But all this had made no dent on the minds of several Senators, and papers had to be prepared for them in July 1949 by Oppenheimer and other scientists 'making mincemeat of the notion that the British didn't know much'.[10] The American public at large was even more ignorant.[11] The British information services should have hammered away at the subject: the fact that they did not may partly have reflected Mr Attlee's dislike of seeing almost anything about atomic energy in print. Certainly in retrospect it is difficult to understand the insistence of the British, as well as of the Americans, that the wartime Quebec and Hyde Park Agreements and the *modus vivendi* should be kept as secret as possible for as long as possible, even after all hopes of international control had faded. The British had a great deal to gain from publicising them. Many years later, officials of the

USAEC remarked that Britain would have profited by some good public relations men in their negotiations.

The third moral is that the British press was almost as coy as the British Government in its attitude to news about atomic energy (see Chapter 2). The attitude of the American press was utterly different. There was of course the well-known ability of its columnists to acquire secret information, reflected as it was in the facetious story that the State Department congratulated itself for getting some top-secret telegrams before Drew Pearson did. The United States press knew pretty accurately the contents of the *modus vivendi* and the arrangements for acquiring uranium. The July meetings were a cause of intense speculation in the American press about Anglo-American atomic relations, and there was some very well-informed reporting. 'The problem of Anglo-American co-operation in atomic energy development', wrote Joseph Alsop of the *Washington Post*, 'is almost as explosive as the bomb itself.' Men attending the first, and supposedly highly secret, Blair House meeting with the President remembered many years afterwards their shock at finding reporters thick on the pavement. The first news the British Embassy had of the meeting and their first inkling of the proposals were from the newspapers, where the whole business created a sensation among Washington correspondents. The British Embassy as well as the US Administration wanted to play the matter down, even though it was soon apparent that newspaper comment was surprisingly objective and sympathetic to the general idea of the exchange of information with Britain and Canada. Carroll Wilson felt that an opportunity was being lost by the British Embassy spokesmen, who failed to stress two facts obscure to most people: the very full nature of British participation in the project during the war, and the mutual advantage to be gained by the exchange of information. Extraordinarily enough, this fever of press interest did not spread to London. There were press reports in England, but they were relatively few and slender. Yet British newspapers were in a position to build up, simply from US official statements and material and Washington press comment, studies of various atomic issues of crucial interest to Britain, about which there was an almost complete ignorance in England.

The fourth moral of the July 1949 talks is that they throw into sharp relief the contrast between the American and British Parliamentary systems. Parliament and all but a very few Ministers knew nothing about the background and problems of Anglo-American atomic relations. At the end of June a Member of Parliament had been persuaded to withdraw a Parliamentary question on the subject. Yet members of the Joint Congressional Committee had been told about the wartime agreements and the *modus vivendi*, and figures about British atomic energy expenditure had been prepared for them.* The point was put with unconscious irony by a Foreign Office official. The Americans at this time prepared and released bulky documents of reference and background material about past history in order to build up informed public opinion in the United States about Anglo–American–Canadian technical co-operation. The British felt the Americans should be helped, but the Foreign Office in London added: 'There is I think no suggestion that any identical or similar release should be made in the United Kingdom. I think this is right: we do not have to work on Parliament as the Americans have to work on Congress. If we did decide to release anything here it should be only the short factual statement about UK development of atomic energy.'

And so, against a background of intense public interest in Washington and almost complete public apathy or ignorance in London, the Anglo-American talks were to begin in September 1949. Even after the Joint Congressional Committee meetings, there had been a delay because the new Secretary for Defense, Louis Johnson, was unenthusiastic over the business.[12] The British said the meetings must go ahead. 'There is a point at which we cannot tolerate without protest the delays and uncertainties which have surrounded the whole question since last February on the US side.' So the talks duly began in September. The British aim, as approved by Ministers, was simply to secure the fullest measure of exchange of information on all aspects of atomic energy development, including the military aspect, and recognition of the British claim to raw material in sufficient quantity to ensure fulfilment of their atomic

---

* Secret information on atomic energy was given, usually orally, to the Public Accounts Committee and the Select Committee on Expenditure when asked for, but was usually unrecorded. The PAC hardly mentions atomic energy in its annual reports. The SCE dealt only occasionally with atomic energy, and then as part of larger inquiries. Its first extensive study of atomic energy was not until 1958–9. Unlike the Congressional Committee, it was of course not a specialist committee, and had no special expertise and no scientific or technical support.

energy programme, which had recently been enlarged (see p. 219) to include a third pile and a low-separation diffusion plant.

The first tripartite meeting – a meeting of the Combined Policy Committee – was on 20 September 1949. It had been one of those weekends which the people involved in the talks were never to forget, the kind of weekend when lights burned late in key Government departments in Washington and London. On 18 September the pound was devalued.* On 19 September evidence was received of an atomic explosion by Russia (see Chapter 7).† The news was communicated to the participants in the talks and, while it was not discussed at any of the meetings, its shadow hung over the minds of everyone there.‡ The British reported that the news had created a sense of urgency about the talks in Washington but that the effect was not wholly in Britain's favour. The explosion emphasised the need for the Americans to obtain all the allies and assistance they could in atomic energy development, but it also emphasised the need for the maximum production of atomic weapons at the earliest possible moment, which the Americans felt could best be achieved by concentrating resources in America. The Russian test further underlined the strategic vulnerability of the United Kingdom.

This went to the heart of the United States proposals, now at last uncovered. The general thesis was that because of Soviet intransigence it was essential 'to maximise the mutual defense effort'. The North Atlantic Pact and the projected Military Aid Programme meant that a pattern of co-operation was emerging among the countries involved; a fundamental principle of this pattern was so to allocate effort in the common defence that it would make the most efficient contribution to the total programme. In atomic energy affairs this meant producing as many atomic weapons and therefore as much fissile material as possible, as soon as possible. The limiting factor would be supplies of raw material, and economy and efficiency

* The tremendous burden on officials can be gauged by the fact that Sir Roger Makins (knighted in June 1949), who led the British team in the atomic energy talks, was also a key member of the Foreign Office economics team and closely concerned with devaluation.

† The explosion was detected through close Anglo-American collaboration (under topic 5 of the *modus vivendi*). However, as explained in the Preface, atomic energy intelligence is excluded from this book. An account is given by Hewlett and Duncan in *Atomic Shield*, pp. 364–6.

‡ Then 21 September was marked by the proclamation in Peking of the Chinese People's Republic.

required that production should be concentrated as far as practicable in the United States. The need to reduce the vulnerability of atomic production to Soviet action reinforced this conclusion.

In specific terms, the United States principles boiled down to the following points about atomic production and weapons storage:

'(*a*) Production and storage facilities should be located with due regard for strategic considerations.
Specifically:
1. To the fullest extent practicable fissionable material, production plants, large-scale atomic energy developments and supplies of strategic material should be located either in the United States or in Canada.
2. All portions of any expanded production programme should be located either in the US or in Canada and present plans for such work in the UK should be modified to include only that portion for which appreciable commitments in the line of construction have been made.
3. To the fullest extent practicable production facilities for fabrication of atomic weapons should be located in Canada or in the US not only to provide for better strategic location but also to supplement US facilities in case of emergency.
4. Nuclear components of atomic weapons should be stored in the UK only to the extent required by common war plans. All other nuclear components normally should be stored in the US or Canada.
(*b*) The programme of the parties should be co-ordinated in such a way as to make the most effective use of joint resources, specifically raw materials and effort:
1. It is recognised that the US will make the major effort of production of atomic weapons as required for joint defence.
2. For the next five years it is expected that the UK–Canadian effort should be on such a scale as not to require more than ten per cent of the raw material currently available and allocation of raw material will be made accordingly.
3. Planning of programmes of research, development and production should be such as to make the most effective use of joint resources of technical personnel and facilities.'

The Americans agreed in their exposition of general principles with a point the British had been urging for some time – that there must be a common atomic policy towards other countries. The British had hoped for some relaxation here, but the Americans said from the outset that they saw grave dangers, with very few compensating advantages, in admitting other countries to any appreciable extent in any exchange of information. It was the Canadians who saw especially clearly that any agreement within an Anglo–American–Canadian 'inner ring' on the atomic bomb was liable to conflict with other defence commitments, undertaken jointly, with NATO allies.

Many different subjects were involved in the discussions and, after the opening meeting of the Combined Policy Committee, the teams divided up into five sub-committees: a sub-committee on strategic policy which became the main steering committee, and other sub-committees on raw materials, exchange of information, intelligence, and the form of an eventual agreement. There were simultaneous discussions between the purely military experts.

A great deal hinged on the production programmes, which were dependent on raw material supplies (see Chapter 11). The United States was planning an expanded atomic weapons programme which, though not large in terms of a percentage increase in capital investment, would give large returns in terms of weapon output. The United States regarded as vital the assurance of enough raw materials to feed this new programme, which would provide the most efficient possible conversion of raw materials into weapons in the shortest time. The British were satisfied that the claims made for this programme were justified. They also soon realised that there was no prospect whatever that the Administration would go to Congress with any proposal which did not ensure that the materials requirements of this expanded programme were met.

So the programme had to be measured against the estimate of raw materials supply and the British and Canadian programmes. The Canadians wished to build a second heavy water pile, primarily to ensure the continuance of their research programme if their present pile should cease to be serviceable, but they would not bring the pile into operation until 1955 and there should be plenty of uranium by then. The British programme had recently, as we saw, been increased from two piles to three piles plus a low-separation plant. According to the raw materials figures, admittedly conservative, the sum did not work out, but supply and demand would balance if the British cut out their third pile. The British negotiators were prepared to recommend to their Government that this should be done.

Even though this concession would meet their raw material needs, some Americans felt it did not go far enough. George Kennan, the friendly and sympathetic leader of the United States negotiating team, said there were three possible bases for an approach to Congress. He listed them in order of increasing difficulty: firstly, the concentration of production of atomic weapons in the United States, which would in return furnish the United Kingdom with supplies of them; secondly, the concentration in Canada of United Kingdom weapon production; and thirdly, the division of production between the United States and United Kingdom, the latter having a balanced atomic energy programme. The British Ambassador, Sir Oliver Franks, and Sir Roger Makins said flatly that the first solution was not discussable. Ministers had in a series of decisions over the past five years settled that Britain would have an atomic energy programme; this was inevitable and necessary to her as a great industrial nation. Moreover, under the *modus vivendi* the United States Government had accepted and agreed to support such a programme and there could be no possible question of abandoning it. The Canadian Ambassador in Washington, Mr Hume Wrong, said that the second solution was not discussable from the Canadian point of view. It was politically quite out of the question to agree that the United Kingdom should operate large industrial facilities in Canada, and in any case it was impossible economically because of Britain's dollar shortage.* Only the third solution, difficult though this apparently was to Mr Kennan, was left. Already the British team with Canadian support had beaten off an American Defense Department suggestion that the British programme should be confined to one pile, to be regarded primarily as a means of acquiring experience. They had pointed out that work on the two piles was already far advanced and that the low-separation plant would not absorb additional ore. Suggestions that there should be only one combined weapons fabrication centre at Los Alamos were also turned down, and it was agreed that there should be a divided programme whereby components for which facilities and experience were already available would be made in Britain while the rest should be supplied by

* Cf. Canada's views just after the war (see Chapter 4).

the United States. Common use of trial facilities would be an essential part of an integrated programme.

The British also firmly withstood the American insistence on the concentration of storage of all weapons and components in North America. The Chiefs of Staff had examined yet again the arguments about the vulnerability of atomic weapons in the United Kingdom, and yet again had found them baseless; it would be senseless to store weapons outside Britain because they would be needed for use in a strategic air offensive at the very moment when the threat would be increasing. If all stocks were stored in the United States, the United States would in effect be in sole control and Britain would virtually be in the position of having to seek their agreement to use her own bombs. Even if the bombs were in British territory in the western hemisphere, the United Kingdom's control would be by no means as complete and satisfactory as if the bombs were stored in Britain, and there would be big risks in transporting them. Dr Penney, Britain's weapons expert, pointed out that the difficulties of inspecting British bombs stored in Canada would be enormous and that it would be preferable to manufacture components there rather than ship them out from the United Kingdom for storage. And so Sir Oliver Franks and Sir Roger Makins told Mr Kennan firmly that there could be no agreement that bombs should not be stored in the United Kingdom; the British could not admit any arrangements which could be interpreted as meaning that the United Kingdom had surrendered to the United States its freedom of action in a vital field of policy. Kennan, however, agreed that the United Kingdom must have a store of bombs under its control in its own country.

After the various conversations the British team hoped and believed that, provided they were prepared to give up their third pile and thus ensure that the Americans' uranium requirements were met, it might well be possible to reach a comprehensive agreement, covering the years up to 1955, with the following ingredients:

(i) Approved production programmes consisting of five piles and a tripling of diffusion output in the United States; two piles and a low-separation diffusion plant in Britain; the present NRX pile and possibly a new heavy water pile in Canada.

(ii) Raw material allocations to satisfy these programmes.

(iii) Each country to modify its programme provided it did not exceed its allocation of material.

(iv) Full technical co-operation without restriction on the information exchanged.

(v) Complete co-operation on the design, production, storage and delivery of atomic weapons, with combined testing of them. In view of the reduction of the United Kingdom production programme, the United States would provide Britain with enriched material and other components for making improved weapons. The weapons would be stored in the three countries 'in accordance with common strategic concepts'.

(vi) Common security standards in the three countries.

(vii) Complete exchange on intelligence matters.

(viii) Classified atomic energy information not to be disclosed to any other countries without prior consultation. Co-operation with Commonwealth and North Atlantic Treaty countries should be mainly through assistance with declassified information, and declassification should be speeded if possible. It might be desirable for political or technical reasons to provide classified information to certain countries.

Postponing the third pile seemed a small price to pay for such an agreement, which would enable Britain to make more efficient weapons and also a greater number if the Americans provided enriched material. Co-operation on this scale would also save a great deal of British effort. The Atomic Energy Official Committee and the Prime Minister therefore supported continued negotiations on these lines. Kennan and some colleagues examined the British searchingly on their draft, especially on their production programme. He concluded that the US Administration could not possibly go to Congress on the basis of such an agreement;[13] they could not be put in the position of justifying the British atomic energy programme and it would be better to advise the continuation of the *modus vivendi* with suitable arrangements to meet the American uranium needs. Makins emphasised that this would be a disappointing result, especially in the present state of the world. Moreover, he urged, it was quite inconsistent to have a close working partnership on defence matters while in this vital area of atomic energy the two countries would be unable to talk to each other at all. Makins implied

diplomatically that if the countries were to go their separate ways
and not have a system of technical co-operation, the British might be
much more cautious over uranium allocations.

The Administration recovered its nerve[14] and proposed that the
Combined Policy Committee should approve a brief interim report
and then adjourn for some weeks while the three Governments
considered the next step. This report simply said that agreement
had been reached on estimates of the supply of raw materials for the
next six years and that they would be adequate for the expanded
United States programme, the Canadian programme, and the British
programme of two piles and a low-separation plant. It added that
the Committee had considered 'on a purely exploratory basis' the
problems of co-operation from the political, strategic, technical and
combined planning point of view and had identified in a general
way the probable desiderata of the Governments and those aspects
which required further consideration.

Only ten days separated the two meetings of the Combined Policy
Committee, and on 3 October the Administration gave the Congressional Committee a factual account of the position reached. Kennan
told Makins afterwards that the atmosphere of the meeting was
favourable, that the position was better than he had expected at the
outset of the talks and that psychologically we were 'over the hump'.
Makins got the impression that if the two countries could agree to
the principle of integration in a weapons production programme,
the rest would be relatively plain sailing. Another meeting with the
Congressional Committee ten days later also went off smoothly and
gave the green light for the resumption of talks.

When he returned to London, Sir Roger Makins reported on the
negotiations at length to his colleagues and to Ministers and analysed
the attitudes of the two other participating countries. He recognised
that a real attempt had been made to formulate a unified United
States policy but that this had not been achieved, partly because of
the number of interests involved and the uneasiness between some
of them, such as the State Department and Department of Defense,
and partly because of the relationship between the Executive and
Congress. It was clear that the United States side believed they had
taken a very long step forward in proposing such a complete system
of co-operation. Some of them, said Makins, seemed sincerely unconscious of the fact that their proposals if taken literally would
involve complete subservience of the United Kingdom atomic effort

to the United States effort. He and Sir Oliver Franks had had again to remind even Mr Kennan, who wondered why the British wanted a programme, that Britain was one of the great industrial nations of the world and necessarily and inevitably wished to develop what might be the great industrial discovery of the twentieth century.

Makins emphasised in London the United States' difficulty in swallowing the existence, let alone the size and scope, of the British programme, even though, if the third pile went, it would not interfere with American uranium supplies. He probed the reasons advanced in Washington – Britain's strategic vulnerability, the need for the fullest rationalisation and efficiency, the burden on the British economy – and said they did not appear wholly convincing even to their exponents. 'There is', he said, 'perhaps an ill-defined and almost unconscious feeling that atomic energy is and should remain an American monopoly, both for military and industrial purposes, and this feeling is rationalised in different ways.' Makins felt some progress had been made in breaking this position down and that probably all the Americans now accepted the fact that the two-pile programme in the United Kingdom was a *fait accompli*.

As for the Canadians, Makins said they now regarded themselves as full atomic partners with the United States and Britain but looked upon the present talks as raising primarily Anglo-American issues. They were determined to increase their programme, but at a leisurely pace, and leave themselves free to develop atomic energy without restraint in the future. They were sympathetic and helpful to the United Kingdom position and supported the fullest measure of technical co-operation and an integrated weapons production and storage plan.

Given these attitudes, Makins considered the possible basis of an agreement. It seemed useless to press the Americans on the important but secondary issue of relations with other countries since there was such unreasoning prejudice on the subject in Washington. Another essential point was clear: any approach to Congress was impossible which did not give the United States the full raw material requirements of its expanded programme. This meant reducing the British programme from three to two piles; in return there was the possibility of full technical co-operation and an integrated weapons programme. On this basis the two outstanding difficulties were Britain's construction of a low-separation plant and her weapons production programme.

Here a distinction could be made between the need for a balanced atomic energy programme in Britain with a view to future industrial development, and the need for production facilities devoted exclusively to war purposes. Facilities for the production of uranium-235 were necessary for industrial development unless an adequate supply of enriched material from other sources could be guaranteed for the next ten years. Since no such guarantee could be replied upon, it was essential to proceed with the separation plant. When it came to atomic weapons, however, certain processes – the fabrication of metal components or initiators – were needed solely for war purposes and were useless for industrial development. Hitherto Britain had held firmly that she must have facilities to produce and test atomic weapons without reliance on any external assistance. But the North Atlantic Treaty and the new emphasis on integration and division of labour in defence now made this position dubious. Under an integrated weapons programme, Britain would have a store of atomic weapons under her own control and complete access to all knowledge necessary for the fabrication of atomic weapons. But probably Britain would send plutonium to the United States, and production of fissile cores and other components for weapons would be concentrated there.

The questions at issue were therefore political and technical. The technical difficulties were not insuperable. But politically, could His Majesty's Government agree to integration of the production and storage of atomic weapons? If they could, said Makins, vague fears about the United Kingdom programme would probably be dissipated and objections to the low-separation plant overcome. As officials, and then the Chiefs of Staff, pondered these questions there were many misgivings. There was, however, one wholehearted enthusiast for the proposals – Sir Henry Tizard. Here was the opportunity to look entirely afresh at the British atomic programme, which was throwing such a heavy burden on an industry struggling desperately to regain the country's position in the world. Britain should keep that part of the programme devoted to the exploration of industrial applications but hand over all weapon production to the United States if they would give her a stockpile of bombs under her own control. Others were much more doubtful. Would constitutional difficulties block the exchange of information as with the *modus vivendi*, or would Congress amend the McMahon Act? If Britain agreed not to undertake certain stages of atomic weapons production, would the Americans, on this very ground, refuse her information on these processes? Britain must prosecute research into all aspects of atomic energy and investigate all processes for atomic weapons production at least on a pilot-plant scale; this would ensure entitlement to information on all aspects of atomic energy, so that if the agreement failed in future she would have the knowledge and ability to develop facilities in the United Kingdom quickly. There was also uneasiness about relations with other countries, especially Australia.

In the international atmosphere of the moment, however, the advantages of Makins's proposals seemed overwhelming. Integration of British defence with the United States was the order of the day and the proposals would close a significant gap in existing arrangements. Such an agreement would be important politically for Anglo–American–Canadian relationships. The Chiefs of Staff were sure it would be wrong and dangerous to rely wholly on the United States for production of atomic weapons. There was a serious risk that Congress might repudiate an agreement. They too felt grave doubts whether Britain would continue to receive information of consequence once she had assumed the position of the poor relation by reducing her own programme so drastically. Nevertheless, the Chiefs of Staff, who had hitherto insisted on a complete atomic programme on United Kingdom soil, now agreed that, in return for full collaboration in all fields and an agreement that Britain should have a store of bombs in the United Kingdom under her own control, the atomic programme should be trimmed. The three piles should be reduced to two, and Britain should look to the United States firstly to supply her with uranium-235 to mix with plutonium for the most up-to-date weapons, and secondly to fabricate the bulk of the cores of atomic bombs and the bulk of the initiators or trigger mechanisms. Britain should reserve the right to build her own high-separation plant if supplies of U-235 from the United States were inadequate and should insist on building prototype-scale plants for cores and initiators. It would be a great mistake, said the Chiefs of Staff, to surrender altogether the right and ability to carry out these processes in the United Kingdom and so become wholly dependent on the United States for atomic weapons.

No one in fact seems to have minded very much about the third pile. If it was dropped, atomic weapons production would fall by the prescribed date (see p. 217) by 20 per cent, but the benefits from the United States under the agreement seemed likely to outweigh this. It was the Chiefs of Staff who emphasised the wisdom of stopping the pile because of the economic situation; it would save £8–10 million in capital expenditure and £2 million in annual expenditure.* Technically it seemed wasteful to build a third pile of the same design, while the resources of Hinton's Production Directorate in administration, design, procurement, staff, building labour and materials were so strained that there would be practical advantages in abandoning the third pile and concentrating on completing the first two. A decision had to be taken very quickly. The concrete raft for the third pile was virtually complete and the structural steelwork was fabricated. The work could be stopped without undue inconvenience and without incurring more than a small percentage of the total expenditure, provided a decision was taken within the next two weeks. Moreover 1,500 tons of graphite costing $615,000 had been ordered from Canada for the pile and its manufacture was due to begin in November. Immediate cancellation might avoid nearly all this liability. Ministers were left to choose among four possibilities: stopping all work on the pile at once and cancelling the graphite contract; completing construction of the pile as a standby but not laying the graphite and cancelling this contract; completing construction and laying the graphite as a standby; proceeding with construction and operation of the pile without regard to the tripartite discussions.

Ministers did not have much difficulty in agreeing that work on the third pile should be stopped forthwith, but there were some qualms about the general basis of the proposed integration. The Foreign Secretary said he had 'great fear of our placing ourselves too much in the power of the Americans on the industrial side of atomic energy no less than in atomic weapons production'. The effective industrial application of atomic energy seemed many years ahead, but some discovery might bring it nearer. It would therefore be false economy, said Mr Bevin, for Britain to make any sacrifice which would impair her ability to deal with the United States on equal terms. In 1946 the United States had wished to prevent Britain from having any atomic energy programme at all, and he doubted whether at heart they had ever departed from this attitude. If there was to be an agreement it must be entered into only on terms of

* The net capital saving was £3½–4½ million because the cost of the low-separation plant had been underestimated by £5 million.

equality and of full recognition of the United Kingdom programme. Similarly, when the Minister of Defence suggested that the principle of integration should be pushed still further, Ministers urged that Britain would be placing herself too unreservedly in United States hands. However, the recent Russian explosion – if, it was said, it was caused by a bomb and not a factory accident – underlined the advantages of the agreement with the United States which would mean that Britain would get a supply of effective weapons sooner than with her own resources. The agreement would not give the United States any greater monopoly than they possessed already. It would certainly be impossible to use raw materials as a bargaining point. Ministers accordingly approved further negotiations on the lines suggested by their advisers: that is, the third pile would be dropped but the low-separation plant would be kept; the United States would get the raw materials for their expanded programme; there would be full technical co-operation; the United States would supply Britain with U-235 if necessary in exchange for plutonium, but Britain would retain the freedom to build a high-separation plant if American supplies were not forthcoming; the United States would fabricate most of the cores and initiators for British bombs, but Britain would retain her freedom to build prototype plants; Britain would not object to the storage of the larger part of nuclear components of weapons in Canada; there would be common test grounds.

Meanwhile at the end of the first round of talks the American team had said they would be very much fortified in their discussions with Congress if one or two of their technical experts could be invited for a tour of British atomic energy establishments in order to be able to report on the technical ability of the United Kingdom to achieve a successful production programme. It was impossible not to issue the invitation because this would suggest that the British programme did not bear inspection, but the British were unhappy about it. It would be necessary to show the visitors everything and they would therefore be able to acquire information in many fields outside the *modus vivendi* before there was any assurance of an eventual agreement. Moreover the visit would be successful only if the visitors derived from it a sense of technical ability, and the risk must be recognised that they would be insufficiently impressed. They were the less happy because the Americans asked that General Nichols should lead the team, and in the past he had shown that he had little or no confidence in British efficiency and ability, while he had been one of the most hostile critics of the British programme in the recent talks. They were also upset that the scientist was to be Weil, whose earlier visit with Zinn had caused so much trouble. The third man, Gordon Arneson of the State Department, had been, however, a very good friend of Britain.

The visitors duly came and were shown everything, but they gave little indication of what they thought of the programme, although General Nichols did tell the Chief of the Air Staff that while on some points the British had something to teach the United States, he was surprised at their lack of information on other aspects. Again there was the constitutional anomaly that Nichols submitted a report about the British programme to the Congressional Committee although the British Parliament had almost no information on the subject.

There was certainly no sign of enthusiasm for the British programme when talks reopened in Washington at the end of November 1949. The British were the more depressed because Kennan, with all his authority, was no longer leading the American team. The raw materials provisions of the *modus vivendi* only went up to the end of 1949 and this date was now so near that interim arrangements for raw material allocations had to be made. Now, according to the figures for 1949 and 1950, there would be more than enough uranium to go round. The British were prepared to agree to the central point – the shipment to the United States of sufficient uranium to meet their full expanded requirements – but they did not intend that the United States should get any more than this. The provisions in the *modus vivendi* for the exchange of information were unlimited in time and the United States said they should continue to be applied as at present until further notice.

The discussions then got back to the long-term arrangements. The British Ambassador emphasised that these arrangements were of the very first importance not merely from the technical but also from the political point of view. 'Many of the imponderables in the Anglo-American relationship were involved in the discussion of this question.' The British were therefore dismayed to find that the American team reverted to the principles they had put forward at the very beginning of the talks (see p. 283) and that they asserted that any proposals which deviated from this body of doctrine would be unacceptable. This confirmed the worst original fears of the British that the Americans had established, before they had sounded out the British at all, a position which they were not able to modify. The Americans might feel that the latest British proposals did not go far enough to justify the American representatives 'putting their heads on the block' in order to get them accepted. To the British, the American conception seemed to be that the United Kingdom's effort should be completely supplementary to the United States programme and should not stand on its own feet. This was intolerable.

The specific American objections to the British proposals were, firstly, that they did not meet the American interpretation of 'most efficient use'; in particular, the low-separation plant was still in their programme. Secondly, the proposals for weapons integration did not give the Americans the advantages for which they had been hoping; in particular, they were anxious to secure the assistance of British scientists in their American establishments.

The Americans gave up the struggle against the British low-separation plant, but it seemed that they had a much better case in wanting to push weapons integration further. The British had proposed that there should be in the United Kingdom substantially all facilities necessary for the production of atomic weapons from ore ('buttons to bombs'), if only in limited numbers. But since the war a large body of scientific knowledge had been generated in the United States and their present atomic weapons were very much more efficient in their use of fissile material, very much simpler and very much more reliable than the weapons Dr Penney had known at Bikini. Moreover a great deal of scientific and engineering effort, a great deal of money (over $100 million) and a great deal of time (nearly three years) had been spent in building up industrial factory production of weapons instead of development in Los Alamos laboratories. This effort had increased the reliability of the weapon by a factor of 10 and had cut assembly time by a factor of 20, but it would hardly be economic for Britain to pay the same price for these results. On the other hand, the number of United States scientific and technical staff of first-class ability was too small and the introduction of key British and Canadian scientists into the United States might have a catalytic effect on existing knowledge and experience. There was need for a more 'basic type of thinking' and the Americans were conscious how much Penney had contributed in this way in the past. The British could make a far bigger contribution to the total effort by bringing new ideas into the large

United States production organisation than by spending their
energies on development which was already obsolete. The Americans were asking for a merged weapon project which would
increase the production of atomic bombs from British fissile material
by a substantial percentage over the next five years.

The British team was impressed with this case and produced some
detailed proposals for Ministers. A small number of first-class British
staff would be sent to work in the United States, participating in all
phases of the United States programme so that they could become
thoroughly familiar with the totality of information and experience.
Britain would continue to develop her planned atomic weapons
research establishment and would work on those parts of the programme which were in the common interest. Britain would be free
to take up any particular developments provided they did not prevent the secondment of an adequate staff of scientists to the United
States. There would be complete freedom to transmit information
between the weapons groups in the two countries. The United
States would provide for Britain's own use the number of atomic
weapons which could be fabricated from the plutonium produced
in the British piles. But to produce the most efficient weapons the
United States would exchange highly enriched U-235 for some of the
plutonium. There would be co-operation in weapon testing.

This weapons integration would be only part of the long-term
agreement the British hoped to achieve. There would be the other
now familiar components: confirmation of production programmes
for fissile material, raw materials allocations, co-operation on military and intelligence aspects, full technical collaboration on plants
for fissile material and new types of reactors for power production,
and agreement on security standards and on relations with other
countries. None of these proposals had yet been endorsed by the
Americans, but meanwhile they had to go through the various
hoops in London. Lord Portal's Atomic Energy Council* and the
Atomic Energy Official Committee thought that on balance the
advantages of the weapons proposals outweighed the disadvantages.
The Chiefs of Staff had two important qualifications. Firstly, it was
of the greatest importance that the British should be free to start up
in the United Kingdom any new processes connected with the
manufacture of atomic weapons, and they should accept no restric-

* See p. 45 above. The Council was composed of the men running the
British project.

tions other than those arising from secondment of their scientists to America. Secondly, the Chiefs of Staff wanted a definite assurance from the United States about the creation of a stockpile of atomic weapons in the United Kingdom. The figure in mind was 'about 20 bombs' in the United Kingdom with any balance in Canada.

Ministers too agreed that the proposals would form a suitable basis for discussion 'if we were to continue to attempt to reach agreement with the United States'. But the crucial point for them remained whether the United States would be willing and constitutionally able to assure Britain the necessary stockpile of atomic weapons. Two possible dangers must be faced in a spirit of realism. There was the attitude of Congress which, after Britain had entered into an agreement with the United States and accepted delay in her own programme, might stop supplies of atomic weapons to her and leave her more vulnerable than if no agreement were concluded. There was also the attitude of the United States Secretary of Defense, Louis Johnson; at the recent meeting of the Overseas Writers' Club, from which British correspondents had been excluded, he had made it clear that it was his purpose to ensure that the British did not start making atomic bombs and that, even if they accepted this, the United States would not provide them with full information on American developments. Several friendly correspondents had told the British Embassy that the British would be suckers to fall for the sort of arrangement Johnson had in mind.

Ernest Bevin was, again, especially unhappy at the idea of any agreement which would place British capacity for atomic energy production unreservedly in the hands of the Americans. If war should break out, it might be a matter of life and death for the British to use atomic weapons, but their supply might be denied by American delays or disapproval of British policy. Moreover, Western Union defence was based very largely on the supposition that when the time came Britain should have all the latest weapons (including atomic bombs) at her disposal.

Ministers agreed that as 'a condition precedent' to the renewal of detailed negotiations the British must get a valid assurance about the supply of atomic weapons to Britain, an assurance which would not be liable to be upset at any time by decisions of Congress and which would have the formal approval of the President, and a guarantee that no subsequent action of Congress could at any time invalidate the agreement.

The British Ambassador in Washington duly handed over to Dean Acheson, the Secretary of State, the draft British proposals and firmly made the point about the stockpile. The discussion was inconclusive. The inference was that the British proposals still did not meet the point which had appealed to the Joint Congressional Committee – that a combined programme involving an integrated effort of raw materials, brains and plant would prove more effective for the defence of the United States and the Western world than would separate activities. The request for a stockpile of weapons stored in the United Kingdom was, said Acheson, 'difficult', even though he understood the British anxiety, while any binding agreement would also be 'difficult'.* In fact, by the time this meeting was held, although the British did not know it, Louis Johnson had 'pitched it all out'.[15] Presumably Dean Acheson tried to keep the possibility of an agreement going; the British heard that the various departments were studying the British memorandum 'with critical and in some cases suspicious eyes' and were formulating counter-proposals. Cables brought niggling queries and the British Embassy and London polished up drafts. But in London even Sir Roger Makins, who had remained so staunchly optimistic, now rated the prospects of a satisfactory agreement as low. Agreement, he said, could be achieved only if Anglo-American relations as a whole were on the most cordial basis, and at present there were a number of serious questions at issue between the two countries which were not conducive to the right atmosphere. The *coup de grâce* to the business came very soon, for on 2 February 1950, Klaus Fuchs,† the naturalised British atomic spy who had worked in Los Alamos, and who had given so much information to the Russians, was arrested. 'This dreadful thing which has risen up to strike both of us', in Acheson's words, made impossible any progress to greater co-operation in atomic energy, especially since Senator McCarthy was also starting his Communist witch-hunts. The recent American decision to make hydrogen bombs had also in any case made weapons co-operation more difficult.

* A pretty, but not completely, accurate version of the British proposals appeared in an article by James Reston in the *New York Times* on 4 Jan 1950. British newspapers did not take the story up.

† The Fuchs case is dealt with in some detail in Chapter 16.

The Doldrums Again

The British were not prepared to acknowledge defeat and they were soon considering a return to the attack. The Fuchs case had not prevented the extension of collaboration through exchange of information in other military fields, including the very secret field of guided missiles where co-operation had hitherto been bad. Indeed a most important agreement for such exchange was ratified in February 1950. By this time too the North Atlantic Treaty arrangements were well established, and within them the United States had expressed their wish to regard the United Kingdom as a country with which they must have the most intimate possible relations. The British Government, economically strong after devaluation and before the Korean War, saw themselves with pride as regaining their position as the principal partner of the United States in world affairs. It had always been anomalous that atomic energy was the one field where no effective co-operation existed, and on any rational assessment it was absurd that the discovery of 'one traitor in the British camp',* when there had after all been traitors in the American camp as well, should be allowed to wreck the policy of co-operation which was in the best interests of all three countries.

The information the British had acquired in the talks about American weapon development had made the desire, indeed the need, for co-operation much more urgent. The methods for producing plutonium which the British were pursuing were no more primitive than American methods, but in the fabrication and design of weapons the United States had leaped ahead, while the British needed the highly enriched uranium which only the Americans could provide for newer types of weapons. The desire for collaboration with America was now no longer a question of wanting simply a full exchange of information. The British were also now convinced by the arguments in favour of a division of labour which would avoid the waste of resources or duplicated effort and enable Britain to concentrate on the matters vital to the common security. The only proviso was that Britain's basic military needs must be guaranteed and that a full industrial basis for nuclear power production must be laid in the United Kingdom.

By the early summer of 1950 it was urgently necessary for Britain

* There had of course also been Alan Nunn May in 1946.

to know whether any chance of tripartite co-operation remained, for decisions on her own programme had to be taken. There was no serious question of resurrecting the third pile, if only because of the shortage of uranium. But it was necessary to know exactly what should be built at the new weapons station at Aldermaston and whether Britain should acquire her own testing range, or set up plant for producing certain materials. With no serious prospect of talks, there was no real alternative to pressing ahead with the complete facilities needed to make some custom-built bombs at Aldermaston. Britain was in a position which Makins summarised: 'We can't hold back on our own production but if we go ahead on our own it will mean additional expenditure for an inferior weapon.'

Dean Acheson and Lester Pearson of Canada were visiting London in May 1950, and because of the importance of the issues the Prime Minister was asked to join a meeting on atomic energy. Acheson had little hope to offer. Fuchs had left United States public opinion in a very sensitive state, and moreover, when the tripartite talks had been suspended, a considerable gap had remained between the two sides. He said the Administration was now convinced that before any such agreement could be put into effect, legislation to amend the McMahon Act must be introduced. This could not be done before Congress adjourned in July and it would not meet again until January.

Meanwhile it had been suggested by the Americans, and agreed by the British, that as a first move to more talks there should be a tripartite conference on security standards with the object of satisfying Congress that British and Canadian standards were at least equivalent to those of the United States. The conference took place in June 1950 and in general the Americans said they had been very pleased to find how close were standards and outlook on personnel clearance between the two countries, although there was a very real difference in procedures. The delegates were satisfied that comparable standards existed for the protection of atomic energy information and materials, but it was clear that the United States was much more thoroughgoing in implementation; here, the British needed to put their house in order.

In August the Prime Minister in a letter to the United States Ambassador urged again the need to resume the atomic energy talks in view of the close collaboration between the two countries 'in all fields of military endeavour'. When the British Embassy asked what the reaction of the United States Government was, it seemed that the State Department had only received a paraphrase of the letter in which all specific reference to atomic energy was deleted.

However, by this time it seemed as if the outbreak of the Korean War in June 1950 had produced a change of heart in the US Administration. In the new international situation where Russia was manufacturing atomic weapons and the likelihood of war was both greater and more immediate than it had seemed a year earlier, the Americans had begun to look on atomic co-operation as primarily a military matter. The omens were still not wholly favourable. The Americans would still not permit the export of a special raw material the British needed for their programme; this refusal would not prevent the development of the programme but would delay it a little, make it a little more expensive and a little less efficient. 'If this is United States policy', wrote Makins, 'it is an unworthy one especially in the light of our present association with the Americans in Korea.' The Americans had their eyes on bigger things. To them, the crucial point was to make the most efficient use of available uranium supplies to build up the biggest possible stockpile of the best possible atomic weapons. Even Louis Johnson and the Department of Defense had got past the stage of wringing their hands over the existence of a competitive programme in the United Kingdom. For they recognised that the British programme of two piles plus a low-separation plant was likely to be more efficient than their existing Hanford piles as a converter of uranium into plutonium and at least as efficient as the 'improved set-up' the Americans hoped to get going very soon. The new head of atomic energy in the Department of Defense, Mr LeBaron, was said to have undergone a full 180° reversal of position on co-operation with Britain.*

The Pentagon itself was hatching a plan by which Britain would produce plutonium and sell or transfer it to the United States, the United States would manufacture plutonium into the best and latest atomic weapons, and these weapons would be used in accordance with mutually agreed strategic plans. The best and most up-to-date weapons would be transferred to Britain and would become her absolute property. It was not clear whether the proposal would cover the H-bomb, but certainly the Americans were still very anxious to have British scientists at Los Alamos where H-bomb work was proceeding. This too would involve amendment of the McMahon

* Later there was evidence that Mr LeBaron blew back again.

Act, but for the first time, the British were told, there was a solid Administration front.* Needless to say, yet again the hopes of agreement receded. Yet again telegrams to and from Washington resumed the familiar pattern of the atomic energy negotiations over the last eight years. There were items of good news which made spirits rise – for example, that General Marshall had succeeded Louis Johnson as Secretary of Defense. There were items of bad news that sent them down again – that the Administration front was not as solid as it seemed and that there was reluctance to agree to provisions for the exchange of information. Another blow fell when Pontecorvo, a naturalised British scientist, fled from Harwell to Russia in September 1950. But above all there were the negotiations between departments in Washington behind closed doors, with few crumbs of news for the British. They realised that after this stage the plan would go to the President and then the difficulties would begin. The Administration had no effective majority in Congress after the 1950 elections and the more the Administration thought about it, the less easy they found it to devise a plan of campaign to handle the Congressional Committee† and open the way for amending the McMahon Act. Atomic energy was still a subject which roused both the passions and the conscience of the American nation, and it was for this reason that the wheels of the Administration had ground almost to a halt.

There was only one thing the British could do beyond needling the Americans from time to time: this was to show that Britain had something to offer in atomic energy. Paradoxically after all the previous hullabaloos, a leak in the *New York Times* in March 1951, to the effect that Britain was building her first atom bomb single-handed and might test it soon, was expected to predispose the Congressional Committee to extend co-operation. The British Embassy begged London to release some information, for example about the functioning of the second British reactor, and to publicise the British programme more forcefully, but the Atomic Energy

* Early in 1950 Lilienthal, the Chairman, and Carroll Wilson, the General Manager, who had both been so sympathetic to the British cause, left the USAEC. Paradoxically it seemed, however, that Britain's chances might in some ways be better under Lilienthal's successor Gordon Dean, because his relationship with the JCAE was much happier. In fact it made very little difference to Britain.

† After the 1950 elections Senator Hickenlooper was again chairman of the Joint Congressional Committee, with a Republican majority.

Council refused to do this. They doubted whether Ministers, in view of their known reticence about publicity, would agree to a specific announcement even in order to restore British prestige in America.

By the summer of 1951 no progress whatever had been made towards collaboration. The Administration seemed in a 'parlous, impotent state' and it was clear that if Congress did not accept the proposals in 1951 there would be no hope in 1952, the presidential election year, by which time the programmes of the two countries 'would have so far diverged that it might be difficult to integrate them'. In June the prospects of advance receded further when the two diplomats, Burgess and Maclean, migrated to Russia, for Maclean had held a key position in handling atomic energy affairs in the British Embassy at Washington from February 1946 to September 1948. There were reports that the US Department of Defense, on whom everything depended, had now become very lukewarm about the original proposals for exchanging plutonium for weapons. Apart from their serious doubts about British security, it was surmised that the Department felt that the United States programme was technically so far ahead of the British, and that stockpiles were increasing so rapidly, that it was not worthwhile for the Americans to try for closer co-operation with the British: it would involve so many political difficulties for a merely marginal addition to atomic potential.

In the end 1951 did, surprisingly, bring an amendment to the McMahon Act, but it was not inspired by any desire for general tripartite co-operation and was of very little help to the British. The Administration had decided to take no initiative itself to amend the Act, but it explained to the Congressional Committee the specific handicaps of the Act upon immediate United States interests and left the Congressional Committee to take action if it wished. The specific American needs were largely concerned with the Canadian, not the British, project. The Canadian NRX reactor had proved to have the most powerful neutron flux of all existing reactors and the United States wanted to use it to irradiate important materials for their weapons programme. They also needed information from Canada about heavy water reactors because they themselves were about to develop this system. All these items of co-operation involved the transmission of 'restricted data' under the McMahon Act. There were two restricted areas where they wanted immediate collaboration with Britain. One was in atomic energy intelligence, where

exchanges had been inhibited by the Act. The other area was in
uranium manufacture, where United States losses of uranium in the
process seemed at the time very much less than in Britain (see
Chapter 22). If Britain could achieve the same standards there would
be a significant saving in uranium.

When Congress moved to amend the McMahon Act for purposes
that so clearly served American interests, it moved very fast. The
amending Bill was introduced on 8 October and enacted on
30 October. Whereas it has been unlawful to export fissile material
from or to the United States, this was now possible if the President
said that 'the common defense and security' were not adversely
affected. If in the unanimous judgement of the USAEC 'the common
defense and security' would be substantially promoted and not
endangered, they might authorise specific arrangements involving
communication to another nation of restricted data on refining,
purification and treatment of source materials, reactor development,
production of fissile materials, and research and development on all
these. But the provisos were daunting. No such arrangement was to
involve communication of restricted data on the design and fabrication of atomic weapons, or to be concluded with any nation
threatening the security of the United States. The restricted data
involved were to be limited and circumscribed to the maximum
degree consistent with the common defence and security and the
recipient nation's security standards must be adequate. These
arrangements were to go to the National Security Council and the
President, while advance warning was to be given to the Congressional Committee.

The Congressional Committee in its covering report to the Bill
made it absolutely clear that the amendments were only intended to
enable the United States Government to pass on the absolute minimum of restricted data in particular cases where this was essential
to secure from the recipient nation tangible and substantial benefits.
There was no intention whatever of making any general extension
of tripartite co-operation, only a few specific arrangements. The
Committee listed twenty conditions which would have to be met
before any arrangements involving restricted data could be made
with another country; one of the conditions on which most stress
was laid concerned security standards. Security became a sore point.
In July 1951, at the request of the Americans, a second tripartite
security conference was held. This was in the shadow of the defec-

tions of Pontecorvo and Burgess and Maclean, and it emphasised the differences in procedures for vetting people in atomic energy work. The United States firmly believed in a double inquiry – record checks, etc., plus 'positive vetting', that is, an open inquiry about loyalty and political views in which the person concerned together with his referees and former employers participated. The British procedure consisted only of the check, the 'nothing known against' system. The British delegates to the conference had believed that acceptance of the American double procedures for all past and future entrants to atomic energy work in all Government departments, as well as in universities and firms which held contracts or consultancies, would do more than anything else to induce the Americans to a freer exchange of information. This was an optimistic illusion, but the negative importance of the business was certainly high since security disasters had recently seemed to do more than anything else to put the Americans off co-operation, and there was no hope of co-operation without revised procedures.

In their last weeks of office, Labour Ministers considered the problem. The Prime Minister himself did not like United States methods with their tendency to disregard the liberty of the subject, and he was not convinced that the introduction of positive vetting would in practice bring higher standards of security. Some Ministers foresaw serious political difficulties, but nevertheless it was agreed to introduce the new procedures for future employees in atomic energy.* On a visit to America, the Foreign Secretary, Herbert Morrison, tried to trade the introduction of positive vetting with the Secretary of State against a prior commitment to amend the McMahon Act and this had gone down very badly with the Americans, who did not feel security was a bargaining counter. The changes in vetting procedure had not been introduced when the Labour Government left office in October 1951, and this point of difference with the Americans was unresolved.

After three years of hope of a new era of combined effort in atomic energy, and after hundreds of meetings and reams of paper on both sides of the Atlantic directed to that end, the final product was almost, if not quite, nothing at all. Raw material allocations continued to be made without too much acrimony on a year-ahead basis, with Britain getting just enough to keep her programme going from the Combined Agency stocks in Britain while all the

* Including university workers but excluding contractors' employees.

current production from the Congo went to the United States. In these years of uncertainty, with British hopes rising and falling but refusing to be quenched, the question arose of day-to-day relations with the Americans. After the end of 1949 no one was very sure for a time whether the provisions of the *modus vivendi* about technical co-operation and relations with other countries were still extant. There was no high-level agreement on this, but at the working level officials of the two countries agreed, for example, to arrange a certain visit in one direction and the transmission of reports in the other and add the words 'These requests are made in accordance with our mutual understanding of the technical co-operation programme under the *modus vivendi*'. This sentence was accepted as an adequate, though brief, recognition of the continued validity of the *modus vivendi*. And so the original addled egg lingered on, becoming of less and less value. The USAEC froze the topics on which information could be exchanged as they stood in February 1950 when Fuchs was arrested. Cockcroft reported that visits in 1949 had been of substantial value, but visits in 1950 much less so. Secret and secret limited reports sent from the United States were so old that they were mostly of very little use, although some unclassified and confidential reports were of substantial importance. Small quantities of a few materials came over the Atlantic. There were the familiar delays or difficulties over visits or reports which the British badly wanted, as, for example, on the effects of radiation on graphite. The export to Britain for atomic energy purposes of certain basic, non-secret materials which were openly available in the United States, notably helium, had been forbidden. There was no hope of any exchange of information on power reactors.

Exchanges were not one-way. After General Nichols's visit in 1949, the Americans had laid great store on getting full supply of all the British reports on the butex process for purifying plutonium and uranium, and the British sent them, even though industrial know-how was involved. It was not only the technical co-operation clauses of the *modus vivendi* that lingered on. So, as we shall see, did the clause restricting the disclosure of information to other countries. At the end of 1951 the general conclusion was that the *modus vivendi* was profoundly disappointing, and some officials at least would have liked to end it. But as we shall see, it was an unconscionable time a-dying.

One request was taken up with the Americans quite separately from all this – the use of American grounds and facilities for Britain's first bomb test. By the spring of 1950 Britain had to think seriously about the test because if she was going to have to develop her own trials facilities, a site would have to be chosen by the autumn, almost certainly in Australia. The sensible and most economical arrangement would obviously be common weapon testing on a common range, whether bombs were made in Britain, the United States or jointly. There seemed some hope that, in spite of the lack of progress on tripartite talks generally, testing could be 'desegregated' as a purely military item to be dealt with between the Chiefs of Staff, especially as it was known that the Americans were most anxious to have the benefit of Dr Penney's knowledge and experience. The request was put to the American Chiefs of Staff in the summer of 1950 but no reply was received for some months, so that the British had to approach Australia for permission to reconnoitre the most likely site there – at Monte Bello.* Preparations at this site were pushed ahead after the Americans replied in October 'in somewhat curt terms' that they were not in a position to consider the loan of test facilities to Britain until they were ready to put forward further proposals for tripartite co-operation.

As the preparations for Monte Bello went ahead, it was clear that the effort would be considerable – and that it would interfere seriously with British naval plans. In the spring of 1951 Ministers agreed that it was essential to retain the option on Monte Bello but another approach should be made to the Americans through the Chiefs of Staff or the Combined Policy Committee. Mr Shinwell, the Minister of Defence, suggested there would be considerable political advantage in going ahead with the Australian tests in spite of the expense and effort, as it would show that Britain was 'not merely a satellite of the United States'. He voiced the general feeling that Britain had given America the use of their airfields in England from which atom bombs might possibly one day be carried, and it was 'very wrong' that the Americans should refuse Britain reasonable facilities in return.

At a meeting of the Combined Policy Committee in August 1951 (the first for two years) the Secretary of State said it was not possible to accede to the British proposals in their present form, since in implementing them there would inevitably be illegal disclosure of restricted data, but it might be possible to revise the test proposals so

* A small group of islands off the north-west coast of Australia.

as not to involve such disclosures. The British had just telegraphed to Washington that this idea was wholly unacceptable and that they would definitely go ahead with 'Hurricane', the Monte Bello test, when telegrams came from Washington putting new United States proposals which would meet the main British needs. The choice was beginning to be an agonising one. Penney flew to the United States for further elucidation. He came back with a detailed interpretation of the American proposals, which began with a general statement that the United States would not give Britain any classified information on United States atomic weapons or any information about techniques, methods or equipment classified as restricted data, and that this restriction would be overriding. Penney believed that the goodwill of the officials and scientists was such that in spite of this rider he could perform a satisfactory test in the United States. It now seemed that on scientific and technical grounds the United States proposals were acceptable, but Britain would lose the underwater test which the Admiralty badly wanted. On the financial side the estimated costs of Monte Bello had come down so far that the gap was narrow. The real problem was a political one. If Monte Bello was abandoned now, the decision would have to be final, and acceptance of the United States offer would mean a big gamble. The officials and scientists Penney had met were no doubt entirely sincere and anxious to co-operate, but would they be allowed to do so when it came to the point? The history of atomic energy negotiations was far from encouraging; an arrangement might start with goodwill on both sides but then a change in political climate or personalities would lead to reinterpretation of basic documents in the strictest legalistic sense until all advantages to Britain had been whittled away. If the American proposals were accepted, the Americans could at any moment 'turn off the tap and leave us helpless'. In general, officials and military experts had become extremely dubious about accepting the American proposals. The decision was left as a piece of unfinished business until after the 1951 General Election, but there was little doubt what the decision would be.

The Use of the Bomb

Most of the negotiations over atomic energy had been concerned with the integration of production programmes and weapon tests. But there was another question so important that it was literally a matter of life and death to the inhabitants of the vulnerable United Kingdom: what collaboration or consultation was there to be over the use of the atomic bomb? The wartime Quebec Agreement, it will be recalled, had laid down that neither the United States nor Britain should use atomic bombs on third parties without the consent of the other. The abortive 1946 agreement had substituted 'consultation' for 'consent'. According to Dean Acheson, the Americans were to wish 'most fervently' that this substitution had been made[16] – presumably because they thought it might have been acceptable to Congress as well as to the British. The right of consent or consultation had been surrendered by the British when the *modus vivendi* was concluded in January 1948. This surrender was part of the price paid for the technical co-operation programme which in the event turned out to be extremely limited.

When in 1950 the British Embassy in Washington heard about the Pentagon plan, whereby Britain would produce plutonium which the United States would turn into weapons to be transferred to Britain, officials there warned London that delicate questions about the use of the bomb would arise. The Americans would want to be satisfied that in the event of a major war Britain would actually use the atomic weapons transferred to her, and would not decline to do so either for fear of retaliation or for some other reason. The British representative in Washington asked the Americans if they were trying to elicit an assurance that Britain would support the United States and use atomic weapons if they embarked on a 'preventive war'. The State Department official replied that the United States would not embark on a preventive war, but pointed to the President's recent statement[17] that he would not hesitate to order the use of atomic weapons in the event of Communist aggression. If they transferred to Britain atomic weapons which were not used in a war against Russian aggression, they would in effect have reduced their stockpile, which they could not afford. The British saw a two-edged difficulty. They themselves might wish to use atomic weapons at the beginning of a war in which the Americans were not yet involved. The Chiefs of Staff felt strongly that once atomic weapons had been transferred to Britain as her absolute property, it must be entirely for her to decide when to use them, though their use would be governed by joint strategic plans. The Defence Committee of the Cabinet had recently endorsed the view that the Western Allies should continue to make it unmistakably clear that they intended to use the atomic bomb immediately in reply to Russian aggression.

The question of the use of atomic bombs transferred to British ownership proved hypothetical because the Americans did not agree to the transfer. But the question of the use of atomic bombs owned by the Americans was terrifyingly real, and was already a matter of urgent concern to the Chiefs of Staff. Anglo-American planning talks on the conduct of any future war had been held at intervals from 1948 onwards, but the most important factor of all – the strategic employment of atomic bombs – was barred from discussion. From the beginning of 1949 the British Chiefs of Staff made requests to the Americans for discussions on the subject, but they always met a blank refusal. They became increasingly anxious about their enforced ignorance and their inability to advise Ministers on the subject in a sudden crisis; they were increasingly conscious that this was not 'an acceptable position'.

The question of consultation on the use of atomic bombs had two aspects. Firstly, there was the question of British control over the launching of nuclear strikes by United States bombers stationed in Britain. Secondly, there was the question of consultation on American use of the bomb from bases other than those in Britain. From 1948 onwards the Chiefs of Staff had been especially concerned about the use of atomic bombs from the American air bases in the United Kingdom. As we have seen, squadrons of American bombers had been allowed bases in Britain at the time of the Berlin crisis in 1948. The initial decision had been taken on 28 June 1948 by a small group of Ministers meeting as a Committee of Ministers on Germany* – a more restricted circle than the Defence Committee. The US Ambassador in London had seen the Foreign Secretary that same day, and was anxious to know at once whether the United States might send to Britain three groups of heavy bombers, as a political gesture and a token of interest in the defence of Europe. Ministers agreed and two groups arrived in July. At the end of July the Ambassador made a further request that the third

* Only the Prime Minister, Mr Bevin, Mr A. V. Alexander and Mr Herbert Morrison, with the Chiefs of Staff. Andrew Pierre (*Nuclear Politics*, p. 79) comments that the quick and uncomplicated acceptance of the American bombers during the Berlin crisis came as a surprise to Secretary of Defense Forrestal and Under-Secretary of State Lovett, so much so that Mr Bevin was asked by Secretary of State Marshall if he had fully considered its implications. Forrestal's diary, says Pierre, shows that he saw it as an opportunity to send aircraft which would become 'an accepted fixture'.

group – then stationed in Germany – should be brought to Britain. Now the reason was military rather than political: air bases in Germany were felt to be too close to potentially hostile frontiers. The Foreign Secretary, Mr Bevin, after consulting the Minister of Defence and the Secretary of State for Air, agreed to this arrangement; the third group moved to Britain in August.

This decision was taken at the time of the first acute crisis in the Cold War and perhaps for this reason, as was noted later, no 'precise objective' was agreed between the American and British Governments. The practical difficulties of the Berlin airlift and conventional air support overshadowed prospects of nuclear war. The American B-29 bombers which came to East Anglia belonged to the US Strategic Air Command which had, in 1946, been given delivery responsibility for nuclear weapons. Moreover, the B-29s themselves were known to be of a type which could deliver atomic weapons. Nevertheless, although the bombers were potential carriers of nuclear weapons, those based in England in 1948 had not been modified to do so.* No specific questions about the storage of atomic weapons at the American bases in Britain or about their possible use from these bases appear to have been raised in 1948 by Ministers, officials, or by the Members of Parliament who showed interest.

Three years later, in September 1951, Herbert Morrison, who was visiting Washington as Foreign Secretary, told the Americans that when the British had agreed to provide the bomber bases, the US Ambassador had said that they would be consulted about the use of atomic weapons. The Foreign Office wrote in 1958 that the US Ambassador had given Mr Bevin full oral assurances in 1948 that the British would be consulted about any plans for the use of the US bombers in Britain, but they said, no contemporary evidence of the assurances existed. In the brief prepared for Mr Churchill's visit to Washington in January 1952 after he had become Prime Minister, these oral assurances were not mentioned. Nor were they mentioned in the 1950 Foreign Office discussions which are set out in the next paragraphs.

The 1948 arrangements for the US bombers had been regarded as temporary, but in 1949 an American request to take over some airfields in Oxfordshire augured a more permanent base. Although Mr Bevin welcomed the presence of US bombers in Britain, he appreciated that to give them permanent peacetime bases involved

---

* In the summer of 1949 some of the B-29s were of the modified type. After mid-1950 all deploying B-29s were of the modified configuration.

quite new principles. He was anxious that the Government should fully safeguard themselves on two points: firstly, Britain's right to terminate the arrangement, and secondly, the position if the Americans ever wanted to conduct operations from the airfields before Britain was at war. His two questions were discussed in 1950. An informal agreement with the Americans, embodied in a letter to the US Ambassador, assured the British right to terminate the arrangement but said nothing about consultation on operational use of the bombers.

Thereupon, a Foreign Office legal adviser suggested that it might be desirable to write to the US Ambassador on this second point. There was no doubt on the legal position: 'it really goes without saying that US or any forces in this country cannot operate offensively from it without the consent of HMG – a consent which certainly does not derive nor can be implied from the existing arrangement *per se*'. The State Department would know this, he said, but it was conceivable that the US Air Force authorities might take the view that they were entitled in the last resort to issue operational orders to their units without reference to any non-American authority. It might be better to say something, for it would be of little use to be able to accuse the United States of an illegality after the event. 'It must not happen at all. Something quite informal and unofficial would suffice so long as it is on record.'

The question at issue concerned all bombing forays, whether atomic or non-atomic, and there was a feeling in some Foreign Office quarters that even most of the senior officials knew very little of American intentions about storing atomic bombs in Britain. The general question of American rights in their use of United Kingdom bases was recognised to be potentially of the highest importance, but there were fears that a letter on the subject might cause suspicion and offence. The question was submitted for ministerial decision, which laid down that matters should be left as they stood, on the grounds that in practice this issue could hardly arise unless British policies had diverged so far from those of the United States that American use of the airfields would have to be reconsidered anyway.

At the end of the year 1950, British official concern about consultation on the use of the atomic bomb focused on the possibility of a nuclear strike in the Far East, for President Truman had said that the use of the bomb in Korea was being considered. However, the immediate issue merged into discussions about a general right of consultation on the use of the bomb.* To allay public anxiety, the Prime Minister rushed to Washington and was able to come back and tell the Cabinet that the President had assured him that he regarded the bomb as in a sense a joint possession of the United States, the United Kingdom and Canada and that he would not authorise its use without prior consultation with the other two Governments save in extreme emergency, such as an attack on the United States, which called for immediate retaliation. Mr Attlee told the House of Commons that 'it was in the spirit and against the background of the wartime partnership that I was able to raise the vital question of the use of atomic weapons and it was in the same spirit and against the same background that I received the assurances which I consider to be perfectly satisfactory'.[19] He refused to give the House of Commons the precise terms of the understanding, but his general reassurance put many people's minds at rest.

However, Mr Churchill was incensed to discover for the first time that the clause of the Quebec Agreement about the use of the bomb had been surrendered and was convinced that the national interest demanded the publication of the agreement, especially in the light of the subsequent arrangements by which United States bombers were stationed in East Anglia. He felt so strongly on the subject that he decided to write to the President himself, asking him to agree that atomic weapons should not be used from British bases without prior British consent. At No. 10 Downing Street, Mr Churchill's belief that because he signed an agreement with President Roosevelt in 1943 he had the right to deal direct with the current President seemed extraordinary, especially as he had not sent the Prime Minister a copy of the letter; it also led to embarrassment in the White House. The United States and Canada were in any case still firmly opposed to publication of the Quebec Agreement and of subsequent arrangements between the three countries.

The situation was worse than Mr Churchill or Parliament knew. The President's undertaking about consultation on the use of the bomb had been given in a short private talk with the Prime Minister, but he subsequently affirmed the gist of it to a full meeting of the

* Several months earlier, in the summer of 1950, 'to meet the contingency of a world war, the Joint Chiefs of Staff moved to reinforce American power in the West. One measure they urged was to store non-nuclear components of atomic weapons in Britain. Then only the nuclear cores would have to be sent if the situation grew worse. . . . The President agreed to the transfer.'[18]

conference. Dean Acheson, Secretary of State, tells us[20] that he himself thereupon pointed out that over and over again the President had insisted that no commitment of any sort to anyone limited his duty and power under the law to authorise the use of the atomic weapon if he believed it necessary in the defence of the country; that he had gone far in declaring that he would not change that position; that if he should attempt to change it, he would not be successful since Congress would not permit it. According to Acheson, he told the President that the undertaking would open a most vicious offensive against him and the British, whereas a programme of keeping in close touch with the Prime Minister in all world situations that might threaten to move towards violence and hostilities of any kind would be widely approved. All agreed with this, says Acheson, 'albeit Mr Attlee a little sadly'. The British record of events was different. It said that the President had indeed affirmed the gist of his undertaking, saying that the understanding on this point was clear, even though it depended on no written agreement and even though he was unable to include in the communiqué a reference to the undertaking. The communiqué simply said that it was the President's hope that world conditions would never call for the use of the atomic bomb, but that he had told the Prime Minister it was also his desire to keep the Prime Minister at all times informed of developments which might bring about a change in the situation.

In these circumstances there was no agreed record of the discussions on this subject, and the Americans would not accept a copy of the British record which included the assurance about consultation on the use of the bomb. They claimed that the wording of the communiqué superseded the President's undertaking to consult. The British made clear to the State Department that they considered an undertaking to consult had been given and was recorded in London. Acheson very much hoped that things would not be said there which might lead to misunderstanding and questioning in Washington; he feared lest the Prime Minister might tell Parliament that the United States had pledged to consult Britain before taking any decision to use atomic weapons. The Foreign Office were able to tell him that in spite of the strongest pressure by the Opposition, the Prime Minister did not go beyond the language that had been agreed. In the last year of his life, Mr Acheson spoke with admiration of Mr Attlee's success in achieving the promise he sought from

the President. 'We had to unachieve that', he added.[21] Once more
the atomic promise of a President of the United States to a Prime
Minister was being broken, and the discussions on the use of the
atomic bomb seemed to have been almost as fruitless as the long
negotiations to integrate atomic energy production.

The Chiefs of Staff saw that, even on the best reading, the Prime
Minister's understanding with the President had not gone far
enough. The Chief of the Air Staff reiterated that it was a matter of
vital importance and extreme urgency that the United States should
agree to immediate joint study of the strategic use of the bomb, and
to a disclosure to Britain of plans for its use. 'The present situation
whereby the United States could launch atomic bomb attacks on
Russia making use of United Kingdom bases and facilities' without
giving any indication of their plans was 'quite intolerable'. If the
international situation deteriorated, Britain might suddenly be faced
with American proposals to use the atomic bomb and she would
have no idea how it was going to be used; nor any assessment of its
effectiveness. Britain had no intention of running away from the
consequence of atomic war should it become inevitable. But the
Government could not accept the possibility that an issue of this
importance should become a matter for hurried *ad hoc* discussion or
last-minute telegraphic discussion, as had happened over Korea.

The Chiefs of Staff and the Foreign Office were conscious that
there might well be differences of opinion between the two countries
if there were such joint discussions. They themselves, for example,
believed it was most dangerous to regard atomic weapons as something entirely new with which aggression would be quickly, easily
and permanently eliminated. There was no guarantee that the bomb
by itself could win a war against Russia in the sense of forcing
capitulation; a general war, whether or not the West ultimately
'won it', would be followed by such appalling consequences on both
sides that it must be a very last resort, an alternative to bloodless
defeat. The Chiefs of Staff and the Foreign Office were conscious
too of a very wide gulf on this subject between public opinion in the
United States and Europe. In the United States, they said, there was
a widespread mystical belief in the atomic bomb as a 'panacea'
which could quickly bring Russia to her knees, restore the rule of
law, and obviate perhaps twenty years of Cold War and its unpleasant economic consequences, without United States troops having to fight once more on European soil, and without any very

serious consequences to anyone else. This idea seemed to be only slightly tempered by the belief that Russia could retaliate with atomic bombs on some United States cities. In the United Kingdom, on the other hand, there was the belief that there was something inherently immoral about the atomic bomb and that the West should never be the first to use it; there was also the very natural fear of retaliation on Britain. The task of statesmanship seemed to be to educate public opinion in the West to the common idea, firstly, that the inevitable effects of full-scale atomic war would be so devastating that it should be launched only as a last resort; secondly, that the last resort must be defined as the only alternative to the surrender of either a vital principle or some vital areas which should be clearly and closely defined; thirdly, that in the last resort the consequences of not forcing the issue would be worse than those of a war – for example, bloodless capitulation to Russian Communist imperialism.

The Prime Minister, the Foreign Secretary and the Minister of Defence entered the discussion and agreed on the need to reach complete and early agreement with the United States about the actual plan for a strategic air offensive, and the conditions and occasions on which atomic weapons should be used. The responsibility for using atomic bombs or issuing an ultimatum could certainly not be handed over to the United States, which was not after all even in the front line. Any military disadvantage of delay must be subordinated to the need for issuing an ultimatum. Ministers were also conscious of the other NATO powers, but thought that the latter might be ready to trust the United States and United Kingdom acting together.

The British applied pressure in Washington for a year on these points to absolutely no avail. In September 1951 the Foreign Secretary, Herbert Morrison, saw Dean Acheson about the strategic air plan. He told him that the long delay was most disturbing; it was intolerable – the oft-repeated and justified word in this context – that Britain should risk annihilating retaliation without being first informed or consulted. He told him, as noted above, that when Britain had agreed to United Kingdom bases for US bombers, the American Ambassador had said she would be consulted about the use of atomic weapons. The President had given the Prime Minister an assurance about consultation before using the atomic bomb, but had subsequently felt unable to refer to this undertaking. Acheson replied that 'as regards the use of the UK bases he personally thought they would consult us and would not use them to launch atomic weapons without our acquiescence'. But, he said, a general undertaking to consult Britain before using atomic weapons from other bases presented great political difficulties for the United States. Politically, the President could not admit that he had accepted any limit on United States freedom to use their most powerful weapon, quite apart from difficulties with the McMahon Act. But, Acheson thought, the difficulty was more apparent than real. The United States would use atomic bombs in a general war but, as a matter of commonsense, would obviously not resort to a general war without consulting their allies. The real issue was, in what circumstances might there be resort to general war?

This conversation, said the Foreign Secretary, 'prodded' the United States into holding some general political–military talks on the whole question. A meeting was held on 14 September 1951, between Sir Oliver Franks (the British Ambassador) and Sir William Elliott* on the one side, and two State Department officials and General Bradley† on the other. Its most important result was a recognition at last that there must be consultation, and that the British must give their prior consent, before the United States used atomic weapons from Britain. The American side accepted that the use of British bases involved British sovereignty and that it was therefore natural that the United States should seek British acquiescence before launching a war from them. The Americans said they were willing to draft a public statement with the British, although the author has seen no draft and no statement. Apart from this vital commitment, the United States side were unwilling – indeed legally unable – to enter into any commitment which would inhibit their sovereign right to make war, if they felt it necessary to do so. They pointed out that the same might be true of Britain. They were prepared to continue general talks with the British about world trouble spots, but they were adamant that they could enter no *formal* commitments about fixed stoplines on one side of which they would in no circumstances resort to general war and on the other side of which they would. Each case would have to be examined on its merits as and when it arose. They wished to hold periodical talks in the politico–military forum and try as far as possible to reach an

---

* Representative in Washington of the British Chiefs of Staff.
† U.S. Chief of Staff.

identity of views about the circumstances in which conflicts might break out and what should be done if they did. General understandings about consultation on the use of nuclear weapons anywhere in the world came after the period of this book.

In October 1951 Oliver Franks, anxious to avoid a situation where the question of the Americans using their British bases to launch atomic attack became a sudden political issue, put a draft formula to the Americans. This concluded with the statement that the question of the use of the air bases and facilities in the United Kingdom in an emergency 'naturally remains a matter for joint decision in the light of the circumstances at the time'. This was submitted to the United States National Security Council who saw no objections to it and agreed that it could be used if required, although they understood the British would not use it unless they needed to. In December 1951 the gist of the formula was given in the House of Commons.[22]

The commitment about prior British consent to the use of atomic bombs from United Kingdom bases – an admittedly partial return to Clause 2 of the 1943 Quebec Agreement – was very important indeed. Otherwise the three years' negotiations on atomic energy with the United States were wellnigh fruitless, anyway in the short run, so much so that it may seem unnecessary to have described them at length. But they are important in illuminating the Labour Government's attitude to nuclear independence and for their place in the Anglo-American special relationship. Before the 1949 negotiations with America, the British Government had believed that Britain must have within her own shores a self-contained nuclear programme, with her own scientists and engineers not only producing fissile material but also fabricating atomic weapons. They simply hoped to get as much information as possible, and perhaps enriched uranium and other special materials, from the United States to make the process quicker and more efficient.

But in the 1949 negotiations this attitude was greatly modified. The news of the Russian atomic bomb explosion, at least three years before the first British test was expected, made the British more anxious than ever to acquire an immediate stock of American atomic bombs under their own control. The effect of the news was still more profound, for it revealed a change in Britain's rating in the technology of weaponry. This was the moment of truth when Britain saw that Russia was a super-power, not only in land mass and size of armies but in atomic warfare as well, and that her own independent atomic deterrent would be much less impressive than she had supposed. This feeling was no doubt strengthened as the British representatives heard in Washington at the end of 1949 of the great progress made by the United States both in the scientific sophistication of weapons and in their industrialised production.

Britain was facing for the first time the implications not just of a gap in the size of armies and the volume of weapons but in techno-logical potential. The difficulties of the British guided missiles programme and the American decision early in 1950 to develop a hydrogen bomb both emphasised this gap still further. In these circumstances the British Government were prepared to set much less store by independence. They were determined to retain all the components for a properly balanced industrial atomic programme – that is, the piles and low-separation plant, which would not only produce fissile material for bombs but also provide the basis for nuclear power. But they now became anxious to sacrifice their independence in fabricating weapons and to leave the processes with a purely military use to the Americans. They were prepared to settle for what they considered the absolute strategic minimum: a stock of bombs under their own control, stored mainly in Canada but partly in the United Kingdom, and the basic ingredients for an atomic weapons research establishment so that they could get production going if the Americans let them down. National pride had become relatively unimportant as a determinant of policy, if only through recognition of the facts of life. The British Government wanted integration rather than independence in deterrence.

But integration was denied them by the Americans, who in these three years of atomic energy negotiations trifled with the British. The Americans had their own difficulties. Some of them were with-in the Administration itself where, as Acheson said, there was not one policy but ten policies. There were divisions between depart-ments and within departments. Within the Atomic Energy Com-mission itself one of the Commissioners was implacably opposed to co-operation. Several individuals did indeed staunchly espouse the British cause and sometimes paid a high price under a later Adminis-tration for having done so. There was plenty of sheer confusion over the issues in Washington departments. The picture was even bleaker outside the Administration, in Congress. Opinion in the Congressional Committee was overwhelmingly against collaboration, and the few who would support it were not strong enough to stick out against the majority. In these circumstances, according to Acheson, everyone who talked truth or sense on the atomic energy business – that there was no secret and so forth – was liable to be besmirched. The succession of British spy cases in 1950 and 1951 made the situation still more difficult, even though the United States had their own black sheep. It seems fairly certain, however, that the negotiations would have failed even if there had been no Fuchs, Pontecorvo, Burgess or Maclean.

Looked at in isolation, these atomic energy negotiations would present a depressing picture of a super-power playing with a satellite. The Americans set a price for an atomic energy agreement which they should have known no self-respecting nation would accept, and yet seemed surprised and even hurt that the British demurred. The Brtish made a sacrifice such as their third pile – admittedly no great loss – and the Americans scarcely acknowledged it. The British exhibited dignity, realism and inexhaustible patience. Nothing, however, seemed likely to satisfy the core of United States opinion which apparently desired that the United Kingdom should do precisely nothing in the atomic energy field.

Yet the atomic energy negotiations were proceeding at a time when, as we have seen, Britain and America were drawing closer and closer together again on nearly every other front. American generosity under the Marshall Plan had been very great indeed. There was full co-operation on foreign policy and on almost all other forms of military policy. There was enthusiasm for the North Atlantic Pact on both sides of the ocean. The Fuchs case did not prevent the ratification of an important Anglo-American agreement for the exchange of scientific and technical information in other military spheres; British and American soldiers fought together in Korea. In talking to the President at the end of 1950, the Prime Minister had heard him acknowledge the Anglo-American partnership as the mainspring of Atlantic defence. As one journalist wrote, if the Anglo-American alliance should be dissolved, every military plan in the Pentagon would have to be torn up.[23]

In 1946 and early 1947 the absence of Anglo-American atomic collaboration had accompanied a general withering of the wartime special relationship between the two countries. In 1948 a general rapprochement brought some thaw in atomic energy relations as well. But in 1949, 1950 and 1951 atomic energy was something wholly apart, something dealt with according to principles quite different from those governing the rest of foreign and defence policy. Later in the 1950s[24] Anglo-American atomic co-operation was at last re-established and became once more an integral part of the special relationship. It will be for a subsequent volume to analyse how far this change resulted from ceaseless British prodding through the post-war decade and how far from Britain's determined demonstration of her nuclear capacity for weapons and industrial power; in particular, progress on Calder Hall, the world's first nuclear plant designed to feed electricity into the national system, was greatly to impress the Americans. As for the years up to 1955, the British found that the United States attitude on atomic affairs defied rational analysis. Perhaps some American experts had the only answer:

The response to this greatest of all triumphs of scientific method and creative intelligence has been in some respects closely akin to the practice of magic among the most primitive of tribes. Having in their possession a fearful image of the god of war, which makes them stronger than all their enemies, the tribe is obsessed with the fear that the image may be stolen or duplicated and their exclusive claim to the deity's favour lost. So a temple is built, ringed about by walls and guarded by untiring sentinels. Those whose function it is to attend the deity are carefully chosen and subjected to purification rites; they are forbidden ever to look upon the whole image or to speak of what they have seen. They are guarded with unceasing vigilance and at the slightest sign of defection condign punishment is visited upon them.[25]

10 Independence Reconsidered: II

BRITAIN's atomic relations with the Commonwealth and Europe had been governed until the end of 1947 by the attitude of the United States, or by fear of their attitude. The Quebec Agreement may have covered only the war period, but its status was dubious and Britain had continued to adhere to the clause which forbade the disclosure of any information to other countries without American agreement. This was not simply a matter of possible legal obligation. Britain realised that her chances of returning to some kind of atomic energy collaboration with the United States would be lost forever if she seemed ready to pass on to others atomic information, even that which she had acquired by her own labours.

By the middle of 1947, with the prospects of a renewal of Anglo-American collaboration apparently as remote as ever, Britain had contemplated taking a more independent line and was planning to investigate the possibilities of atomic energy collaboration and even integration at least with the Commonwealth. The sudden resurrection of hopes of a new Anglo-American agreement put these proposals into cold storage and policy towards other countries was determined once more by American wishes, which were embodied in the *modus vivendi*. When the *modus vivendi* was reconsidered in 1949, the British again hoped that the way would be opened to greater atomic collaboration with their friends and relations in the rest of the world, but the agreement that Britain was prepared to contemplate with the Americans in 1949 provided almost no relaxation of restrictions and, as we have seen, it was in any case abortive. The spirit and even the actual provisions of the *modus vivendi*, that curious document with so indeterminate a term, continued to govern Britain's atomic foreign policy for years. We shall return to these problems in a moment.

Canada

The one exception to all this was, as ever, Canada, who was a party to the *modus vivendi* and was deeply involved in the 1949 negotiations as well. As we have seen before, Britain's atomic relations with Canada could be considered only as part of the triangle of which the United States was the third corner. All kinds of possibilities were open for collaboration between Britain and Canada which did not depend on American concurrence, but when any major question of policy came up it was often influenced by United States needs and wishes. Canada was sometimes torn between her friendship and ties with the two countries, and indeed there was conflict between her own interests since they were involved with both countries. Britain had a constantly recurring fear that United States policy would, whether accidentally or by design, drive a wedge between her and Canada.

In the immediate post-war period, it will be remembered, Canada had been anxious to continue a combined Anglo-Canadian project, and all kinds of misunderstandings had arisen over Britain's refusal to contemplate this. Britain had wanted collaboration rather than integration, and by the end of 1947 collaboration with Canada was working very well and to the advantage of both sides. The British Government had helped Canada to acquire W. B. Lewis to run her project, and British staff were staying long enough to enable Canada to make the transition to a fully Canadian-run project. On the other side of the account, the use of Chalk River facilities was absolutely indispensable to the United Kingdom project. The NRX reactor with its high intensity of radiation was invaluable for testing materials and for providing certain isotopes. Above all, Dr Spence was able to do in Canada all his essential experiments on the basis of which the chemical separation plants at Windscale were to be built. He and his chemistry team remained in Canada until the autumn of 1947, when the essential features of the process had been worked out, but the chemical engineering team remained at Chalk River until 1950. The two friends, Cockcroft at Harwell and Lewis at Chalk River, corresponded frequently, warmly and at length,* swapping ideas on immediate and future problems, especially nuclear power, and concealing no technical details from one another. The

---

* Cockcroft's letters to Lewis seem to be the longest he wrote to anyone.

transatlantic atmosphere at this latitude was now extremely cordial not only between the scientists but between all the other people concerned in the project.

But though collaboration was very close, what had once been an integrated international project had split into two national projects. In the early summer of 1947, it may be recalled, the British wished to move back towards a joint project or anyway two projects jointly planned together. At this stage indeed they were beginning to think in terms of a joint project of all the white Dominions. It was the Canadians who had now drawn back. They were very anxious not to frighten the Americans, who were proposing the tripartite talks that were to lead to the *modus vivendi*, by suggestions for widening the charmed atomic circle (see p. 150). As for the British suggestions about joint planning, it seemed that the interdepartmental complications in Ottawa were too great and Dr Mackenzie thought it would be possible to meet all the specific requests the British had made by administrative action. Though Mackenzie was extremely co-operative, this pragmatic approach did not provide for the integration of high-level policy which the British now desired.

The *modus vivendi* did not in itself make any difference to Anglo-Canadian co-operation, which was not circumscribed by any rules. Nor did it make much difference to Canadian–American co-operation. The Canadians may have got rather more information from the Americans, but there were still complaints that the American liaison officer at Chalk River would stand by and let them make mistakes he could have prevented. The Canadians themselves had always been, and continued to be, entirely open with the American liaison officer who could obtain, and pass on, virtually any information he wanted. Of course the Canadians depended on the United States for the defence of North America, but they were in any case generous and lacking in pettiness. The British felt much less happy about the Canadian magnanimity as it often meant that British information was passed to the Americans with no reciprocity. 'The leak through Chalk River is a running sore which should be healed or else cut out', exploded one scientist as late as 1952.

Nevertheless, information flowed freely between the two countries and every opportunity was taken to make intelligent use of each other's facilities. The Canadians sent Britain milligram quantities of plutonium – with American permission, as the uranium slugs had been given by the United States to the Anglo-Canadian project –

and as each country's range of activities grew, there was a general exchange of isotopes and materials.

At the end of 1948 Britain and Canada began discussions about atomic energy collaboration in the event of war. In particular, the British were hoping that Canada might provide reserve supplies of polonium* and plutonium as well as certain weapons research facilities. In order to provide the reserve supplies, a new pile of high power would have to be constructed. This fitted very well into Dr Mackenzie's ideas, for he had been worried that Canada was supporting a project as expensive as Chalk River purely for research. Canada's project was now on such a scale that it was necessary to move forward, but since nuclear power was not imminent and Canada did not wish to make atomic bombs, there was no obvious reason for building another pile. The British request might strengthen the case for further development at Chalk River.

It was some months before the discussions went any further, and by this time, the summer of 1949, the British seemed interested only in ensuring reserve supplies of polonium. They appeared to have lost interest in Canadian plutonium, even though they had recently decided to build a third pile of their own to increase the output of plutonium to meet the Chiefs of Staff's requirements. There is no evidence that anyone suggested that Britain should buy plutonium from Canada instead. Canadian output from their NRX reactor and chemical plant was limited at this time and really useful supplies would require another reactor; the immediate dollar cost would probably have put such a proposition out of court, although in terms of the materials and men that might have been released for export work in Britain, the idea might not have involved a greater drain on foreign exchange. In fact, as we have seen, Britain abandoned the third pile in the 1949 tripartite negotiations, though it was generally agreed that Canada should go ahead with her own second pile.†

Britain did, however, make a formal request to Canada for polonium, on the understanding that she herself would supply the technical information. The Canadians said they could meet Britain's polonium needs from their existing pile, but they were very anxious

* Polonium is needed for atomic weapons, but as it has a short half-life it has to be constantly replenished.

† Britain's third pile – a carbon copy of the Windscale piles – would, however, have been ready long before the Canadian pile, which would not be ready until 1955 when uranium was expected to be plentiful.

to build another pile if only they could make the project economic by finding an outlet for the plutonium, which was quite useless to them. The Canadians said they had suggested to the United States Atomic Energy Commission that Canada should build her second pile and dispose of polonium to Britain and the plutonium to the United States.

In the summer of 1950 Mackenzie wrote to Cockcroft that Canada was hoping to get, within a month or so, an undertaking from the United States for the sale of their excess plutonium, a deal which was essential if she was to go ahead with the second pile. The British showed no particular concern about such a contract, and they must have known it had gone ahead, because soon afterwards Lewis told Cockcroft he was now making detailed plans for constructing the new reactor and he asked if someone from Harwell would independently duplicate the Canadian experiments to ensure that the answer to the crucial question of critical size was right.

Meanwhile Britain's own immediate requirements for Canadian plutonium for research had been going up from milligram to gram quantities, and now, in the middle of 1950, Cockcroft asked for solutions from Chalk River containing 1 kilogram of plutonium in order to push ahead with pilot-plant studies on the purification and extraction of plutonium metal: Britain would barter uranium metal for the plutonium. The Canadians agreed to this proposal. At the end of 1950 the British request for Canadian plutonium was pushed up to a loan of 5 kilograms in order to help with work on the fabrication of metal, preparatory to Britain's first weapon test. This new request was put in the context of a greater Canadian interest in the military aspects of atomic energy and a desire for closer rapprochement with Britain in this field. This interest could be encouraged not only by the request for plutonium but also by the loan of Canadian scientists to the British weapons research organisation and the provision of an atomic weapons test range for trials subsequent to Monte Bello. The Canadians could only provide half the British needs, but they promised to do so as long as this did not interfere with their plutonium agreement with the United States.

It was only now that the British became aware that this agreement committed to the United States all Canadian plutonium from both the existing pile and the new pile, except for the small quantities needed by Canada and the United Kingdom for experimental purposes. They had shown so little inquisitiveness earlier, when the

Canadians talked about the imminence of agreement, that the sense of injury they now displayed was misplaced. Clearly the agreement was of very great importance to Canada: the proceeds from the sale of plutonium to the United States would be enough to amortise the whole of the capital expenditure involved in the expanded programme and also to yield Canada a substantial annual profit from which to finance further experiments. Nevertheless, Britain's rage was justified when the Americans showed every sign of refusing to allow the Canadian loan of 2½ kilograms* of plutonium to her. Lord Tedder, Chief of the Air Staff, was in Washington and told the Americans very bluntly that if they were to throw a spanner into the supply of Canadian plutonium to Britain, 'London's patience would go through the roof'. However, Mackenzie went to Washington and persuaded the Americans to see reason and allow the loan to Britain.

This plutonium business, on top of the long-standing arrangement whereby all Canadian uranium went direct to the United States and was not even allocated by the Combined Policy Committee, seemed to threaten to build barriers between Canada and Britain in atomic energy affairs. The amendments to the McMahon Act in the United States at the end of 1951 were an even graver threat. They had been made largely to facilitate co-operation on specific projects between the United States and Canada, and the British could foresee that the Americans would make it a condition of co-operation that Canada would not pass on to Britain restricted data received in this way. There was a real risk that the atomic ties between the two North American countries would become closer and that Britain would be left out in the cold.

There was general agreement that the best way of countering this threat would be to try to integrate the United Kingdom and Canadian programmes. This might be achieved by offering to have a unified project with Canada on the development of nuclear power and to promise her enriched material from the British diffusion plant. This point was not reached, however. The head of the British scientific mission in Washington saw Dr Mackenzie and said it would be difficult to convey on paper his great cordiality. Mackenzie said he attached the utmost importance to free interchange between Canadian and British scientists not merely of results but of plans for future work, and that he had made this clear to the United States.

* i.e. 2·5 kg including the 1 kg already promised.

He intended to maintain this. For example, United States reports on uranium refining might be supplied to Canada on the understanding they went no further, but the plant would be a Canadian one and he would no more consider excluding British scientists from it than from Chalk River. The British concluded that the dangers that a wedge would be driven between Canada and Britain seemed remote as long as Britain continued to show Canada full consideration and co-operation.

Co-operation remained extremely close in interchange of staff, facilities, information and materials and was eased by a barter account which enabled individual transactions to be arranged directly between Cockcroft and Lewis without detailed reference to the Treasuries. Over five years Britain had incurred the extremely modest net liability of $25,000. There was also to be an implicit division of labour in the countries' nuclear power programmes. Britain, for example, informally forswore an interest in heavy water power reactors because this was Canada's province.

Co-operation could not go much further than it did, but it was still not the same as unification. There had been a unified project in 1945 but it had split into two at the wish of the British and could not be put together again now. There had been much anxiety in Canada in 1945 about the country's ability to carry single-handed this immensely demanding project which she had undertaken in 1942 out of goodwill rather than careful forethought. But now in 1951 there was great and justifiable confidence in Canada's ability to run an independent project successfully. Atomic energy had helped to carve a new status for Canada in the post-war world. It had brought her to the top diplomatic tables and it had demonstrated and enhanced her underlying scientific technological and industrial strength. The NRX reactor – planned by a wartime hotchpotch of Canadians, British, New Zealanders, and French and other European refugees – was the most successful experimental pile in the world. In these circumstances Canada was relaxed and generous, ready to help the British and the Americans without bothering too much whether she got back as much as she gave. An odd twist of wartime fate had made her into an important country atomically speaking. She wanted full collaboration, but she now valued her independence as well.

The Rest of the Commonwealth, and Europe

Just before negotiations for the *modus vivendi* began, the British Government had decided to organise an integrated Commonwealth atomic energy project so that as time went on, new tasks could be allocated to various members on grounds of expediency and availability of resources. This decision was engulfed by the *modus vivendi* talks (see p. 149). At the time there was no question of any similar atomic rapprochement with any European country; Belgium and France had both refrained from asking for any such co-operation since the early months of 1947, when both had been rebuffed (see pp. 152–8).

When the *modus vivendi* talks began, the British team had the impression that any resulting exchange of information would not be confined to the United States, Britain and Canada. The strong Communist elements among the French scientists made it unlikely that France would be included in any arrangements, but the extension of collaboration to Belgium seemed possible and desirable. The British also wanted to press the Dominions claims for the information they needed for the next stage of their atomic energy development. However, the United States team were very hesitant about passing on any information to any other countries; they felt they were already stretching the McMahon Act a long way in agreeing to the exchange of information with the United Kingdom and Canada. Their reluctance seems to have been little affected by their realisation of the important part the Dominions would play in the future provision of uranium. In the event, the *modus vivendi* said that classified information would not be disclosed to other countries without due prior consultation. However, it was recognised that scientists from New Zealand, Australia and South Africa had worked in the British atomic energy project during the war years as part of the combined effort and since then at Chalk River, in the United States and at Harwell. Since these countries were also co-operating on raw materials, certain areas of co-operation with Dominion scientists were recognised: the parts of the proposed declassification guide that were suggested for immediate declassification, that is, health and safety, research uses of isotopes, the detection of distant nuclear explosions, survey methods for raw materials and research on ore treatment; in addition, information on the design of research reactors and general research experience with the Harwell

Gleep reactor were to go from the United Kingdom to New Zealand. Co-operation was subject both to the proviso that the Dominions must adopt common security standards and to the principle of current usability.

This meant that the British were free to talk slightly more openly to the Dominions about some aspects of atomic energy, but it would certainly leave Australian demands for information unsatisfied and it was certainly a far cry from the proposals for an integrated Commonwealth project. These proposals were indeed soon dropped. As for Europe, there was no provision for any exchange of information at all – even in the case of Belgium who, by stopping the export of Congo uranium, could have brought disaster on the American and British projects. In these negotiations, therefore, Britain's relationship with the United States had again taken absolute precedence over relationships with the Commonwealth and Europe. The complete disregard of Europe is the more noteworthy since it was in January 1948, almost at the same moment as the conclusion of the *modus vivendi*, that the Foreign Secretary wrote his eloquent Cabinet paper calling for a Western European Union, of which Britain would be part, and to which she would give leadership in a way that would show clearly she was not subservient to the United States or the Soviet Union.

The restriction of atomic energy co-operation with other countries to a bare minimum was part of the price the United Kingdom paid for the *modus vivendi* which, it was hoped, would provide a growing-point for more and more technical co-operation with the Americans. This hope was disappointed but the price was not always, in practice, as heavy as it seemed. There were, for example, no immediate specific needs from the white Dominions that could not be met under the agreement. In particular, Britain could help New Zealand with the construction and material for a research reactor. A few more scientists from these Dominions came to Harwell where they worked without restriction, although none was in the weapons establishment or on the production side. The scientists could not transmit classified information home, but their brains carried it back on their return. There seemed no possibility of any wider arrangements with the Dominions. In the summer of 1948, for example, the Ministry of Defence was making preparations for a meeting early in 1949 of the Commonwealth Advisory Committee on Defence Science. The Dominions wanted to raise the use of atomic energy for military purposes, but it was concluded, because of the *modus vivendi*, that any paper would have to be confined wholly to declassified items – that is, putting together information already made public.

The *modus vivendi* made no provision at all for any exchange of information with the non-white Dominions or with Western Europe. At the end of 1948 the Atomic Energy Official Committee was becoming increasingly concerned about this. Dr Bhabha, the eminent Indian physicist and chairman of the newly-formed Indian Atomic Energy Commission, said that India would like atomic collaboration with the United Kingdom; indeed collaboration in such matters was one of the features which made membership of the Commonwealth worthwhile. India was anxious to be in a position to use atomic energy for power when that was practicable, and she wanted to build a research reactor to get pile technology experience. Alternatively she would like to send one or two scientists to Harwell for training; there was the threat that if they could not go to Harwell they might go to France.

As for Western Europe, Cockcroft had found at a series of recent physics conferences that several countries were eager to push ahead. France was working on a very modest scale but had nearly completed her first heavy water research reactor and was developing the manufacture of uranium metal and pure graphite: she was getting on well in spite of the British refusal to help in testing graphite. France wanted official collaboration with the United Kingdom and the United States, but realised it might not be possible and as an alternative would like to establish collaboration with other Western European nations. Belgium was establishing a nuclear industry but her programme was vague. Norway had a programme to build a low-power heavy water reactor and had asked Britain whether she would purify ore for them. Again, if Britain did not do it, France no doubt would. Sweden would like to build a low-power reactor and get information from Britain about its construction.

All these projects were being set up on a semi-secret, semi-military basis and were thus spreading an unwholesome atmosphere of secrecy in atomic energy throughout Europe. One way of dealing with this and the Indian problem was to declassify information about low-power heavy water reactors. Cockcroft believed that Britain should go further and offer to supply uranium metal for such reactors. This might well increase effective security by stopping individual projects for making uranium metal, and would enable Western Europe to obtain immediate research benefits from atomic energy. Britain might also offer to hold conferences from time to time to discuss, in general terms, progress towards the development of power-producing reactors.

Britain was in a position to be the leader of atomic energy in Europe. Scientists in several countries were 'raring to go'; some of them had spent the war in Britain, for which they had a strong affection, and they all naturally wanted to discuss their progress with British scientists and get British co-operation. It was positively embarrassing to the British to evade their questions and requests. At the beginning of 1949 the Official Committee was sure that on political grounds it was most important that Western European countries should look to Britain for assistance in atomic energy development and that she should be able to exercise a guiding and co-ordinating influence over their efforts and over India's. The United Kingdom should seek United States agreement to the adoption of a more positive policy to atomic energy development in Western Europe and India. However, news from Washington at this time was that there were such differences of opinion within the Administration about collaboration with Britain that these questions had to be left for the time being. Dusty answers had to be given to European and Indian requests.

The question was left until the negotiations with the United States in the autumn of 1949. In the long preliminaries it was agreed by the Americans that atomic relations with other countries would be an important item on the agenda, but the item turned out to be very subsidiary. The Americans said at the outset of the talks that they did not want to include other countries to any appreciable extent in any exchange of information. Britain felt she could not press the issue because it would compromise the possibility of agreement on the major issues such as integration of weapons production. So even if an agreement had been reached, it would not have made relations with other countries any easier. As it was, all that remained was the restrictive *modus vivendi* which seemed to make impossible wide co-operation with any country except Canada.

At the end of 1951, as British officials reflected bitterly on the three wasted years of fruitless negotiations with the Americans, some would have liked to denounce the *modus vivendi* so that Britain could acquire what she had never had – freedom of action in atomic energy with the Commonwealth and Western Europe. This was the first time* that anyone had suggested giving British atomic relations with other countries priority over the possibility, however remote, of an agreement with America. It was paradoxical that this should happen at a time when in terms of global policy it was recognised by Ministers that Britain's relationship with the United States was more important than her relations with any other country or group of countries, while the *modus vivendi* had been concluded at a time when Britain's relationship with Europe was beginning to seem as if it might come first in order of priority.

The suggestion about denouncing the *modus vivendi* was not pursued. It was simply proposed that in future Britain should not feel constrained on all occasions to consult the Americans before having dealings with other countries. She should use her discretion and take a flexible view of this aspect of the *modus vivendi* as the Americans had done on all other aspects of it. Since the drying-up of the exchange of technical information, much of the British development had been the fruit of her own unaided effort and she could reasonably claim to share it with her friends if it was politic so to do (see p. 264). This proposal did not go to the Labour Ministers, who were, as it happened, just about to lose the General Election. As we shall see, this policy of continuing to try for agreement with America while exhibiting slightly more flexibility towards other countries was favoured by the Conservative Government. As we shall also see, the *modus vivendi* lingered on; even though it was operated rather less restrictively, it was still the point of reference for relations with other countries in 1954.

Within this framework of policy, how did co-operation with individual countries work out? Britain's atomic relationships with countries in the Commonwealth was founded not only on ties of kinship but on the prospect of uranium supplies in the Dominions. This was especially true in the case of South Africa, which seemed likely to be one of the biggest sources in the world of low-grade ore.

In the 1950 and 1951 negotiations for her uranium, South Africa had asked for technical assistance in exchange. A request for a 'special position', first made to Britain in November 1949, was repeated at the Colombo Conference in January 1950; it was in very general terms and was based on a feeling that because she was likely to become one of the world's greatest producers of uranium,

* As far as the author has seen.

she had some claim to be brought into the inner circle on the same basis as Canada. The Americans insisted that the approach must be to both the United States and United Kingdom Governments, that the question of a 'special position' should be kept quite separate from the contract negotiations, and that South Africa should not be given any more advantages than Belgium, who had after all been supplying uranium for years with no other recompense than the commercial profit from Union Minière operations and the benefit of a modest export tax. The Americans thought that the South Africans should not be offered any privileges but should be asked exactly what they had in mind. However, the South Africans, apart from wanting to be a member of the club, had only the haziest ideas of what they wanted and were motivated mainly by nationalist feeling and jealousy of Canada. The American attitude softened to some extent and by the end of 1950 they agreed to give South Africa a special treatment not less favourable than Belgium's, and to make a definite offer. Mr Dönges, the chairman of the South African Atomic Energy Board, who visited Washington in December, was, after some brief and unpromising discussions and on the eve of his departure, given a comprehensive memorandum hastily drawn up by American officials and British Embassy staff. This memorandum described the historical background and the origins and functions of the Combined Policy Committee and Combined Development Agency, and explained the position of Canada (based not on her uranium production but on the fact that she had been involved in atomic energy research from the outset) and the position of Belgium. It then outlined the raw materials situation and the prospects of atomic energy, including nuclear power – said to be ten to twenty years away – and finally offered the following privileges:

1. Assistance in placing selected South African students in American and British universities for advanced nuclear studies.
2. Access on a priority basis to American and British declassified information.
3. Visits of selected South African scientists and engineers to see unclassified atomic energy work in the United States and United Kingdom.
4. Assistance in obtaining equipment and materials for scientific research in the atomic energy field.
5. Exchanges of technical information, as agreed upon from time

to time, on the exploration, mining, processing and extraction of radioactive ores.

6. Information necessary for the development and design of low-power research reactors, if South Africa wanted them.

In short, the United States and Britain would supply to South Africa whatever technical information and assistance was being given, or would be given, to the Belgians (see Chapter 11). Mr Dönges took all this back to South Africa to study.

Sir John Cockcroft, when he saw these proposals, pointed out that the United Kingdom was already co-operating with South Africa in the provision of isotopes, priority access to declassified reports, information on defence against atomic weapons and on the processing and extraction of radioactive ores, and the attachment of scientists to Harwell. He therefore suggested an extension of the 'Dönges memorandum', but the Americans were reluctant to make another move before the South Africans. In fact the South Africans appeared to be satisfied with the explanations and others made to them, and did not raise the matter again. Early in 1952 Cockcroft heard privately that the Dutch were planning to build a research reactor and were offering scholarships to technical people in South Africa, and this stimulated the British to set up a Commonwealth research fellowship scheme; research fellows from Canada and Australia were already working at Harwell, and South African applications were being sought at the beginning of 1953.

Australia also had uranium deposits, although they were not as great as those of South Africa. She also now had as chairman of her atomic energy committee Mark Oliphant, pupil of Rutherford, intimate friend of Cockcroft and prominent member of the wartime British atomic team in America, who had recently returned for good from England to his native land. Oliphant was very anxious to begin a nuclear power project in Australia and naturally hoped for help from Britain.

The Australians had asked as long ago as 1947 for help in building a low-power experimental pile, but though the British agreed in principle to help with information and materials, there was as yet no uranium metal to spare, and classified information could not be given until an assurance of satisfactory security arrangements was received. Soon afterwards, Australia and New Zealand agreed on a joint programme in which Australia would build a cyclotron and

New Zealand a research reactor, but political pressure for a reactor in Australia was too strong, and the joint programme was abortive.

By the beginning of 1951 Australia was thinking not of a research reactor but of a large-scale reactor, using native uranium, which would be used to generate power. This plan was discussed by the Prime Minister, Robert Menzies, when he visited London in January; it was explained that since, under existing rules, this would be a classified project, the agreement of the United States and Canada would be required before Britain could help and that the Americans and Canadians would be very exacting about security. Later the Australians wrote asking for advice on security organisation and procedures, and a voluminous letter of guidance was sent in May 1952.

After Mr Menzies' visit he and Mr Attlee exchanged telegrams about the promising Radium Hill uranium prospects in South Australia and about arrangements for technical co-operation, and Mr Attlee reaffirmed Britain's desire to collaborate to the best of her ability but pointed out the limitations imposed by the tripartite agreement with the United States and Canada. In effect, apart from technical co-operation on uranium ore treatment, she could give Australia virtually nothing of real interest to her, though Australian scientists were able to gain experience at Harwell both as research fellows and on attachment to the staff, where they worked *inter alia* on production processes.

Britain's inability to do much to help the Australians was unfortunate not only because she hoped for supplies of Australian uranium. She was also anxious to prevent Australia from becoming too closely aligned with the United States (now increasingly co-operative with uranium-producing countries) to the exclusion of Britain. Above all, she was conscious of being greatly indebted to Australia in a most important matter. In 1950, when it seemed likely that Britain's first atomic bomb test could not be held in United States territory, Britain looked to Australia instead. The Australians were most co-operative in finding, and helping to survey, a suitable site – the Monte Bello Islands, a small group off the northwest coast of Australia; Mr Attlee finally wrote to Mr Menzies in March 1951 that it had been decided not to wait any longer for the Americans, and the British Government would be grateful for the Australian Government's agreement to the use of the site for a weapon test in October 1952, and for help in preparing and carrying out the test. Exploding the bomb would contaminate at least some of the islands with radioactivity, and for about three years the area would be unfit for habitation, or even for visits by the pearl fishermen who went there from time to time.

The Australians agreed to this without striking a hard bargain over technical collaboration, and were most co-operative throughout (see Chapter 24), even when later on the British, through no fault of their own, were in an agony of indecision whether they should hold the test in Australia after all or should accept the belated American offer in September 1951 of a test in Nevada. The Australians were extremely forbearing in making requests for observers at the trial, since the possibilities were strictly limited by security considerations. They gave every possible assistance in areas where security difficulties did not arise, such as meteorology and radiological safety, and they set up a small radiochemical laboratory at Perth expressly for the test. The situation was full of irony. The British wanted to help the Australians, because of Commonwealth ties, uranium hopes, and her dependence on Australian sites for weapon testing in 1951 and probably later too.* Their desire to help was frustrated largely by their commitments to the United States and by American distrust of Australian security. However, the Americans themselves were much less inhibited than the British; they tended to be much more forthcoming to the Australians than they would allow the British to be, so that the Australians might well have felt that their hopes lay in the United States.

New Zealand was simpler. Possibilities were mooted of the development of heavy water in New Zealand geothermal steam, but in general the only problem about co-operation had been solved without difficulty. Britain had helped New Zealand with the design of her research reactor. A team of five New Zealand scientists had been responsible for the design of the low-powered piles in Canada and at Harwell; the United States and Britain had therefore agreed that subject to adequate security arrangements, New Zealand should be allowed to build such a reactor if she wished, and the provision of technical information for this purpose was specifically covered in the *modus vivendi* of January 1948. Mr Attlee, in reply to an inquiry from the New Zealand Government, said he thought such a

---

* Penney wrote in March 1952: 'If the Australians are not willing to let us do further trials in Australia, I do not know where we should go.'

development would be advantageous from a Commonwealth point of view. New Zealand – unlike Australia who was interested in the prospects of nuclear power – wanted a reactor primarily to produce radioisotopes for medical, biological and agricultural research.

India was also seeking collaboration with Britain on the development of reactors. In 1948 Joliot-Curie had approached Professor Bhabha with proposals for close atomic collaboration with France, but Bhabha had replied that they would first go for a working arrangement with Britain; only if that failed would they turn to France. However, a request to Britain at the end of 1949 could only be partially satisfied with information that was being declassified. A year later Professor Bhabha wanted Britain to collaborate in the development of a beryllium-moderated reactor, in exchange for which India would make beryl available to Britain. The Official Committee was anxious, for political reasons, to be as forthcoming as possible, but there was delay because of security questions. In the meantime India negotiated an agreement with the French for this purpose, and both of them suggested that Britain should share in the experiments. Britain simply took a 'friendly' interest in them and invited India to send scientists to courses in the school of reactor technology that was soon to be established. In the case of India too, Britain had her eyes on material supplies – in this instance thorium, which India could produce in abundance. She foresaw, in the future, collaboration in power reactors, especially the breeder reactors that were likely to interest India, in return for thorium. Mercifully, by the time this became a practical proposition declassification policy would probably have changed.

In Western Europe, Britain had been forced by the American attitude into a 'masterly inactivity' in atomic affairs throughout the years 1946–51.* This again ran right across the grain of global policy, for the United States had been only too anxious in this period that Britain should combine with Europe economically, militarily and politically. The British made the best of a bad job. They wanted to bring in Western European countries and help them to build small research reactors, but they were told that feeling in the USAEC made this very difficult. They therefore tried to help by means of declassification. When heavy water as well as graphite research reactors were declassified it was easier to meet requests, and at the end of 1951 the Americans relaxed sufficiently to agree that

* The words are Cockcroft's.

the development of research reactors in Europe could be assisted by the provision of small quantities of materials. Perhaps equally, if not more, important, was Cockcroft's personal friendliness and helpfulness throughout the post-war years to the scientists of Europe. This kept channels of communication open and held several countries at least potentially within the British orbit.

This was true of relations with France herself. In January 1948 a letter had gone out from the Foreign Office, emphasising the urgent need to draw Britain's relationship with France closer both politically and militarily. But this did not extend to atomic energy. The French in fact made no more requests to the British for specific help with their project. Bertrand Goldschmidt, who had played such an important part in the early chemistry work at Montreal, had, however, been to Harwell several times; he had seen a good deal of Cockcroft who, though giving no classified information away, was able to advise him on the right pattern for the French to follow. Other old friends from Montreal days went over to give the French some help – for example, on the organisation and production of isotopes. Cockcroft in turn knew exactly what was going on in France and no secrets were kept from him. The spirit of the times was illustrated by a telegram the French sent when their first research reactor went critical. It was sent to Gleep and Bepo c/o Cockcroft at Harwell and said: 'Greetings from your little sister Zoe.' The reply was: 'Congratulations from friends at Harwell. Hope little sister is doing well.' For the rest the French were in the same position vis-à-vis the British as the British were vis-à-vis the United States: they had to work out scientific answers themselves and do a certain amount of detective work to find out facts that the British could have told them in the course of a telephone talk. For example, the French found out the name of the solvent to be used in the chemical plants at Windscale by discovering by chance from a chemical salesman that large orders were being placed for it.*

The French project as a whole was of course under deep suspicion because of the presence in it until May 1950 of Juliot-Curie, a confirmed ideological Communist. Indeed, in 1948 an American in the State Department said he personally felt the time had come to examine ways and means of dislodging Juliot, possibly by a direct approach to the French Prime Minister or by indirect pressure in

* This was especially ironic as Bertrand Goldschmidt had been the key person in the early chemical separation work at Montreal.

connection with French applications for commodities useful to atomic energy projects, such as a mass spectrometer they wanted. The British suggested that if the French were to be expected to sacrifice Joliot at the behest of others, they might first want to know what benefit in the form of collaboration they would secure thereby. They also questioned whether the removal of Joliot himself was of much significance from the security point of view. France had many Communists in many walks of life and it would not be much good cutting off only one head from the hydra. The British spokesman in Washington who took part in these conversations was Donald Maclean, who later fled to Moscow! The Atomic Energy Official Committee agreed that it was quite impracticable to dislodge Joliot in view of his high prestige in France and his importance to the French atomic energy project, which would be unlikely to succeed without him.*

The French behaved impeccably in adhering to their obligations to the British. Goldschmidt pointed out that the French were far behind the Russians in research and possessed no secrets worth keeping from them. Nevertheless, the French acceded to the British request that they should not allow a Norwegian chemist to work in their project lest this should disseminate classified information obtained in the wartime project. They kept strictly to the same declassification policy as the United States and the United Kingdom, even though this was difficult for them since they were given so little information about the policy and few warnings about any changes in it, and even though it involved some sacrifice. For they sometimes felt obliged to withhold results of their own work which they would have published if they had been sure it would not be objectionable to Britain. Yet they had no means of knowing what the British would release except by observing the literature, and if they waited for this they might lose priority in publication. It was only in 1951 that it was agreed with the Americans that there could be unclassified informal talks on declassification with France – and other Western European countries – and that no major changes in declassification policy would be adopted without informing France well in advance.

Britain's enforced atomic inactivity in Europe had left the field

* The French Government decided finally, in May 1950, to dismiss Joliot-Curie because of his active participation in the propaganda against the official French policy towards NATO.

largely to the French, who were, however, for a variety of reasons, unable to seize their opportunities. The possibility of a French-led European project was not popular among other European countries and France simply engaged in the negotiation of bilateral collaboration with a number of countries – with Norway, Sweden, Switzerland and Italy. Ultimately, Britain's lead in Europe was not supplanted by the French as it so well might have been. Even during the period of this book Britain did manage – but only after months, even years, of negotiation – to achieve a deal with the Norwegians and the Dutch.

At the end of 1947 Dr Gunnar Randers, the Norwegian physicist who had worked on radar in Britain during the war, asked for an unclassified visit to Harwell, but there was difficulty in agreeing even to this because of American susceptibilities. Early in 1948 Randers said the Norwegians were planning a low-power heavy water reactor. Would Britain trade Norwegian heavy water against 5 tons of uranium metal and help on some points of design? Though Cockcroft was anxious to help, and pointed out the advantages, Britain decided that, quite apart from any strategic objections to an atomic energy pile in Norway, she could not possibly spare any uranium metal. The Norwegians then asked in the autumn of 1948 whether Britain would purify uranium ore into oxide for them. This was a negligible request in terms of British processing capacity, while if the Norwegians erected their own ore-purification plant it would be available to any foreign power which might occupy Norway in the event of war. However, the United States had to be consulted. The Foreign Office in London wrote to the Embassy in Washington: 'We hope you will be able to face this minor deviation from the straight and narrow paths of Anglo–US harmony but even an undertaking to refine some oxide for Norway in 2/3 years' time could not by any stretch of the imagination be regarded as a danger to security.' Predictably, however, the US State Department did not like the idea at all, since their present mood was to look with disapproval on any steps by Western European countries to develop atomic energy. The British did not dare to defy them and their chagrin was increased when they heard that Norway was going to send the ore to France for processing in return for heavy water.

Norway, however, was reluctant to send the ore to France for political reasons. The next stage was that Norway and Holland were going to collaborate in erecting and operating a pile in

Holland. The Dutch likewise were not anxious to collaborate with the French, and the two countries asked Britain whether she would turn some tons of uranium oxide into metal for them. This was to be a straightforward transaction without any bartering for heavy water. By this time it was late in 1950 and the Atomic Energy Official Committee agreed they should meet the Dutch–Norwegian request. The world situation had changed considerably since 1948; Russia had exploded an atomic bomb and relations between Western European countries were closer. These countries were going to develop low-powered reactors with or without Anglo-Saxon assistance. 'If we don't help, the French will.' There was considerable discussion whether the United States should be informed in advance or presented with a *fait accompli*, and it was decided that there should be no question of seeking US approval but that the United States should be informed. This time the Americans did not object. In 1951 the uranium metal arrived and was received with gratitude by the Norwegians, as it had saved them a year in time and a whole lot of difficulties. Dr Randers asked whether Britain would supply further uranium metal rods for their pile, this time in exchange for their value in heavy water. Harwell wanted the heavy water for experimental work and this proposal would provide them with it at least three years earlier than any other source. However, since Britain could not use uranium acquired through the Combined Development Agency for this purpose they had to move very carefully, and the whole business took over a year to settle.

The most difficult problems in atomic co-operation with European countries arose over Belgium. Belgian ideas even for a small research reactor were far less advanced than those of the other Western European countries, but of course Belgium had performed an inestimable service to the United States and United Kingdom by signing over to them in 1944 the option on all the Congo uranium for ten years ahead, and indeed by selling it to them at a most advantageous price. The agreement assigning the option had, it may be recalled,[1] said that if the United States and United Kingdom decided to use the ores as a source of energy for commercial purposes, Belgium would be 'admitted to participation on equitable terms'. This was Clause 9(*a*). Legally Belgium had no contractual rights until nuclear power was being taken seriously, but morally Belgium felt, soon after the war was over, that she deserved some return for her services. It was also politically important that the

Belgian Government should be able, if called upon, to demonstrate that the agreement was not one-sided. From the end of the war the Government was being constantly harassed about the agreement by the Communists, who inferred that Belgium's wealth had been lightly and cheaply signed away. Disclosure of the agreement would have been worse for the United States and the United Kingdom than for the Belgians, because the Belgians might well have been forced to denounce it. Moreover news of this exclusive long-term purchase would have been highly embarrassing while the United Nations Atomic Energy Commission was sitting. Even when it was realised that many of the details of the agreement were known, it was believed that full disclosure would stimulate speculation on amounts, tempo of ore shipments, and the relation of the Congo to the overall procurement programme, and that all this might help to fill gaps in Russia's estimate of the West's bomb production. In fact the Belgian export-tax statistics gave much of this information anyway. The Belgian Government loyally fought off all the pressure for disclosure of the agreement, and they deserved some thanks and recognition for that alone. In retrospect it is surprising that the Communists relaxed their pressure for publication and did not leak the actual document. There were fairly accurate accounts of the agreement, especially in United States newspapers, while Donald Maclean had full access to all information about the agreement and raw materials affairs while he worked on atomic energy in the Washington Embassy from February 1947 to September 1948.*

From 1948 onwards the Belgian Government's pressure for some tangible evidence of technical assistance grew, for repeated expressions of 'sincere appreciation of the steadfast manner' in which the Belgian Government had executed the agreement had palled. M. Spaak told the British Ambassador that he could not help feeling the United States had little incentive to press forward with researches in the commercial uses of atomic energy, while the position in Europe was quite different and indeed he understood Britain had made important steps towards powerful atomic piles. He also believed there were by-products of great value. The Ambassador, somewhat out of his depth, reported 'he mentioned the word "isotypes" (which I confess however I do not understand) and also spoke about something called plutonium'.

* He worked in the Embassy from the spring of 1944 to September 1948, and was British Secretary of the CPC from February 1947 until he left.

In the summer of 1948 the British and Americans joined in talks with the Belgians in Washington. In spite of the 1944 agreement and the fact that the uranium was pouring from the Congo to the United States, the Amercians considered they could not go far with Belgium without infringing the McMahon Act. The Belgians might have been forgiven for exploding, but they did not, and they seemed happy to discuss declassified information. They heard discouraging estimates of the period before atomic power became a reality, but various minor offers were made. Belgian scientists could take a United States isotopes course, students could go to US universities, the supply of isotopes and equipment would be hastened. Thereafter Belgium did enjoy a privileged status in isotope work in the United States, and Union Minière took over the distribution of isotopes in Belgium.

In the autumn of 1949 the Belgian Government read the press reports of the tripartite Anglo–American–Canadian talks and learned about the programmes of technical co-operation, which must be industrial since they excluded atomic weapons, and also about the distribution and use of the uranium, largely supplied by the Belgian Congo. The Belgian Foreign Minister said it was imperative to re-examine ways of implementing Clause 9(*a*) of the 1944 agreement. It was inconceivable that Belgium, as a principal supplier of uranium, should be put in an inferior position to anyone, especially Canada, in information about atomic energy. It was one thing if information was exchanged between the United States and the United Kingdom, but Belgium was not prepared to see Canada – a country about equal in importance with Belgium – a full partner, while she herself was excluded. The Belgians wanted to send at least a dozen of their first-rate atomic energy scientists to America to participate fully in the study of nuclear development, and they wanted to become a full partner in the exchange of information on the industrial uses of atomic energy. They also wanted the price of their uranium reconsidered and more publicity about their agreement.

Talks were held early in 1950 between the United States, the United Kingdom and Belgium. Belgium went to them with a long list of specific requests for information and facilities. She realised that the industrial use of atomic energy was still a distant and speculative prospect, but when it came she wanted to be in a position to use it. The Belgians felt that although they were the world's main uranium supplier, they were falling behind other countries in knowledge of atomic energy. France and Norway would both have given Belgium reciprocal facilities in exchange for some uranium, which she could not supply because of the monopoly she had granted to the Americans and the British. The United States took the leading part in the talks. They stuck to the line that the utilisation of atomic energy for commercial purposes was still remote and that therefore the obligations envisaged in Clause 9(*a*) 'were not susceptible' of implementation at present. They turned down most of the Belgian requests – requests to send Belgians to work in USAEC establishments, requests for certain information, requests for assistance in building a small pile. They were adamant that they could pass no classified information at all to Belgium. They only relented about the possibility of financial adjustments.

The British in Washington were unhappy about the uncompromisingly negative and uncooperative attitude of the United States, which seemed to them politically unwise and capable of leading to serious trouble with Belgium. All this reflected the wide and growing differences between American and British attitudes to co-operation with third countries. Apart from their fears of trouble when the Belgian agreement came up for renewal later, the British were conscious that Belgium was now an ally of America and Britain in the North Atlantic defence organisation, in which the ability to deliver atomic weapons was an essential element. While there might be good reasons at present why the manufacture and use of atomic weapons should be confined to the United States (and to the United Kingdom when its programme got that far), it was bound to have a bad effect on the alliance if the Anglo-Americans excluded their allies even from the elements of nuclear energy work. Exclusion might drive the smaller Western European countries into a group which would go ahead on its own. The North Atlantic alliance might be split into two camps on atomic energy, with all its political and psychological importance. But the British in Washington felt they could do very little – partly because the Belgian requests were primarily, indeed wholly, addressed to the United States and partly because the post-Fuchs atmosphere made it impossible for the British to suggest any relaxation of the interpretation of the McMahon Act.

The British in London felt much less sympathy for Belgium, who seemed to be 'opening her mouth very wide' and asking for much more than she was entitled to under the 1944 agreement. It would create difficulties with other powers if Belgium was given special treatment. In any case the impending declassification of small research reactors would help Belgium, and if the United States could not assist with uranium metal because of the McMahon Act, Britain could.

The Belgians then threatened to amend the 1944 agreement. The American Secretary of State pointed out sharply that while Belgium had indeed honoured her obligations, the United States had not been an idle beneficiary but had devoted resources now totalling $5 billion to the production of atomic weapons serving the common security of the United States and Western Europe. Belgium was at this time spending a far smaller percentage of her national income on armaments than any other member of the Brussels Treaty group. However, the Secretary of State let it be known orally to the Belgians that when the McMahon Act could be amended, Belgian requests for financial and other aid would be sympathetically considered, while declassification would also help them.

At further talks in London, the Americans and the British emphasised that it was not their fault if Belgium lagged behind other European countries which had developed atomic energy programmes entirely from their own resources. They would be willing to see how they could help Belgium if only she would draw up a programme, for information acquired under Clause 9(*a*) would be valueless if she was not equipped to use it. This the Belgians agreed to do.

Subsequently there were some very difficult negotiations indeed about finance – that is, about some financial recompense for the fact that implementation of Clause 9(*a*) had been delayed for longer than anticipated in 1944; this was so involved with general questions of uranium pricing that it is dealt with in the next chapter. There was from now on, however, much less dispute about technical assistance. In the autumn of 1950 information about most small research reactors was declassified and it was agreed that the announcement should be delayed and that Belgium should get this information before the rest of the world. The Belgians also began to take much more interest in Harwell and the British project, and to ask for Cockcroft's advice. The British were ready to offer whatever facilities they could. In 1951 the Belgians said they wanted to build a reactor like Harwell's Bepo, and as these larger reactors were declassified in the spring of 1951, there was little difficulty. Britain was also prepared to supply uranium metal, help with graphite and give lectures on reactor technology in Belgium. It was clear that the Belgians would rely on the United Kingdom for help in building their reactor, and Britain wanted to do everything she could to give them this help. The negotiations with Belgium had gone on for months and formal agreement was only reached in a communiqué issued in the summer of 1951 (see Appendix 12, pp. 397–9). Even so, Britain's interpretation of it differed from that of the United States.

The difference in the attitude of the two countries to the treatment of other countries in atomic energy persisted for some years yet and was a cause of friction. The British Embassy in Washington wrote wearily in August 1951 of the 'tactics of delay, evasion and of trying to get the maximum from the other fellow without giving anything which the United States have pursued in the Belgian negotiations and indeed in all their dealings with other countries in atomic energy'. The American policy, to which Britain had perforce submitted, had meant that no rational line could be taken in atomic energy policy towards European or Commonwealth countries. Any concessions made had to be justified in terms of immediate concrete benefits received in exchange, and even when the benefits were large, as in the case of Belgium, concessions were made unwillingly. Discrimination in itself led to difficulties. A British official complained in 1951: 'We are getting into a sad state of confusion by trying for political reasons to give various European countries and others a special position in one sense or another in atomic energy.' This meant, for example, that Belgium, because of the Congo uranium, was given a privileged status which extended even to such a small matter as getting advance notice of declassification changes, while France was given no privileges at all even though it was her scientists who had instigated Britain's slow-neutron project in 1940 and indirectly Canada's project as well. Similarly, South Africa because of her uranium had a privileged status for a time compared with Australia, and it was only the prospects of uranium finds in Australia which encouraged real atomic co-operation with her. In the long run, expediency was an unsatisfactory substitute for rationality and principle.

In the end, Britain had managed to make acceptable arrangements with the white Dominions and with Norway, Holland and

Belgium; to that extent the influence of the *modus vivendi* had proved less constricting than it seemed. But the effort involved and the delays incurred had been wholly disproportionate.

In these post-war years there was great generosity in many of the United States dealings with other lesser nations, whatever their underlying motives. This makes the contrast the more striking: in atomic relationships it was too often the arrogance rather than the magnanimity of power that was apparent. Yet even here there were contradictions. The United States was extremely niggling in handing over any information that might conceivably be classified, but they poured out to the world from their atomic laboratories a great flow of unclassified scientific findings, which was the foundation of other countries' research. The British flow of papers was far smaller and she was sometimes guilty of the same faults as the Americans where classified information was concerned. She found it difficult to steer a balanced course between her own self-interest and her different loyalties and commitments, but as time went on she was far more conscious than the United States that safety did not lie in an atomic secrecy that seemed more like the attitude of a dog in the manger.

11 The Area of Interdependence: Uranium

The Indispensable Element

THROUGHOUT all discussions of external policy, uranium supplies have been a dominant theme. Proposals for international ownership of uranium featured prominently in the unsuccessful plans for international control of atomic energy. Anglo-American collaboration in uranium survived as the one area where the two countries continued to co-operate throughout our period. Britain's concessions on uranium allocations and her possible influence with producing countries seemed the only bait to tempt the Americans to technical exchanges; even so, they consumed the bait while avoiding the hook. Britain's own programme was influenced – though beneficially – when she forwent a third atomic pile to ensure uranium supplies for the United States. In the formulation of policy towards Europe and the Commonwealth, uranium was the criterion which divided the sheep from the goats; irrespective of any wider political considerations, countries were treated more or less favourably according to whether or not nature had endowed them with uranium-bearing rocks.

This chapter interrupts the main narrative of policy formation to focus directly on the problems of securing uranium supplies during our period. For uranium was indispensable. There were some possibilities of choice for the other materials in nuclear piles – for the moderators or coolants – but there was no foreseeable alternative to uranium as fuel (see p. 464). Uranium had long been known,* but before the 1938 discoveries about the effect of splitting uranium atoms, it had seemed an unimportant by-product of radium production from pitchblende. Uranium occurs in many different forms and often in complexes with other metals, especially gold, silver, copper, nickel, vanadium and lead. It is as abundant as lead, much more

* Uranium was discovered in 1789 and the first metal isolated in 1869.

abundant than mercury, copper, or silver. Uranium, usually as oxide, constitutes 4 parts per million of the earth's crust, but rich ores are rare, the main deposits being, in the 1940s, in the Congo, in Canada and in Czechoslovakia. Elsewhere uranium was known to be present only in much lower-grade ores, containing less than 1 per cent uranium, compared with 30–70 per cent in the rich ores of the Congo. Very large quantities of low-grade ores have to be excavated and processed* for a small output of uranium-rich concentrates.

The American wartime project had been well provided with high-grade uranium ores from the Belgian Congo, thanks to M. Edgar Sengier, the managing director of Union Minière du Haut-Katanga. Fearing a German invasion of the Belgian Congo, he had shipped uranium oxide ores to America for safety in 1940 and had thereafter agreed to further shipments, so that raw material was the least of the wartime project's many obstacles.

The question of post-war supplies, however, quickly became a major preoccupation. The United States had a vast new complex of atomic plants to be fed; Britain had none but needed uranium stocks to initiate an atomic energy project. Both countries were anxious to locate and secure all accessible supplies and to deny this strategic material to others, particularly Russia. During the war and afterwards uranium gave rise to much urgent and secret activity among geologists, chemists, diplomats, engineers, businessmen, miners, construction workers and speculators. Uranium mining, unlike a gold rush, would provide not only wealth but atomic weapons and perhaps, one day, limitless power.

Governments, having decided to involve themselves directly in procurement, were concerned much more directly and deeply than they had been with other minerals and mining even in the heyday of colonial expansion; their search for uranium extended to five continents and the Antarctic.† All kinds of difficult political and economic questions soon arose. Countries possessing uranium found

---

* This processing has to be done at or near the minehead to avoid costly transport. 15,000 tons of low-grade ore, say 0·1 per cent, would yield about 15 tons of uranium oxide in the form of concentrates, from which 12 tons of oxide might be extracted. This in turn would produce about 10 tons of uranium metal.

† It has sometimes been suggested that more geological effort was expended on uranium than on all other metals since the beginning of civilisation. This is an exaggeration of the kind often found associated with atomic energy.

themselves faced with political conundrums. Once the war was over, was it compatible with the United Nations spirit to supply material for atomic bombs to one power or group of powers? How would such action affect relations with Russia, especially in the case of neighbouring countries such as Sweden? If publicly known, what would be the domestic political reaction to such action, particularly in countries such as Belgium with strong left-wing parties? How did uranium contracts affect Belgium's relations with her colony in the Congo? In the case of Czechoslovakia, the political implications were perhaps infinitely more serious; it was commonly believed that her rich uranium mines were one of the reasons for Russia's determination to draw her firmly into the Eastern bloc.

Economic questions were scarcely less difficult than the political ones. There was not, as in other mining booms, a free market to determine prices and govern output. America and Britain wanted all the uranium they could get, even from high-cost, low-grade ores. Yet hungry though they were for supplies, they had no intention of paying more than they were obliged to. They never contemplated paying a uniform price, but from the outset made individual arrangements with each country and for each mining area. This led to hard and detailed bargaining.

For countries not prepared to sell to Russia, America and Britain acting together were the only immediate, major customer; the French felt justifiably aggrieved when they were not allowed into the market, but their uranium demands at this time were small. However, the producers possessed plenty of countervailing power; they must have realised this if only because of the buyers' eagerness, which was apparent except in the cash offered. The cycle of American production in the post-war period, if not entirely dependent on Congo uranium, would have been greatly affected without it.* The country and company owning it were therefore in a very strong position. Possessing such an extraordinarily rich mine, the Belgians might have felt bound to weigh short-term against long-term economic returns. With scientists talking of the promise of atomic energy for peaceful uses one day, should a country with uranium reserves risk exhausting them before that day dawned? Would it be selling its 'birthright to the golden key of the future' for a mess of pottage?[1]

* Though without Congo uranium they would undoubtedly have developed North American resources more rapidly.

Such questions were less pressing to the owners of low-grade ores, who could make no immediate contribution but were being persuaded and helped to develop future production. They were usually reluctant at first. After political agreements had been made with governments, prospectors and mine operators had to be enlisted to find and exploit the ore, and they were not always easily convinced of the advantages of producing uranium, possibly at some cost to gold or copper mining; the British were for long loath to offer cash incentives to prospectors, and secrecy hampered discussions with them. Much effort was needed to locate uranium deposits and estimate their potential, while large capital investment in mining machinery, treatment plants and so on was necessary in promising areas. Meanwhile little was known about the extraction of uranium and the plants could not even be designed without the results of laboratory research.* There were so many uncertainties that mining companies considering production might want capital assistance and also a long-term guarantee of a profitable market. Even then the future of uranium seemed uncertain (as indeed it was to prove); if international disarmament were achieved, military requirements might come to an end while, to the less optimistic, peaceful uses seemed remote and highly speculative. The outcome of these trials of strength between producers and consumers will emerge later in the chapter.

Combined Operations

The Anglo-American wartime arrangements for obtaining and sharing uranium supplies continued after the war. The Combined Policy Committee set up by the 1943 Quebec Agreement had included among its functions the allocation of 'materials, apparatus and plant in short supply, in accordance with requirements of the programme agreed by the Committee'. The 1944 Declaration of Trust (see Appendix 10), signed by President Roosevelt and Mr Churchill, had established the Combined Development Trust† to secure control of uranium and thorium within the participants' own

---

* 'It may require years of time and a revolution in extraction technique to produce a usable product, and the cost factor may have to be completely disregarded', said a May 1946 report by an American and a Canadian expert.

† Renamed the Combined Development Agency in January 1948 at the suggestion of M. Sengier of Union Minière (see note, p. 367). In this chapter it will unavoidably be referred to sometimes as the Combined Development Trust (CDT) and sometimes as the Combined Development Agency (CDA).

territories – the United Kingdom taking responsibility for the British Commonwealth (excluding Canada) and the Colonial Empire – and to seek to acquire control of uranium and thorium resources in third countries (known as 'CDT territories'). The Trust had wide powers to carry out surveys and explorations; to acquire mines or mining concessions and provide equipment; to conduct research into production methods; to acquire, treat, stockpile and dispose of uranium and thorium; more generally, to undertake any operations conducive 'to the effective carrying out of the purposes of the Trust in the common interest'. Though the Declaration referred to 'the successful prosecution of the present war', it had recommended that as soon as possible after the war the agreement should be extended and revised to cover post-war conditions and meanwhile should continue in full force. In accordance with the Declaration's spirit of equal partnership, Britain had borne half the cost of uranium supplies even though they all went in wartime to the United States, and she had shared expenditure on capital investment and research and development.*

Canada had participated in the atomic energy project from the beginning and was a major uranium-producing country. Though not a signatory to either the Quebec Agreement or the Declaration of Trust, she was represented both on the Combined Policy Committee and the Trust but had no financial role in the latter.

The Trust consisted of two United States, two British and two Canadian members,† under United States chairmanship and with a joint secretariat. With no permanent staff, it acted largely through the staff of the three Governments. The British members were provided by the Embassy in Washington, with technical support from Arthur Storke, a most able and highly regarded mining engineer who was a part-time consultant on metals and minerals to the Ministry of Supply until his death in an air crash in 1949, and from Dr C. F. Davidson, of the United Kingdom Geological Survey and Museum. By August 1945 the Trust was well established and had produced a survey of world uranium sources based on field

---

* The British had paid $1,165,000 by December 1945.

† The British members between 1945 and 1952 were, at various times, Sir Charles Hambro, F. G. Lee, Roger Makins, Gordon Munro, A. D. Storke, Frederick Hoyer Millar, Christopher Steel and J. G. Bower, and the British secretaries were Dr W. L. Webster, J. F. Jackson and P. J. Eaton. The first chairman was General Groves.

work and literature researches, had concluded the first Trust contract for uranium from the Belgian Congo, and had negotiated two further contracts.* It was, however, 'a very imperfect instrument of co-operation' since it was regarded by General Groves and his staff purely as an aid to American operations, to be used when convenient and otherwise ignored. It met only spasmodically and the British members had a constant struggle to be consulted or kept informed. Few in number and overworked, they had to try to hold the British position far from their base in the face of large American staffs with massive technical support.

The Trust was essentially a procurement agency, directed by the Combined Policy Committee which determined policy on raw materials and was responsible for allocating them. Allocation had not been an issue during the war, for it was agreed that all Trust uranium should go to the United States. Since this would leave the British with no uranium, it was agreed in July 1945 that any excess material not needed for weapons during the war should be held in trust for later allocation or disposal. By late 1945 the British were planning an atomic energy programme but had no uranium for it,† even though they had played a vital part in Trust activities – particularly in negotiating the Belgian agreement and the Congo contracts and in marshalling information about world uranium resources – and had shared the costs equally.

The combined machinery had been set up as an equal partnership to deal with the wartime situation in which there was only one uranium user, one major supplier, and one type of ore. Only one important change was made in the arrangements when the war ended – that is, in finance. After some tough arguing it was agreed in May 1946 that shipments before the Japanese capitulation should be paid for equally; thereafter each Government should advance half the cost but should in the long run pay only for what it received for its own use; thus the country receiving less than half would get a refund from the Trust. However, the 50:50 division still applied to agreed Trust expenses such as geological survey and research and development, and the cost of capital assistance was for a time shared equally, though later the British contribution was reduced.

Otherwise, the wartime machinery continued in the post-war decade in a complex and rapidly changing situation – with compet-

* Signed on 27 Oct 1945.
† Except for 100 tons allocated for research purposes.

ing demands, escalating American requirements, an increasing imbalance of British and American resources, new sources of supply, new kinds of ore, and new problems of politics, price policy and technical methods. The machinery worked, though not very well; it was tinkered with, neglected and misused, and had some disadvantages for both sides. The British found themselves involved in unwelcome financial commitments, often without proper consultation – for the Americans, hard pressed, were sometimes careless about consulting their junior partner. The Americans would often have liked to be free of any obligation to consult the British, consider their point of view or concede their claim to a share in supplies.

Both sides at different times thought of scrapping the agreement. Late in 1947, frustrated by the deadlock on technical atomic cooperation, the British sought legal advice about the effect of terminating the Trust upon the all-important arrangements with Belgium. The answer was that the Trust could not be terminated unilaterally, only by agreement, and that if it ceased to exist the Belgian agreement and contracts would become void. So the British decided to make the best of a bad job. Two years later the Americans also thought about going it alone; in 1949 their inexplicably tardy realisation that the British were determined to produce plutonium for bombs (see Chapter 9) aroused such alarm in some quarters that it was suggested that the United States should abrogate the raw materials arrangements and deal separately with Belgium. However, American officials, too, realised the risks involved.

For all the attractions of independence, the two countries were bound together by the Belgian contracts and by other common interests as well. As we shall see, despite the original exclusion of the Commonwealth from the 'CDT areas', South Africa and Australia were treated as such, and the British operated independently only in the colonial territories, where no significant deposits of ore were ever found. Britain, however, was believed to hold 'the key to the Commonwealth'; South Africa seemed the greatest potential source of uranium in the world, and the Americans relied on the British to help obtain it. Britain regarded South African uranium as her trump card (see p. 378), although this was probably an illusion, especially after the anti-British Malan Government replaced the Smuts Government in 1948. In practice, South Africa, Australia and the United States showed a tendency – natural enough, but disturbing to Britain – to get in touch with each other without informing London, and no Dominion would have been likely to refuse to deal directly with the United States for dollars.

The United States received clear advantages from the arrangements. They acquired nearly all the available uranium, considerably aided by the British, especially in negotiations with the Belgians and South Africans. Moreover they were able to buy more cheaply because joint procurement kept prices down and the British negotiators generally drove a hard bargain. In addition Britain financed half the CDT/CDA-sponsored research and exploration, undertaken mostly by the Americans, and contributed largely to capital expenditure in the Congo, Portugal and South Africa.

The British sometimes felt the arrangements were disproportionately helpful to the Americans, but they themselves benefited greatly. Co-operation on raw materials was a unique link when all other Anglo-American collaboration in atomic energy had practically ceased. Without joint action they would probably have failed to get uranium for their own project; unlike the United States they had neither domestic uranium* nor access to Canadian supplies, and they would have been outbid in competition with the Americans, who were prepared to pay any price, and in dollars. Thanks to the combined machinery the British got the uranium they needed, and for sterling. It was, as we shall see, the cheapest and the highest-grade uranium from 1946–7 Congo deliveries; here they had an advantage over the Americans, for later Congo deliveries were more expensive. Another benefit to the British was in sharing the results of American research on raw materials. A third benefit, incidental but of real importance in Britain's financial straits, was the 'dollar windfall'; she paid her 50 per cent share of the cost of CDA uranium in sterling, but her programme was only one-tenth of the American size and she was reimbursed in dollars for material allocated to the United States.†

If the South Africans and Australians had realised this situation they might well have felt that Britain was defrauding them of dollars, as well as influencing them to sell their uranium in the

* Such small deposits as were found in the United Kingdom at this time were negligible and were not worth developing.

† The Americans were well aware of it and favoured the arrangement, which did them no harm and helped Britain's serious dollar shortage; the only sufferers were the supplying countries who, in principle, should have reaped the dollar benefit.

belief that much of it was for British use. Then too, in later years, Commonwealth countries might well feel that Britain had helped to strip them of an irreplaceable asset, only to build up a gigantic American monopoly, especially as the United States would have a valuable source of future uranium supplies in accumulated residues (see pp. 360, 364).

By the end of 1952 some people in Britain, including Lord Cherwell, felt that the CDA partnership, formed mainly to purchase Congo ores in wartime, was out of date. Nevertheless, the CDA survived for many more years and its existence was beneficial to both countries and vital to Britain's programme (see pp. 390–2).

The Pattern of Supply and Demand

By the time the war ended, it was estimated that the Trust nations controlled 97 per cent of the world's uranium output. Their policy was to secure all the available material for their own use and to deny it to other countries;* General Groves was determined to stockpile while the going was good. There was no precisely calculated demand, merely a general determination to get all the uranium possible. The British could only guess at American needs for plants and programmes which were wrapped in secrecy. They themselves had no existing plants but were determined to have their own project for which, as Chadwick emphasised, adequate supplies must be ensured. 'We must by hook or by crook', he wrote, 'divert some of the Congo material to England.' Cockcroft in Montreal also stressed the overriding importance of getting a share of raw materials; technical problems could be solved without American co-operation after some delay, but lack of uranium would be catastrophic.

* The Trust also had agreements covering some 65 per cent of the world supply of thorium (an element, found mostly in monazite sands in India, Brazil and the Netherlands East Indies, which was in use, decreasingly, for making gas mantles and as an industrial, etc., catalyst). Thorium featured in the terms of reference of the CDT and in the 1946 US Atomic Energy Act; it received a good deal of attention as a cheaper and more abundant material which might serve as a partial substitute for uranium, if a reactor could be developed based on a thorium/uranium-233 cycle instead of a uranium-235/plutonium cycle (see Technical Note, Appendix 14). Thorium was, however, of no practical importance during our period – the system was not developed until 1960, at Indian Point, USA – but the British and Americans feared that if the Russians were short of uranium they might have concentrated on thorium research and development, and might be ahead in this field.

The need to secure uranium supplies was the more urgent because the total amount of ore available to the United States, Britain and Canada might only just suffice in the near future. Though the whole of the Belgian Congo output up to 1956 was contracted to the Trust, the proved deposits being worked at Shinkolobwe were nearly exhausted; as we saw in Chapter 4, after 1947 further supplies would depend partly on whether the rich pipe extended to lower levels than had been proved, and partly on building new plant to process the lower-grade ores. The only other important sources of supply were the United States and Canada, whose output for several years was to go to the United States. South Africa was extremely promising for the future but would not produce uranium for several years, while Portugal was not yet producing and offered very limited prospects. Unless some new and unexpected source of high-grade ores were found quickly, a period of acute uranium shortage would intervene until Congo production rose again and South African deliveries began.

This is the background to the Anglo-American negotiations on uranium allocations which were themselves part of the wider discussions on atomic co-operation. They have been described in earlier chapters and are now briefly recapitulated. Chadwick had been largely responsible for the success of the negotiations in 1946, when the British decided that they must bid on grounds of equity, not current needs, for a share of the Congo ores. He had been very anxious about uranium during the war and had urged that the British should strengthen their bargaining position. He had repeatedly stressed the small British contribution in the search for new supplies and the development of methods of surveying and chemical analysis compared with the massive American effort;[*] to play a worthy part in this aspect of the Trust's work was 'quite as important as the negotiation of contracts'. Uranium supplies were a sore point with him because he felt that his advice had not been taken seriously enough.

Chadwick's proposal, which the Americans accepted in May 1946, was that all the 850 tons of ore acquired by the Trust from the Congo since the end of the war, together with 600 tons of material captured in Europe, should be firmly allocated to the United States.

[*] But there was an acute shortage of suitable manpower – especially of geologists and analytical chemists – throughout the Commonwealth (see below).

For the rest of 1946, 1,350 tons each should be allocated to the United States and Britain while Congo ore should be shipped alternately to the United States and the United Kingdom. By the end of 1946 the British had received their full 1,350 tons and a further 500 tons had gone into an unallocated stockpile at Springfields, near Preston, the site of the British uranium metal factory. These 1946 shipments provided the basis for the British project. At the end of 1946, in the absence of a general agreement on atomic co-operation, General Groves agreed to issue instructions for alternate shipments from the Congo to continue up to April 1947 and this arrangement was twice extended, so that a further 1,400 tons was shipped to the United Kingdom in 1947, making a total of 3,250 tons delivered, 1,3500 tons allocated for British use and 1,900 tons to be stockpiled for the Trust.

In the autumn of 1947 unmistakable hints were received that the Americans were seriously concerned about the division of Congo ore and the size of the stockpile in Britain. The USAEC and the State Department were under severe political pressure. Congressmen had been surprised to find that domestic ores were insufficient for America's atomic energy plants, and then alarmed and angry to learn that half the Congo output was being shipped to Britain. It seemed that the Americans were running short of ores, and would soon raise the question of future shipments and perhaps ask for unallocated ores to be transferred from Springfields. The stockpile in Britain was worrying not only the Americans; Britain was in dire financial straits and the post-war $7½ billion loan was almost exhausted. The Treasury warned that it might be necessary to 'take a dollar view' and that Britain might not be able to afford a half share, unless her atomic energy project would otherwise be seriously impaired.

This was the position when the Anglo-American-Canadian discussions on atomic co-operation, which led to the *modus vivendi* of January 1948, began. This agreement incorporated new provisions for uranium allocations. As we saw in Chapter 8, the Americans' appetite for uranium was the main reason why they reopened discussions.

For the first time, instead of bargaining in general terms, the three parties discussed actual supplies and requirements, and the Americans disclosed figures of stocks and of quantities needed to feed their plants. These facts shattered the British intention of claiming both the Springfields stockpile and a substantial share of Congo production. American requirements were much larger than the British had guessed and their supplies were practically used up. To maintain their programme, they would need more than the total estimated 'free world' output up to 1952, and nearly twice that figure for their planned expanded programme. The estimate of output was admittedly conservative, but estimates of the total deficit ranged between 4,800 and 13,000 tons.

The British knew there was an element of extravagance in the American estimates, for their project had been going for six years already and, in spite of the critical scarcity of uranium, they had as yet no plant to recover uranium from residues. However, the British did not press the point, for the American piles were after all working, while the British, with their Springfields metal plant not ready for some months and with their 1946 allocation untouched, could not in all conscience ask for any new deliveries. They were, however, anxious to keep in the country the Springfields stockpile of unallocated ore, some or all of which the Americans wanted to move to the United States at once. A compromise was reached: the Americans should have all the 1948 and 1949 Congo production, as well as the unallocated material held in the United States, and only if their reserves fell below an agreed level should they ask the Combined Policy Committee for shipments from the United Kingdom. This agreement, embodied in the *modus vivendi* (see Chapter 8 and Appendix 9), ended any British illusions about equal shares or an inalienable right to the Trust stockpile at Springfields. But that stockpile was to remain in British hands and in the event no transhipments were necessary. Moreover the British programme had been accepted in principle and its modest raw materials requirements recognised as valid. Above all, the uranium concession seemed a small price to pay for the new era of Anglo-American co-operation which the *modus vivendi* seemed to augur.

When the Americans proposed further discussions on atomic co-operation in 1949, their main reason was, once more, desperate anxiety over the shortage of uranium, which was indeed said to be the limiting factor on their atomic bomb programme. They were planning a greatly enlarged programme – a 60 per cent increase in plutonium production and a trebling of uranium-235 output. However, in any case, the raw material provisions of the *modus vivendi* were soon to expire and must be replaced.

In these next uranium discussions the estimates of prospective supplies in the next six years were 40 per cent greater than they had been in December 1949. It was now assumed that Congo supplies would improve in 1950, that American and Canadian production would be better than foreseen, and that small quantities would come from Portugal from 1951 on, although there would be no South African uranium until 1953. Even these supplies would not support an expanded American programme, a small Canadian project and a British programme comprising three piles and a diffusion plant; however, there should be ample if the British postponed one pile. As part of an Anglo-American co-operation package, Ministers in London agreed to give up the third pile, and this decision stuck even when the package disintegrated (see Chapter 9). It was agreed that most of the 1950 Congo production should go to the United States, but that if there was a surplus a small tonnage should be shipped to Britain.

By June 1950 the plant at Springfields had been working for some months, the original 1,350 tons was almost all used and only four months' supply remained. Unallocated stocks at Springfields now amounted to some 1,900 tons. This stockpile was very important to the British. Admittedly they could not use the material until it had been allocated, and there was always the threat of transfer to the United States under the *modus vivendi*, but physical possession was reassuring; it would be easier to get ores from the stocks than from new shipments or from the United States.* The British also saw the stockpile as a bargaining counter, and had even suggested privately in Washington in 1949 that, failing a satisfactory general agreement on technical co-operation, the British attitude on Congo stocks in the United Kingdom 'might change'. The American response was that the raw materials question was 'by far the most sensitive and delicate point' for the United States and 'if the idea emerged that the United Kingdom was putting pressure on the United States Government by threatening to withhold supplies of raw material necessary for their production plans, this would certainly lead to very serious trouble'. Legality apart, it is hard to imagine a situation in which it would have been politically possible for the British to seize the unallocated stocks at Springfields. In the end, all the uranium

---

* Any shipment of uranium ores, even jointly owned, from the United States would be practically prohibited by the McMahon Act.

for the British programme up to 1955 was supplied from the Spring-fields stockpile of – duly allocated – low-cost Congo ores.

Since no general agreement on atomic co-operation was reached between 1949 and the end of the period of this book, uranium continued to be allocated on a year-to-year basis. In 1950 the Americans readily agreed to allocate 505 tons of the Springfields stockpile to the British for current needs, although they warned that 'as a result of the deepening world crisis', their own uranium requirements would increase drastically. For 1951 the United States requirement was over 5,000 tons, nearly twice the 1950 figure; the British were asking for 800 tons, and only about 1,400 tons remained unallocated at Springfields. The combined deficit was more than 1,800 tons. The British bid was very severely scrutinised by the Americans, who were highly critical of Springfields uranium process losses (see Chapter 22). Eventually the British were allocated 561 tons, and supplies for the Springfields plant were assured for another year. For 1952, with supplies beginning to improve, the British easily obtained a further allocation of 500 tons, and foresaw no supply difficulty with annual requirements at that level.

In 1949 the Combined Policy Committee's raw materials experts had agreed that 1951–3 would be the lean period for uranium supplies, with 1951 as the year of greatest deficit, but that a substantial surplus was likely by 1955. Free-world production in 1954, estimated in 1949 at under 3,500 tons, seemed in 1952 likely to be nearer 8,000 tons. However, demand increased even more than supply. There was, said the Embassy in Washington, no ceiling to American requirements – already 10,000 tons a year of uranium oxide, soon perhaps rising to 12,000 tons – regardless of cost.

Britain, with her modest needs of 500 tons a year or less, was not in the same league as the United States. But not only did she have to fight extremely hard for supplies; as a junior partner in the Combined Development Trust she was also involved in the ruthless drive for uranium. Britain was engaged in a joint effort of exploration, research and development; she bore half the cost of all CDT/CDA-sponsored work, whether British or American, and she was committed to a great deal of capital expenditure, 50:50 in the Congo and one-third in South Africa and Australia. It was only by helping to increase supplies, especially from Commonwealth countries, that Britain could make her own small claims for raw material heard. These efforts – in geological investigation and exploration, scientific and technical research, political and commercial negotiations, and capital development – are described later in this chapter.

Until 1952 the uranium needs of the three countries were met exclusively either from CDT-procured Belgian Congo ores, or from Canadian and United States domestic ores which were neither purchased through the CDT nor allocated by the Combined Policy Committee. From 1946 to 1952 the Belgian Congo delivered over 20,000 tons of uranium oxide; some 16,800 tons were shipped to the United States and some 3,250 tons to Britain. Canadian and United States production, and captured stocks, added over 3,000 tons to United States supplies (see Appendix 13, Table 1).

Throughout most of this period there was intense anxiety, especially in the United States, about the threatened shortages of uranium, though a surplus was expected in the mid-1950s when South Africa would be producing on a large scale, extensive new Canadian mines would be in operation, and Australian and Portuguese supplies would be arriving. In fact the huge American production programme never broke down for want of raw materials and the Americans never had to call on the beleaguered Springfields stockpile. The small British project was affected by the uranium shortage in that the third pile had to be cancelled in 1949, and every ton of the British allocations had to be fought for, but there was in the end always enough uranium for all three countries. The original 1946–7 shipments lasted Britain for nearly ten years; indeed for a time her slow rate of consumption was so embarrassing that some material was partially processed before storage, to improve the plant throughput figures.

The fears of shortage were, however, real, not imaginary. Various unforeseen developments meant that the worst never materialised. Firstly, the output of Congo ore, which was the main source of supply, was much better than had been expected (see Appendix 13, Table 2). This was not due to inefficient forecasting; the geologists' forecasts in 1947 and 1949 were rightly conservative, based on the available evidence of deposits which could be relied on rather than merely hoped for. Secondly, intensive exploration and incentives for prospectors in the United States had led to the discovery of many new deposits, so that domestic output of low-grade uranium ores increased more than tenfold, from about 70 tons in 1946 to over 800 tons by 1952. Thirdly, new and extensive reserves were discovered in Canada, where production continued to contribute some 200 tons a year. Even though supplies from South Africa were not available before 1953, and supplies from Portugal fell short, free-world production was much better than the 1947 and 1949 forecasts.

Meanwhile uranium consumption increased rather less than expected. This was partly because uranium was processed more efficiently, but mainly because the United States ran down its reserves – both pipeline and warehouse stocks. American requirements were calculated with a generous thirty months' reserve, and twenty-four months' reserve was an emergency level at which the Combined Policy Committee might authorise the transfer of stocks from Springfields. However, when the Americans could have asked for this, they did not do so because the amount involved was marginal from their point of view and not worth shipping. Large American requirement figures thus not only represented the increasing needs of their old and new plants, but also included very big quantities to restore their stocks to the thirty months' standard; supplies during this period met the growing current needs for plant consumption but did not rebuild these feedstocks. In effect, the Americans were working for years on a 'crash programme' basis, with ore feedstocks below the theoretical emergency level. Though the programme did not break down during the crucial years, the raw materials staff of the US Atomic Energy Commission lived in a state of continuing crisis, and were frenetically determined to secure more and more uranium ores, at any cost. British requirements in comparison were minute, and not urgent except for the need to secure uranium 'before the Congo tap was turned off'. As we have seen, the original 1946–7 shipments lasted Britain until 1955; the British rate of consumption, though artificially accelerated, was, the Belgians thought, 'pathetic'.

While uranium was so scarce, the Americans had large potential supplies unused in dumps (see above). Uranium fuel rods had to be withdrawn from the plutonium production piles after only a small proportion – perhaps 2 per cent – of the fissile uranium-235 atoms* had been used up in the fission process. When plutonium is extracted, if the unused uranium is not recovered from the fuel, replenished with fissile uranium and recycled in the pile, the material is poorly utilised (see Chapter 22). The American process for treating irradiated rods extracted most of the plutonium, but left the depleted uranium contaminated with fission products so that it could not be

* Themselves 0·7 per cent of the uranium atoms.

used without further separation. To economise in uranium, the British programme from its outset envisaged recycling as soon as uranium enriched in U-235 could be produced for the purpose; the British plutonium separation process was therefore designed also to remove fission products from the depleted uranium.

The British urged on the Americans the need for recycling, for they realised that the depleted uranium accumulating in the underground waste tanks in the United States was like a huge mine which could be later exploited but was lying idle at the time of maximum scarcity. The Americans had originally, in wartime, chosen the method of separating plutonium most certain to succeed, but after the war they developed a new method similar to that adopted by the British (see Chapter 22) to separate plutonium, uranium and fission products from each other. However, the new American process did not come into operation until six months after the British plant, in spite of superior American industrial resources. A plant for separating the uranium from the fission products in the accumulated dumps began to operate in November 1952.

Securing Present Supplies

The Belgian Congo

The Shinkolobwe mine, in the Belgian Congo, was the richest source of high-grade uranium ore in the world. The Trust had secured its output up to 1956, by a secret agreement in September 1944 with the Belgian Government giving the United States and United Kingdom Governments an option on virtually all uranium and thorium ores produced in the Belgian Congo, together with three contracts between the Trust and the mining company, Union Minière du Haut-Katanga. The first of these contracts, signed in September 1944, provided for capital payments to the company for reopening the mine* and diverting resources from copper production; it covered the purchase by the Trust of 1,720 short tons of uranium oxide at a price of $1·45 per pound. The second and third contracts were signed in October 1945; the second was for up to 10,000 tons of oxide at $1·90 a pound and the third was for as much more oxide – price and tonnage unspecified – as could be economically mined before the inter-governmental agreement expired

* Closed in 1935 because it no longer paid to produce radium in the face of competition from newly developed radium mines in Canada.

in 1956. Payment was to be half in dollars and half in sterling, and an undertaking was given that the material was for military use.

Congo supplies were nevertheless precarious for three reasons. First, the rich ores so far proved would not last much beyond 1947, and after that supplies depended partly on building new plant to use lower-grade ores and partly on opening up new deposits at a deeper level; this would mean delay and expense, and the extent of the deeper reserves was conjectural. The other two reasons were political: Washington was alarmed when at the beginning of 1946 a Bill to nationalise Belgian uranium supplies appeared imminent; any departure from the *status quo* seemed to be to the common Anglo-American disadvantage, and the Americans wanted Britain to try to dissuade the Belgians. The British thought this suggestion unrealistic; Belgium was merely proposing a course adopted in several other countries and contemplated by the United States and Britain. However, the question answered itself when the Belgian Parliament was dissolved and the Bill dropped. There was, finally, a real possibility that the Belgian Government might be forced to repudiate the agreement, since the Prime Minister, M. Spaak, was under strong left-wing pressure to disclose the terms on which Congo uranium was being disposed of, and was fiercely criticised for secret diplomacy, betrayal of Belgian interests and pursuance of a policy inconsistent with United Nations principles.

Production prospects improved. Shinkolobwe reached peak production – over 4,400 tons – in 1946, by clearing up surface dumps as well as mining new ores. By mid-1946 Union Minière, with CDT finance, were drilling deep and reserves of high-grade ores looked better than expected. A further report in September 1947 was even more hopeful and the output of high-grade material seemed likely to last until the plant for treating low-grade ores was ready. As deliveries under the second contract neared completion, further negotiations with Union Minière were necessary to fill out the details of the third contract. The Trust contemplated a firm contract for 10,000 tons and were prepared for a much increased price, partly to cover higher costs of production from low-grade ore and the amortisation of capital for the new plant. Moreover, by this time the Belgians would be aware that much higher prices were paid for Canadian and United States domestic ores. The Americans expected the Belgians to ask for $8 or even $10 a pound, although the British members of the Trust were not willing to go above $5. However,

M. Sengier* agreed to extend the second contract from 10,000 to 15,000 tons – all the ore then known to be available – at a price of only $1·90 a pound for the first 7,500 tons and $2·90 a pound for the rest, provided that it was for military use only.

Even more encouraging reports about the mine reached the Trust before the end of 1947; production and development work had exceeded expectations, 1947 output was 3,000 tons and output was likely to average 2,000 tons for the next four years. Towards the end of 1948 new ore bodies were discovered at Shinkolobwe and remaining reserves seemed likely to total 10,000–13,000 tons. The new deposits, being deeper, would be more expensive to mine; future production costs were very uncertain and it was difficult for the Belgians to commit themselves on price. M. Sengier was prepared to contract for a further 5,000 tons to the CDA but wanted, firstly, a capital grant for opening up the lower deposits and extending the plant, and secondly, a higher price, because of both increased operating costs and the higher prices paid for Canadian and American ores. Provisional agreement was reached for a further 5,000 tons of uranium oxide at $3·40 a pound, and the CDA was to pay $5 million towards prospecting and development costs. The British now proposed that the capital expenditure should no longer be shared equally by the American and British Governments, but should be proportionate to the allocation of supplies† – a further departure from the original equal partnership.

Meanwhile the Belgian Government had suffered increasing criticism at home about the 'US monopoly' of Congo uranium and the 'derisory price' received. In July 1947 M. Spaak had defended his policy strongly in the Belgian Senate:

It was necessary during the war to provide the Allies with as large a quantity as possible of materials essential to the development of atomic energy. Consequently, with the full approval of the Belgian Government, arrangements were concluded for the uranium ore of the Congo to be placed at the disposal of the

* It was in the course of these discussions that M. Sengier suggested a change of title for the CDT, because the word 'Trust' was associated in the public mind with powerful privately owned monopolies and might cast an unnecessarily sinister light on his company's transactions if these ever became generally known in detail. The CPC approved a change and the title 'Combined Development Agency' was adopted in January 1948.

† It was later divided on a 2:1 basis.

United States and United Kingdom. By these arrangements,
the legitimate interests of Belgium were fully safeguarded. They
are still in force, and the Belgian Government hopes that an international agreement concerning the control of atomic energy will
be concluded as a consequence of the work of the Commission
created within the United Nations. As soon as these results are
obtained the Belgian Government will quickly proceed to modify
all its legislation on uranium accordingly.

Meanwhile the Belgian Government had just imposed a tax,* retrospective to the beginning of 1944, on all uranium oxide exported
from the Congo. Criticism was renewed during 1949, and the
Belgian Government was attacked both for making secret agreements on uranium with other governments and for accepting an
unfair price.

The CDA argued that the higher unit prices paid elsewhere
related to higher production costs, and the Union Minière price was,
'taking all relevant factors into account', as good as that paid by the
Agency or its members to any other producer. However, M. Sengier
was under great political pressure and in October 1949 he asked for
a retrospective increase of 45 cents a pound on all deliveries. The
Agency representatives resisted, on the curious grounds that the
motives were purely political and so any approach would have to be
made by the Belgian Government.

The Belgian Ambassador in Washington soon formally asked for
re-examination of the unit price, for payment of a bonus to the
Belgian Government, and for implementation of an article in the
1944 tripartite agreement according to which, in the event of the
Governments of the United States and of the United Kingdom
deciding to use the ores as a source of energy for commercial purposes, they would admit the Belgian Government to participation
on equitable terms. The Americans and the British stalled on the
last two points (see Chapter 10), and also refused a straight price
increase; they would discuss the price again in relation to production
costs. Sengier argued that the price for Canadian uranium had been
raised to $6 a pound and that even more might be paid to South
Africa, but the CDA continued to resist the idea of a world price
and to emphasise the relation of prices to production costs.

---

* 60 fr. per kilogram of contained uranium oxide; increased to 85 fr. in
May 1948.

A year later, in October 1950, more tripartite talks with the
Belgians took place in Washington. The Belgians, aggrieved and
conscious of the important part they had played in the project from
the beginning, argued for substantially increased export duties. They
said that the price of uranium had been kept artificially low and was
out of date; that it ought now to be based on real market values; that
the price of all other strategic raw materials had increased considerably; that the users could pay twice as much for uranium without
appreciably increasing their total atomic energy budgets; and that
radioisotopes had greatly reduced the value of Belgian radium,
as a by-product of the uranium mine at Shinkolobwe.* Belgium
could not afford to go on alienating her uranium deposits on uneconomic terms; the Belgian authorities, they said, were open to
criticism for neglecting Belgium's legitimate interests, and political
pressure in the Belgian Parliament or by 'subversive elements' might
well jeopardise preferential deliveries to the Agency. The Belgian
case got short shrift from the CDA, but the Americans repeated an
earlier offer to contribute towards the cost of a Belgian research
programme and to give information on low-power reactors (see
Chapter 10).

At this time, however, the Americans, desperate for every ton of
uranium they could get, were urgently discussing with Sengier the
possibilities of increasing production by mining lower-grade ores
and extending the ore-treatment plant, even though the price would
inevitably be higher, more capital assistance would be needed, and
mining for maximum tonnage would entail uneconomical working,
erratic production and more rapid exhaustion of the mine. These
negotiations took place between American representatives and
M. Sengier; the British were not invited to participate in what was
clearly CDA business but were asked at the last minute to concur in
the agreement, which they did. The days of asserting equal British
rights were long past. An agreement signed on 27 October 1950,
and an addendum of 28 December, allowed for price increases up to
$3·90 for later deliveries, while the CDA would pay the cost of
extending the low-grade ore-treatment plant, estimated at $8 million.
By mid-1951 extension plans had been completed, and the extra

---

* Radium production was worth their while as a by-product of uranium
mining, though not as the main product. The uranium contracts specified
that the radium-bearing residues should be returned to Union Minière for the
radium to be extracted.

capacity would be working early in 1954; by then there would be stockpiles of low-grade ores to keep the plant going for ten years.

During these discussions about production and price with M. Sengier, negotiations had continued with the Belgian Government on their claim for assistance towards an atomic energy programme. A memorandum of understanding signed on 13 July 1951 (see Appendix 11) provided retrospectively for a special tax of 60 cents a pound on Congo uranium, beginning with the later deliveries under the second contract.

The CDA was by now financially involved in long-term developments at Shinkolobwe, and heavily dependent on Congo uranium as the main source of supply for some years ahead. The renewal of the 1944 agreement with the Belgian Government and the Union Minière contract, both due to expire in 1956, were therefore extremely important and urgent to the Americans, who already, in 1952, wanted to begin negotiations with the Belgians. The British Embassy in Washington warned London of the need 'to see that we take a fully equal part in the negotiations whatever happens, and also that no ridiculously extravagant prices are paid in the American zeal to clinch the matter'. Recent experience, they said, showed that the American anxiety for supplies 'bordered on hysteria'; by displaying such eagerness the Americans played into the hands of the producers and encouraged excessive prices.

In yet another round of discussions in Washington at the end of 1952, Sengier made a case for a greatly increased price, similar to the figures embodied in other offers, notably to South Africa. Apart from questions of fairness, costs in the Congo had risen steeply as lower-grade ores were worked. Sengier suggested $8 as the new price and the Americans, desperately anxious for an agreement, were ready to settle quickly for $6·30. The British wanted to drive a harder bargain but left it to the Americans since they would be using and paying for the uranium. In December 1952 the existing Congo contract was extended and the price of the later deliveries was raised from $3·90 to $6 a pound. None of these increased prices affected the British who, until 1953, were still using the cheap uranium oxide – at $1·90 a pound – delivered in 1946–7. Britain also left the Americans to resist Union Minière demands for a 58 per cent increase in the advances for prospecting and development work and plant extensions.

By this time Britain no longer fought for full consultation and equal participation in Agency affairs. As the junior partner, with requirements less than one-tenth of those of the United States, Britain had been relieved first of the cost of supplies not allocated to her, and later of her liability for 50 per cent of capital costs.

Without Congo uranium Britain could not have produced fissile material or atomic bombs in these early post-war years and the American programme would have been seriously affected, to say the least. Congo supplies represented an abundant source of ore, secured by long-term agreement at advantageous prices; they presented no difficult processing problems, and moreover the CDA had to deal with only one highly expert company and with a sympathetic manager, M. Sengier, of extraordinary authority. The United States and Britain both acknowledged his services to them by awards in their Honours Lists.

The relationship between the atomic powers and the Belgian Congo raises a number of questions. The former undoubtedly drove a hard bargain; was it an unfair one? In 1947 the Americans expected to be asked $8 or $10 a pound, and even the British were prepared to go up to $5, but Sengier settled for $2·90; why did the Belgians as the main producers not press their advantage more strongly? They must have realised that the Americans wanted uranium urgently, at almost any cost.

The transactions were not purely commercial.[2] The supply of Congo ore had begun during the war and the Belgians had regarded it as a part of the Allied war effort. Possibly in October 1945, when the second and third contracts were signed, it was seen as something of a thank-offering. Thereafter, during the Cold War, it was seen as a contribution to Western defence. As Lilienthal said: 'We must continue to make [Sengier] feel, as he has in the past, that this is more than a commercial transaction – that he is contributing to stopping Communism.' The uranium was supplied on the explicit understanding that it was for military purposes only and that a new agreement would be necessary if it was to be used commercially. Nevertheless, Sengier could have provided the uranium needed to stop Communism and still demanded the higher price which in 1947 even the British were ready to pay. Possibly the politics of the Cold War affected relative bargaining strengths. If the CDA needed to buy, the Congo needed to sell and there was no other big customer in sight except Russia. Sengier once complained to a CDA representative, 'Where else would you get it so cheap?' only to be asked where else he could sell.

The concept of a fair price is moreover one of theological subtlety. In the case of the Congo ores an inordinately eager buyer bargained with a willing seller. It is just possible that the Belgians did not fully realise their strength because they did not know how large were the American requirements and how low their stocks, but American eagerness was nevertheless ill-concealed. However, Sengier himself said in 1949 that the prices were 'commercially satisfactory'.

Certainly the CDA were successful in avoiding paying a price in line with prices elsewhere, which would have given huge profit margins to the low-cost Congo producers. Congo prices were very low* compared with prices paid for American and Canadian ores and with those promised later to South African and Australian suppliers.† This reflected low Congo costs: Shinkolobwe was a going concern, the high-grade ores were so rich that they could almost be picked out by hand, and labour was cheap in European terms. Mining, processing and transport costs for 80 per cent ore are of course much less than for low-grade ore. Costs in the other countries were high and prices were worked out separately for them on a complicated cost-plus basis.

The United States and Canada

In a few years the United States and Canada were to be the two largest producers of uranium in the world, with South Africa in third place. During our period they were much less important than the Congo, though in these seven years United States domestic output increased tenfold as new ore deposits were found and opened up in Colorado, Utah, Wyoming and New Mexico.

In Arctic Canada, on the shores of the Great Bear Lake, the Eldorado Company had been mining pitchblende for radium since

---

* Between 1944 and 1953 the basic price of Congo uranium had risen from $1.45 a pound to $1.90, then $2.90, $3.40, $3.90 and finally $6. These prices, however, excluded the Government taxes, mostly imposed retrospectively.

† Sengier, in a letter to Lilienthal,[3] says: 'My whole life has been devoted to the industrial and social development of Katanga, the mining district of the Belgian Colony, with a policy of putting the general interest of the country and the welfare of white and native populations above the financial interest I was responsible for. The pleasure derived from such a policy turned out to be the most valuable dividend I received for my work.'

1933, but in 1940 the mine closed. It was reopened in 1942 to produce uranium, and before long the Canadian Government assumed control of prospecting, mining and the sale of uranium, and took over the Eldorado Company. Eldorado began an extensive prospecting programme in collaboration with the Geological Survey of Canada, numerous private prospectors followed, and in the next few years many deposits were discovered around Beaverlodge Lake, Saskatchewan, and Great Slave Lake, Athabasca. Much development was needed before the new mines and mills produced ores, and up to 1952 only the original Eldorado mine at Great Bear Lake contributed to the American project. The biggest uranium strikes, in the Blind River area of Ontario, were still to come, in 1952 and later.

The British tried to buy 50–100 tons of uranium from Canada in 1946, but the Canadians were selling all their output direct to the United States* and for various reasons preferred to do so. By the time they had some to offer at $12·50 a pound the British did not really need it, as they had stocks of cheap Congo ore. So Canada's uranium did not closely concern the British; it was not sold through the CDA, or allocated by the Combined Policy Committee, and the British received none for use in their project.

Britain was even less concerned with the United States' rapidly growing domestic production from low-grade deposits, and she had only occasional very sketchy information about it. North American output mattered to Britain only because by supplementing supplies from the Belgian Congo it increased her own chances of getting uranium.

Securing Future Supplies

Exploration

The Congo, the United States and Canada kept the CDA member countries supplied with uranium until 1952, but all this time the CDA was seeking other sources, first of all to deny them to other powers, then to meet the growing demand and to replace the original reserves if and when they were exhausted. Every possible method of exploration was used. Geiger and scintillation counters greatly speeded up the geologists' systematic exploration, and enabled almost anyone to become a prospector for uranium; they reduced the

* Immediately after the bombing of Hiroshima the Russian authorities tried to obtain 50 tons of ore from Canada, as Mutual Aid or as a commercial sale.

chances of missing inconspicuous outcrops of the ore and helped to determine the position and thickness of the deposits. Nevertheless, although these instruments were indispensable, exploration still depended on detailed field geology and laboratory research. The British were supposed to investigate and explore Commonwealth* and colonial territories, and the Americans, the United States; 'third countries' were to be divided between them and the cost of agreed projects to be equally shared. This arrangement led to various arguments, when the British were asked to pay half the cost of investigations they had not been consulted about – including some in British colonies – or which they considered worthless. In this search the Americans deployed much greater forces, but the British effort, though small, was efficient, and the Ministry of Supply's mining consultant, Arthur Storke, played a key role in all important uranium negotiations until his death in 1949 (see p. 353). He was for a time a British member of the CDA, but as an expert adviser he served both the Agency and the British representatives. He was succeeded as British consultant by J. G. Bower. His United States counterpart was Anton Gray, on loan to the Agency from an American copper-mining company, who was later to become a consultant to the United Kingdom Atomic Energy Authority.

The Ministry of Supply – unlike the US Atomic Energy Commission, which directly employed 120 geologists by 1952 – had no geological staff. It relied wholly on an atomic energy division in the United Kingdom Geological Survey and Museum (UKGSM), which in turn depended on the Chemical Research Laboratory at Teddington for analytical support. The division was small and always under-strength; even by 1952 it had only 9 professional staff – 8 short of a complement authorised five years before – while the United States Geological Survey had about 500 geologists on atomic energy work, besides 50 geologists in American universities working on US Atomic Energy Commission contracts. British and colonial mining houses had only 3 geologists in this field, compared with at least 25 in American firms; altogether the British were outnumbered by about 50 to 1. In the United States more than 8 per cent of the total atomic energy budget was spent on raw materials exploration, compared with 0·1 per cent in Britain. By 1952 the French employed 100 geologists on atomic energy work. C. F. Davidson, leader of the

---

* There were some small deposits in the United Kingdom, but these were not economic.

GSM team, was extremely critical of the scale of effort, but half the division's vacancies could not be filled owing to a serious post-war shortage of geologists. In the circumstances the division's achievements were creditable. Their job was not to prospect but to use their specialist knowledge to advise prospectors and evaluate discoveries, and to assist the staffs of local Geological Surveys in the colonies.

Davidson and his colleagues worked indefatigably on theoretical investigations, literature searches and the examination of thousands of mineral samples a year sent from all over the world, and they also travelled extensively to the United States, Canada, South Africa, Portugal, Australia, and nearly every British colony. They ran training courses for colonial geologists on leave in the United Kingdom; they collaborated with Harwell in the development and provision of surveying equipment such as borehole counters and car-borne detectors for colonial officials to use on their routine travels; they took part in international conferences on raw materials; they published a *Prospectors' Handbook to Radioactive Mineral Deposits* of which 10,000 copies were issued; and they devised new techniques of exploration which were widely used in America and the Dominions.

The British geological staff were hard-working and highly qualified, but not infallible. Davidson – well informed, cautious and trenchant in his opinions – rejected the idea of aerial prospecting (using radiation detectors in aircraft) on which Harwell did a good deal of work, although this later proved extremely effective in Canada and Australia. He was habitually sceptical about American geologists' reports, which he usually thought wildly sanguine, but results often belied his own conservative, even gloomy, forecasts. Nevertheless, the small British staff made a useful contribution. It was the misfortune and not the fault of the British geologists that apart from South Africa (see pp. 378–83) no uranium deposits were found comparable in importance to those of North America; extensive searches throughout the colonies revealed no deposits capable of early development. Much of the GSM's time and effort was devoted to Portugal (see pp. 386–90), one of the 'third countries' for which under CDA arrangements Britain was responsible; this was never of major importance and the ores, which could not conveniently be used in the British metal plant, were transferred to the United States.

Davidson, and also Linstead of the Chemical Research Laboratory, criticised the British raw materials organisation not only for its small scale and slender resources. In their opinion the Ministry of Supply should have had a technical director of raw materials, as did the US Atomic Energy Commission; the British organisation, they said, was too diffuse, involving too many different bodies, and lacking strong and expert central direction. Davidson also thought that the slight interest shown by British mining houses, unlike the very active and enterprising American firms, resulted from the official policy of not offering special incentives for ore discovery; there was little inducement to prospectors to search for uranium in any British colony, though prices offered by the Ministry of Supply improved after 1951, when it was feared that news of the South African prices might leak out. Davidson himself had at one time opposed the idea of rewards for prospectors, but he changed his mind and admitted that it was the offer of a £20,000 reward that led to the discovery of uranium at Rum Jungle in Australia.

Research

New kinds of ores called for new processes. Sources of high-grade ore were few but low-grade ores were common, and extensive low-grade deposits represented large tonnages of uranium if only methods of recovery could be devised. Unfortunately the process used for the rich ores of the Congo and Great Bear Lake was not applicable to low-grade ores which might contain less than 0·1 per cent of uranium oxide. Mining experts were accustomed to such difficulties; entirely new techniques of recovery had been developed for copper, tin and zinc when expanding demand led to the mining and treatment of lower-grade ores. As atomic energy was going to have to depend more and more on low-grade uranium ores, a simple and economic process was needed to produce high-grade concentrates from them.

The technical problem had to be solved before the promise of vast new South African and Australian supplies could be realised, and laboratories in the United States, Britain, Canada, South Africa, and later Australia, all took part in a co-operative effort. In Britain the work was divided among the GSM, Harwell and the Chemical Research Laboratory. The GSM, which had a small ore-dressing laboratory, studied physical methods of treating ores – by automatic sorting, gravity methods, flotation and so on – and later, in 1949, an ore-dressing laboratory was set up at Harwell; it went there rather than to the DSIR for reasons of secrecy, but although it was well equipped it was never fully used.* Mineral dressing by physical means turned out to be of comparatively little value for uranium ores, and the development of chemical methods became increasingly more important.

Chemical treatment was studied in Britain by the Chemical Research Laboratory at Teddington, which had a staff of 35† or so on atomic energy work. After developing a method of treating Portuguese ores, they turned their attention in 1948 mainly to the problems of low-grade South African ores. This programme, financed by the CDA, was far smaller than the CDA project on South African ores at the Massachusetts Institute of Technology. Research was also pursued in Ottawa, and the South African Government financed work at its own Metallurgical Laboratory. There was much traffic between the four countries – shipment of ore samples, visits of staff, exchanges of reports and results – and co-operation was useful if imperfect.

The first part of the chemical treatment consisted of a suitable acid or alkaline leach, according to the composition of the ore, followed by processes to extract uranium, and any other associated metals worth recovering, from the solution. Possible processes included precipitation, usually using ammonia; solvent extraction from nitrate solutions using such solvents as ether or butex; ion exchange, especially useful for low concentrations in sulphate solutions; and electrolysis, useful with carbonate solutions. The Chemical Research Laboratory studied all these methods, while ICI (Widnes) and Springfields were also working on solvent extraction for a quite different purpose. The CRL's major preoccupation was the application of ion-exchange resins to uranium recovery and purification, a method to which the American firm, Cyanamid, devoted much effort. It was first used in the South African plants, and subsequently in Australia.

This was the most important single part of the CRL's work, but they worked on methods of chemical analysis and also undertook many subsidiary long-term studies, such as a Harwell contract on the possibilities of extracting uranium from sea water; the extraction

* It was later transferred to the DSIR in order to handle non-radioactive mineral studies, but there was little UK demand for mineral dressing.

† 1951–2 figure. In 1947 they had 11 people on analytical work and 25 on extraction research and development.

of uranium from phosphate ores as a by-product of the fertiliser industry, which the Battelle Institute in the United States was also investigating for the CDA; and bacterial leaching, first used in 1953 in the Portuguese plants. The CRL's support of the UKGSM has already been mentioned, but they also co-operated closely with Harwell and Springfields, and in particular helped to solve the troublesome Springfields problem of uranium losses in processing (see Chapter 22).

South Africa

At the end of the war the most promising new uranium territory, perhaps almost as good as the Belgian Congo, seemed to be the South African Rand.[4] It had no potential uranium mines, but there were vast quantities of uranium in the gold mines and in their accumulated wastes. A Canadian-born geologist named George Bain, who worked for the United States Manhattan Project, had brought back some specimens of gold ore from a field trip to South Africa in 1941. Some years later, as a consultant to the Manhattan Project, he became interested in uranium, examined the gold ore specimens with a Geiger counter, and found they were slightly radioactive. This important discovery was reported to the CDA, and an approach was made to the South African Prime Minister, General Smuts, in 1945, suggesting a visit by Bain and Davidson. They both went to South Africa in September 1945 and preliminary radiometric surveys in the Rand and Orange Free State indicated extensive uranium reserves, probably between 65,000 and 168,000 tons. It was a far cry to uranium production, but the news was most welcome to the CDA, anxious about future Congo supplies.

The British were especially delighted as South Africa, being a British and not a 'Trust territory', could be regarded as an independent source of uranium for Britain and as a trump card in bargaining with the United States. Later, Roger Makins wisely warned against relying on this card which was after all not in Britain's hand but South Africa's. Moreover, he said, 'if . . . we fail to secure an arrangement with South Africa by our unaided efforts we might be glad of an agreement with the Americans which gave us a claim in the world pool of uranium including such South African supplies as we might jointly be able to extract from the Union'. Smuts did indeed send 'a dusty answer' when Mr Attlee asked him to grant the United Kingdom an option to purchase

South African uranium over a term of years; in the present state of knowledge of the economic possibilities, he said, no government could undertake an obligation with unforeseeable implications, but he would ensure that supplies did not fall into 'hands that might abuse' this 'new source of frightfulness'. Pressure from London was soon renewed, for prospects of South African ore seemed crucial in Anglo-American discussions on technical co-operation. Then, in February 1946, Storke returned from a visit to South Africa with the depressing news that chemical analysis of ore samples suggested that the previous estimates had been far too high; South Africa might not be very important after all. Bain, however, now believed that the deposits there were probably the most important in the world.

General Smuts, in London in May 1946 for the Dominion Prime Ministers' meeting, told Lord Portal he believed that the prospects were better than Storke feared, and he intended that in future South Africa should 'face two ways', towards uranium as well as gold. The British decided to pursue the matter vigorously; South African uranium might be vital to their programme, and if they did not secure a lien on it the United States might ignore agreed procedures and act unilaterally.* During June 1946 Brigadier Schonland,† director of the South African Department of Scientific and Industrial Research, and Professor Taverner, director of the South African Government Metallurgical Laboratory, came to London for discussions; it was agreed that, unless costs were prohibitive, production plans should go forward and a pilot-scale purification plant set up in South Africa.

South Africa began to recruit staff, obtain equipment, and carry out laboratory investigations of ore-dressing methods. At the same time the research on low-grade ores was going on at the Massachusetts Institute of Technology. Many arguments arose: Taverner considered research on South African ores should be done in South Africa; the Americans believed progress could only be made in the United States; the British were unwilling to go on paying for the MIT work unless Taverner thought it of value for South African ores; Taverner, lacking information on what MIT was doing, could not say. Eventually, however, most of the difficulties were smoothed

* Shortly afterwards the British Secretary of the Trust was concerned to note direct communications between Bain and the South African authorities.
† Later on he became the second director of Harwell.

out and an ore-dressing conference, the first of several, was held in New York at the end of the year, with American, South African, Canadian and British participation.

South Africa was not a Trust territory, but the British were uncertain whether they were under an obligation to share uranium from non-Trust areas with the Americans, and whether South African supplies should be subject to allocation by the Combined Policy Committee; they decided to assume tacitly that the answer to both questions was 'no'. However, because of secrecy the South African Government knew nothing about the Trust and Anglo-American raw materials arrangements, and the British could not tell them. So the South Africans saw no impediment to discussing uranium direct with the Americans, who – through reports, visits, supplies of equipment, and so on – were much more in evidence in South Africa than the British. Impatient with the apparent lack of progress, the Americans were vigorously studying problems of extraction from South African ores; Professor Taverner was surprised to find fifty people engaged on this work at MIT, many more than in South Africa.

Meanwhile General Smuts had held private meetings with leaders of the mining industry. There were hopes of some production in 1948 and about 1,000 tons a year by 1952, provided extraction research was successful; costs were likely to be less than in Canada. A British offer in May 1947 to buy up to 1,000 tons a year met at first an encouraging response, but Smuts again deferred discussions because technical production difficulties were still unresolved and the gold-mining industry would have to be fully consulted. The Americans, although impatient for results, were prepared for the time being to leave negotiations to the British. Smuts, confident that once extraction problems were solved both British and American needs could be met, said he intended to treat both countries equally. South African mining companies now appreciated the advantages, provided gold recovery was not impaired, of extracting gold and uranium oxide simultaneously from newly mined ores and, possibly, extracting uranium from the huge accumulation of mine residues. Prices, Smuts added, would probably have to be on a cost-plus basis because of uncertainties and variable production costs from mine to mine.

Nothing could be settled until the technical problems were overcome. Research continued and by mid-1947 MIT had developed a process which was expected to extract 98 per cent of the gold and 65 per cent of the uranium content from the ores – a process which was improved over the next five years. In the spring of 1948 Schonland and Taverner came to London to discuss uranium prices and quantities, the problem of mines with poor ores and high production costs, the recruitment of technical personnel, and the development of South Africa's chemical industry. Talks continued in Washington with the CDA and it was agreed that South Africa would supply a total of 10,000 tons of uranium oxide, not less than 400 tons a year at a maximum price of $9 a pound, and up to 150 tons at a maximum price of $25; this formula was designed to secure a balanced development of the richer, low-cost, mines and the poorer, high-cost, mines. Payment would be half in dollars and half in sterling.

Final contract negotiations were to take place in South Africa towards the end of 1948, but in June the anti-British, nationalist Mr Malan replaced General Smuts as Prime Minister. Contract discussions were not renewed until the end of 1949 and then proved disappointing: the new Government disliked Smuts's projects; gold production was now more attractive and there were new gold prospects in the Orange Free State; uranium extraction problems were still intractable; there were radical differences on price questions, especially on apportioning mining costs between gold and uranium. The talks were deferred once again for six months.

Other political complications arose. Smuts had mentioned earlier the question of a 'special position' and now South Africa asked for recognition, as a major supplier of uranium, in atomic energy counsels. Britain, acutely aware of the 'special position' problem in relation to Belgium and the Commonwealth countries, consulted the Americans who thought any discussion of it should follow, not precede, negotiations for a uranium contract. South African aspirations were eventually satisfied by the arrangements for collaboration already described in Chapter 10.

Not until November 1950 was a uranium agreement signed. Then it was between the South African Atomic Energy Board* and the CDA, not Britain. It covered virtually the whole output, for various periods up to 1964, of four named producers – a restriction

* As this was not an inter-governmental agreement, it could be secret and did not have to be registered with the United Nations under Article 102 of the UN Charter.

to prevent the introduction of too many high-cost mines. The CDA offered to advance the entire capital for the project, nearly $20 million, and priority arrangements were to be made for constructing ore-treatment plants. A price formula* was agreed – a basic price per pound of oxide, plus 70 per cent of the cost of production, within a ceiling figure; this formula combined the advantages of a fixed price with the flexibility of a cost-plus price, while giving the producers an incentive to keep their costs down. The average price was expected to work out at about $7.70 a pound – much more than the Congo price but decidedly less than the Canadian – and payment was to be two-thirds in dollars and one-third in sterling.† The agreement also provided for secrecy as to contract terms, processes and output, for technical exchanges, and for sharing research results.

Plant construction at the West Rand mine was expected to be complete by January 1953, and at the other mines by mid-1954. Uranium production should begin in 1953 at 200 tons a year, rising to 800 tons by 1955; after that, output in the required grade and cost range would probably reach 1,500 tons a year. The 1950 agreement cleared the way for action. By March 1951 two more South African producers had come into the scheme, and it had been agreed that the United States and British Governments should make loans direct to the mining companies; of the capital required, estimated at some $30 million, Britain was to provide one-third.

By October 1951 further expansion of the United States defence programme made the 1950 agreement inadequate, and CDA representatives went to South Africa to discuss means of increasing production. The American delegates wanted production at any price; the cost, however high, would be as nothing to the billions of dollars invested in the American plants. Output might possibly be increased to 3,000 tons a year by the end of 1956, but technical staff in South Africa were so loaded with work on uranium that gold production was suffering, and there were serious shortages of artisans, of native labour, of electrical power and of such essential materials as steel and cement. The British were alarmed, partly by the implied financial liabilities to themselves and partly lest American pressure endangered the balance of the South African economy;

---

* There was a variation or 'kink' in the price formula in cases where mining was primarily for uranium, with only incidental gold recovery (as in the West Rand mine).

† All figures are given in dollar equivalents.

they were nevertheless determined to play their part in the CDA, the only remaining area of Anglo-American co-operation.

A revised agreement was concluded in December 1951. South Africa decided that in spite of the serious impact on the economy she would undertake to produce 3,000 tons a year by 1956; increased output would come partly from the high-uranium low-gold West Rand area, partly from new sources in the East Rand and Orange Free State. There would be steep price increases to cover the mining companies' risks and to compensate for diverting resources from gold operations; a new and more complicated price formula gave an average price of nearly $10 – a 30 per cent increase. Capital expenditure over the years 1951–6 would be about $126 million, of which the British would contribute one-third. Once again, the 1951 agreement was hardly concluded before the Americans were agitating for a planned output of 4,000 tons instead of 3,000: the British, not wishing to appear obstructive, accepted the proposal.

South African uranium did not contribute to either the United States or the British atomic energy programmes during our period, but the development of South African production was a major preoccupation from 1945 onwards and of great importance for the future. Though South Africa was a Commonwealth country and not a 'CDA territory', it was in practice treated as a CDA territory, with agreements negotiated by the Agency, and with the United States closely involved.

In South Africa uranium was generally not a main product – as in the Congo, Canada and Portugal – but the by-product of the profitable and very important gold industry. The technical problems of extracting uranium in very low concentrations from the gold-bearing ores were novel, and the new process of ion exchange (which was to have wide industrial applications later) was first used there. The South African situation was further complicated because several companies were involved, and numerous mines with widely varying conditions and production costs; the consequent price problem was solved by formulae allowing for variable production costs while providing low-cost incentives, a device that was also to prove useful in Australia.

Australia
Australia was another promising Commonwealth country, technically not covered by the CDA. A hopeful but subsequently

disappointing prospect had been explored there by the British Government in 1944. Two important sites were, however, found soon after the war, at Radium Hill in South Australia and at Rum Jungle in the Northern Territories. Early in 1948 the South Australian Director of Mines claimed that Radium Hill could produce 540 tons of uranium oxide, an estimate rejected by the cautious Davidson. The Australians persisted nevertheless, and in 1951 told the British that 500 tons could certainly be produced and that they intended to develop the mine for industrial power. Once more the contradictions of Britain's relationship with the United States were apparent. She did not adopt Australian proposals for joint development because it was not an opportune time to seek American agreement on sharing classified information with the Australians. The Prime Minister of South Australia, Sir Tom Playford, therefore approached the United States Atomic Energy Commission direct for advice on the South Australian deposits, and the Commission replied direct that the United States might buy the uranium. Playford went to Washington, where the workings of the CDA were explained to him and the British joined in the talks. The Americans said that they were willing, in co-operation with the British, to discuss a contract for all the uranium that could be produced, at a price related to production costs, and they urged that production at Radium Hill should begin as soon as possible.

The understanding that Commonwealth countries should be dealt with by Britain, and not by the CDA, had by now disappeared without trace. Australian uranium was barely treated as a CDA concern except for purchasing arrangements, but rather as a private United States–Australian business. British officials were unhappy, but as a matter of practical politics they realised that no one could prevent the Americans from buying uranium where they could. In January 1952 the Australian Government invited a United States mission to examine all Australian uranium occurrences. No invitation was sent to London, but the Americans, from now on meticulous about joint negotiations, agreed that Davidson should join them. In April 1952, in Canberra, the mission initialled an agreement on the South Africa model (but for 175 tons a year compared with 4,000). It was to run for seven years,* but gave South Australia the option, after delivering 600 tons, of reducing the term to safeguard reserves, since they were then determined on an industrial

* From the date of full production, or from January 1955.

power programme. The CDA was to buy the Radium Hill output at $5·04 a pound plus 70 per cent of the cost of production, and the price was expected to work out at nearly $14 a pound. Payment was to be two-thirds in dollars and one-third in sterling; the Australians would have preferred dollars only, but the Americans firmly upheld the British position on sterling payment. The CDA also agreed to give technical assistance, and to make a loan for mine development and chemical plant construction. The Australians were to do their best to ensure the secrecy of the terms, production processes, grades of ore, tonnages, and so on.

From South Australia the delegation went to the Northern Territories, to see a new ore discovery made at Rum Jungle by a kangaroo hunter. Their inquiries, and the reports of Australian geologists, convinced even the sceptical Davidson that these deposits were really valuable. It was too early for a development and production agreement, but a contract was made for the sale of development ores to the CDA.

In the summer of 1952, when the Australian Prime Minister, Mr Menzies, visited Britain and the United States, both countries stressed the urgent need for uranium and the importance of Rum Jungle, possibly one of the world's major uranium sources. He affirmed Australia's desire to contribute to the common defence, but emphasised that Australia wanted to save ores for future use and also wanted technical help; she had power problems and was much interested in the industrial potential of atomic energy. American officials in Washington offered Mr Menzies a scheme for Rum Jungle, providing for the immediate design and construction of an ore-treatment plant, and proposed that the CDA should buy all the Rum Jungle output for ten years, again with an option to terminate to safeguard reserves. The price formula was similar to the Radium Hill agreement, but with a ceiling of $16·80; to finance the initial exploration and development the CDA would make advances against future production up to the value of $5 million.

The British, though by now extremely chary of new financial commitments, could not afford to stand aside from a major project in a Commonwealth country, and accepted the draft agreement. It was signed in January 1953, with an additional clause permitting termination if the material were no longer needed for military purposes; the Australians were determined not to sell uranium for the common defence, and then see it, put to commercial use.

The Anglo-Australian position was difficult. Constricted by the *modus vivendi* with the Americans, the British could not co-operate effectively with the Australians, who not surprisingly felt that their best course was to establish a close tie with the less inhibited United States. This, combined with the insatiable American demand for uranium, could easily have led to a direct relationship between the two countries, excluding Britain. It did not, partly because the Americans took great care to ensure British participation; nevertheless, in all defence matters Australia had tended since 1941 to turn to the United States rather than Britain. Generally, Britain's hold over Commonwealth countries was proving much less strong than she, or the United States, had assumed.

Production began in 1953 at Rum Jungle, and in 1954 at Radium Hill (where extremely difficult ore-dressing problems arose), and it continued into the 1960s. It was not until 1954 that the important 'Mary Kathleen' deposits in Queensland, which were later to supply the United Kingdom Atomic Energy Authority, were discovered.

Portugal
Oddly enough, the British played a less dominant role in uranium-producing Commonwealth countries – Canada, South Africa and Australia – than in Portugal. British interest in radium mining there dated from 1926, and during the war a British Government agency* had acquired the controlling interest in the concessions to prevent them from falling into German hands. In April 1945 it was agreed that the minority shareholders should be bought out and that the Combined Development Trust would take over the mining company,† which the Ministry of Supply would run with a local board of directors in Lisbon. There were sixty unused concessions and three mines in working order, the most important at Urgeirica. There the lode had been lost in a fault and the mine was on a care and maintenance basis, but some exploration continued; by mid-1946 all the concessions had been examined and in July a British geologist, James Cameron, rediscovered Urgeirica's lost lode. Anton Gray visited Portugal and estimated the total yield, very accurately, at some 1,000 tons‡ of oxide.

The potential production, though not great, seemed worthwhile

* The United Kingdom Commercial Corporation (UKCC).
† Companhia de Radium Limitada (CPR).
‡ Total ore production 1951–62 was 1,325 metric tons.

when uranium was so urgently needed. But first an assurance was required that the Portuguese Government would permit export. It fell to the British, with old political and commercial associations with Portugal and already established at the mines, to act for the CDT; later the Portuguese were told informally on various occasions of American interest, but not about the CDT or the secret Anglo-American agreements.

In June 1947 the British Ambassador in Lisbon, Sir Nigel Ronald, informed Portuguese officials of the potential value of the uranium reserves, and sought approval for exploitation of the mines and the export of ores and concentrates, of which a balance would be left for Portugal's own use. The ensuing polite discussions between Portuguese and British experts made little progress, and by the end of 1947 Washington, as well as London, was becoming impatient.

In Lisbon Sir Nigel Ronald was pressing once or twice a week for an answer. The Portuguese readily gave formal assurances that they would not permit the export of uranium to countries suspected of being unfriendly towards the United Kingdom, but they refused to grant a monopoly; Portugal, lacking natural resources, could not hand over the control of this most important mineral 'even to her ancient ally'. In May 1948 Ronald at last obtained an interview with the Prime Minister, Dr Salazar, who he realised, feeling that his country had been caught out too often over mineral concessions, would drive a hard bargain.

Dr Salazar asked searching questions about the British atomic energy programme, and about the principle on which the British and the Americans had divided the world's uranium sources between them, as Pope Alexander Borgia had divided the New World between Portugal and Spain. What advantages would Portugal gain from the plan? When told that Portugal would be helping to maintain order in the world, the Prime Minister wanted more tangible benefits for his country. No agreement was reached.

For nine more months Ronald importuned the Portuguese Government. Meanwhile the mine was losing staff, and the Americans were increasingly critical. At last, in February 1949, came a favourable reply. In July, after two wearisome years of negotiation, letters were exchanged providing for 100 tons a year of uranium oxide to be exported for seven years from 1951. The plant for preparing ore concentrates was to be installed by the end of 1950; a daily quota was imposed on production; the number of concessions which could be worked at any one time was restricted; finally, secrecy was to be guaranteed.*

The Americans accepted the terms and the CDA formally noted the agreement in September 1949; until then the British took full responsibility. The Portuguese Government, though certainly aware of American interest, regarded it as an Anglo-Portuguese agreement; the British believed that it was entirely due to their position as Portugal's ancient ally and felt sure that United States intervention would not have helped.

Great activity then began at the mines, with keen competition for employment. Labour relations were good, improved health precautions reduced the risks to the miners, and much attention was paid to welfare. The installation of the new ore-treatment plant was tackled urgently. But imported materials and equipment were constantly delayed in Customs, and skilled steel erectors were very scarce in Portugal. The senior staff worked under abnormal pressure; early one Sunday morning a visitor† to Urgeirica saw the senior engineer in charge of plant construction, together with his surveyor, working on the site preparing templates for foundation bolts.

But despite all efforts the plant could not be completed by the beginning of 1951, as stipulated, and, reluctantly, the Portuguese authorities twice extended the time limit by six, and then by three, months. By that time, fortunately, the plant was finished, and the first ore consignment was shipped in February 1952. Before this, however, the Americans were urging a revised agreement, doubling production and exports, and permitting more extensive exploration.

The British, unwilling to seek an increased quota even to make up eight or nine months' output lost by the late completion of the plant, were still more reluctant to ask for the quota to be doubled; moreover any big increase would mean building new plant when the original plant was only just running. However, Sir Anthony Eden and Dean Acheson agreed to approach Dr Salazar separately during the NATO conference held at Lisbon in February 1952. Dr Salazar, though sympathetic, told Mr Acheson that the main stumbling-block was payment in sterling; besides, he wanted to conserve

* Security at Urgeirica was, however, an almost insoluble problem; the mine was near a well-known holiday hotel for whose guests a visit to the mine was a local attraction.

† Mr J. G. Bower, then British representative on the CDA in succession to Mr A. D. Storke. This visit was in November 1950.

Portugal's reserves, for the price was sure to rise when the present armament fever was over and uranium could be used for non-defence purposes.

The British and the Americans were agreed on the objective – increased output – but not on the means. The British wanted maximum production without new construction or further surveys; the Americans wanted a considerable plant extension and an aggressive programme of exploration. The Atomic Energy Commission – under pressure from the Defense Department, Congress and the President – could not tolerate a British dog in the Portuguese manger. If the British feared more capital expenditure, the Americans would go it alone; a further approach to the Portuguese might fail, but the Americans wanted a free hand at least to try. However, by late 1952 they decided that it might not be worth the effort; negotiating the 1949 agreement had taken two years, and if it took as long to revise it would then be near expiry. By then, too, South African and Australian uranium would be in production.

Meanwhile the Portuguese mine had worked well. In the first ten months nearly 100 tons of oxide had been shipped. Output went steadily on, but after all the high-powered negotiation, the diplomatic manoeuvring, and the immense toil of the construction and mining staff, Portuguese uranium was no longer of vital interest. Senior people who, under extreme pressure, had been heartened by thinking that their task was of great importance to Britain, now found their efforts eclipsed by South African prospects. Portuguese uranium was used only in research quantities in Britain; stocks of it even became an embarrassment, and later consignments, too low in concentration for the Springfields plant to use economically, were shipped on to the United States.

This small project, involving only one, British-controlled, mining company, produced the expected tonnages efficiently and cheaply.* Technical problems of ore treatment were solved† well before the plant was designed or commissioned. Portugal herself profited both from the employment provided and from a levy imposed in 1955 which yielded some $10 million, and eventually, in 1962, she received the mine and plant free of charge as a going concern. Nevertheless, the story of the Portuguese project exemplifies not

* At prices between $6.50 and $8, one of the CDA's cheapest sources of supply, apart from Congo ore.
† By the Chemical Research Laboratory.

only the tensions and complexities of the Anglo-American partner-ship and the dilemmas of uranium-producing countries, but also the tremendous efforts devoted to gaining even small tonnages of uranium.

Conclusions

By 1952 the search for new sources of uranium had been in progress with increasing momentum for more than a decade. At the begin-ning pitchblende was the only type of ore and the Belgian Congo was the only major uranium source for the Western world. An intensive world-wide search, depending not only on official surveys but also on the awareness and interest of mining houses and private prospectors, led to new discoveries, mostly associated with known mineral deposits – especially gold, copper and vanadium – rather than in virgin territory. The time-lag from exploration to production was eight to ten years; apart from the time needed to negotiate agreements, open up mines, build plant and provide such facilities as transport and housing, much technical research was necessary for ores which could not be treated by existing methods. By 1952 many years of effort were beginning to pay off and a world-wide mining industry was established, important both to the atomic powers and to the economies of the producing countries. Insatiable demand in the early days for uranium, however costly, led to instability. The industry was to enjoy a uranium boom (primarily weapons-based) in the 1950s, followed by falling demand and some ghost towns during the sixties. There was some small recovery in the late sixties, but a new boom based on nuclear power is unlikely before 1980.

By 1952 the primacy of the Belgian Congo was drawing to a close, and the United States and South Africa were emerging as the main sources of uranium in the West, soon to be joined by Canada. From now on the atomic powers were going to have to depend not on the rich Congo material but on low-grade ores with higher mining and treatment costs. But by the late 1950s demand had ceased to rise and the day of the very high-cost producer was over for the time being.

To the growth of this new industry Britain had contributed less than the United States, which had not only the more compelling need but also much greater resources of men, money and material, as well as domestic reserves of uranium. But the British had helped in exploration and research, by the efforts of their own geologists,

chemists and mining experts and also by paying – sometimes reluctantly – half the cost of CDA-sponsored survey and research. In
Portugal, a minor source, the British were responsible for virtually
all the prospecting and development; in the Commonwealth, however, they had been little involved in the Canadian uranium discoveries, while in the South African and Australian discoveries the
Americans were as much concerned as the British. However, British
experts made an important contribution to the treatment of South
African and Australian low-grade ores, and especially to the development of practical ion-exchange methods of purification; they also
developed new instruments, including a very useful borehole
counter, but were less successful than the Americans in commercial
exploitation.

Financially, in spite of her economic problems, Britain contributed
much: half the cost of the CDA's administration and its research
and exploration programmes, and a share of the CDA's capital
expenditure – half in the case of the Belgian Congo and Portugal,
and one-third in South Africa and Australia. As commitments
increased, the Treasury, though conscious of the need for Britain to
maintain a role in CDA, scrutinised new proposals with great
severity; in 1952 the Chancellor of the Exchequer ruled that Britain
should not participate in any further CDA projects except in
Commonwealth countries. One reason why the Treasury was prepared to accept so much in the way of CDA commitments was the
'dollar windfall' already mentioned (see p. 356), which was a net
source of dollar income until 1958.

British participation was especially strong in policy and negotiation. The all-important Belgian Congo contracts were skilfully
negotiated by British representatives, and the British handled most
of the difficult and protracted discussions with the South Africans
in the early stages, and with the Portuguese. It is impossible to say
whether equal success would have been achieved if their American
partners had dealt with the business; the British thought not and
the Americans certainly believed, at any rate in the early days, that
they depended on Britain's good offices. Without the British they
would probably have had to pay much more, for the British discouraged the Americans from betraying over-eagerness in the
negotiations, and it was largely British hard bargaining and in-
genuity in price negotiations that kept prices low and prevented the
emergence of a world price.[5]

The United States got most of the Congo uranium and all the Canadian uranium (until 1956), and were expected to receive most of the South African and Australian supplies when they began to flow in. It might well seem that the CDA was disproportionately advantageous to the United States and that Britain's raw materials activities and expenditure were largely for American benefit. But the British were not being altruistic; they had weighed up the pros and cons of collaborating on raw materials and decided that on balance it was worthwhile. This was the only matter in which atomic collaboration with the Americans continued, however uneasily, and the British, imbued with an unfailing desire for cooperation, regarded it as a unique link, to be preserved and strengthened – the one thing which made them partners, not just poor relations.

More practically, though the Americans got most of the uranium, without joint action the British might have got no uranium at all; unlike the United States they had no domestic production, and they would have been beaten if they had had to bid competitively against American dollars.* The CDA machinery survived because it was advantageous to both countries, but it was more essential to the British than the Americans.

* 'We dare not expose the £ to the $ in open competition for limited supplies' said an official paper of May 1952.

DECLARATION OF TRUST, 13 JUNE 1944

This Agreement and Declaration of Trust is made the thirteenth day of June One thousand nine hundred and forty-four by Franklin Delano Roosevelt on behalf of the Government of the United States of America, and by Winston Leonard Spencer Churchill on behalf of the Government of the United Kingdom of Great Britain and Northern Ireland. The said Governments are hereinafter referred to as 'the Two Governments';

Whereas an agreement (hereinafter called the Quebec Agreement) was entered into on the Nineteenth day of August One thousand nine hundred and forty-three by and between the President of the United States and the Prime Minister of the United Kingdom; and

Whereas it is an object vital to the common interests of those concerned in the successful prosecution of the present war to insure the acquisition at the earliest practicable moment of an adequate supply of uranium and thorium ores; and

Whereas it is the intention of the Two Governments to control to the fullest extent practicable the supplies of uranium and thorium ores within the boundaries of such areas as come under their respective jurisdictions; and

Whereas the Government of the United Kingdom of Great Britain and Northern Ireland intends to approach the Governments of the Dominions and the Governments of India and of Burma for the purpose of securing that such Governments shall bring under control deposits of the uranium and thorium ores within their respective territories; and

Whereas it has been decided to establish a joint organization for the purpose of gaining control of the uranium and thorium supplies in certain areas outside the control of the Two Governments and of the Governments of the Dominions and of India and of Burma;

Now it is Hereby Agreed and Declared as Follows:

1. (1) There shall be established in the City of Washington, District of Columbia, a Trust to be known as 'The Combined Development Trust'.

(2) The Trust shall be composed of and administered by six persons who shall be appointed, and be subject to removal, by the Combined Policy Committee established by the Quebec Agreement.

2. The Trust shall use its best endeavours to gain control of and develop the production of the uranium and thorium supplies situate in certain areas other than the areas under the jurisdiction of the Two Governments and of the Governments of the Dominions and of India and of Burma and for that purpose shall take such steps as it may in the common interest think fit to:

(a) Explore and survey sources of uranium and thorium supplies.

(b) Develop the production of uranium and thorium by the acquisition of mines and ore deposits, mining concessions or otherwise.

(c) Provide with equipment any mines or mining works for the production of uranium and thorium.

(d) Survey and improve the methods of production of uranium and thorium.

(e) Acquire and undertake the treatment and disposal of uranium and thorium and uranium and thorium materials.

(f) Provide storage and other facilities.

(g) Undertake any functions or operations which conduce to the effective carrying out of the purpose of the Trust in the common interest.

3. (1) The Trust shall carry out its functions under the direction and guidance of the Combined Policy Committee, and as its agent, and all uranium and thorium and all uranium and thorium ores and supplies and other property acquired by the Trust shall be held by it in trust for the Two Governments jointly, and disposed of or otherwise dealt with in accordance with the direction of the Combined Policy Committee.

(2) The Trust shall submit such reports of its activities as may be required from time to time by the Combined Policy Committee.

4. For the purpose of carrying out its functions, the Trust shall utilize whenever and wherever practicable the established agencies of any of the Two Governments, and may employ and pay such

other agents and employees as it considers expedient, and may delegate to any agents or employees all or any of its functions.

5. The Trust may acquire and hold any property in the name of nominees.

6. All funds properly required by the Trust for the performance of its functions shall be provided as to one-half by the Government of the United States of America and the other half by the Government of the United Kingdom of Great Britain and Northern Ireland.

7. In the event of the Combined Policy Committee ceasing to exist, the functions of the Committee under the Trust shall be performed by such other body or person as may be designated by the President for the time being of the United States of America and the Prime Minister for the time being of the United Kingdom of Great Britain and Northern Ireland.

8. The signatories of this Agreement and Declaration of Trust will, as soon as practicable after the conclusion of hostilities, recommend to their respective Governments the extension and revision of this war-time emergency agreement to cover post-war conditions and its formalization by treaty or other proper method. This Agreement and Declaration of Trust shall continue in full force and effect until such extension or revision.

(Signed) FRANKLIN D. ROOSEVELT
On Behalf of the Government of the United States of America

(Signed) WINSTON S. CHURCHILL
On Behalf of the Government of the United Kingdom of Great Britain and Northern Ireland

Appendix 11

MEMORANDUM OF UNDERSTANDING WITH
BELGIUM, 13 JULY 1951

It is the understanding of the Governments of Belgium, the United Kingdom, and the United States of America, that

1. The attached Joint Communiqué sets forth the understandings reached by the three Governments as a result of negotiations on the Memorandum of Agreement of September 26, 1944. The Communiqué will be published simultaneously, in whole or in part as agreed, and on an agreed date, if and when the Belgian Government finds it advisable.

2. The method of bringing about the increase in revenue described in paragraph 3 of the attached Joint Communiqué will be an increase on the special tax on uranium ore exported from the Belgian Congo of $0·60 per pound, commencing with the coming into effect of Part C, Tab 2 (Rev).

3. The final paragraph of the Annex to the Joint Communiqué is to be interpreted in the sense that when the three Governments are agreed that the United States and United Kingdom Governments have decided to employ uranium ores for commercial purposes, the Belgian Government will have an equal right to utilize uranium ores for the same purposes.

In connection with the foregoing understandings, the Belgian Government pointed out the fact that it retains the right to make further tax adjustments on the seller. The United States and United Kingdom Governments recalled that under existing contractual provisions all taxes, including export taxes, are to the account of the seller. Accordingly the United States and United Kingdom Governments undertake to amend the existing contractual arrangements with the seller so that the special tax of $0·60 per pound will be borne by the buyers.

GOVERNOR-GENERAL PIERRE RYCKMANS   SIR OLIVER FRANKS
Belgian Commissioner for   British Ambassador
Atomic Energy

GORDON DEAN
Chairman, United States
Atomic Energy Commission

Appendix 12

JOINT COMMUNIQUÉ AND ANNEX
RE AMERICAN, BELGIAN AND BRITISH
UNDERSTANDINGS IN THE ATOMIC ENERGY FIELD,
13 JULY 1951

1. Understandings have been reached among Belgium, the United Kingdom and the United States as the result of talks the three countries have had from time to time to review arrangements governing the sale of Congo uranium ores to the United Kingdom and the United States. These arrangements, which sprang from war-time necessity as a military measure, are incorporated in a Memorandum of Agreement dated September 26, 1944, and expiring early in 1956. The substance of the Memorandum is attached. Through these arrangements, Belgium and the Belgian Congo have made an important contribution to the common defense of the democratic nations.

2. In the talks, the three Governments discussed methods of implementing the Anglo-American undertakings to Belgium included in the 1944 arrangements regarding eventual utilization of Congo ores as a source of energy for commercial power. The American and British representatives stated that the commercial use of atomic energy was still some appreciable distance away. It was decided, however, that Belgium and the Belgian Congo should take those steps best calculated to prepare them to make use of the advantages which it is envisaged will stem from the Anglo-American undertakings. To this end and in accord with the spirit of their obligations, the American and British Governments have agreed to furnish financial and technical assistance in support of a Belgian atomic energy program as outlined in paragraphs three and four respectively.

3. Uranium is a Belgian Congo resource, and substantial sums have accrued to the Belgian Congo Government through the medium of the duty and surcharge on the export of uranium ores. In addition thereto, and taking into account the special position accorded Belgium by the 1944 arrangements, the Governments of the United Kingdom and of the United States recognize that there should be a considerable increase in revenue accruing to the Belgian Congo

from uranium to support a Belgian atomic energy research program which will enhance the value of this Congo asset. Accordingly, besides duties levied in accordance with existing legislation and in consideration of the circumstances mentioned in paragraph 2, a supplementary amount, which, if deliveries continue at the anticipated rate during the remainder of the agreement, would produce about $2,500,000.00 per annum, will be paid during this period to the Belgian Congo.

4. As regards technical assistance, it has been decided that the most valuable contribution the United States and the United Kingdom can make for the time being would be assistance directed towards the prompt development of a well-trained corps of Belgian scientists and engineers in the field of atomic energy. To this end, the American and British Governments have agreed to:

(A) Assist selected Belgian students to find facilities for advanced study and research in unclassified fields in American and British universities;

(B) Facilitate Belgian access to American and British declassified material and facilities, including visits to unclassified work being carried out under the auspices of the United States Atomic Energy Commission and the British Ministry of Supply;

(C) Furnish Belgium certain declassified technology, equipment and materials needed for its atomic energy research program, which program might include a research reactor;

(D) Arrange for close Belgian participation as agreed upon from time to time in the mutual exchange of technical information on the exploration, location, mining, processing and extraction of radioactive ores;

(E) Give advance notice to Belgium concerning the distribution as between the United States and the United Kingdom to be made of any shipments from the Belgian Congo of such ores.

5. In order to facilitate the carrying out of these measures, the Belgian Government has added to its Embassy staffs in Washington and London liaison officers with appropriate background and training in these scientific fields. These officers maintain liaison between the official organization in Belgium responsible for the direction of atomic energy activities and the United States Atomic Energy Commission and the British Ministry of Supply.

6. The assistance outlined above is regarded as an initial step towards closer co-operation among the three governments in keeping with the spirit of the 1944 arrangements; it is agreed that further talks will be held from time to time with a view towards devising means whereby a closer association may be brought about as soon as future developments warrant.

ANNEX

Substance of Memorandum of Agreement of
26 September 1944

The Belgian Government agreed with the Governments of the United States and the United Kingdom as to the desirability during the war against Germany and Japan, as well as in the future, that all uranium ores wherever located should be subject to effective control for the protection of civilization. To this end, the Government of Belgium undertook to insure effective control of such ores located in all territory subject to the authority of Belgium.

The Belgian Government also agreed that Congo uranium ores should be made available to the United States and the United Kingdom through commercial contracts. The Belgian Government further undertook to use its best endeavours to supply such quantities of uranium ores as might be required by the Governments of the United States and the United Kingdom.

To aid in the reopening and development of the Congo uranium properties, the Governments of the United States and the United Kingdom undertook to facilitate the delivery to the producing company (the Union Minière du Haut-Katanga) of such materials and equipment as the parties to the contracts thought necessary.

The arrangements outlined above were arrived at on the understanding that Belgium would reserve for herself such reasonable quantities of uranium ores as might be required for her own scientific and industrial purposes. The Belgian Government, however, in deciding to utilize such ores as a source of energy for commercial power, would do so in consultation and in agreement with the Governments of the United States and of the United Kingdom. The latter, on their part, agreed that the Belgian Government should participate on equitable terms in the utilization of these ores as a source of energy for commercial power at such time as the two Governments should decide to employ the ores for this purpose.

Appendix 13

TABLE I   Estimated Uranium Requirements, Deliveries and
Allocations, 1946–52 (in tons of uranium oxide – U_3O_8)

United Kingdom

	Estimated requirements	Deliveries from the Congo	Allocations	Unallocated stockpile
1946	–	1,857	1,350	507
1947	–	1,390	–	1,897
1948	580	–	–	1,897
1949	555	–	–	1,897
1950	650	–	505	1,392
1951	650	–	561	831
1952	561	–	503	328
	2,996	3,247	2,919	

111 tons were delivered from Portugal to the UK in 1951 and 1952, and were allocated to the United Kingdom, but were later transferred to the United States.

United States

	Estimated requirements	Deliveries from the Congo	Allocations*
1946	?	2,698	1,350†
1947	?	1,911	–
1948	2,547	2,781	All Congo ores
1949	2,547	2,066	delivered
1950	2,422	2,356	1948–51
1951	5,259	2,520	
1952	?10,000	2,500	All Congo and South African ores delivered 1952
		16,832	

* Unallocated supplies were also available to the United States from Canada and from domestic production, and these provided about 1,250 tons and over 200 tons respectively in fiscal years 1947 to 1952.

† In addition to (a) all the uranium received in the United States up to March 1946, and (b) 600 tons of uranium captured in Europe and stored in Britain.

TABLE 2 Belgian Congo Uranium Deliveries: Forecast and Actual
(tons of uranium oxide)

	Dec 1947 forecast (a)	Sep 1949 forecast (b)	Actual deliveries (c)	
1946	–	–	4,555	
1947	–	–	3,301	
1948	2,200	–	2,781	
1949	1,200	1,700	2,066	
1950	1,200	2,500	2,356	
1951	1,200	2,200	2,520	
1952	1,200	2,200	2,500	*Total* 20,079

1951–1952

12 'Winston is Back' – and Cherwell

WHEN Mr Attlee's Labour Government gave way to Mr Churchill's Conservative Government in October 1951, the pioneering or heroic period of the atomic energy project – the period to which the participants would always look back nostalgically – was almost over. Despite shortcomings in the machinery of government, and shortages, crises and difficulties of every kind, the programme was coming along almost exactly to time. The uranium metal plant was working smoothly. The Windscale piles were working too and were so simple to operate that it was difficult to remember 1946 fears about piles. The chemical separation plant at Windscale, the first of its kind in the world, was about to begin its near-faultless operation. The first billet of plutonium was to be produced within five months. The gaseous diffusion plant to enrich uranium was under construction. Penney's team had almost finished working out the bomb design and bomb mechanics. The first military stage of the project was almost complete and the Government had simply to wait for the programme to reach its terrifying pyrotechnic culmination. Much thought had already been given to the possibilities of nuclear power.

Thus the new Conservative Government's immediate atomic problems were tidying-up ones. But they also had to decide how to develop their nuclear inheritance. What should be the next stage in military developments? Had the time come to launch a nuclear power programme? What was the right organisation for this new phase? Mr Churchill had not concerned himself with the details of the project during the war, but he had always taken special pride in his Quebec Agreement with President Roosevelt in 1943. After the war he had put profound faith in America's possession of the atomic bomb which had, he believed, prevented the Russians from sweeping across Europe. His interest in atomic affairs remained on the broad strategic level. Conscious of Britain's extremely vulnerable position as the aircraft-carrier for the United States atomic bombers, he had probed justifiably but unsuccessfully into Britain's right to be consulted about the use of the bomb. It was in this connection that he had pressed for the publication of the Quebec Agreement, but once the Americans had reiterated 'no', he unhesitatingly accepted the answer.

Otherwise he did not appear to have a marked interest in the progress of Britain's own project. During 1949 there had been a series of defence discussions between the Government and the Opposition, but the atomic bomb had not been mentioned at any of the meetings. Early in 1951 Mr Churchill had taunted the Government with their slow progress in making atomic bombs. Certainly the Labour Minister of Defence had been conscious of the shadow of Mr Churchill during the 1949 discussions with the Americans, in which it had been proposed that Britain should give up making atomic bombs. Mr Churchill was part of the 'quite big political repercussions' that such a proposal might incur.

When Mr Churchill returned to 10 Downing Street, he was surprised and impressed by the size of the atomic energy project built up by the Labour Government. He found with a mixture of admiration, envy and the shock of a good parliamentarian that his predecessors had spent nearly £100 million on it without informing Parliament. He felt he would have been branded as a warmonger for a similar feat, and one of his early minutes on his return to office was to ask the Permanent Secretary of the Treasury how this very large sum had been hidden away in the accounts. Nevertheless, he maintained the same policy, albeit with a qualm. When Lord Cherwell supported the new Minister of Supply's refusal to reveal the figures of atomic energy expenditure on the grounds that the actual figure would give away something to the Russians while it would not impress the Americans, Churchill commented: 'There are also the British. But I agree to the answer.'

Mr Churchill was not now in practice a strong advocate of an independent British project, even though in November 1945 he had assumed agreement that Britain should make atomic bombs.[1] In November 1951 he sent a minute to Lord Cherwell: 'I have never wished since our decision during the war that England should start the manufacture of atomic bombs. Research however must be energetically pursued. We should have the art rather than the article. A large sum of money will have to be provided for this.

There is however no point in our going into bulk production even if we were able to.' He had already arranged a visit to Washington for January and he had no doubt that he could then 'arrange to be allocated a reasonable share of what they have made so largely on our initiative and substantial scientific contribution'.

Such a belief showed Mr Churchill's remoteness from realities. He was obsessed with the Quebec Agreement. His concern was now not so much about the lapse of the clause which had given Britain a right of consent over the use of atomic bombs. He thought that Britain had been unfairly treated and forced into spending vast sums of money on her own project simply because Attlee was 'feeble and incompetent' and had not told the Americans the facts about the wartime agreements. He seemed ignorant of the temper of the United States in atomic affairs in the post-war years.

For the most part Mr Churchill's minutes on atomic energy in the months after his return to office show the deterioration of his powers. But he had Lord Cherwell, his Paymaster-General, at his side. By 1952 Cherwell had had, as he himself proudly said, eleven years' continuous connection with the project. During the Labour Government he had been a member of Lord Portal's Technical Committee and knew a great deal about the programme and its problems. He was in close touch with several of the key people and, living at Oxford, he saw a good deal of Harwell. Cherwell believed fervently in the atomic energy project. He had no doubt whatsoever that Britain should possess atomic bombs. Apart from military necessity, he felt, like most members of both front benches, a deep dislike of any prospect that Britain might 'rank with other European nations who have to make do with conventional weapons'.

Lord Cherwell was much less sanguine than the Prime Minister about the dependability of the Americans and he believed that even if any offer of bombs were forthcoming from the United States, Britain must continue to make her own. For, he said, 'If we are unable to make bombs ourselves and have to rely entirely on the United States army for this vital weapon we shall sink to the rank of a second-class nation, only permitted to supply auxiliary troops, like the native levies who were allowed small arms but not artillery.' But Cherwell's enthusiasm for the whole project was founded as much on its industrial as on its military promise. 'Our prosperity in the Victorian era', he wrote, 'was due largely to the men who had the imagination to put and keep England ahead for sixty to eighty years in the use of steam power for industrial purposes. It is quite likely that our prosperity in the coming century may depend on learning how to exploit the energy latent in uranium (1 pound = 1,000 tons of coal).'

Cherwell entirely approved the Labour Government's decision to make atomic bombs in Britain and he also thought the scale of effort was correct – that is, manufacture on a medium scale to accumulate a stock of bombs 'not without military significance' by 1957. This seemed to him a correct balance between the importance of the matter and Britain's economic difficulties. He told Mr Churchill roundly: 'If you had been in power and had heard the whole story I am sure you would have come to the same conclusions.' Cherwell believed moreover that Churchill was unfair to Attlee in castigating him both for his failure to publish the Quebec Agreement before the McMahon Act was passed and for his agreement to drop the Quebec clause giving the right to consent to the use of the bomb. This was, he pointed out, an exchange for dropping the unfortunate Quebec clause which had left British industrial development of atomic energy at the mercy of the President of the United States. No one could say that the correspondence between Churchill and Cherwell on such matters was sycophantic or inhibited.

Cherwell's criticisms of the atomic project under the Labour Government were directed not at the decisions of policy nor the scale of effort, but at the pace of progress. He believed progress had been slow and delays intolerable because the administrative structure of the project was all wrong. He believed atomic energy was uniquely different from all other Government scientific projects, so much so that it justified quite exceptional treatment. He had become dedicated to the idea of taking the whole business out of the Civil Service, and in July 1951 he had successfully moved a resolution to this effect in the House of Lords.[2] When the Conservative Government was formed, Cherwell was determined that the resolution should be translated into action. While Mr Churchill's atomic obsession was the Quebec Agreement, Lord Cherwell's was an independent corporation. We shall return later in this chapter to a discussion of these administrative problems. As we shall see, for a time the unsatisfactory administrative structure became more confused than ever, especially in relation to ministerial responsibility. Nevertheless, with all its faults the new Cherwell regime had one advantage. There was now a Minister who was very knowledgeable about atomic energy, its past history and its future possibilities and who could exert that central grip on the project which Ministers of Supply and Controllers of Atomic Energy had hitherto been unable or unwilling to do.

Unfinished Business

What were the tidying-up problems, the unfinished business, left for the Conservatives? Final decisions were needed on security procedures and on the location of the first British bomb test. There were also the perpetually unfinished atomic negotiations with the United States and their corollary, atomic negotiations with Commonwealth and European countries.

The Government decided without any difficulty to approve the proposals of the head of the Civil Service for new procedures for those employed in classified atomic energy work – that is, there would be positive vetting or an open inquiry in which the person himself and his referees would be required to declare whether he had Communist associations. Ministers recognised that it was inevitable that this procedure would also have to be applied to holders of key posts outside atomic energy, but they concluded, like the Labour Ministers, that the procedure could not be applied to people not in direct Government employment. They emphasised that the new system would be put forward as a means of improving security and not as a sop to the Americans. Nevertheless, the primary motive was to improve the prospects of co-operation with the United States.

The question about the location of the British bomb test seemed by now equally uncontentious. The inherent stupidity of an independent test in Australia, when the Americans had such well-developed test sites, had led to long meetings and cables and a final transatlantic dash by Penney. But though the Americans had finally expressed their willingness to help, they had felt bound to impose so many restrictions and conditions under the McMahon Act that the Chiefs of Staff and all the departments concerned had unanimously concluded that the test should be held after all in Australia. Immediately after the General Election, Cherwell minuted Churchill that he entirely agreed with this view. There was more likelihood of American co-operation, he said, 'if we show we are not entirely dependent on them now'. He added that there was always the chance that something might go wrong with the bomb so that it did not detonate properly and 'it would be disastrous if this happens in full view of all the United States newspapers'.

However, Mr Churchill did not grasp the real significance of the situation. 'As to your experiments surely the question is not urgent', he said. He thought the preference for Australia rather than Nevada was quite right, but he thought it had all better wait until he had talked to President Truman. 'I am sure when we produce the Treaty we made in the war and demand that it shall be published we shall get very decent treatment from Truman and his military advisors. I do not consider the matter is urgent but nothing avoidable should be done to discourage active and continuous research.' Cherwell replied immediately with a long summary of the atomic energy position and relations with America which showed the impossibility of Churchill's desire to develop the art but not the article. He begged the Prime Minister to accept the unanimous official advice and decide in favour of the Australian test. A month later he had had no reply and he curtly wrote again that he trusted, unless he heard to the contrary, that the test in Australia might go ahead; he was now told by Mr Churchill to proceed.

Mr Churchill, accompanied by Lord Cherwell, was to visit Mr Truman in January 1952. Atomic energy was to be only one subject in the discussions, which were to range over the whole field of Anglo-American relations. The keynote of the new Government's policy towards the United States was the same as that of the Labour Government: they wanted to obtain recognition that in the eyes of the United States Administration at any rate the United Kingdom was regarded and treated as America's principal and most reliable ally in the world. But while to the Labour Government this specially intimate relationship had been desirable largely on grounds of practical interest, to Mr Churchill and some other members of his Government it was part of a long, if sometimes one-sided, love-affair. The primary and general aim of the January talks was an improvement in the 'tone' of the Anglo-American relationship.

There was some apprehension in Washington that the visitors might not be sufficiently aware how greatly circumstances had changed in the United States since the war, and there was anxiety that the atomic energy briefing in particular should be realistic. Certainly Cherwell had his feet firmly on the ground. He reminded Churchill that the wartime agreements had been superseded and that nothing would be gained by referring to them now. Mr

Churchill annotated this with a question mark and he put 'no' and a variety of exclamations against Cherwell's statement that in view of the ferocious penalties of the original McMahon Act it would be quite inconceivable that the Americans should give Britain any information about bomb design, still less an allocation of bombs.

There were three separate questions to be explored with the Americans: technical co-operation in atomic energy – the issue that was now nearly ten years old; questions of strategy and tactics arising from the use of atomic weapons about which the Chiefs of Staff were becoming more and more anxious; co-operation in intelligence matters. In the briefing on technical co-operation there was a warning, especially from Hinton, against any tendency to go 'cap in hand'. As far as production of fissile material was concerned, Britain's programme was successful and the few items of assistance and material needed from the United States were marginal to it. Data about atomic weapons were needed most but were expressly prohibited by the recent amendments to the McMahon Act. The case for full co-operation rested primarily on pure commonsense. Here was this new invention, mainly the product of Anglo-American effort, the development of which might be vital in war and ultimately also in peace. Yet the two countries were working in watertight compartments and thus wasting effort, scientific manpower and resources. A situation had arisen where the United States was exploding an atomic bomb in the Pacific and the British Commonwealth one in the Indian Ocean.

Nevertheless, it was futile to expect the United States Administration to seek a new amendment to the McMahon Act in election year. Cherwell therefore advised that the British should try to get the Administration to recognise the waste of effort and resources involved in non-co-operation, and to agree to end it as soon as possible and to establish the maximum co-operation and exchange of information permissible under existing legislation, with specific examples. Finally, the British should convince the Americans that their programme was comprehensive and that they would make a significant contribution to the joint effort, but that co-operation must not be limited to what suited the United States but must be fully reciprocal.

Technical co-operation was now much less urgent than discussions on the strategy and tactics involved in the use of atomic weapons. Here the situation was increasingly absurd and dangerous. The

British were allowed to know nothing at all about crucial American calculations of the effects of atomic bombs, on which to base their civil defence and any counter-measures. British students were excluded from American military courses because atomic weapons were discussed, while the most vital element in the common defence could barely be mentioned between the British and American Staffs. The development of tactical atomic weapons would make things even worse: artillery weapons, the torpedo, the submarine and other items of warfare would be withdrawn from the area which could be discussed between Staffs until all talks were quite unreal. Over and above this was the life-and-death question of the United States' strategic air plan and Anglo-American consultation on the launching of atomic warfare. The stationing of American atomic bombers at British bases might bring a terrible retribution on Britain. Surely Britain should be consulted about the use of atomic bombs and receive details about the American strategic air plan.

As we have seen, Mr Attlee's attempt to regain some right to consultation on the use of the atomic bomb had been partially successful. The Americans had agreed that the use of the United States bases in the United Kingdom to launch an atomic attack would be a matter for joint decision between the two Governments. They had also bound themselves not to put their strategic air plan against Russia into action in a war in which NATO was involved without consulting the other NATO powers. But the Americans would admit no curb on their right to drop atomic bombs from other bases in non-NATO wars – possibly, for example, in the Middle East or the Far East – even though this might call forth the same retribution on Britain for harbouring United States Air Force bases. The American view was that a general war would immediately bring into operation their strategic air plan involving a full-scale atom attack on Russia, but they could not accept any commitment limiting their right to make war. British efforts had therefore concentrated on trying to get agreement about the circumstances in which the launching of a general war would be justified.

The brief for Mr Churchill on his visit to Washington suggested that the United States be asked to agree to consult Britain fully before launching a general war, to reaffirm their assurances that the use of their United Kingdom bases for an atomic attack was a matter for joint decision, and to agree about the issue of an ultimatum before an atomic attack was launched. On top of this the

British wanted to be informed more fully of the details of the strategic air plan, about which they knew something but far too little. It was hardly possible for the British to judge whether in any given circumstances they should agree to the use of United Kingdom bases if they did not know what the strategic air plan was, what the targets were, what the effect of the bombs was expected to be and with what accuracy they could be delivered.

Mr Churchill's talks with President Truman produced little improvement in assurances about the use of the bomb, but they marked the beginning of a willingness to talk about the strategic air plan. The President said he had special responsibility and powers vis-à-vis the strategic air plan and atomic weapons, but that in the exercise of these powers he was tied by very considerable legislative halters. He assured the Prime Minister that he was just as reluctant as the British Government to see atomic weapons used and he hoped the time would never come when he might have to give the decision to wipe out a whole population not in the firing line. But this feeling would not prevent his taking the decision if and when it proved necessary. In any case, he said, those countries 'lined up with the United States' should be consulted first. His Secretary of Defense said that it was inevitable that the atom bomb would be used in the Third World War but there was no question of British bases being used without British consent.* Mr Churchill would have liked more than this assurance. If ever they came to a conference with the Russians which broke down, he said, the immediate sequel should not be an atomic conflict. There were two aspects to the outbreak of war. If the United States heard that Russia had started across the North Pole, they would have to act and there would be no hindrance from the British Government. But if it should rest with the United States to bring the situation to a head there should be consultation. However, the Americans gave no further promises whatever on this point. The Secretary of Defense did nevertheless promise Mr Churchill a personal briefing on the strategic air plan, and he was apparently told as much about it as Dean Acheson, the Secretary of State, knew.

In these military relationships Mr Churchill's visit produced 'a far better and more sympathetic feeling' towards Britain in Washington, and in the favourable climate thus created the US

---

* This assurance was published for the first time in the communiqué after the conference.

Secretary of Defense authorised joint discussions on the strategic and tactical aspects of the air plan, while steering clear of the technical field barred by the McMahon Act. By the end of 1952 the Chiefs of Staff had received on a highly personal basis a great deal of information about the plan, although they were unable to convey any of it to British commanders-in-chief for planning purposes.

In 1952 there were also in Washington further politico-military discussions of the 1951 type about the assumptions underlying the American and British approaches to a decision to launch a general war, the use of atomic weapons and the issue of ultimatums. Sir Oliver Franks, the British Ambassador, emphasised again the British fears that most of the American general public had come to believe that the use of atomic weapons in a general war would bring quick and easy victory, without counting the terrible consequences of general war for Western Europe. He also reiterated that British public opinion felt a real moral difficulty about using atomic weapons and that it would be dreadful if the West were the first side to use them. The talks were still inconclusive on these supreme issues, but at least they were continuing. A suggestion that the British Government might educate British public opinion about the nature and effects of atomic warfare was ill-received in London: the Foreign Office thought that a campaign to disabuse United States public opinion of excessive light-heartedness and optimism was desirable but that a campaign in Europe to popularise atomic warfare would be unwise.

Mr Churchill's talks with President Truman had helped along these highly important politico-military discussions which had begun under the Labour Government. The talks had, however, proved no more successful than any previous talks in securing greater technical co-operation in atomic energy. Mr Churchill had made no attempt to rake up the past or make reproaches. He did not ask for amendment of the United States law but simply that the President should say he wished for maximum co-operation within the limits set by the McMahon Act. The President agreed and was prepared for Lord Cherwell to pursue discussions on this, but he warned that 'the rather hysterical feeling in America on this subject' limited his own power to act independently. He thought the news that the British Government had agreed to stiffen its anti-Communist procedures would help very much.

Mr Churchill also saw Senator McMahon, the chairman of the

Joint Congressional Committee on Atomic Energy, and went over all the past agreements from Quebec onwards with him. McMahon told him that the recent amendment to his Act should make immediate progress in co-operation possible until it covered 90 per cent of the field, but he agreed with Mr Churchill's understanding that Mr LeBaron of the Defense Department 'was stiff in these matters'. So it proved. Lord Cherwell and a British team met Commissioners and senior officials of the USAEC and Mr LeBaron and others of the Defense Department. It was clear that hopes for maximum co-operation within the McMahon Act were very slender. The relatively friendly and sympathetic USAEC emphasised that they operated under the restriction not only of the McMahon Act but of Congressional interpretation of it. It would only be possible at best to get exchange of information on specific details, for example the canning of uranium rods, rather than on broad fields such as reactor technology, and then there was the difficulty of proving in advance that such an exchange would be of substantial advantage to the United States. Even this doctrine was much too radical for Mr LeBaron, who said that since nearly all atomic energy activities in both the American and British programmes were directed to producing atomic weapons, it would be impossible to approve the exchange of practically any atomic information.

The meeting simply became an open dispute between the USAEC and the Defense Department. Lord Cherwell's suggestion that he should ask Mr Churchill to take the matter up with the President was so badly received by the Americans that he dropped it. Mr Acheson asserted, contrary to the British record and recollection, that the President had made no agreement for maximum co-operation within the law but had simply expressed the view that the possibilities of fuller co-operation should be explored. The differences on crucial points in the British and American records of the meetings of the two heads of government were so great that they seemed as if they could not apply to the same gathering.

It was agreed that Cockcroft should visit Washington and put forward some specific cases to test the McMahon amendment and also follow up a proposal that data on atomic weapon effects should be declassified or made available to Britain for civil defence purposes. Cockcroft produced a longish list of topics to be discussed – to the dismay of Hinton, who believed that on most of them the United States would gain more than Britain, partly because the

British would not be shown the crucial development work being done in the laboratories and factories of the big American firms which carried out most of the industrial-scale work as agents of the USAEC.

However, such apprehensions proved unnecessary because it was quite clear that there was going to be no real progress in co-operation. The British found that the machinery of the McMahon amendment was so cumbersome that the Americans would be unwilling to set it in motion for anything less than a major operation. In any case, even if the British had a bright idea it would have to be very bright indeed before the Americans were interested, because of the large amount of money tied up in existing atomic capital equipment. It might dislocate the American programme less to use a well-established process than to introduce a theoretically superior one. Moreover there was the general difficulty that to prove 'substantial advantage' to the United States, full unilateral disclosure by the United Kingdom to the United States would be necessary. It was a member of the USAEC who summed it up as a 'Big Brother–Little Brother' attitude. Big Brother had a right to know everything Little Brother was doing, but there was no need for Big Brother to disclose what he was doing.

Inevitably, therefore, Cockcroft's discussions in Washington were extremely one-sided, and practically fruitless. The only concrete result was some valuable co-operation in intelligence. For the rest, some remnants of co-operation left by the *modus vivendi* survived. Declassification had solved many problems but in only one classified area – chemical extraction – had co-operation remained worthwhile. The success in this area was thought to be due largely to the determination of the eminent American leader of this work, Glenn Seaborg, to be as open as possible. Hopes occasionally sprang up to be quickly dashed. In May 1952, for example, Longair of the British Mission in Washington wrote to Cockcroft: 'On Friday, 2nd May, the heavens opened, a great light shone (metaphorically) and there lying on my desk was a fully authorised licence to export 50,000 cubic feet of helium.' However, this turned out to be 'a premature administrative action' – someone had made a mistake and the licence was not to be used. Longair was seeking a gold frame for it. However special the Anglo-American relationship had again become in political and military affairs, it had progressively declined in technical co-operation on atomic energy.

dislike of the Anglo-American agreements which, they said, 'deliberately make it more difficult than necessary for small countries to follow developments in a field like atomic energy'. Eventually and reluctantly the Americans agreed, provided the Belgians (whose uranium would be making the metal) were squared. So the Norwegians got their metal from Britain and yet another step was taken towards helping atomic energy projects in Western Europe. A feeling was gaining ground that atomic energy had an important political side and was one way of drawing other countries into the British sphere of influence. However, although during 1952 Britain became somewhat more friendly, atomically speaking, to Commonwealth and European countries, her policy was still governed primarily by her relations with America. Hope still sprang eternal in the breasts of Mr Churchill and many officials, if not in Lord Cherwell's, that Anglo-American collaboration would revive once more, and the election of General Eisenhower as President in November 1952 sent the hopes soaring again.

Towards a New Organisation

Lord Cherwell had thought that the general size and shape of the Labour Government's atomic energy programme had been right, but he was very critical of the speed of its fulfilment. Russia's explosion of an atomic bomb three years before Britain's test seemed to him the main proof of unwarrantable delays in the British project. To Cherwell these delays had one root cause – the faulty organisation of the project. Certainly, as we have seen, the organisation of the project had been very peculiar according to any of the accepted principles of the machinery of government. Cherwell believed a panacea was at hand; the chief source of trouble, he believed, was the Civil Service machine and what was needed above all was to make the project into an independent corporation.

The question of a public corporation had already been raised under the Labour Government. Even during the war Sir John Anderson had favoured such an organisation for the post-war project in the interests of the freedom and flexibility which were needed to keep in the van of progress. However, when the war ended, advice on nearly all sides favoured lodgement of the project in the Ministry of Supply (see Chapter 2). Early in 1950, in the aftermath of the Russian atomic test, Sir John Anderson, Lord Cherwell and Lord

Portal all favoured reopening the question. There were particular difficulties at the time over the recruitment of senior scientists and engineers for the project because the salaries offered were not competitive with those of industry. The Treasury had agreed to certain *ad hoc* improvements, but this had caused much dissatisfaction elsewhere in the Civil Service. Even when the Treasury was prepared to allow salaries above the Civil Service rate for certain individuals, the delay was so great that the candidate had almost certainly lost interest by the time approval was given. Other Civil Service rules about subsistence allowances, removal expenses or house purchase seemed also to have hampered recruitment of scarce senior men.

Mr Attlee had set up a working party under Sir Edward Bridges, Permanent Secretary of the Treasury, to go into the whole business, and it reported in July 1950. The team went into various possibilities, in terms of pay and conditions of service, for overcoming the difficulties of recruiting and retaining highly qualified technical and professional staff in atomic energy. One suggestion was to segregate the project from the rest of the Civil Service within a 'ring fence', openly depart from Civil Service standards within the fence where necessary, and withstand the inevitable consequent claims from the rest of the service. This system would be impossible. But the device of a largely independent corporation was not much less difficult. The existence of a body of public servants wholly paid out of money provided by Parliament, but not employed on the conditions laid down for the main body of civil servants, would produce a sense of grievance and pressure on Ministers to accept repercussions in the Civil Service.

The working party recognised that the last months had been especially difficult. Recruitment difficulties to atomic energy had increased with the scale of the project and had shifted from the field of basic science to that of technology, where comparisons with industry were important. At the same time the Civil Service had been closely controlled in the interests of the Government's wages policy* and the Treasury had been obliged to refuse special treatment for particular posts. This had accentuated disparities in the pay of scientists and technologists compared with pay in the outside

---

* In September 1948 the Chorley Committee (Cmd 7635) on salaries of senior civil servants had recommended large increases, but the Government postponed their payment, in stages, until October 1950–October 1951 (see Chapter 14).

world, and if policy on Civil Service salaries were relaxed, much of the trouble in atomic energy might disappear. All the same a committee of the Treasury and Ministry of Supply might be set up to try to settle special establishment problems concerned with atomic energy 'across the table'. The Ministerial Atomic Energy Committee agreed with the analysis of the difficulties of establishing a corporation and with the doubts whether it would achieve its intended objectives. They decided that in the first instance the special committee should be set up in the hope that this, possibly with a relaxation of the Civil Service wage freeze, might largely solve the problems.

The new Treasury–Ministry of Supply Committee worked satisfactorily except for salaries at the highest level, and most of the salary complaints disappeared. But the problem of recruiting experienced high-level staff for the Industrial Group was not solved. Lord Portal and Lord Cherwell remained as convinced as ever of the need for a separate corporation. In February 1951, at the Technical Committee, Cherwell proposed a resolution in favour of an independent body; permanent officials on the Committee were not allowed to vote and the resolution was carried. At about the same time various disturbing facts were drawn to the attention of the Prime Minister: Lord Portal was to leave the project in the autumn of 1951 and also Mr Perrin, one of his two deputies; Sir John Cockcroft had been asked to take over Sir Henry Tizard's post as Scientific Adviser to the Ministry of Defence and was disposed to accept; Dr Penney, whose work was so vital to the military side, was likely to be offered a professorship at Oxford and would be tempted to accept. The loss of these men would in itself be a heavy blow to the project and it would be worse if their departure started a snowball of resignations. Disappointment at the Government's rejection of the proposal for a public corporation had been the consideration which had made Perrin at least decide to leave the project.

Even more disturbing, the Ministry of Supply seemed to be showing no special anxiety about the departure of these key people. There were a good many people, apparently, who would be glad if the special position of the atomic project and its special priorities were brought to an end, from the Chiefs of Staff and Sir Henry Tizard downwards. But if it was time for the atomic energy project to be deprived of the special position it had occupied since 1940, this should result from a deliberate decision taken on its merits after a careful review of all the arguments on both sides, not incidentally, through the disappearance of some of the outstanding personalities 'who had hitherto resisted attempts to submerge it into the ordinary run of administration'.

A fresh review by Ministers of the whole future of the project was suggested even though it was not long since the ministerial decision of 1950. It was argued that those most enthusiastic about the project* had become convinced that some looser form of control, on the public corporation model, was the only solution of their difficulties. Previously stress had been laid chiefly on salaries, but now the main complaint was the general frustration at the meticulous controls and the delays in getting things done which seemed inseparable from departmental organisation.† There was another more fundamental question which had not been examined. The atomic energy project was in the Ministry of Supply but not of it.‡ This exclusiveness must tend to arouse the jealousy of the very people in the Ministry on whom the project depended for facilities, and must mean that the atomic energy project was getting the worst of both worlds. 'Even Lord Cherwell, I think, is not in this actuated by political motives', commented one senior official who advocated a review.

Mr Attlee found the problem difficult because in the last analysis only experiment could prove whether one form of control was better than another and many of the causes of complaint were intangible. Nevertheless, he agreed to a new ministerial inquiry. The Minister of Supply was most emphatic that the separation of atomic energy work from his other defence research activities would have most serious consequences and that news of a fresh inquiry would create trouble and discontent where none existed at present. The inquiry had barely begun when Lord Addison, who was to lead it, became ill. In July 1951, Lord Cherwell put down his motion in the House of Lords (see p. 408) regretting the slow progress in developing atomic energy and calling on the Government, while maintaining broad control, to transfer the work to a special organisation, more

* This shows the limitations of this advice: people in the project were not in favour (see p. 429).

† Most of these frustrations had by now been overcome.

‡ This presumably refers to the special status of the project within the Ministry and Lord Portal's right of access to the Prime Minister. In strictly departmental terms the project was definitely part of the Ministry during the Labour Government.

flexible than the normal Civil Service system, under the direct
control of the head of the Government. As we saw, the motion was
passed – against Government opposition. Three months later Lord
Cherwell was in office as Paymaster-General.

Very shortly after the change of Government, Mr Churchill told
the Minister of Supply, Duncan Sandys, that until the 1946 Atomic
Energy Act was altered his Ministry would remain responsible for
atomic energy and financially accountable for it. However, Lord
Cherwell was to advise the Prime Minister on atomic energy matters
and Mr Sandys was to consult Lord Cherwell on all important
questions of policy. The two Ministers came to an amicable arrangement about the division of labour. The Ministerial Committee on
Atomic Energy disappeared and nothing took its place. Atomic
energy matters appeared slightly more often on the Cabinet's
agenda.

A month after the advent of the new Government, Lord Cherwell
had ready a memorandum proposing the transfer of responsibility
from the Ministry of Supply to an Atomic Energy Commission. He
repeated his conviction that progress in the project had been slowed
down by the need to observe normal Civil Service rules in pay and
employment conditions, and that the project was so vital to the
future of the nation that wholly exceptional methods were required.
Reorganisation would make it possible, without reference to the
Treasury, to pay such salaries and special expenses as were necessary
to recruit key men and to get a single-purpose organisation in which
the security problems could be handled satisfactorily. The Treasury
and Parliament would simply control the total amount of money
voted yearly. These objects would best be achieved by transferring
the project to a nationalised corporation, but this was inappropriate
because it was a vital defence business, the project would earn a
negligible revenue and none of the staff of the corporation could be
civil servants. The alternative of an independent Ministry was ruled
out as giving the worst of both worlds, and so Cherwell contemplated a semi-Government organisation or Commission financed by
a grant-in-aid and so designed that its staff could include civil
servants and others. The Commission would be responsible to the
Ministry of Defence who would give it an annual directive for its
programme and issue any directions to it. Non-civil servant staff
earning over £1,500 a year could be on industrial-type contracts
with personal salary rates.

Cherwell hoped to get a Bill through Parliament in the current session. But the Treasury was quick to point out the snags. Parliament was showing itself very sensitive to extensions of grants-in-aid and was demanding very strict control over capital expenditure by grant-aided bodies. Once there was a separate Commission there would have to be full disclosure to Parliament of the amounts to be spent on atomic energy, which had hitherto been avoided. The Treasury was equally doubtful about employing civil servants and industrial contract staff side by side. To have 'an organisation which consists of sheep and goats who are specifically so labelled and who have different conditions of service' was a very difficult concept indeed. Meetings of the special Treasury–Ministry of Supply Committee set up in 1950 to get quick decisions on special cases had rarely been asked for but they had settled on the spot all the points put to them. Special security rules could also be made without a special commission.

The strength of the opposition and the lack of time for a Bill in the current year led Cherwell to accept that direct government control must continue for the present. He was, however, determined that a new start should be made somehow. The ideal way would be to put the whole undertaking directly under the Prime Minister, but it would be very difficult to make him responsible for a considerable spending department. The best course, Cherwell said, would be to transfer all responsibility from the Ministry of Supply to the Ministry of Defence; he himself would act on behalf of the Minister of Defence in atomic energy and, subject to the Minister's formal authority,* report directly to the Prime Minister. If this was accepted it would redeem the House of Lords resolution.

Treasury officials warned the Prime Minister about difficulties in this solution as well. Apart from certain legal problems, the Ministry of Defence, as organised, could not provide any of the common services given by the Ministry of Supply. Over 10,000 people were employed on atomic energy and were serviced by staffs experienced in contracts, recruitment and employment of industrial workers, housing, etc. Separate staffs for these purposes would be larger and more costly. The Ministry of Defence was, besides, a co-ordinating department and responsibility for atomic energy might impair that

---

* At this time the Minister of Defence was the Prime Minister, but this arrangement was not expected to last for long and Lord Alexander of Tunis became Minister of Defence in March 1952.

function. It would also give atomic energy an even more warlike flavour. At present atomic expenditure was all treated as civil expenditure in the Ministry of Supply estimates, but it could not remain so in the Ministry of Defence. As an alternative a special Atomic Energy Board was suggested – under Lord Cherwell, with its own organisation and its own Accounting Officer, but remaining within the Ministry of Supply.

Lord Cherwell, conscious that Mr Sandys did not like to be responsible in form only, was not at all happy at the prospect of consulting and persuading him on all occasions. He doubted whether, even with Churchill's driving force behind it, the scheme would work and, without that, all élan would be lost and the project, concerned as it was with the biggest step to man's mastery of nature since the discovery of fire, would sink to being one of the many sub-departments of the overtaxed Ministry of Supply. Cherwell was irritated on personal grounds. He pointed out that though he was responsible in the eyes of the public and the staff, he had no power; confusion of counsel and uncertainty about the future were having a bad effect.

The Prime Minister was being pulled in two directions, by Cherwell on one side and the Treasury on the other. Cherwell was furious that promises made to him one day seemed to be countermanded the next. He fought passionately to get the business moved to the Ministry of Defence, but he failed. Churchill said flatly that he did not see how it was possible to move 11,000 atomic energy staff to the Ministry of Defence, which was not an administrative department. Cherwell was to be responsible for atomic energy, but the accounting and detailed administration was to be done in the Ministry of Supply.

There was some acrimony between Lord Cherwell and Mr Sandys as a Prime Minister's directive on the division of responsibility was drafted. The final document appeared in April 1952. It said that the Paymaster-General was responsible for advising the Prime Minister and Cabinet on atomic energy policy matters and would preside over an atomic energy board comprising senior officers of the project. He would take all ministerial action required in research, development and production; provision of buildings and facilities for these purposes; appointments of staff (within Treasury ceilings) and allocation and supervision of their duties; and all other atomic energy matters not specifically entrusted to the Minister of Supply

by the Prime Minister. On all matters within his sphere of responsibility the Paymaster-General would deal directly with the officials
of the Ministry of Supply and would issue the instructions considered necessary, keeping the Minister of Supply informed of any
important decisions he took. The Minister of Supply would be
entirely responsible for day-to-day administration – contracts, staff
management, accounting questions, security and public relations –
and such other atomic energy matters as the Prime Minister, on the
advice of the Paymaster-General, might entrust to him. Within this
sphere the Minister of Supply would be responsible for any administrative action asked for by the Paymaster-General to give effect to
policy decisions taken by the latter. In the House of Commons, the
Minister of Supply would answer parliamentary questions on atomic
energy matters, other than those the Prime Minister decided to
answer. While the Minister of Supply would be responsible only for
matters entrusted to him by the Prime Minister, he would formally
retain the powers and duties conferred on him by statute and would
have access to all atomic energy information.

For collectors of curiosities in the history of the machinery of
government this bizarre document is important, cutting clean across
the hallowed canons of ministerial responsibility. Complicated
though it was, it did not cover all the complexities. Three months
after it was issued, Lord Alexander,* now Minister of Defence,
reminded Lord Cherwell that the Chiefs of Staff were responsible
for advising the Prime Minister and Cabinet on the military and
strategic aspects of atomic energy; this advice should go through
the Minister of Defence and the Defence Committee. He therefore
asked Lord Cherwell to bring before the Defence Committee any
atomic matters with a defence aspect, so that the Chiefs of Staff
could express their views. Lord Cherwell replied coldly that, while
he was altogether in favour of close consultation with the Chiefs of
Staff on the military aspects of atomic energy, he himself had never
been informed of discussions between the Chiefs of Staff and the
project's departmental heads which had led to recent recommendations about nuclear weapon development. 'If the Chiefs of Staff
desire that any advice I may give should coincide with theirs', he
wrote to the Minister of Defence, 'this is certainly not the best way

---

* Lord Alexander of Tunis, not Mr A. V. Alexander, later Lord Alexander
of Hillsborough.

to proceed. In the circumstances I would suggest any grievance there may be is not on the side of your Ministry.'

So the machinery for governing the atom became more, rather than less, irrational under the new Government. The lines of responsibility of the senior people in the project were more confused than ever. A further curious result was that the Atomic Energy Board, which replaced the Atomic Energy Council, was chaired by Lord Cherwell, a Minister, but on some major policy questions it reported to the Atomic Energy Official Committee, whose chairman – an official – usually reported back to Lord Cherwell. The Atomic Energy Board was organisationally the same as the old Council but it was a more effective body with its new chairman. Sir Frederick Morgan, who had replaced Lord Portal as Controller of Atomic Energy, was pushed completely to one side. Nevertheless, in spite of all these new organisational faults, the heads of the atomic energy project found great benefits in having Lord Cherwell at the helm; he was knowledgeable about their problems and the most determined and ruthless exponent of the exceptional nature of the project. Hinton was especially relieved at his advent. Since the project started, for example, there had only been one ministerial visit to Risley. Cherwell visited the northern factories* and showed great interest in them. For the first time Hinton felt he was responsible to somebody who could really understand what he was talking about and appreciate his difficulties.

Cherwell needless to say did not intend to accept the existing system. He himself was now in a very powerful position, but he was not concerned with personal power. He reverted to his original idea of an independent corporation and a clean break with the Civil Service and was now strengthened in his advocacy by his closer acquaintance with the Ministry of Supply, which was heavily engaged on conventional rearmament and seemed to pay far too little attention to the needs of atomic energy.

During the summer of 1952 support for Cherwell's views had grown inside the project itself. When he had led the agitation for a corporation in 1950 and 1951, eager support had come from Lord Portal and Mr Perrin, who were not representative of the project as a whole. Dr Penney also seems to have favoured a corporation for a time. But at the end of 1951 the staff at Harwell and Risley and the

---

* He had of course to wear a white coat and cotton over-shoes to go into radiation areas, but with them he wore his characteristic bowler hat.

weapons establishment were almost wholly opposed to the idea. Hinton, for example, had told Lord Cherwell so, vigorously, at the end of 1951. His production division had worked entirely satis- factorily within the Ministry of Supply. It was meeting its pro- grammes, its morale was high and it got good service from other branches of the Ministry and from other Ministries, notably the Ministry of Works. The Treasury had never kept it waiting for capital cost sanctions and salary scales were now satisfactory. Many members of the staff would consider their career prospects impaired if the project were hived off from the Civil Service and would leave. The change to a corporation would involve very big organisational problems, the solution of which would take up much senior staff time and mean a loss of efficiency. The scientists at Harwell and in the weapons establishment had similar feelings. The weapons people felt that their technical collaboration with other Ministry of Supply establishments had undoubtedly stimulated friendly competition and invigorated large regions of armaments research. The creation of an atomic energy corporation would be interpreted by these colleagues in armaments research as nominating atomic weapons research staff as a *corps d'élite*; collaboration with the Ministry of Supply, although no doubt still formally correct, would be affected by the resentments which would undoubtedly appear.

But in 1952 these views changed. Hinton was especially con- cerned at the lack of strength at the top of his organisation. The total salaries of his 13 top staff, running an organisation which would by 1956 have an invested capital of £86 million, came to £30,000 a year compared with £350,000 for 75 staff of equivalent grade in ICI, which had only three times the capital investment; of course ICI had marketing functions as well, but on the other hand it dealt largely with routine industrial plant. Not one man of industrial standing had been brought into the project after the beginning. Hinton was now very anxious to try to appoint to his staff, as his own ultimate successor, Mr C. F. Kearton, the talented scientist- engineer from ICI who had been associated with gaseous diffusion from the early war days. This would involve paying Kearton rather more than Hinton himself and very much more than Hinton's two deputies. These other salaries would have to be adjusted too, but the Treasury refused to raise the deputies' salaries. Rather than under- mine the team spirit which had been so important in the success of the production division, Hinton had dropped the scheme to appoint

Kearton. He now felt that although many of his objections to a nationalised board remained, his inability to deal satisfactorily with top-level staffing problems made the change necessary. Cockcroft also felt that promises to carry out certain administrative changes so that the organisation could keep pace with the increasing scale of work had not been fulfilled. He, however, favoured a separate Ministry directly responsible to a Minister. There was also consistent support for Cherwell from F. C. How, the senior administrative civil servant in the atomic energy headquarters.

During the summer of 1952 Cherwell's staff searched for all the evidence they could find of delays and staffing difficulties in the organisation. There was some evidence of course, but not nearly as much as Cherwell had hoped to find. Indeed the case for reorganisation was weak in so far as it was based on the past seven years. Problems of staff recruitment had been acute because there had been serious national shortages, but losses of scientists and engineers to other employment had been less than in several big firms noted as good employers. Considering all the difficulties, losses in the project had been low – latterly only 5 to 6 per cent a year of total strengths in all the establishments. There had been in the early days many troubles over housing and hostels, but such frustrations and difficulties were probably inevitable in the circumstances of post-war Britain and the Ministry of Supply had been remarkably successful in using the administrative machine to overcome a host of shortages and complications. It is difficult to believe that any independent corporation or industrial organisation could have done better than the Ministry or could have succeeded where it had failed, for example in getting the British Electricity Authority to complete on time the power stations needed for the gaseous diffusion plant. Again there had been a 'dragging' effect on the project arising from the constant hope of closer co-operation with the United States, but, as one official wrote, 'that a corporation would succeed in this field where we have failed is a pious hope'. The same official noted that delay on the political side – the failure to get early decisions from Ministers – had increased since the change of Government because the channel of responsibility was less well defined. The project in the initial stages, from which it was only just emerging, had done as well as, and almost certainly better than, it would have done under any other organisation in terms of speed, efficiency and economy.

The organisation on paper had looked crazy, but, whatever the inadequacies of ministerial and parliamentary participation, the executive machine had worked. It had proved in the end an example not of Civil Service red tape but of extreme Civil Service flexibility, even if the flexibility had been induced by unrelenting pressure from top people inside the project. Cherwell urged that there had been no integration of the project below the level of Permanent Secretary, and not even there or at the ministerial level in practice; the meetings of the directors and the Controller had been advisory only, and the three branches of the project had gone their own way with little oversight, while the headquarters administrative services formed a fourth branch. Yet the project had integrated itself at the working level and had achieved common ends without strong central co-ordinating machinery.

However, a new phase of the project was beginning and it seemed open to question whether, for reasons of size alone, the machine that had served well in the past was now the right one. As Cherwell came back to the attack, he based his case on the failures of the past and the needs of the future. In September 1952 he sent to Mr Churchill a paper which he wished to circulate to the Cabinet, advocating the removal of the atomic project from the Civil Service. He said he sincerely hoped Mr Churchill and the Cabinet would accept his advice, since no one else had such long and continuous experience of the matter. He added that he wished to make it absolutely clear that he had not the slightest desire or intention to control, or take any part in running, any corporation that might be formed. Still less did he covet a part in any interim Ministry which might be set up to prepare the transfer. Mr Churchill agreed that the paper should be circulated, but the Monte Bello trial was at hand and he added: 'wait to see whether your bomb goes off or not'.[3]

Cherwell's Cabinet paper went over the past history. He repeated to his colleagues his conviction of atomic energy's immense importance to civil life (less than a hundred tons of uranium yearly might generate the whole of the nation's electricity) and to political and military affairs (it might effect changes in international relations as great as those wrought by gunpowder in the political structure of Europe). Such an enterprise, he said, required vision, elasticity and rapidity of decision. Britain alone among nations had chosen to put her atomic undertaking under the control of an ordinary government department. 'We have subjected it to the same rules as the collection of customs.' Full control by Treasury rules was fatal to the conduct of a high-pressure industrial undertaking employing a host of wholly novel techniques whose development in turn depended on physical and chemical research pursued on the frontiers of knowledge. Cherwell asked his colleagues to agree to set up a corporation with a small executive board, financed by grant-in-aid, with complete freedom within an annual budget and investment programme and subject to directions which might be given to it. A separate Ministry should be organised to arrange the handover.

Cherwell was sure that the critical time to decide upon and announce the change would be just after the Monte Bello test. For the size, and to some extent the character, of the project were about to change. The size would increase owing to the switch from experimental to production weapons, Chiefs of Staff demands for increased fissile material, and the new programme for industrial power reactors. The character would be changed by increasing co-operation with industry. Hitherto, although industry had provided the organisation with virtually all its ironmongery, it had participated only to a limited extent in development and conceptual design. This would soon have to be changed. Sheer size of the undertaking would probably force the Government to entrust part of the development and management of nuclear plants to industry – a policy the Americans had followed from the outset. This would be difficult if the project remained embedded in a Government department.

Cherwell was convinced that if his proposals were accepted Britain would make far quicker progress and regain the place in nuclear development to which the outstanding achievements of her scientists entitled her. 'If these proposals are rejected and the *status quo* maintained', he concluded, 'the new Industrial and Military Revolutions will pass us by. Quietly and imperceptibly we shall lose our place among the nations of the earth.' Oliver Lyttelton, Colonial Secretary, entirely shared Lord Cherwell's views.* Duncan Sandys

---

* e.g. 'Standardised rates of pay in the Civil Service for various grades have insuperable disadvantages. Civil Service salaries rise like the tide and once a Civil Servant in the Ministry of Supply got a higher salary than a Civil Servant in the Ministry of Pensions disorder would follow and civil disturbance would soon be detected in the Athenaeum Club.'

rebutted the criticisms of the Ministry of Supply and rehearsed the former arguments against an independent corporation. He agreed with the new point about the importance of relations with industry, but pointed out that the Ministry of Supply had been able to co-operate most effectively with firms over a wide field, for example in aircraft and guided weapons.

Lord Cherwell was incensed when Mr Churchill told him that he did not think there was any hurry about deciding to free atomic energy from the Civil Service. He wrote an angry minute going over the familiar ground. The bomb test was now over, but it was no use pleading this as proof of success. With a different organisa-tion it would have been held two or three years earlier* and a diffusion plant could have been working already so that output would have been three to four times greater. Cherwell said that the tactics of those with vested interests in the present organisation would be to hold up any change in the hope either that there would be a change of Government 'or at least that I shall have vanished from the scene'. He hoped the Prime Minister would not let earlier decisions be frustrated in this way. He accompanied the minute with a handwritten note in effect threatening resignation – 'you will I am sure not wish to place me in the invidious position of carrying out a policy which I notoriously consider to be wrong'. Churchill addressed a sharp reply to 'my dear Prof':

> I certainly do not feel that I am pledged in this matter which I frankly admit I have not mastered in all its variants and still less that I made a bargain with you about it when you took office. We all have to try our best to deal with our problems as they come along. I should however be quite willing to propose to the Cabinet a small Cabinet Committee of 3 or 4 to examine the matter with you.

This is what happened at the Cabinet meeting in November. The Cabinet tended to favour Cherwell's proposal† but wanted the facts more thoroughly investigated before they took the decision. A three-man committee under the Lord Privy Seal (Captain Crookshank) was asked to do this and its recommendation in favour of a corpora-tion was to lead to the establishment of the Atomic Energy Authority in 1954.

There is no doubt that Lord Cherwell, as his biographer says, won

* This is not true (see Chapter 21).
† The Chancellor of the Exchequer voiced the strongest opposition.

the establishment of the Atomic Energy Authority single-handed or anyway supported by a few very enthusiastic Civil Service advisers, and we are told that this must be regarded as his 'political monument'.[4] In so far as this monument was built on a misreading of the past – on the belief that an organisation outside the Civil Service would have made the first atomic bombs more quickly and in greater numbers – it was ill-founded. In so far as the future was concerned, Cherwell when he died in 1957, just after the world's first nuclear power station had been opened at Calder Hall, would probably reflect that his judgement had been right.

It is impossible to say whether, if the Ministry of Supply had retained control, progress would have been any slower: there was no inherent reason why it should have been unless the very able top people who had remained with the project had left in default of the decision to establish a corporation. Indeed the crucial work on Calder Hall itself had been done before the Authority was established and the people at Risley who were in charge of it would certainly not have left before it was finished. The changeover to an Authority put a very heavy additional administrative load on the senior people in all parts of the project. It is in the nature of political monuments, moreover, that they tend to be transitory. Lord Cherwell had seen the Authority as the panacea for all the problems and difficulties of the atomic energy project. He had not contemplated, any more than Lord Portal before him, that atomic energy could in a short time become just one of many military projects, as far as the British were concerned, and just another industry as far as industrial power was concerned. He underestimated the advantages given to a project by the wider discussion and criticism of a big Ministry. A mere ten years after the establishment of the Authority for which Cherwell had fought so tenaciously, its existence was being questioned outside, if not inside, government, and within fifteen years or so its dismemberment was being officially considered. It was to be found that redistribution of functions within atomic energy and between atomic energy and other Government activities was more difficult when they were embedded in a large independent corporation established by Act of Parliament rather than in a Ministry.* It was

* In 1950, at a ministerial discussion, the point had been raised that if a corporation were established and atomic energy later lost its high priority, the Corporation would not be equipped to deal with other defence matters that might take the place of atomic energy.

to become apparent that the crucial problems connected with the exploitation of atomic energy could not be solved simply by forms of organisation.

Towards a New Programme

The Conservative Government had taken office in October 1951 as a new phase of the atomic energy project was about to open. Although the project had started as an open-ended one – the fissile material might be used either for bombs or for nuclear power development – it had become in its first phase primarily a military project directed to making a certain number of atomic bombs. But the first bomb was to be tested in a year's time and the military programme itself had to be analysed anew. The strategic background was changing all the time, and once having embarked on a policy of atomic weapons the Services would not be satisfied simply with an increasing supply of the first primitive bomb. Meanwhile the scientists and engineers at Harwell and Risley had on their own initiative forged ahead with their studies of nuclear power. Although the work of the whole project had been very largely in aid of weapons, much of it was also potentially useful for a nuclear power programme. At the end of 1951* the effort which had been devoted specifically to power was, however, very small; from now on it began to increase.

In 1952 there were three main problems connected with the weapons programme. Firstly, production was going to move up from a laboratory scale, if not to mass production then to production runs which were the province of the engineer rather than of the mathematician and physicist. How was this to be organised? Secondly, what types of weapons were to be developed after the Mark I bomb? Thirdly, what was the scale of production to be? An answer to the first problem was becoming pressing. Penney's organisation was making only the radioactive components for bombs, while the other components were made by the Royal Ordnance Factories and the Royal Aircraft Establishment at Farnborough, but the organisation was also responsible for co-ordinating production of the finished weapons. The organisation, which was still called High Explosive Research, would continue to be respon-

* See Chapter 18, also J. D. Cockcroft, Joule Memorial Lecture, Nov 1951. The figures in this lecture for the division of effort are not clear.

sible for the radioactive pieces, but it was not intended or suited for organising and inspecting the production of complete bombs on any scale. The production responsibility for 'sealed' or firm designs could either be transferred to the appropriate Controller of Supplies in the Ministry of Supply or to a special Director of Weapons Production appointed within the project; the answer was to appoint a Director of Weapons Production within the project, but it was very difficult to find the right person and no one had been appointed when the first British bomb was tested. There was also the question whether the Royal Ordnance Factories should take on the whole production job or whether the American system of sub-contracting the work to large industrial companies should be followed; it had been decided to concentrate production in the ROFs.

The second military problem was the choice of future types of weapons. Until 1951 there had been very little serious study of the military implications of atomic weapons or their future development. Until then military calculations had taken account only of the British atomic bomb as a deterrent which, by threatening unacceptable damage, would prevent enemy attacks. As we have seen, because of ignorance about the American strategic air plan, even the military calculations surrounding the production of the first bombs were very rough and ready. There had been no discussions about future types of atomic weapons and their uses.

However, in 1951 the Defence Research Policy's Sub-Committee on the Strategic Aspects of Atomic Energy (see Chapter 2), had produced a report on 'Military Aspects of Atomic Energy' which began to ask some of the leading questions concerned with atomic weapons. In particular, what uses were there for atomic weapons other than blasting and burning cities, and what types of atomic weapons, subject to the inescapable design features peculiar to atomic weapons, were required for these other uses? Mathematical studies in Britain had shown that a wide choice in the design and performance of atomic weapons was possible, especially if both plutonium and U-235 were available. Tactical weapons to be used against troops and artillery had to be considered as well as strategic weapons. At present only one type of weapon was being developed and three years must be allowed for the development of a new type; at most only two types could be developed at the same time, so that difficult choices lay ahead. It was recognised that methods of operational research must be used to discover the best distribution of weapon production. The choice could not be delayed too long because Penney's establishment would soon be ready to start development work on the next type of weapon. The choice had to be related to other questions about methods of delivery, targets and so forth.

It is clear that the enterprise was entering a far more chilling phase where all kinds of horrible possibilities could be bandied about in terms of so much military hardware. Men whose job it was to protect their country were in the process discussing calmly the efficiency of these appalling weapons in terms of cost, fissile material and destructive power, related to weight and dimension. They also proceeded to think about the 'unthinkable' – the hydrogen bomb. Its feasibility, the Strategic Aspects Sub-Committee said, was not yet established. Its development was believed to be an immensely difficult technical problem, while the design and manufacture of a carrier for it would be almost comparable in difficulty. The limiting factor to hydrogen bomb production would be the production of the artificial element tritium. This could be made only by irradiating lithium in a pile with a large surplus of neutrons. The effects of two types of hydrogen bombs were considered – one equivalent to 1 million tons of TNT and one equivalent to 10 million tons. Even with the smaller of these Molochs, the Sub-Committee said, the whole area up to perhaps 5 miles would probably experience a fire storm; it was unlikely that anyone in it would escape, and there would be 1–2 million casualties. Radioactivity would cause high dose rates and serious contamination of water and crops, but, they said, the widespread contamination would not present a serious threat to the population of the world at large.

Following this report, a working party was set up to advise the Chiefs of Staff on the operational use of atomic weapons, and to assess the best policy for future weapon production; the various Services submitted reports on what they considered their atomic requirements to be. As a result of the working party's interim report in April 1952, the Chiefs of Staff gave some guidance on the priority for the development of various types of bomb. As time had gone on, there had been increasing doubt about the possibility of making hydrogen bombs in Britain. Quite apart from the difficulties of producing enough tritium, Penney, the chief expert, doubted whether the country's resources, especially of scientific manpower, could stand the strain of such an additional development programme. Cherwell told the Prime Minister at the end of 1952 that work at present on the hydrogen bomb was, he believed, 'quite beyond our means'.

At the end of 1952 it was apparent that the machinery for discussing these weapons questions was not working well. For security reasons, the Services had appointed to the working party officers of a very high rank who could not give the necessary time to study operational problems in great detail. Penney's suggestion for a small full-time joint Services working party, composed of high-grade officers of colonel or equivalent rank, was therefore accepted. At the same time Lord Cherwell made it clear that he wished to know personally much more about what was going on in this field. He was not being informed of the various studies that were being made and of the decisions being taken on the operational use of atomic weapons. He pointed out that the answers to these operational problems had great military, economic and political implications. It was impossible for him to put forward recommendations to his colleagues in the Cabinet if he did not know all the arguments leading up to the various conclusions. Moreover he was uneasy about some of the technical-military decisions: he thought, for example, that too much stress was being laid on designing the bomb to fit the aircraft rather than the other way round.

Discussions about these technological questions, about types of weapons, were developing a relentless momentum of their own, separated from the discussions on global strategic policy. But it was global strategy that determined the total size of the military atomic effort and in 1952 a new global strategy document was drawn up. The world outlook was still very bleak. The NATO countries and the countries in the Soviet bloc glared at each other and the volume and sophistication of military hardware were multiplying. In Korea, war still raged. When the Conservative Government returned, their policy was the same as that of the Labour Government – to prevent the Cold War turning into a hot war, though not at any cost.

When Mr Churchill went to Washington in January 1952 he was seeking United States agreement that the long-term strategic aim was to reach an accommodation between East and West. The short-term aim was to concentrate on building up positions of strength and then to negotiate local and limited settlements which recognised the strength of these positions. But this had to be done against a new factor – that is, the effect of rearmament programmes on the economy of the West. In Britain the Conservative Government had been obliged to cut defence estimates for economic reasons and further substantial cuts were possible or likely. The Chiefs of Staff were conscious that there was great danger that the countries of Western Europe, including Britain, might burst themselves economically; this, it will be remembered, was the same metaphor Sir Henry Tizard had used when he recalled Aesop's frog. Forces were being built up which it might well be impossible to maintain. One of the problems in Britain was that atomic strategy was being imposed on conventional strategy. Did this make sense?

In the early summer of 1952 the Chiefs of Staff held a conference at Greenwich to study global strategy and took atomic experts with them.* The resulting document identified two main changes since defence policy was last considered – the economic situation and the notable increase in United States atomic power. The policy itself was still to prevent Russia and China from gaining their ends by infiltrating and disintegrating the free world, and to prevent war. The concept of policy was to restore the economic strength of the free world, create a self-confident spirit in it, and build up alliances against aggression and military strength by rearmament. When the existing strategic policy was established it had been thought that Russia might be contemplating an early attack. But now it was thought that Russia was unlikely to embark on a war which would lead to catastrophic devastation, although there was a danger of either side being provoked into precipitating war as a result of a minor incident. War was unlikely if the Cold War, which was likely to be prolonged, was conducted by the Allies in a patient, level-headed and determined manner, and the United Kingdom must use her influence to this end.†

The chief reasons, according to the document, why war was unlikely were the increased strength of Western Europe and the atomic deterrent. The strength of Western Europe was shown in NATO. In the background of NATO policy was the vague assumption that

* I have never found any reports of the actual conference.

† One of the Chiefs of Staff had pointed out that one unfortunate but inevitable result of British withdrawal of forces for economic reasons was the predominantly decisive influence of America, whose experience, judgement and internal political system were ill adapted to her enormous responsibilities and her capacity to determine the fate not only of the Western Allies but of most of Asia as well. This put a grave responsibility on Britain who, to an extent that was underrated, had more influence on the United States Administration than any other of their allies.

the United States had built up large stocks of atomic bombs which they could drop on Soviet key points. Only America had this formidable weapon, whose power was so closely guarded that with the sole exception of Britain, and possibly Canada, NATO countries knew very little about it. But Britain had good reason to rate much more highly than before the effectiveness of the United States strategic air plan, and the number of its atomic weapons.

This knowledge had a frightening obverse. The document said that it was now clear that there was in the foreseeable future no effective defence against atomic air attack. Since there was no defence, said the Chiefs of Staff, the primary deterrent must be Russian knowledge that any aggression would involve immediate and crushing atomic retaliation. This meant that the Allies must give the necessary priority to air striking forces. The number of atomic bombs was no longer the crux, but rather their delivery. The complementary deterrent was Allied ability to hold up a Russian advance against Europe.

The British part in this strategy was fourfold: to exercise influence on Cold War policy, to meet NATO obligations, to prepare for war in case the deterrent failed and to play a part, albeit a small one, in the main deterrent, the air offensive. This fourfold problem must be solved without ruining the economy.

What of the British part in the atomic deterrent? The deterrent at present rested entirely in American hands. The document concluded that, largely for economic reasons, it must remain there. But, said the Chiefs of Staff, it would be quite wrong for the United Kingdom to take no share in it. It was not possible to rely on the Americans to deal adequately with targets not of direct strategic interest to the United States. 'We feel that to have no share in what is recognised as the main deterrent in the cold war and the only Allied offensive in a world war would seriously weaken British influence on United States policy and planning in the cold war and in war would mean that the United Kingdom would have no claim to any share in the policy or planning of the offensive.' There is no doubt that the recent discussions in Washington on the use of the atomic bomb had seemed to prove the great political disadvantage Britain would continue to suffer until her own contribution entitled her to claim a share in controlling what might be the decisive strategy in any future war and in determining any peace terms. The alternative – a supply of United States bombs to Britain under her own control –

had been ruled out by the Fuchs betrayal, said the Chiefs of Staff. They seemed to think, probably wrongly, that only that betrayal had prevented agreement with the United States. They saw a possibility of reviving the abortive agreement after the 1952 presidential election and the first British atomic test, while it was 'probable' that if war came a stock of United States bombs would be made available for RAF use. However, it would in any event be most unwise for the United Kingdom to be completely dependent on the United States. Britain must press forward with her own atomic development, giving priority to small bombs where she could make the best contribution to scientific development and production.

In 1950 the threat of atomic air attack had tempted the Chiefs of Staff to downgrade Britain's own atomic deterrent in favour of more obviously defensive items. Now the threat was greater, but, increasingly, means of offence, notably the strategic air offensive, were seen again as a main method of defence, of reducing the scale of air attack on Britain. 'It has always been a cardinal point in British air policy', wrote the Chief of Air Staff, 'that the counter-offensive is an indispensable element in air defence', a view which the Second World War had vindicated. The rethinking of strategy had already led, some months before the Chiefs of Staff review, to new announcements on priority. Now almost for the first time very special emphasis at all levels was laid on the need to build up the bomber force, particularly the V-bombers. In March 1952 the Cabinet had confirmed an earlier directive from Mr Churchill giving priority to a limited number of items of defence equipment which were lagging – the latest type of aircraft, ammunition for aircraft, the radar chain, Centurion tanks, guided weapons, certain anti-mine equipment. Atomic energy was not mentioned, but it was later confirmed that its priority was equal to these super-priority items. Later in the year the Prime Minister agreed that the super-priority rating might be used for those parts of the newly approved programme for nuclear power development, where it was necessary to avoid great delay in the provision of key items.

In the latter half of 1952 the military and industrial programmes had partly converged. The heightened concern of the Chiefs of Staff for defence-through-offence, that is, for the strategic air offensive, had led them to urge the need for greater production of fissile material in Britain. They said in their global strategy document that their attention had been drawn to the possibility of doubling the present output of plutonium within three years or doubling output of uranium-235, the latter in the Commonwealth because of the power requirements. In these ways, they said, the United Kingdom could greatly increase its resources for atomic warfare at relatively small cost. 'This action would naturally increase British influence on United States policy in peace as well as being an asset of great value in war.' Moreover the fissile material would not be a wasting asset, for as the danger of war receded it would be available as a source of power.* The Chiefs of Staff recommended investigation into the possibilities and implications. Presumably the atomic experts had drawn the attention of the Chiefs of Staff at the Greenwich Conference to the possibility of increasing fissile material production. Certainly this pronouncement came at a crucial time. For at much the same moment the first reactor programme specifically aimed at developing nuclear power had been put forward.

What had been happening to the industrial programme? Research on reactors to produce nuclear power had been proceeding apace in 1951 and 1952, and by the spring of 1952 the Harwell and Risley experts had a clear idea of the immediate programme they wished to follow. The rationale of the programme was not, as we have seen, a mirage of very cheap power. In the long term, fast breeder nuclear reactors might yield substantially lower power costs, but in the medium term, with slow-neutron reactors, nuclear power was unlikely to be much, if any, cheaper than power from coal.† The experts were increasingly concerned with the economic aspects of nuclear power in this medium term – though they apparently did the sums themselves and did not call in professional economists. They refused to accept the argument voiced in many quarters that it was important to build something irrespective of cost. Indeed it would undoubtedly have been difficult to push a case for nuclear power if the evidence showed that it was going to be definitely more expensive than power from coal.

The rationale of the programme was not the cost of power but the inadequacy of coal supplies. Requirements for electric power

* There was also the point, emphasised in the project, not by the Chiefs of Staff, that the cost of fissile material was lower than that of conventional explosive for a given size of explosion, in view of the saving in aircraft costs by the use of atomic bombs.

† The 1952 calculation about the cost of power from natural uranium piles is given in Chapter 19.

were likely to increase rapidly for many years; electricity consumption had doubled in the previous decade and yet the consumption of electric power per operator in United States industry was still three times that in the United Kingdom. The British Electricity Authority estimated that they would require another 13 million tons of coal a year by 1960, but it seemed doubtful whether this expanding demand could be met from existing sources. Oil was still not mentioned at all in any of these papers.

Coal shortage was the reason why efforts must be made to produce electric power from atomic energy. Ever since the subject had been discussed in the war, it had been generally agreed that in the long term the best method would be the fast fission breeder reactor, which would produce both heat and power and at the same time breed more fissile material than it burned. Such reactors might produce power equal to the total national consumption of electricity at that time with appreciably less than a hundred tons of uranium of thorium a year. The design, construction and operation of these reactors posed many new and difficult problems, but a first experimental reactor of this type in the United States was already said to be producing a few hundred kilowatts of electric power. Harwell had also taken the first step by building a very low-power reactor, Zephyr, to investigate the nuclear characteristics of such systems, and this would be ready by March 1953. The next step would be to design and construct a full-scale reactor which would develop 50 MW of electrical energy. Harwell and Risley were already producing tentative designs; if accorded high priority it might be in operation by 1956.*

There was, however, no certainty that the long-term power breeder reactor would succeed. A more immediate solution to nuclear power development would be to improve the existing design of the Harwell experimental reactor (Bepo) and Windscale-type piles. It was likely that with a throughput of 100 tons of uranium a year in such piles, a million tons of coal could be saved and electric power production be increased by 3 per cent.

After the Harwell Conference of September 1950, which had endorsed the idea of beginning a nuclear power programme with natural uranium reactors to produce power and plutonium simultaneously, a Harwell design committee had considered many differ-

---

* The Dounreay fast reactor producing 14 MW of electric power went critical in 1959 (see Chapter 19).

ent types of moderator and coolants for such reactors (see Chapter 19). It had concluded that a graphite-moderated reactor, like the Windscale piles but cooled, unlike the Windscale piles, by gas under pressure, was the most likely to evolve reasonably soon into a practicable design and to be an economic proposition. At the beginning of 1952 the British Electricity Authority and selected engineering firms had been invited to help design a small pilot reactor and steam plant of this type, to produce 10 megawatts of power and also about 20 kilograms of plutonium a year: this was the project called Pippa.

There was a third item in the reactor development programme planned in the summer of 1952. Harwell needed a much more powerful research reactor, especially to support fast reactor development, for Bepo did not provide an adequate neutron intensity and the Chalk River facilities were overloaded. A heavy water research pile, Hippo, at first seen as a copy of the Canadian NRX pile, was then planned. This would produce abundant isotopes for sale for industrial use, as well as about 20 kilograms of plutonium.

Meanwhile the development of a nuclear reactor for submarine propulsion, which had been high in the order of priority in 1950 and 1951, had become less urgent. A design study had been going on for some time and the outlines of the problem were clear. But the Admiralty would not have a submarine ready for some years and the reactor would be extremely expensive in highly enriched uranium; it was therefore to be subsidiary to the breeder reactor project.

The three-pronged power programme consisting of Zephyr, Pippa and Hippo would be expensive – the capital cost would be £17 million in the years 1952–7 – and would absorb over 10,000 tons of steel and a peak site labour force of 2,500. The Treasury noted the proposals with alarm from the investment point of view, especially as the heaviest expenditure would occur in 1955 when the national housing programme would be at its peak. They were dubious about both Hippo and Pippa. However, their qualms were overcome and the programme was endorsed by the Chancellor of the Exchequer and finally the Prime Minister. Meanwhile, for the first time, the question of allocating plutonium between military and civilian uses arose – for 12 to 15 kilograms of plutonium were needed on loan for Zephyr. The Ministry of Defence therefore had to agree to this diversion from weapons, and although they did so readily they sensed possible conflicts of interest in the future.

The Chiefs of Staff were, as we saw, at this very moment asking, or at least hoping, for a doubling of plutonium output within three years. They had suggested, alternatively, doubling the output of uranium-235 by building a plant in the Commonwealth – a proposal that appalled Cherwell if only because of the capital cost. At first it was assumed that the plutonium requirement would be met by building a third production pile, a replica of the Windscale piles, on the platform already built and then abandoned during the 1949 Anglo-American negotiations. This, plus the plutonium from Hippo and Pippa, would meet the Chiefs of Staff requirements; a new plant for separating the plutonium from the fuel rods would also be needed. Indeed such a pile was the only way of greatly increasing plutonium production within three years. The prospect of building a third Windscale pile was greeted with gloom, because by engrossing so much constructional effort it would greatly delay the fast reactor programme without itself advancing nuclear technology.

If, however, three years were regarded as a general indication of the Chiefs of Staff time-scale, rather than an immutable requirement, the way would be open to consider meeting it wholly or partially from new types of pile such as Hippo or Pippa. A Hippo pile might possibly be built within three years, but it was unlikely that even the small Pippa originally proposed could be built in much less than four years, and design studies might continue for several months yet before an enlarged Pippa could be firmly recommended as a plutonium producer. Hinton opposed especially strongly the suggestion of building a Chinese copy of the Windscale piles. These piles, he said, had never had anything to recommend them except that they could be brought into production more quickly than any other type. They used uranium and graphite extravagantly and were expensive to run. Apart from this, of course, the heat of fission simply went up the chimney. This had been realised when their construction was first suggested, and it had been proposed that only one such pile should be built and should be followed by a pressurised power-producing pile. This idea had been turned down because of the urgent demand for plutonium, but design studies for a pressurised reactor had continued at Risley and had reached an advanced stage when the sanction of the third (later abortive) pile had halted it.

There had thus been two occasions on which the urgent demand for plutonium had set back development of a reactor of more advanced engineering design, and it would be a great pity if this happened a third time. The construction of a third Windscale pile ought to be avoided and the Chiefs of Staff requirement met by building power-producing piles. Hinton deprecated reliance on plutonium produced from the research reactor, Hippo, since its operation for this purpose would conflict with its operation for research. He believed that the successful design and operation of pressurised piles were no more problematical than the design and operation of the Windscale piles in 1947. Such piles, however, could not be completed within the three years specified by the Chiefs of Staff; if finally sanctioned in January 1953, the piles might become divergent in mid-1956. In fact only half the Chiefs of Staff demand could be met within three years from Windscale-type piles because they were so greedy in graphite, which was difficult to produce. The recommendation to build pressurised gas-cooled piles was based on the military demand for plutonium. But power would be a by-product. The cost of two Pippas to meet plutonium needs, including extensions to the fuel plants and chemical separation plants, would be £23 million.

Lord Cherwell met the Chiefs of Staff and asked if they would accept a four-year, instead of a three-year, programme. Apart from the wastefulness of the Windscale-type piles and their extravagance in uranium and graphite, power production would have a good psychological effect on public opinion. The Chiefs of Staff were content to wait. Pippa had thus moved very rapidly from the stage of a design study for a very small pile, primarily intended to produce power, to a project for two full-scale piles intended primarily to produce plutonium. There was by now very little technical doubt about the piles. The uncompleted studies mainly concerned the economics of power production, and now that power production was not the main aim, these were not crucial.

The prospect of useful power within the next few years had suddenly become very much more hopeful. It would have, it was thought, a good effect on morale in the project, on public relations and on prestige vis-à-vis the Americans. There were, however, some effects to be weighed on the other side, in particular the delay in introducing industrial firms into nuclear technology. One of the main reasons always urged for pushing ahead with the little Pippa was to train industry and the British Electricity Authority. The importance of this participation was held to outweigh any additional costs in time or money. However, now that plutonium production and speed were the essence of the big Pippas, there was little doubt that Risley would build them best and most quickly. Risley would make the maximum use of outside industry, particularly in designing the conventional power plants, but would itself design the reactor and the factory as a whole. However, Hinton suggested that when built, the Pippas should be operated not directly by Risley but by BEA as their agents.*

The concentration of the work on Risley would also slow down design work on the fast reactor, but with the compensation that results would first be obtained from Zephyr and essential metallurgical and heat-transfer investigations could be completed.

Everyone in the atomic energy project believed by October 1952 that the Chiefs of Staff requirements should be met by building two Pippas. A month later such a firm recommendation was not possible, because of doubts whether the plutonium so produced would be suitable for military purposes: the reactors would run at such high temperatures that the proportion of the plutonium isotope 240, which was subject to premature fission, might be unacceptable. The decision had to go back for further calculation and consideration. Meanwhile Cherwell put to his ministerial colleagues in the Defence Committee a formal proposal for meeting the Chiefs of Staff requirements. While it was not possible to specify the exact type of pile, it was proposed to build to new designs which would be more economical and net producers of power, designs which would be a significant step in the development of the civil use of atomic energy.

To the dismay of everyone, and Cherwell's rage, the Prime Minister would not at present support the doubling of plutonium output, whatever the means. He had no intention of doing so until he had the opportunity of discussing Anglo-American atomic co-operation with the newly elected President Eisenhower. It had always been his understanding, he said, that the Americans would supply the British with atomic bombs for their own use and he felt that the recent success of the British bomb test, together with the change of Administration, might make this possible. It was unwise, he said, to embark on costly expansion at home until this new approach had been made. Design studies might continue in the meantime but there must be no commitment.

---

* The decision to build the Pippas also brought to a head controversy over the roles of Harwell and Risley (see Chapter 18).

Lord Cherwell wrote a patient minute to the Prime Minister but told him plainly that he was shocked by his attitude at the Defence Committee. He emphasised the need for the new piles for civilian purposes. 'Unless we are to sacrifice all hope of holding our own in this vital field of exploitation of nuclear energy we shall have to spend almost the same amount of money whether we make atomic bombs or not.' For without plutonium and uranium-235 no progress in industrial applications could be made. Whether the materials should be put into bombs or reactors need not be decided in advance: this was one of the advantages of atomic compared with conventional weapons, which could only be scrapped when no longer needed. Even if Eisenhower gave Britain 50 atomic bombs, Cherwell said, the new dual-purpose piles would still be needed not only for plutonium but also to learn how to design and use reactors for making electricity. The extra cost, averaging £6 million per annum over four years, was negligible compared with the £1,500 million spent annually on defence or the £250 million spent on food subsidies. 'If it is decided not to make atomic bombs of our own and to rank with other European nations who have to make do with conventional weapons', Britain might be able to save about £7 million a year on Penney's establishment. But there would be no other major saving unless all serious work on atomic energy was given up. 'I cannot believe', wrote Cherwell, 'you would contemplate adopting such a disastrous line which might well in the long run spell national suicide.'

Pippa was to be eventually sanctioned and become famous as Calder Hall. But for the moment, as 1952 ended, the refrain was only too familiar: Britain's project was waiting yet again for the atomic negotiations with the United States.

Meanwhile the first British atomic bomb had been exploded at Monte Bello in Australia on 3 October 1952. An extraordinary research and industrial effort involving £150 million or so of expenditure had gone into it and, as the next part of this book will suggest, the programme had been executed with great skill. The explosion brought telegrams from the Prime Minister to Cockcroft, Hinton, Penney and their staffs. The explosion seemed to the project, to most politicians and probably to most members of the public a matter of congratulation and relief – a demonstration of scientific and technical competence, a proof of Britain's status as a great, if not a super, power. It would surely win greater respect from the

United States, and Britain would surely be militarily more secure through possession of the supreme deterrent of the day.

And yet. . . . Congratulation was muted as the explosion brought to the fore serious questionings about the morality of making atomic bombs at all. Relief was muted because only a month after Monte Bello the United States exploded their first thermonuclear 'device' and in August 1953 the Russians tested their first thermonuclear bomb. Britain was just acquiring atomic bombs as the United States and Russia were acquiring the infinitely more powerful hydrogen bombs. For Britain it was a race of the Red Queen's variety. To add to the chagrin, the United States was not even particularly impressed. Dr Solandt of the Canadian Defence Research Board wrote to Sir William Penney,* saying he had been in Washington just after the British test and found there – and indeed in Canada – a feeling that the British weapon programme was merely a propaganda effort to interest the United States authorities. When early in 1953 an American newspaper polled Congressmen about interchange with Britain on atomic energy, one of them said: 'We would be trading a horse for a rabbit.'⁵ These immediate North American reactions later gave place to second thoughts, and the British demonstration of the success of their project with their limited resources was probably one of the factors which encouraged the much fuller American co-operation of the mid-1950s.

Nevertheless, victory, it seemed, had yet again more than a taste of ashes. But it did have its sweetness too. The present achievement was in terms of a primitive but wholly terrifying bomb and the whole project had been hitherto dominated by military considerations. Yet the essence of atomic energy is that it is dual-purpose – that the vast energy released by the fission of the nuclei of uranium can be used either for industrial power or bombs. The Monte Bello explosion was a token that Britain possessed the plants and the expertise which would make it possible to proceed apace with the fair instead of the foul purposes, and it was in this new direction that the energies of most people in the project were now bending.

* Penney was knighted immediately after the test.

Appendix 14

TECHNICAL NOTE

Atoms

All matter is made up of atoms, each of which is like a tiny solar system but unimaginably small – about one hundred millionth of a centimetre in diameter and consisting largely of empty space. Each atom has a nucleus which is the analogue of our sun and, round this nucleus, particles called electrons move in orbits just as planets move around the sun. The orbits of these electrons are arranged in a succession of 'shells' each capable of containing a fixed number of electrons; only the outermost electrons are affected by chemical reactions.

The nucleus of every atom is made up of nucleons or sub-nuclear particles, of which protons and neutrons are the most important. The neutrons are electrically uncharged, but each proton carries a positive charge of electricity; the whole nucleus therefore has a positive charge. The number of protons in the nucleus ranges from one in hydrogen* to 92 in uranium, and more in the so-called transuranic elements which do not exist in nature. In the lighter elements the number of protons and neutrons is generally about equal, but in the heavier elements there is an increasing ratio of neutrons to protons, until in the heaviest natural element, uranium, the nucleus has 92 protons and more than 140 neutrons. This neutron surplus makes possible the chain reaction which is described below.

Electrons, though about 1,850 times lighter than protons, carry an equal but negative charge of electricity. In a normal atom the number of electrons is equal to the number of protons, so that the charges balance one another and the atom as a whole is electrically neutral, but an atom can temporarily acquire a net charge, negative or positive, and it is then called an ion. The chemical properties of an atom and its place in the periodic table† are determined absolutely

* An atom of hydrogen weighs less than one seventeen-million-million-millionth part of an ounce.

† The chemical elements when arranged in order from lightest to heaviest exhibit a recurrence of chemical properties at regular or periodic intervals, hence the name 'periodic table'.

by the number of protons in its nucleus; thus an atom with 6 protons must be carbon, and an atom with 26 must be iron. This number, usually symbolised by the letter Z, is called the atomic number.

The nucleons – protons and neutrons – constitute almost the entire matter of the atom, and their total is called the atomic mass number.* The atomic mass number (A) is therefore equivalent to the atomic number (Z) plus the number of neutrons (N). Atoms which have the same number of protons, and therefore the same chemical properties, may have different numbers of neutrons, and therefore different atomic masses and different physical properties. Such atoms are called isotopes† of the same chemical substance. Nearly all elements occur in several isotopic forms; thus carbon-13 and carbon-14 both have 6 protons, but one has 7 neutrons and one 8, while uranium-235 and uranium-238 have atomic number 92 and contain 143 and 146 neutrons respectively. Tin has ten naturally occurring isotopic forms, but a few elements – including sodium and aluminium – have only one.

As protons are positively charged, the atomic nucleus would tend to fly apart because of electrostatic repulsion between similarly charged particles, but the nucleus is held together by powerful binding forces.‡ Some of this binding energy is released as kinetic energy of the fission fragments when heavy nuclei are fissioned, and this kinetic energy is converted into heat which can be used to generate electricity in a nuclear power station (see below). The energy released in the fission of one atom is thousands of times greater than that released from one atom when merely changed chemically, e.g. in the process of burning.

---

* The atomic mass of the nucleus is, however, somewhat less than the sum of the masses of the nucleons, and this difference is called the mass defect. It corresponds (remembering Einstein's Law, which states that mass and energy are interchangeable) to the forces binding the nucleus together (see below).

† A name – originated by the chemist, Frederick Soddy, who discovered isotopes over seventy years ago – derived from two Greek words meaning 'the same place', i.e. occupying the same place in the periodic table. To distinguish isotopes, the atomic mass number is often placed after the name of the element, e.g. uranium-235, cobalt-60. When chemical symbols are used, the atomic number and mass number are generally placed before the symbol, e.g. $^{60}_{27}$Co designates the isotope of cobalt which has 27 protons and 33 neutrons, and thus atomic mass number 60.

‡ This energy is equivalent to the mass defect referred to in footnote* above.

Radioactivity

In some naturally occurring heavy atoms, described as radioactive, the arrangement of protons and neutrons in the nucleus is unstable; such atoms tend to emit radiation. There are four types of radiation:

1. *Alpha particles*, which are positively charged and consist of two protons and two neutrons – in fact a helium nucleus. In passing through the air they collide with molecules, slow down and eventually acquire orbital electrons to become stable helium atoms. Meanwhile the atomic mass number of the radioactive parent atom, by the loss of an alpha particle, has decreased by 4, and the atomic number by 2, so that a new element has been formed two places lower in the periodic table.*

2. *Beta particles* are high-speed electrons, travelling at almost the speed of light; these particles are created within the nucleus of a radioactive atom in a process of 'beta decay' by which, in an unstable nucleus, either a neutron is transformed into a proton or a proton into a neutron. Beta decay of the former kind yields an isotope of a new element of the same mass but one atomic number higher: for instance, tritium, an isotope of hydrogen (one proton), yields an isotope of helium (two protons), and bismuth-210 (83 protons) is transformed into polonium-210 (84 protons).

   Beta transformation of the second kind produces an element with unchanged mass but of atomic number lower by one; e.g. phosphorus-30 (15 protons) is transformed into silicon-30 (14 protons).

3. *The neutrino* is a particle which has neither mass nor charge and which is emitted in radioactive beta decay along with an electron.

4. *Gamma radiation* is a form of electromagnetic radiation similar to X-rays, emitted by a nucleus, and is a way of releasing unwanted energy from the nucleus.

Alpha particles can be stopped by a thick sheet of paper or a few inches of air; beta particles can be stopped by a thin sheet of metal or a few feet of air; some gamma radiation is extremely penetrating and several inches of lead may be needed to stop it. These radiations

---

* e.g. uranium-238 (Z = 92, A = 238) emits an alpha particle (2 protons + 2 neutrons) to become thorium-234 (Z = 90, A = 234).

are all called ionising radiations because they can eject orbiting electrons from atoms which they encounter, and so produce positive and negative ions or electrons along their paths. These ions or electrons can be readily detected in instruments such as Geiger-counters, crystals and ionisation chambers; consequently it is possible to detect very tiny amounts of radioactivity.

The radioactive elements which occur in nature form three series, the parent elements being uranium (92 protons), protactinium (91 protons) and thorium (90 protons). In each series, radioactive decay consists of a succession of transformations in which alpha or beta particles are emitted, until a stable isotope of lead is reached. The uranium series is shown in the table below.

The Uranium Decay Series

Element	Atomic Number	Mass Number	Particle emitted	Half-life
Uranium	92	238	α	4,500 million years
Thorium	90	234	β	24 days
Protactinium	91	234	β	1·1 minutes
Uranium	92	234	α	248,000 years
Thorium	90	230	α	80,000 years
Radium	88	226	β	1,600 years
Radon	86	222	α	3·8 days
Polonium	84	218	α	3 minutes
Lead	82	214	β	27 minutes
Bismuth	83	214	α and β	20 minutes
Polonium	84	214	α	0·000164 second
Thallium	81	210	β	1·3 minutes
Lead	82	210	β	21 years
Bismuth	83	210	β	5 days
Polonium	84	210	α	138 days
Lead	82	206	None	Stable

Every radioactive substance is characterised by the type and the energy of the radiation emitted and also by the physical 'half-life' – the time taken for half the atoms in any given quantity of a radioactive substance to change, so that its activity is reduced by half. Half-lives, which are invariable and cannot be affected by chemical or physical processes, range from fractions of a second to millions of years. Uranium-238 has a half-life of 4,500 million years, while the half-life of polonium-214 is only 0·000164 seconds.

Radioactivity is measured in curies. This unit, named after the famous woman physicist, is that amount of activity which decays at the rate of 370 thousand million disintegrations a second. The specific activity of a substance is usually expressed in curies per gram.

Radioisotopes

Radioactive substances – including some elements not found in nature – can be made artificially by changing atomic nuclei; this can be done in high-energy machines called particle accelerators, or by neutron bombardment in nuclear reactors. An isotope of a stable element can be transformed into a radioactive isotope of the same element if the nucleus gains a neutron while the number of protons, and hence the atomic number, remains unaltered. For example, when an atom of stable sodium-23 captures a neutron and a gamma ray is emitted – the so-called neutron-gamma (n, γ) reaction – it becomes radioactive sodium-24; stable cobalt-59 becomes radioactive cobalt-60 by a similar reaction.

However, neutron capture may transmute one element into another. An added neutron may make the nucleus unstable so that a proton is ejected – by the so-called neutron-proton (n, p) reaction – thus reducing the atomic number by one; for example, sulphur-32 (16 protons) becomes phosphorus-32 (15 protons). Or the nucleus may emit an alpha particle – the neutron-alpha (n, α) reaction – reducing the atomic number by 2 and the atomic mass by 3;* thus lithium-6 (3 protons and 3 neutrons) becomes tritium, an isotope of hydrogen (1 proton and 2 neutrons).

In some instances a required isotope is obtained as a decay product of a radioisotope produced by neutron capture; for example, tellurium-130 (52 protons) becomes tellurium-131 by the (n, γ) reaction and then changes by beta decay (see above) to iodine-131 (53 protons). Only a small proportion of the atoms actually absorbs neutrons, so the radioactive substance formed is mixed with the inactive target (or 'carrier') material. To obtain a pure product – or one of higher specific activity – further processing is necessary to separate the radioisotope from the 'carrier'.

A few important radioisotopes can only be produced in

* The loss of 4 nucleons in the alpha particle is offset by the one neutron captured, so that the net loss is 3.

cyclotrons, but the main method is irradiation of target materials in a reactor. A third possibility is the extraction of fission products which are formed in reactors when the fuel is irradiated; this method is not used in Britain, though plans for it were considered.

The production of radioisotopes is important because of the value of these substances in scientific, especially biological, research; in medical uses, both diagnostic and therapeutic; and in industrial applications (see Chapter 20). The two most important methods underlying these numerous applications are (1) the employment of radioisotopes as sources of radiation, or ionising agents, and (2) their employment as tracers. The ionising effects of radiation on the body are utilised when, for instance, a cancer is irradiated by a cobalt-60 source in a teletherapy unit, or when yttrium-90 pellets are implanted in the pituitary gland.

Radioisotopes may be used as tracers because of two properties: their chemical behaviour is identical with that of the non-radioactive isotopes of the same elements; and they decay by the emission of radiation which can be detected and measured so as to identify their position and quantity. Thus any substance, whether chemically identical or not, in which a small quantity of radioactive material is mixed, is 'marked' or 'labelled', and its subsequent progress through any mechanical, chemical or biological system can be readily followed. This is of the greatest significance in medical and biological research – for instance in metabolic studies.

At the present time, tracer applications, in diagnosis and research, are much the most important uses of radioisotopes in medicine, if not in agriculture and industry as well.

Ionising Radiations

Human beings have always been subjected to ionising radiations, mainly from cosmic rays and from the radioactivity of the earth's rocks, and the body itself contains a certain amount of potassium which is weakly radioactive and which contributes to the total dose. The natural background radiation varies considerably, according to altitude and geological conditions. Cosmic radiation is three times greater at 10,000 feet than at sea-level, and radiation from the earth's rocks is much more intense in certain areas, particularly parts of India and Brazil, where the levels may be 100 times higher than those normally observed in Great Britain.* Even in areas of low natural radioactivity the natural background is the greatest source of radiation (when averaged over all the population), while the largest contribution from man-made radiation is due to diagnostic radiology.† A few people who work with radiation sources – radiologists, radiographers and workers in the atomic energy industry – receive radiation doses higher than background, but when averaged over the whole population they contribute only a small amount to the population dose.

Man-made ionising radiations can have useful physiological effects, and if administered in controlled doses can be used to cure cancer by stopping the multiplication of malignant cells. However, ionising radiations can also be harmful, whether originating inside or outside the body. Radioactive isotopes may enter the body by inhalation, or they may be swallowed or absorbed through the skin so that they become incorporated in the tissues. The effect of ionising radiation depends partly on the type of radiation, partly on the total dose and its distribution in time (a dose delivered over a period, instead of instantaneously, permits some recovery), and partly on which cells and body tissues are irradiated. Large doses can cause acute damage such as radiation burns or severe radiation sickness, and death if the dose is high. Small doses, or chronic low-level exposure, may produce no acute symptoms but may increase the risk of late-developing malignancies such as leukaemia, bone sarcomas, or cataracts. Exposures to the germ cells of individuals – the genetic dose – increase the risk of mutations or other undesirable effects in future generations.

Since ionising radiations may produce biological damage which may not be apparent for perhaps twenty years – and their genetic effects, if any, for several generations – the danger is insidious. But though they cannot be detected by the senses, very small amounts of radiation can easily be detected by simple instruments; this fact makes radiation often less hazardous than some chemically toxic materials. Radioactive material, however, cannot be rendered inactive; it inexorably emits radiation until its period of radioactive decay is complete, perhaps after hundreds or thousands of years.

---

* Investigations have not shown any correlation between levels of natural radioactivity and the incidence of genetic defects or diseases associated with radiation.

† The usefulness of these medical techniques is such that any attempt to curtail their use would create much greater health hazards than it would remove.

These various characteristics are important from both occupational and public health and safety viewpoints (see Chapter 15), and rigorous precautions have to be taken at all stages in handling radioactive substances and ionising radiations. The specialists concerned with radiological safety were originally known as 'health physicists'.

Units of Radiation

Various units are used in radiation dosimetry and radiological protection. The *roentgen** – the original unit of exposure – is defined in terms of the amount of electric charge released in air by the ionisation caused by X- or gamma-rays. More useful to the health physicist is the *rad*, which is the unit of absorbed radiation dose and is measured in terms of the amount of radiation energy absorbed. For the effect of radiation on biological tissues, the unit is the *rem* (for *r*oentgen *e*quivalent *m*an), that is, the quantity of any radiation that produces the same biological effect in man as that resulting from the absorption of one rad of X-rays or gamma rays. This unit takes into account the greater relative biological effectiveness (RBE) of irradiation by alpha particles, protons or neutrons compared with gamma rays and X-rays.

To indicate the orders of magnitude, a single absorbed dose of 300 rads to the whole body, delivered within a few minutes, is likely to be fatal within a few weeks in 50 per cent of cases; the upper limit for occupational exposure to external radiation is 3 rem in 13 weeks, and not more than 5 rem a year on average; and the exposure to natural background radioactivity in this country is about 0·1 rem a year.

Fission and Fissile Material

The most effective particle for inducing nuclear changes is the neutron. It is heavy and, being uncharged, is extremely penetrating, as it can move freely, unchecked by forces of electrostatic attraction or repulsion, until it collides with an atomic nucleus. If atoms of a heavy unstable element such as uranium† are bombarded by

---

* Named after the discoverer of X-rays.

† Both thorium and protactinium also undergo fission when bombarded by fast neutrons. The advantage of uranium is its abundance (compared with protactinium) and its susceptibility to fission by slow neutrons. For thorium, see below.

neutrons, some of these atoms may split into roughly equal fragments, creating new atoms of lighter elements. Because, as described previously, lighter elements have a lower proportion of neutrons, some neutrons will become surplus,* and will be emitted. Some of these free neutrons may go on to collide with other uranium nuclei and cause further fissions, and in this way a 'chain reaction' is created. At each fission a large amount of energy is released, mainly in the form of kinetic energy of the neutrons and the fragments. As they are slowed down by interaction with surrounding material, heat is generated. If every fission results in exactly one new fission, a chain reaction will be maintained at a steady rate; to achieve this, each neutron causing a fission must liberate enough neutrons to replace itself and also to compensate for neutrons which will be unproductive for some of the reasons explained below. In a steady reaction of this kind the multiplication factor (known as k) is 1; if the multiplication factor is less than 1 the reaction will die out. However, if each fission yields enough neutrons to cause *more* than one new fission, the multiplication factor is more than 1, and therefore the neutron population and the number of fissions will increase exponentially in a 'divergent chain reaction'. The system is then said to have excess k. The rate of exponential growth will depend on this excess k; if each fission leads on average to 1·5 new fissions, the multiplication factor is 1·5 and the excess k is 0·5. The excess k can obviously be increased by minimising neutron loss as well as by increasing neutron yield.

Atoms consist largely of empty space, and if an atom were magnified to the size of a house the nucleus would still appear to be smaller than a pinhead; the wonder is that neutrons ever hit nuclei. Some nuclei present better targets than others and the likelihood that a nucleus will be effectively hit is measured by what is called its nuclear cross-section. Cross-sections vary from element to element, between isotopes of the same element, and also according to neutron energy; boron-10, for instance, is 100,000 times likelier to absorb slow neutrons than is boron-11, and 10 million times likelier than deuterium (hydrogen-2). Each nucleus has several different cross-sections: for protons, neutrons or other particles; for particles moving at different speeds; and for elastic collision, absorption or fission. A chain reaction is only possible with material in which free neutrons

* The number of neutrons per fission in uranium-235 averages 2·5.

are most likely to collide with nuclei and to split them. Neutrons are ejected in the fission process at very high speed – 10,000 miles a second – but they can be slowed down by 'elastic collisions', i.e. by the sort of collision that takes place between billiard balls. Very slow neutrons moving at a mile a second are called 'thermal neutrons'* and these are the ones most likely to cause fissions in uranium-235.

Of unproductive neutrons, which fail to cause fissions, some may be lost by escaping entirely from the system and some may be captured in non-fissionable nuclei. Neutron escape, like loss of heat, is a surface effect which depends on size and shape, so that loss is greater from a flat plate than a sphere of the same weight, and relatively greater from a small sphere than a big one. The larger the system, the smaller is its surface in relation to its volume, and the less likely is it that sufficient neutrons will escape to cause the chain reaction to die out. The size at which the production of free neutrons by fission is just able to maintain the neutron population at a constant level, after having provided for neutron loss by escape and non-fission capture, is called the critical size of the system. Below this critical size no chain reaction is possible.

One isotope of natural uranium – uranium-235 – is fissile. But natural uranium consists mostly of uranium-238, and uranium-235 constitutes only 0·7 per cent, or one part in 140. It is, however, only the presence of this small proportion of uranium-235 which makes a fission chain reaction possible in natural uranium. Uranium-238 is not fissionable, but it will absorb free neutrons by non-fission capture.

In order to sustain a chain reaction in natural uranium, a super-critical quantity of very pure metal is needed. This metal is usually disposed in a lattice arrangement in a material which will slow down the emitted neutrons to thermal velocities. At these velocities they are more likely to be captured by a uranium-235 nucleus and bring about fission, and less likely to be captured and absorbed by an atom of uranium-238. Materials called 'moderators', which have low atomic weights and a low propensity for capturing neutrons, are used to slow the neutrons down. The two best moderators are heavy water† and very pure graphite. The spacing in the lattice is carefully

---

* The velocity of movement of molecules is related to temperature, and thermal neutrons are moving at speeds appropriate to their ambient temperature.

† Heavy water is a better moderator than ordinary 'light' water which has

calculated to slow the neutrons sufficiently without wastage, and both uranium and moderator must be pure and free from contaminants that would capture neutrons. Next, some means of control is needed so that the reactor can be started up and shut down at will, and its reactivity varied during operation. This control is usually provided by rods, containing a neutron-absorbing material such as boron, which can be progressively inserted or withdrawn to give a very precise degree of control. Finally, arrangements must be made to remove the heat of fission by means of a liquid or gaseous coolant.

Fissile material: isotopic separation

Since uranium-235 and uranium-238 are chemically identical, they cannot be separated by any chemical means, but only by a process which exploits the slight difference in atomic mass. Four methods of isotopic separation were tried by the Manhattan Project (the United States atomic bomb programme) during the war. Of these, electromagnetic separation is no longer used industrially; thermal diffusion is used for separating isotopes of carbon; the centrifuge method is only now becoming successful; gaseous diffusion plants are operating on a large scale.

In the diffusion process a gaseous compound of uranium (uranium hexafluoride) is made to diffuse through a series of very finely porous barriers. The molecules containing the lighter uranium-235 nuclei tend to pass through the membrane a little more readily. The enrichment at each stage is extremely slight and a 'cascade' of many successive stages is needed. The end-product contains a higher proportion of fissile uranium-235 atoms than the feedstock, the degree of enrichment depending on the number of stages used in the cascade.

In a high-speed centrifuge the forces acting on the two isotopes are slightly different because of their different atomic weights, so that the heavy nuclei tend to go to the periphery. Again, many stages are necessary.

By using slightly enriched uranium in the sort of nuclear reactor which has been described, the critical size of the reactor can be reduced.

---

a greater tendency to absorb neutrons. In heavy water, which is present in ordinary water as about one part in 5,000, the hydrogen atom is replaced by deuterium or heavy hydrogen (hydrogen with one neutron).

Fissile material: plutonium production

If a slow-neutron controlled chain reaction is sustained in a uranium reactor, plutonium is produced in the following way. Many of the neutrons liberated by the fission of uranium-235 nuclei are captured by uranium-238 to form uranium-239. This has a half-life of 23 minutes, and decays* to form neptunium (93 protons). In its turn, the neptunium – with a half-life of 2·3 days – decays to form plutonium-239 (94 protons). This plutonium, which has a half-life of 24,000 years, is fissile (or fissionable). A material like uranium-238 from which fissile material can be produced is called 'fertile'.

Besides plutonium, fission products are also formed in the reactor. These are mostly radioactive isotopes of elements in the middle of the periodic table, and some of these fission products may decay to form radioactive daughter products. Fission products include strontium-90, caesium-137 and iodine-131.

Irradiated fuel elements taken from the reactor will therefore contain uranium (depleted in its fissionable uranium-235 isotope), plutonium and various fission products. These can be separated from one another by a complex chemical process (see Chapter 22) to obtain plutonium; the depleted uranium can then be restored by enrichment in a diffusion plant† and can be recycled through the reactor.

Bombs

A fast-neutron, uncontrolled chain reaction in almost pure fissile material can be used as a super-explosive. Assembling either uranium-235 or plutonium-239 in a more than critical mass can initiate a divergent chain reaction which releases tremendous quantities of energy in a period of time measured in millionths of a second. A few kilograms of uranium-235 in the bomb dropped on Hiroshima had an effect equal to some 20,000 tons of TNT; in that bomb, two sub-critical pieces of uranium-235 in a gun-like assembly were shot together so that they suddenly became one supercritical mass. In the plutonium atomic bomb a different device was used.

* By the loss of an electron; it gains one positive charge by losing a negative one, thus changing from atomic number 92 to 93.

† It is uneconomical to enrich uranium by adding uranium-235. In practice uranium-238 is removed in the plant.

A hollow sphere of plutonium was placed in the centre of a much larger sphere made up of TNT and other conventional explosives; when these conventional explosives were detonated, they compressed the ball of plutonium so that it became supercritical, and an atomic explosion resulted.

Nuclear Reactors

As we saw, a controlled chain reaction in a natural or enriched uranium reactor can be used to produce plutonium. The fission of nuclei in such a reactor releases a vast amount of energy, and the heat energy liberated has to be removed from the reactor to permit safe operation. A gaseous or a liquid coolant, with a low-capture cross-section for neutrons – air, light or heavy water, carbon dioxide, helium or liquid sodium – can be used. If the hot coolant leaving the reactor is then passed through a heat exchanger, it can boil ordinary water and so raise steam to drive a turbine. An atomic reactor can thus be used simply as a new way of boiling water, replacing the coal or oil furnace of a conventional electrical power station. Reactors can be designed, with different characteristics, as either plutonium producers or power producers – or indeed as dual-purpose plants, though they cannot be optimised for both purposes at the same time (see Chapter 19).

A considerable range of nuclear reactors is theoretically possible using various combinations and permutations of coolant and moderator, various forms of fuel element, and various degrees of fuel enrichment. Within the core of a reactor all the materials used – for moderating, cooling, fuel canning or structural purposes – must be chosen with an eye to their low absorption of neutrons, so that k is not wasted. For example, if ordinary water is employed as a coolant instead of heavy water, its greater appetite for free neutrons has to be compensated for by using enriched uranium as the fuel. The highest standards of purity are necessary to avoid the absorption of neutrons by impurities, and particular care must be taken to exclude impurities that, like boron, have high neutron capture cross-sections.

The only reason that a moderator is needed in reactors which use natural or slightly enriched uranium as a fuel is to minimise the probability that too many neutrons will be absorbed in uranium-238, and too few will be available to cause further fissions in uranium-

235. This problem is avoided if uranium-238 is not used in the core. Thus, with pure (or nearly pure) uranium-235 or plutonium as the fuel, the chain reaction can be maintained by fast neutrons and a moderator is not required. Such a reactor is called a fast reactor because the neutrons are not slowed down to thermal velocities. Neutrons in excess of those needed to sustain the reaction may be absorbed in a 'blanket' of natural or depleted uranium surrounding the core, and so may be used to form more plutonium. It is possible in this way to breed more fissile atoms than are used up in the core; hence the name 'fast breeder reactor'.

Thorium

Atomic energy is initially dependent on uranium, but thorium (see Chapter 11) may be important in the long run. Thorium is an abundant material, found entirely in the form of thorium-232 (90 protons). By absorption of a neutron, a thorium-232 atom changes to thorium-233, which then gives off a β-particle and becomes protactinium-233 (91 protons); this in turn gives off another β-particle and becomes uranium-233 (92 protons). This new isotope of uranium, not found in nature, is fissile. So natural thorium, like uranium-238, is fertile. Unlike natural uranium, it does not contain a proportion of fissile atoms to supply free neutrons to initiate a reaction. Therefore, in order to use thorium for atomic energy purposes, it must first be subjected to neutron irradiation in a reactor, in which the source of the neutrons may be either uranium-235 or plutonium; if plutonium is used it can only have been produced by the fission of uranium-235. Uranium-235, the only fissile material found in nature in usable quantity, is thus (until thermonuclear fusion processes are industrially possible) the only possible starting-point for atomic energy.

CHRONOLOGY OF EVENTS: APRIL 1945–OCTOBER 1952

1945

General	*Atomic**
April	
President Roosevelt dies	
San Francisco Conference	
(24 April–26 June)	
May	
War with Germany ends (7th)	
June	
United Nations Charter	
July	
Potsdam Conference	First atomic bomb test in New
(17 July–2 August)	Mexico (16th)
Labour Government takes office in	
Britain (27th)	
August	
USSR declares war on Japan (8th)	Hiroshima bombed (6th)
	Nagasaki bombed (9th)
Japan surrenders (14th)	US Smyth Report ('Atomic Energy
USA terminates Lend-Lease	for Military Purposes') published
	(16th)
September	
Gouzenko defects from Soviet	First Canadian research reactor criti-
Military Attaché's office in	cal. Work on NRX reactor begun
Ottawa and reveals spy ring	
Council of Foreign Ministers, Lon-	
don (10 September–2 October)	
October	
UN organisation comes into being	French atomic energy organisation
	(CEA) announced
	British decision on atomic energy
	research establishment (AERE) an-
	nounced; also transfer of atomic
	energy to Ministry of Supply (29th)
	Second and third contracts for Bel-
	gian Congo uranium

* British atomic energy events are italicised.

1945

General	Atomic
November	
	President Truman, Mr Attlee and Mr Mackenzie King meet in Washington
	Washington Declaration on atomic energy (15th)
December	
Anglo–American financial agreement; US loan of £3,750 million	*Ministers approve one atomic pile for plutonium production*
Council of Foreign Ministers, Moscow (16–27 December)	Council of Foreign Ministers agree to propose a United Nations Atomic Energy Commission

1946

General	Atomic
January	
First UN meeting, in London	*Chiefs of Staff report on Britain's atomic bomb requirements*
	United Nations General Assembly sets up UN Atomic Energy Commission
	Decision to set up an atomic energy production organisation under Hinton, and to appoint Lord Portal as Controller announced (29th)
	Cockcroft's appointment as Director of AERE announced
	Penney appointed Chief Superintendent, Armament Research
February	
Hungary declared a republic	*Atomic Energy Production Division set up at Risley, Lancs. Preliminary production plans drawn up*
Canadian spy case	
March	
Mr Churchill's Fulton speech on Anglo-American fraternal assistance against Soviet expansion	*Arrest of atomic spy Alan Nunn May Uranium-processing plant at Springfields (near Preston, Lancs.) announced (28th)*
April	
	US Bill on Atomic Energy presented by Senator McMahon
	Work begins on AERE site at Harwell, Berks.

1946

General	Atomic
April (*contd.*)	
Council of Foreign Ministers in Paris (25 April–15 May and 15 June–12 July)	Lilienthal Report (US) on international control of atomic energy
	Anglo–US–Canadian atomic co-operation breaks down at Combined Policy Committee meeting (Washington)
May	
	British Atomic Energy Bill introduced
June	
	UN Atomic Energy Commission begins work; Baruch Plan (US) published
July	
	US atomic weapon trials at Bikini atoll – British scientists participate
August	
	US Atomic Energy Act (McMahon Act) becomes law
	Air Ministry send requisition for atomic bomb to Ministry of Supply
October	
	The Radiochemical Centre set up at Amersham, Bucks.
	Preliminary work on gaseous diffusion plant approved
November	
	US Atomic Energy Commission set up to take over the atomic energy project from the Army
	Atomic Energy Act passed (6th)

1947

General	Atomic
January	
General Marshall becomes US Secretary of State	*Ministers decide on a British atomic bomb*
British coal mines nationalised	
February	
	Prime Minister gives directive on priority for atomic energy

1947

General	Atomic
March	
Anglo-French fifty-year alliance (Treaty of Dunkirk)	
USA takes on British commitments in Greece and Turkey	
Truman Doctrine on foreign policy enunciated	
Council of Foreign Ministers in Moscow (10 March–24 April)	
April	
	Long-term atomic energy design and construction programme produced
	First Bill on Radioactive Substances (withdrawn)
May	
	Plan for two air-cooled (instead of water-cooled) piles approved
June	
Partition of India and Pakistan announced	Negotiations with Portugal for uranium production begin
General Marshall speaks on the European Recovery Programme (ERP)	*First meeting of atomic bomb staff*
July	
USSR rejects Marshall plan	*New atomic energy site at Windscale (Cumberland) announced (23rd)*
August	
India and Pakistan become Dominions	*First experimental pile at Harwell (Gleep) goes critical*
September	
Sixteen nations accept Marshall Plan	*Work begins on Windscale site*
Britain announces withdrawal from Palestine	*First British radioisotopes delivered for hospital use*
October	
Cominform established in Belgrade	
November	
Council of Foreign Ministers in London (25 November–15 December)	
December	
Council of Foreign Ministers adjourned *sine die*	Anglo–US–Canadian atomic co-operation – tripartite discussions in Washington

1948

General	Atomic
January	
Burma leaves the British Commonwealth	*Modus vivendi* concluded – tripartite agreement on atomic energy (8th)
Gandhi assassinated	*First uranium cast at Springfields using Canadian material*
February	
Communist regime established in Czechoslovakia	
April	
British electricity supply industry nationalised	
World Health Organisation (WHO) set up	
Organisation for European Economic Co-operation (OEEC) set up	
May	
Independence of Israel proclaimed	*British atomic bomb decision announced in the House of Commons*
South African elections – General Smuts's party defeated	*Radioactive Substances Bill introduced in the House of Lords*
	UN Atomic Energy Commission wound up
June	
Dr Malan becomes South African Prime Minister	*Windscale graphite shop in operation*
Soviet blockade of Berlin (18 June 1948–12 May 1949)	*Radioactive Substances Act passed*
July	
Britain's National Health Service comes into operation	*Second experimental reactor (Bepo) goes critical at Harwell*
US bombers based at British airfields	*First press visits to Harwell*
October	
	First uranium cast at Springfields using metal from Congo ores processed at Springfields
November	
President Truman re-elected as US President	*Windscale graphite shop starts work on redesigned lattice*
	Filters added to Windscale chimneys

1948

General	Atomic
December	French experimental pile Zoe goes critical

1949

General	Atomic
January Comecon (Council for Mutual Economic Aid) founded in Moscow	
February	*Prime Minister's second priority directive on atomic energy* *Enlarged programme approved, with third pile and LSD**
April NATO set up	
May Council of Europe established Berlin blockade ends Council of Foreign Ministers in Paris (23 May–20 June)	
June	*Applied research establishment for Risley decided upon* *Completion of Harwell's 'hot' laboratory announced*
July	Agreement reached with Portugal on uranium exports US meeting at Blair House on Anglo-American atomic co-operation
August	First Russian atomic weapon test
September The pound devalued (18th) Detection of first Russian atomic weapon test announced by President Truman (19th) People's Republic of China proclaimed in Peking (21st)	Washington talks on Anglo–US–Canadian atomic co-operation begin (20th) *Prime Minister's third priority directive on atomic energy* Tripartite scientific conference in Canada on permissible doses of radiation

* Low-separation gaseous diffusion plant.

1949

General	*Atomic*
October	
GDR (German Democratic Republic) established	*Windscale teams sent to Canada for work on experimental plant*
	Graphite lattice for first Windscale pile finished
November	
	New atomic site at Capenhurst (Cheshire) announced – purpose not stated
	Atomic energy exhibition at Whitehaven, Cumberland
December	
	Tripartite talks in Washington continue
	Work on third Windscale pile suspended
	Harwell cyclotron given first full trial

1950

General	*Atomic*
January	
	American decision to develop an H-bomb
	Arrest of the Harwell spy, Klaus Fuchs
	Washington talks break down
February	
US–UK agreement on guided missiles	
Thirty-year alliance between USSR and China	
UK General Election – Labour Government returned to power with much reduced majority	
April	
British Chiefs of Staff global strategy review	*Aldermaston site taken over for atomic weapons work*
	The Radiochemical Centre comes under Harwell control
	Advisory Council for Scientific Policy makes recommendations to Ministers on nuclear power development

1950

General	Atomic
June	
Korean War begins (25 June 1950–14 July 1953)	*Windscale pipeline is laid*
	Anglo-American conference on (atomic) security standards
July	
	Experimental loading of first Windscale pile
	Graphite lattice for No. 2 pile completed
August	
	Second tripartite conference on permissible doses of radiation, held near Harwell
	Cartridges discharged from Windscale No. 1 pile for modification of fins
September	
Britain undertakes general rearmament programme	*Fin-clipping operation completed at Windscale*
	Defection of Harwell scientist, Bruno Pontecorvo
	First British nuclear power conference
	The British Chiefs of Staff ask for US bomb-testing facilities
October	
	Tripartite talks with Belgium in Washington: further agreement on Congo uranium
	US McMahon Act amended to permit rather more co-operation
	US bomb-testing facilities refused
	Windscale's No. 1 pile goes critical
November	
	Agreement with South Africa on uranium supplies
December	
Mr Attlee flies to Washington to see Mr Truman about the Korean War and the bomb	*Windscale No. 1 pile operating at low power*
First production order placed for Valiant bombers	

1951

General	*Atomic*
February	
	British Chiefs of Staff agree on a shipborne atomic bomb trial at Monte Bello in late 1952
March	
Mr Bevin resigns as Foreign Secretary (and dies a month later)	*Isotope School set up at Harwell*
April	
	Chemical separation plant completed
	Windscale No. 1 pile operating at normal power
June	
British Foreign Office officials, Maclean and Burgess, defect	*Windscale No. 2 pile goes critical*
	Windscale's highly active storage plant commissioned
	First inactive run in chemical separation plant at Windscale
July	
	Ministers approve HSD*
	Second inactive run in chemical separation plant
	Dutch–Norwegian experimental pile near Oslo goes critical
August	
	US proposals about weapon test facilities for Britain not accepted
October	
UK General Election – Conservative Government formed under Mr Churchill	*Windscale's No. 2 pile commissioned*
November	
British Government's retrenchment campaign	
December	*First billet of pure metal produced at Harwell from Canadian plutonium*
	Revised South African agreement on uranium

* High-separation gaseous diffusion plant.

1952

General	Atomic
January	
Mr Churchill visits Mr Truman for general discussions	*Chemical separation plant at Windscale takes first irradiated slugs*
British Chiefs of Staff review global strategy	
February	
King George VI dies, and Queen Elizabeth II succeeds him	*Plutonium separation plant commissioned at Windscale*
	Announcement of forthcoming test ('Hurricane')
	First ships of 'Hurricane' expedition sail
	First consignments of uranium ore from Portugal
March	
NATO Conference at Lisbon	*Plutonium finishing plant commissioned at Windscale*
Mr Churchill issues priority directive on defence	*First billet of metallic plutonium made at Windscale (28th)*
April	Agreement with Australia on Radium Hill uranium
	Scheme for dual-purpose pile (for power and plutonium) under consideration
May	*'Hurricane' assemblies completed*
June	*Main flotilla sails for Monte Bello*
August	*Plutonium for bomb delivered to weapons establishment*
	Main 'Hurricane' party reaches Monte Bello
September	*Planned shutdown of No. 1 pile at Windscale: overheating from Wigner effect observed*
October	*'Hurricane' – first British atomic weapon test at Monte Bello, Australia (3rd)*
November	
US presidential election – General Eisenhower elected	US H-bomb test at Eniwetok

References

Chapter 1: August 1945: Retrospect and Agenda

1. See Mark Oliphant, *Rutherford: Recollections of the Cambridge Days* (Elsevier, 1972) chap. 10; also *Nature*, 16 Sep 1933, pp. 432–3.
2. See, e.g., Geoffrey Barraclough, *Introduction to Contemporary History* (C. A. Watts, 1964) chap. iv.
3. See *Britain and Atomic Energy, 1939–1945, passim.*
4. Richard G. Hewlett and Oscar E. Anderson, *History of the USAEC*, vol. 1: *The New World, 1939–1946* (Pennsylvania State UP, 1962) pp. 624–42 *passim.*
5. See *Britain and Atomic Energy, 1939–1945,* chap. 13.
6. Ibid., chap. 8.
7. *The War Memoirs of Charles de Gaulle: Unity, 1942–1944* (Simon & Schuster, 1959) pp. 273–4.

Chapter 2: Labour's Machinery of Government

1. See, e.g., R. H. S. Crossman's Introduction to W. Bagehot, *The English Constitution* (Fontana, 1963) and Barraclough, *Introduction to Contemporary History*, p. 142. The latter says: 'It is well known that the decision to proceed with the A-bomb was taken by Mr Attlee on his own initiative, without reference to the Cabinet, and was not revealed to Parliament until the first bomb had been tested in 1951.' The decision was not made by Mr Attlee on his own initiative; it was revealed, if obliquely, to Parliament in 1948 (see below, Chapter 6) and the first bomb was tested in 1952.
2. HOC Deb., 29 Oct 1945, vol. 416, col. 1908.
3. See *Britain and Atomic Energy, 1939–1945*, p. 237.
4. HOC Deb., 1 May 1946, vol. 422, col. 200 (for second reading debates, see HOC Deb., 8 Oct 1946, vol. 427, cols. 43–98, 113–46).
5. Letter from R. E. Peierls and P. B. Moon in *The Times*, 8 Oct 1946.
6. See Peierls and Moon letter, ibid.
7. e.g. Alice Kimball Smith, *A Peril and a Hope* (Chicago UP, 1965).
8. HOC Deb., 8 Oct 1946, vol. 427, col. 528.
9. See Select Committee on Estimates, Fourth Report (1945–6) on 'The Form of the Estimates'. Giving evidence to the Select Committee on 19 Feb 1947, the Permanent Secretary of the Ministry of Supply said: 'Our Estimates in respect of other research activities are on the same basis. If you want to know how much we are spending on guided projectiles you will not find it on the face of the Estimates but the Department will be only too willing to disclose it to the Committee.'
10. HOC Deb., 19 Apr 1948, vol. 449, cols. 1425–7.
11. HOL Deb., 16 Oct 1945, vol. 137, cols. 285–94. See note 29 below.

12. See, e.g., *Atomic Scientists News*, vol. 1, no. 4, p. 44.

13. HOC Deb., 4 Mar 1944, vol. 448, col. 574.

14. HOC Deb., 2 Aug 1946, vol. 426, col. 1371.

15. Reported in *News Chronicle*, 9 Aug 1945.

16. *New York Times*, 26 Sep 1945.

17. *Observer*, 21 Oct 1945. Liddell Hart later noted that British public and Parliamentary concern about the vulnerability of the British Isles was surprisingly slow to develop (quoted by Andrew J. Pierre in *Nuclear Politics*, Oxford UP, 1972, p. 163).

18. Letter from Stephen King-Hall to *Manchester Guardian*, 13 Sep 1945.

19. *Christian Science Monitor*, 6 Feb 1948.

20. *Manchester Guardian*, 23 Apr 1946.

21. *Manchester Guardian*, 19 July 1949.

22. *Daily Express*, 26 Sep 1949.

23. According to the *Christian Science Monitor*, 8 Mar 1949.

24. *Economist*, 24 Mar 1951. The article went on, 'It is difficult to feel enthusiastic about the idea', and argued that there was no strategic reason for Britain to have atomic bombs and that such a programme would be a burden on the British chemical and engineering industries.

(Reference supplied by C. E. S. Franks, Kingston University, Ontario.)

25. *Daily Mail*, 11 Oct 1945.

26. *Manchester Guardian*, 23 Apr 1946.

27. The *Christian Science Monitor*, 6 Feb 1948, said of the British Government: 'Reportedly, the attitude is not that of delving into an exciting unknown, but rather that of simply making sure Britain doesn't fall behind other nations.'

28. *Irish Times*, 20 July 1949.

29. e.g. 'Tuesday's debate in the Lords on the atomic bomb was a sorry affair. All the old comfortless clichés were brought out for the occasion' (*Manchester Guardian*, 18 Oct 1945).

30. *New York Times*, 25 July 1948: 'Atomic energy is not only the government's business, it is the business of every citizen.'

31. *Christian Science Monitor*, 6 Feb 1948.

32. *Daily Express*, 14 Dec 1949.

33. *Daily Mail*, 20 June 1949 (quoting the *New York Daily News*).

34. *Christian Science Monitor*, 18 July 1949.

35. *New York Times*, 21 July 1949.

36. *Manchester Guardian*, 18 July 1949.

Chapter 3: External Policy: Brief Hope of Interdependence

1. *Britain and Atomic Energy, 1939–1945*, pp. 353–71.

2. The text was published in Francis Williams, *A Prime Minister Remembers* (Heinemann, 1961).

3. The books which were the origins of the controversy were Herbert Feis's three books, *Churchill, Roosevelt, Stalin* (Princeton UP, 1957), *Between War and Peace* (Princeton UP, 1960) and *Japan Sub-* dued (Princeton UP, 1961). The first of the revisionist histories was Gar Alperovitz, *Atomic Diplomacy: Hiroshima and Potsdam* (Secker & Warburg, 1966).

4. Hewlett and Anderson, *The New World*, pp. 419, 455–9.

5. See also accounts in Williams, op. cit., pp. 102–9, and John Wheeler-Bennett, *John Anderson* (Macmillan, 1962) pp. 336–8.

Chapter 4: External Policy: Hopes are Dupes

1. See, e.g., Bertrand Goldschmidt, *Rivalités Atomiques* (Fayard, 1967).

2. *The Journals of David E. Lilienthal*, vol. II: *The Atomic Energy Years, 1945–1950* (Harper & Row, 1964) *passim*; the quotation is from p. 39.

3. Hewlett and Anderson, *The New World*, p. 478.

4. Text in H. S. Truman, *Year of Decisions* (Signet edition) pp. 581–4.

5. Bill No. HR 4280.

6. See Smith, *A Peril and a Hope*, and Hewlett and Anderson, *The New World*, chap. 4.

7. 19 Apr Report to accompany S1717, Senate 79th Congress, Calendar 1251, Report 1211. The Committee print including the new wording was dated 11 Apr (Committee Print No. 5).

8. House of Representatives Debate, 17–20 July 1946.

9. Public Law 585, 79th Congress, approved 1 Aug 1946.

10. Congressional Record, vol. 92, pt 7, 18 July 1946. The speaker was Mr Fulton.

11. Dean Acheson, *Present at the Creation* (Hamish Hamilton, 1970) p. 167.

12. Hearings before Special Committee on Atomic Energy pursuant to S.Res. 179, pt 2, p. 291.

13. Hewlett and Anderson, *The New World*, p. 481.

14. Cf. Congressional Record, vol. 92, pt 7, p. 9626, Mrs Luce: 'It seems to me there is nothing to be gained by this House trying to deceive itself or the American people about the true intent of this legislation [McMahon Bill] which is to secure and promote for so long as we can or until international atomic control is achieved, our national monopoly of this fearful weapon.' There were also commercial reasons for the monopoly, e.g. p. 9273, Mr Elston: 'When in all the history of the nation has it been required that anything developed for the benefit of American industry, shall be shared with other nations?'

15. Smith, *A Peril and a Hope*, p. 519. This detailed account of the scientists' pressure movement to get the McMahon Bill passed does not mention any concern for Britain.

16. See Sir Leonard Owen, 'Nuclear Engineering in the United Kingdom: The First Ten Years', *Journal of the British Nuclear Energy Society*, Jan 1963.

17. See P. M. S. Blackett, *Studies of War: Nuclear and Conventional* (Hill & Wang, 1962).

18. See Lilienthal, *Journals* passim.

19. Lilienthal, *Journals*. There was 'some surprise at learning that Great Britain and Canada actually had had men participating with all four feet on the development of the bomb itself, during the war. Senator Connally said then "you mean that England knows how to make the bomb. The answer is certainly 'yes'"'. (p. 175.)

Chapter 5: External Policy: The Commonwealth and Europe

1. *Britain and Atomic Energy, 1939–1945*, chaps. 5, 6 and 10, and p. 171.

2. Ibid., p. 300.

3. Ibid., chaps. 6 and 10.

4. Ibid., p. 289.

5. Ibid., p. 288.

6. *Britain and Atomic Energy, 1939–1945*, pp. 298, 307–11.

7. Ibid., pp. 49–52, 289.

8. Ibid., pp. 209–13.

Chapter 6: Deterrence

1. *Britain and Atomic Energy, 1939–1945*, pp. 329–32.
2. Ibid., chap. 12.
3. Ibid., e.g. pp. 168, 174, 324 ff.
4. Information from Lord Hinton. See Sir Leonard Owen, 'Nuclear Engineering in the United Kingdom: The First Ten Years' (*Journal of the British Nuclear Energy Society*, Jan 1963). He says: 'The remit given to the new organisation was the production of plutonium for military purposes.'
A written remit was never given.

5. HOC Deb., 7 Nov 1945, vol. 415, col. 1300.
6. Ibid., col. 1379.
7. But Alfred Goldberg, 'Military Origins of the British Nuclear Deterrent', *International Affairs*. Oct 1964, p. 601, says the Ten-Year Rule was adopted in the winter of 1946. I have not found evidence of this and the Hansard reference given in the article provides no support for it.
8. Quoted by Pierre, *Nuclear Politics*, p. 124.

Chapter 7: Deterrence Recalculated

1. USAEC, *In the Matter of J. Robert Oppenheimer*, p. 467.
2. Lilienthal, *Journals*, p. 571.

3. Ibid., *Journals*, p. 486; see also *Journals*, p. 376.

Chapter 8: The Anglo-American Modus Vivendi

1. Richard G. Hewlett and Francis Duncan, *History of the USAEC*, vol. II: *Atomic Shield, 1947–1952* (Pennsylvania State UP, 1969) p. 279 and *passim*.

Chapter 9: Independence Reconsidered. I

1. Lilienthal, op. cit., pp. 457, 550–552; Hewlett and Duncan, *Atomic Shield*, p. 297.
2. Lilienthal, *Journals*, p. 465.
3. Ibid., p. 455.
4. Ibid., p. 555.
5. See Hewlett and Duncan, *Atomic Shield*, pp. 209–303.
6. 'The issue did not go to the Committee on Foreign Relations or to the Committees on the Armed Forces, but was decided, in practical effect, by a committee whose jurisdiction was limited to the Atom.... My present point is that so portentous a question of foreign policy of the United States was dealt with decisively by a specialised committee dealing with the Atom rather than by the Committee on Foreign Relations. The fact that

on the Joint Committee were senators who were also members of the Committee on Foreign Relations did not, I submit, change the basic point of the unsuitability of having a Joint Committee on the Atom having a decisive role in so critical an issue of our foreign policy....' Lilienthal, *Change, Hope and the Bomb*, pp. 120–1.
7. Lilienthal, *Journals*, pp. 543–5, 547–8.
8. Ibid., p. 548.
9. Ibid., p. 557.
10. Ibid., p. 551.
11. Ibid., p. 551, quoting Senator Vandenberg at one of the July meetings: 'It may be the UK does have all the knowledge but the people of this country don't know that; they

think that they are the sole possessors of the secret. They will react violently if they hear that we gave that to the British.'

12. See ibid., pp. 508–10, for a description of Mr Johnson.

13. Ibid., p. 574. Kennan had apparently reported to the President earlier that day that the UK–Canadian talks had failed.

14. Ibid., pp. 574–5. It is clear from this that Lilienthal, intuitively understanding the underlying British feelings, did the stiffening. 'If we take the course of the hard-boiled banker or try to blackjack the British, or deprecate them, they will respond as almost any human beings would respond, by almost being difficult, by insisting on doing things automatically that would not be the most economical division of labors and of materials between real partners, but just to assert their pride and place in the world. This is what Hickenlooper and Strauss and others have accomplished with their pecking away at technical co-operation and the kind of things that were said at the time of the last Blair House [i.e. the July] meeting.'

15. Ibid., p. 615.

16. Acheson, *Present at the Creation*, pp. 164–8.

17. At a press conference on 30 Nov 1950. See Hewlett and Duncan, *Atomic Shield*, p. 532, and Williams, *A Prime Minister Remembers*, p. 233.

18. Hewlett and Duncan, *Atomic Shield*, pp. 521–2.

19. HOC Deb., 14 Dec 1950, vol. 482, col. 1356.

20. Acheson, *Present at the Creation* p. 484.

21. 'Dean Acheson Talks to Kenneth Harris', *The Listener*, 8 Apr 1971.

22. HOC Deb., 6 Dec 1951, vol.

494, col. 280 (written answers). The Prime Minister who answered the question was by then Mr Churchill.

23. J. Alsop, *Washington Post*, 22 July 1949.

24. Agreement for Co-operation on the Civil Uses of Atomic Energy signed at Washington on 15 June 1955 (Cmd 9560); Agreement for Co-operation on the Uses of Atomic Energy for Mutual Defence Purposes (Washington, 3 July 1958 (Cmnd 537).

25. James R. Newman and Byron S. Miller, *The Control of Atomic Energy* (McGraw-Hill, 1958). Cf. Lord Ritchie-Calder in Lord Sherfield (ed.), *Economic and Social Consequences of Atomic Energy* (Oxford UP, 1972) pp. 76–7, writing of a World Health Organisation study group in 1957 on the mental health aspects of the peaceful uses of nuclear energy meeting at Geneva. The group agreed that, 'confronted with immeasurable power from the infinitesimally small nucleus, civilised man tends to cower, like his Neanderthal ancestors "in the dark caves of his own emotions" or, in the less poetic terms of the psychologists, "The tendency to relapse into more primitive forms of thought and feeling which is characteristic of most of the reported reactions of the public to nuclear energy can be ascribed to a psychological mechanism known as 'regression'." Our primitive ancestors dreaded, and sought to appease, the elemental gods of thunder and lightning and fire, but the elemental gods of the new mythology are radioactive, unseen, unsmelt, unfelt, unheard, and all-pervasive. They are also man-made. In our retreat into "the childhood of mankind" (to quote the study group) we revive a

cosmic guilt about tampering with things we should not. This exists in the myth and legend of every culture: Adam and Eve eating the forbidden fruit of the Tree of Knowledge; Prometheus stealing fire, the prerogative of the gods; Pandora opening the box; Faust trafficking with the Devil; and the Ancient Egyptian saying, "When Man learns what moves the stars, the Sphinx will laugh and all life upon earth will be destroyed".'

Chapter 10: Independence Reconsidered. II

1. *Britain and Atomic Energy, 1939–1945*, p. 310.

Chapter 11: The Area of Interdependence: Uranium Supplies

1. Article in Belgian Communist newspaper, 17 Apr 1946.
2. Lilienthal, *Journals*, p. 437.
3. Ibid., p. 438.
4. See *Britain and Atomic Energy, 1939–1945*, p. 315.
5. Some specimen prices during this period (excluding royalties, taxes, levies, etc.):

Belgian Congo – $1.45, $1.90, $3.40, $6.00.
Portugal – $6.50–$8.00.
Canada – $3.50–$12.50.
South Africa – $7.70–$9.94 (averages).
Australia – $21.27 (Radium Hill average).
$17.60 (Rum Jungle ceiling price).
United States – $12.50 (average).

Chapter 12: 'Winston is Back' – and Cherwell

1. HOC Deb., 7 Nov 1945, vol. 415, col. 1300.
2. 'That this House regrets the slow progress made in this country in developing atomic energy for peaceful and for war-like purposes and calls upon His Majesty's Government, whilst maintaining broad general control, to transfer work on this subject from the Ministry of Supply to a special organisation more flexible than the normal Civil Service system under the direct control of the head of the Government.' HOL Deb., 5 July 1951, vol. 172, cols. 670–9, 684–707.
3. See Earl of Birkenhead, *The Prof. in Two Worlds* (Collins, 1961) p. 307, which says that Cherwell had been rebuffed by the Prime Minister in August and was reluctant to press the matter further but was urged by his advisers to do so. Hence the paper to the Cabinet. The biographer's emotional description of this episode – 'This was the act of high moral courage which must remain memorable as long as the atomic story is told' – is scarcely warranted by Churchill's minute. It seems clear that Mr Churchill did not care very much one way or the other but did not like being bullied. The paper was certainly not circulated to the Cabinet against Churchill's wishes.
4. Ibid., p. 315.
5. *Washington Star* poll, 2 Jan 1953, Representative Harrison of Wyoming.

Index

Cunningham, Admiral Sir John, 25n.
Cyanamid, 377
Cyclotrons, 112, 120, 336; *see also* Particle accelerators
Czechoslovakia, 92, 213
  uranium, 77n., 350–1

Daily Express, 52–4
Daily Mail, 53
Daily Telegraph, 52–4
Daily Worker, 54
Dale, Henry, 25n., 53, 163
Dalton, Hugh (Chancellor of the Exchequer), 21, 133, 167n., 182
Daniels, R. J., 113n.
Darwin, Charles, 16, 45n.
Davidson, C. F., 353, 374–6, 378, 384; *see also* Uranium
Davis, E. D., 44
Dean, Gordon, 302n., 396
Declassification, 112, 247, 270–1, 287, 329, 331, 335, 338, 340, 346, 415–416; *see also* Secrecy
Dee, P. I., 45n.
Defence Committee, 23, 56, 58, 174, 214, 222, 231, 233, 309–10, 428, 448
Defence estimates, 20, 218n.
Defence expenditure, 51, 187, 214, 218, 229–30, 234–5, 439–41
Defence policy, 19, 20–3, 26, 32–7, 51, 56, 115, 147, 183–9, 195–206, 213–15, 290, 321
  Conservative Opposition discussions with Government, 406
  rearmament, 214, 440; economic effects of, 439
  See also Atomic weapons, United Kingdom, Chiefs of Staff, Strategic air offensive, Strategy, United Kingdom (economic difficulties)
Defence research, 5, 32–6, 188–9, 225–8, 323
Defence Research Policy Committee, 22, 33–4, 36–7, 56, 59, 188, 224–8
  sub-committee on Strategic Aspects of Atomic Energy, 34, 437–8
Denmark, 10; *see also* Bohr, Niels
Department of Scientific and Industrial Research, 5, 16, 26, 40, 47, 377; *see also* Tube Alloys
Devaluation (of the pound), 282, 299

Dickson, William, 251
Dominions Office, 30; *see also* Commonwealth
Dominions, Secretary of State for, 23; *see also* Addison, Lord
Dönges, Mr, 334–5; *see also* South Africa

Eaton, P. J., 353n.
Economist, 54, 190
Eden, Anthony, 5n., 388
Einstein, A., 67
Eisenhower, General, 98, 117–19, 275, 277–9, 421, 448–9
Eldorado Company, 372–3; *see also* Canadian atomic project (uranium production)
Electrical industry, 168, 239
Electricity:
  atomic energy requirements, 218–219, 224, 431
  demand generally, 443–4
  See also Coal, Nuclear power
Elliott, William, 317
Ellis, C. D., 163
Emeleus, H. J., 45n.
Engineers, *see under* Manpower
Evatt, H. V., 147
Exports, 168–9, 186–7, 219; *see also* United Kingdom (economic difficulties)

Feather, N., 16, 45n.
Federation of British Industries, 48
Fermi, Enrico, 1
Fisk, J. B., 116, 245, 272
Fissile material, *see* Canadian atomic project, United Kingdom atomic project, United States atomic project, Uranium 235, Plutonium, Thorium
Fission products, *see* Plutonium separation
Foreign Office, 5, 30–1, 37, 48, 52, 55, 69, 93, 96, 108, 115, 119, 123, 150, 156, 281, 311–15, 339, 341, 414
  British Embassy in Washington, 31, 47, 108–10, 116, 150, 244, 250, 256, 259, 280, 282n., 298, 300, 302–3, 309, 327, 341, 343, 347, 353, 362, 370
  See also Franks, Oliver, Halifax, Lord, Inverchapel, Lord,